Let Truth Be Told

Let Truth Be Told

50 Years of BBC External Broadcasting

Gerard Mansell

Weidenfeld and Nicolson
LONDON

© 1982 Gerard Mansell

First published in Great Britain by
George Weidenfeld & Nicolson Ltd,
91 Clapham High Street, London SW4

ISBN 0 297 78158 8

Printed and bound in Great Britain by
Butler & Tanner Ltd
Frome and London

Contents

Illustrations

All of the pictures (except Nos. 13, 15 and 16) are used by kind permission of the BBC.

Preface

This book could not have been written in the relatively short time available since my retirement from the BBC without the willing help of a great many people. I place on record here my gratitude for their kindness to me personally and for their readiness to go out of their way to assist me.

While a great deal of the primary evidential material on the development of the External Services is to be found in the BBC's files at the Written Archives Centre and elsewhere, biographies such as Andrew Boyle's studies of Reith and Brendan Bracken and autobiographies such as those of Harman Grisewood and Sir Robert Bruce Lockhart have been invaluable in casting light on people and events. Asa Briggs's massive four-volume *History of Broadcasting in the United Kingdom* is, of course, a unique and indispensable work of reference as well as a most authoritative account of the history of the BBC as a whole, and within it the External Services, and I have consulted it at every point. Reith's 'Diaries' and his autobiography, *Into the Wind*, have also been a key source of information and insights on the early days.

However, it would have been impossible to give this book the flavour of reality as it was experienced by those involved at the time without the personal recollections of a number of key witnesses, particularly as concerns the start of foreign language broadcasting and the wartime story. I have had access to much information made available orally by the first Director of External Broadcasting, Sir Ian Jacob, and by my predecessor Oliver Whitley. Among those who kindly devoted time and effort to providing me with answers to my many questions – even in some cases going to the trouble of drafting many pages of detailed recollections for my benefit – were Arthur Barker, his sister Elizabeth Barker, George Camacho, Tom Chalmers, Donald Edwards, Martin Esslin, Bill Galbraith, Josephine Gaman, Felix Greene, Sir Hugh Greene, Harman Grisewood, Donald Hodson, Tahu Hole, Maurice Latey, Clare Lawson Dick, Alexander Lieven, Gregory Macdonald, Leonard Miall, Bernard Moore, Robin Scott, Leo Shepley, Donald Stephenson, Michael Sumner, Konrad Syrop, W. A. Tate and Halvor William Olsson. On the all-important technical side, Edward Pawley's admirably comprehensive account of the development of the transmitting capability of the External Services in his jubilee study, *BBC Engineering 1922-1972*, has been my constant guide, supplemented for the more recent past by the always lucid advice of the present Chief Engineer of the External Services, Bill Dennay. On the wartime French Service, I am indebted to Cecilia Gillie, *née* Reeves, whose husband, the late Darsie Gillie, was the BBC's French Editor, for permission to draw on the material included in her unpublished monograph on the subject. She was also one of those involved in the selection of texts for the magnificent five-volume account of the war as told through the broadcasts of the French Service, *Les Voix de la Liberté – Ici Londres 1940-1944*, produced by La Documentation Française under the direction of Jean-Louis Cremieux-Brilhac, himself a wartime French broadcaster from London.

I am grateful also to Andrew Walker, the External Services Commonwealth and Defence correspondent, who generously made available to me material he had collected in the course of an earlier project.

Among those who have contributed a great deal to smoothing my path are first and foremost the staff of the Written Archives Centre headed by Jackie Kavanagh. It might seem invidious to single out one individual among them, for they have all invariably been welcoming and helpful, but I must make a special mention of Dennis Perry, whose patience and resourcefulness in tracking down particular documents and answering my enquiries never flagged. Shelley Hardcastle at the Records Management Centre at Acton, Pauline Mills at the Bush House Registry and Pam Edwards at the Central Management Registry kindly found me temporary desk room and allowed me to delve at leisure through relevant files. Leonard Miall and Pat Spencer in the BBC History Unit were unsparing in their efforts to guide me towards useful sources of material. Both read my manuscript, as did also Sir Hugh Greene. All three made many valuable comments and suggestions for improvements. Special thanks are also due to the BBC's Librarian, David Evans, for his relentless pursuit of the books I needed and for his forbearance in letting me keep them well beyond the due date for return.

Alexander Lieven, an old and trusted friend, was kind enough to undertake the onerous duty of reading the proofs, and I asked more of my former Personal Assistant at Bush House, Diana Burnett, than I was entitled to, but was always confident I could.

Rosemary Shaw, Jennifer Iles and Kathleen Sargent typed my manuscript, and I am particularly grateful to Kathleen Sargent, who carried the main burden, for her readiness to spare no effort to finish typing the last chapters against a tight deadline. She did so with her usual efficiency.

GERARD MANSELL
London, June 1982

1
Origins

So far as the British public was concerned Saturday 19 December 1932 was an unexceptional broadcasting day. The BBC was operating two radio networks – the National and Regional Programmes. During much of the day, they transmitted the same programme and did not separate until after the six o'clock news. Though the 'Daily Service' went out as usual at 10.15 in the morning, the day's broadcasting did not really start until 1.00 pm. The main offering of that afternoon was live coverage of a Rugby International between Ireland and South Africa. Much of the evening's broadcasting on the National Programme was taken up by a live relay of *The Barber of Seville* from the Prince of Wales Theatre in Birmingham. John Barbirolli was conducting and Heddle Nash sang the role of the Count. Later there was vaudeville, with Tommy Handley topping the bill, while on the Regional Programme the young Harman Grisewood was one of those taking part in 'Yes, and Back Again', described in the *Radio Times* as a dramatic sequence for broadcasting adapted from Walter de la Mare.

But that morning, at the unusually early hour of 9.30, well before the start of the normal broadcasting day, one studio at least in the newly built Broadcasting House was busy. Sir John Reith, the Director-General, was there, and so were a number of his most senior colleagues. It was ten years almost to the day since he had been placed on the payroll of the British Broadcasting Company. The occasion was the start of the Empire Service, the BBC's first venture into international broadcasting. The first transmission lasted two hours and was beamed at Australia and New Zealand, where it would be heard in the evening. Four further transmissions followed in the ensuing fifteen hours, beamed at different parts of the Empire at times thought suitable for local listening, which meant the evening. Given the shortage of available resources these first transmissions consisted largely of programmes relayed from the two home networks, some gramophone records and a news bulletin.

The service formally opened with a message from the Rt Hon. J.H. Whitley, the former Speaker of the House of Commons, who had become Chairman of the Board of Governors of the BBC two years earlier. Whitley set the tone for the new service, a tone which was characteristic of the high-minded attitude to the role of broadcasting which prevailed among those in charge of the BBC at the time: 'This wireless,' he said, 'one of the great gifts of Providence to mankind, is a trust of which we are humble ministers. Our prayer is that nothing mean or cheap may lessen its value, and that its message may bring happiness and comfort to those who listen.'

Whitley was immediately followed on the air by Sir John Reith, who had been Director-General of the BBC since 1926, and the first General Manager of the British Broadcasting Company at its creation in 1922. The Empire Service had been Reith's idea, and he had fought to bring it about for five years. His own address matched the importance of the occasion with the solemnity of its style. Radio, he asserted, was

an instrument of almost incalculable importance in the social and political life of the community. Its influence will more and more be felt in the daily life of the individual in almost every sphere of human activity, in affairs national and international. Now it becomes a connecting and co-ordinating link between the scattered parts of the British Empire. Here at home, from the earliest days, it has been our resolve that the great possibilities and influences of the medium should be exploited to the highest human advantage ... The service as a whole is dedicated to the best interests of mankind.[1]

Reith had been compelled to read his message live at the microphone five times, at the start of each successive transmission at 9.30 am, at 2.30, 6.30 and 8.30 pm, and 1.00 am the next morning, an experience which, not surprisingly, he did not enjoy: 'I was very bored with it,' he noted in his diary, 'and with having to speak for about twelve minutes.'[2] But there was no avoiding it. Recording was still in its infancy, and too much reliance could not be placed in the three German-made Blattnerphone steel tape recorders which had been installed at Broadcasting House shortly before, specifically to meet the programme needs of the Empire Service. These machines, the forerunners of the modern magnetic tape recorder, were technically unsophisticated and liable to mechanical breakdown.[3] Reith was not taking any chances.

There had been other technical problems, and these were only gradually being solved. Starting a regular service on short wave at that early stage was something of a gamble and Captain P.P. Eckersley, the BBC's first Chief Engineer, had consistently advised caution. He was principally worried by the unreliability of short waves as a means of transmission. By the mid-twenties short wave broadcasting had not gone beyond the experimental stage. Fading, distortion and interference were common phenomena, and engineers did not yet fully understand the complex characteristics of short wave propagation. Eckersley's advice to Reith, given in an internal memo dated 16 May 1927,[4] just prior to the Colonial Conference at which proposals for Empire broadcasting were to be discussed, was that the BBC was in no position to guarantee decent audibility if it were to set up a regular short wave service in the immediate future. False hopes would be created and listeners would become discouraged, thus damaging the long term prospects of the service. American stations came in very well 'as a noise', Eckersley pointed out 'but it is tantalisingly imperfect'. That point of view was supported by Major C.F. Atkinson, who was responsible for the BBC's international relations. In a memorandum written at about the same time, he deliberately took up the position of devil's advocate and stressed the dubious wisdom of attempting to broadcast music on short wave in the existing imperfect state of the art. There was undoubtedly an element of excited wonder in listening to performances taking place on the other side of the earth, he wrote: 'but is it in the interest of radio to send out poor musical transmissions all over the world in order that certain sections of the world may have the satisfaction of knowing that the performance originates in their mother country?'[5]

By the time the Colonial Conference opened on 20 May 1927, Eckersley's advice had become BBC policy. The Rt Hon. W. Ormsby Gore, Parliamentary Under Secretary for the Colonies, pointed to the existence of pressure from the colonies for the development of empire broadcasting: 'I have heard in my various travels,' he said, 'that there are great complaints, that they can get on to Philadelphia, but they never can get Daventry or 2LO. Bournemouth they occasionally get, but it is pretty bad.'[6]

The BBC delegation at the conference was led by Vice-Admiral Carpendale, one of the legendary figures of the corporation's early years, who, as Controller, was also Reith's deputy and spoke with Reith's full authority. He assured the conference that the BBC was alive to the desire to see empire broadcasting developed. He was aware that this desire was given added stimulus by the availability of short wave broadcasts, however technically imperfect, from other countries such as Holland and the United States. But he was firm in his response: 'The BBC technicians consider this work can only be the outcome of continued short wave experiments. We have not until now been entirely satisfied that we should be justified in spending large sums of money in erecting an experimental station and in conducting these experiments, which are necessarily costly.' He strongly advised against 'going wildly ahead to give the colonies merely what you can receive today from America on the short waves, which is unsatisfactory and distorted'.[7] He was backed by Eckersley, who spoke with the full weight of his authority as Chief Engineer:

We definitely feel it would be a great pity to raise hopes. Other people are forcing our hand by experimenting. Whatever is received, and however bad, is taken as marvellous because it has been received from such a long way, and the impression in the empire that America is very far ahead of us is due to the fact that they have rushed in at an imperfect thing, whereas we have been more cautious and are waiting for the perfect thing.[8]

Eckersley found his caution startlingly vindicated only a few months later.

The Postmaster General had authorised a private operator, Gerald Marcuse, a pioneer of low power communication over long distances and Honorary Secretary of the Radio Society of Great Britain, to conduct a once-only experiment. Against the advice of his officials he agreed to Marcuse transmitting a concert arranged by him from his transmitter at Caterham for relaying by stations in Australia and New Zealand. The Australian High Commissioner returned specially from a conference in Geneva to broadcast a short address to Australian listeners. The BBC had strongly objected because the broadcast would give the impression of the start of a new service and not an experiment. Eckersley described Marcuse's activities scathingly as 'not experiments but dabbling'.[9] Reith's information chief went as far as to observe that: 'It would be of great assistance to us if Sunday's affair was a fiasco.'[10] And so it proved to be. Eckersley had taken the precaution to cable a friendly Australian Station manager for a first-hand report on audibility. The report was unequivocal. Reception had been poor and broke down completely after about eleven minutes. 'Satisfactory relays of such transmissions at present not practical proposition', the cabled reply concluded.[11] Yet, only a few days before, the first Empire relay had taken place from Australia, on 4 September 1927. Dame Nellie Melba, the Australian Prime Minister, and the Governor of New South Wales had read messages at the microphone of Station 2FC Sydney. The programme had been carried by the Sydney short wave station 2ML on thirty-two metres and had been picked up at the Keston relay station and relayed to British listeners by 2LO.

Eckersley remained profoundly sensitive to suggestions that he was dragging his feet. He wrote twice to *The Times* in August 1927 to justify his attitude:

> At isolated moments it is possible in almost any part of the world to pick up somewhat distorted music and speech transmitted by short wave stations. On only some of these rather isolated occasions reception is reasonably good. Neither the time nor the duration of these admittedly unsatisfactory moments of reception can be anticipated. Therefore every factor essential to service is absent.[12]

This was a rigorous professional judgement, backed by a strong determination not to be deflected from what seemed to Eckersley to be the proper, responsible view for a public corporation to take. But there was another consideration to which Carpendale drew the attention of the assembled colonial officials. 'Our money is for listeners in England', he pointed out.[13] There would be a need for some assurance that financial support would be forthcoming from official sources before the BBC could feel justified in embarking on the expenditure involved in conducting the necessary experiment. Would the colonies, he asked, be prepared to consider some reciprocal financial basis? Although the BBC secured the warm support of the conference for an experiment, the question of funding was to remain unresolved for the next four years. In the end it was Reith who solved it in his own manner.

In a sense the BBC was caught in an uncomfortable dilemma. Ideally it needed time and money to work at leisure on learning more about why short wave signals behaved with such apparent unpredictability and on solving the problem of providing a signal of dependable service quality. On the other hand it was being pressed by the Colonial Office – albeit without offers of financial help; it had the warm support of colonial governors; there was public lobbying for British programmes to be made available to the empire, and there was ominous pressure from some interests for the Wireless Association to be entrusted with the task instead of the BBC. If the decision was deferred these interests might steal the initiative.

The problems facing the BBC's engineers were formidable. The ability of short wave signals to travel long distances was a relatively recent discovery. It had been believed at first that radio waves travelled in a straight line along the earth's surface. Long waves – or 'low frequencies' – were thought to be the most suitable for transmitting over long distances. They were indeed in common use for international radio telephony and wireless telegraphy in the early twenties. It was largely thanks to experiments carried out by radio amateurs that the fallacy of this belief was discovered, and this itself happened fortuitously, arising as it did from the decision made after the First World War to set aside the short wave bands for the use of wireless amateurs because they were thought to be useless for professional communications purposes. Sir Edward Appleton, whose researches led to the identification of ionised layers in the upper atmosphere against which short wave signals could be bounced back to earth, described in a BBC talk for overseas listeners how the breakthrough took place:

> A very remarkable thing happened. Suddenly round about 1921 British amateurs found themselves in communication with their American colleagues. Some of these short wave stations, though operating with a very small power indeed, were heard across 7,000 miles of the globe with only a simple two-valve receiver. In October 1924 the greatest distance of all was spanned when communication was established between Mr F. Bell of New Zealand and C.W. Goyden, a London schoolboy. Thus began what I have often called the short wave revolution.[14]

C.W. Goyden later became a professional radio engineer, joined the BBC Research Department and eventually became Chief Engineer of All-India Radio.[15] In 1924 Sir Edward Appleton and Dr Miles Barnett were able to demonstrate that the reflecting ionospheric layer truly existed and established that it was about sixty miles above ground level. Two years later Sir Edward Appleton went on to discover the existence of yet another layer, this time 150 miles from the ground, and he was able to show conclusively that it was this layer which embodied the characteristics most conducive to effectiveness in bouncing short wave signals back to earth. So it became established that these signals were capable of travelling very long distances by a series of 'hops' between the earth and the ionosphere and back again. The transmitter power required was much below that which would be needed to achieve the same result by long wave, assuming this to be possible. Both capital and running costs would thus be a great deal lower.

Appleton's discovery was still very recent when the possibility of empire broadcasting was first formally discussed at the Colonial Conference of 1927, and despite its crucial importance as a turning point in the history of communications a great deal remained to be learnt about the variations in the performance of individual frequencies with each phase of the eleven-year sunspot cycle, with the passing of the seasons and of the years, and with the time of day. At that very early stage engineers were only just beginning to foresee the possibility of being able one day to predict, fairly accurately, which frequencies would be most effective for a particular path at a particular moment in time. This was the main reason for Eckersley's caution and for his feeling that much research would be necessary before he could be confident that a moderately reliable service could be provided.

American broadcasters suffered from no such inhibitions. In keeping with the free enterprise system under which broadcasting had been developing in the United States, a number of experimental short wave stations – at Pittsburgh and Schenectady – began to operate on American soil from the early twenties. As has already been shown, their activities drew attention to the absence of a corresponding short wave service from Britain, notwithstanding the haphazard nature of their technical performance. Their development remained equally haphazard and subject to the whim and enterprise of individuals. No systematic development of international broadcasting took place until America's entry into the Second World War, when all private short wave stations were gradually brought under government supervision and eventually merged into the Voice of America, operating under the control of the Office of War Information.[16]

Holland was another country where early developments took place which played their part in stimulating the authorities in Britain to agree to the desirability of a British short wave service. As in the case of the original British Broadcasting Company it was manufacturing interests which were responsible for priming the pump. In this case it was the Dutch firm of Philips, which having moved into the designing of short wave transmitters, launched a regular daily service in 1928 from a transmitter at Heuzen, on the Zuyderzee, to the Dutch East Indies in order to demonstrate the effectiveness of its transmitters. Its call-sign was PCJ – which stood for 'Peace, Cheer and Joy'. The service was the precursor of today's Radio Nederland 'Happy Station'.[17] There was a ready-made audience for it in the Dutch colonial empire in the East Indies, and the distance – 9,000 miles – was almost ideal for short wave. Reith was well aware that similar opportunities existed in the British Empire. It came naturally to him to think in an imperial rather than on a parochial scale, and he shared the national sense of pride in the Empire which was reflected by the British Empire Exhibition in 1924. He had a particular interest in India which was to lead him in later life to the ultimate personal ambition of becoming Viceroy, having briefly toyed in 1934 with the thought of offering himself as a candidate for the job of putting Indian broadcasting on its feet and then staying on for good. The Chairman of the Governors, J.H. Whitley, talked him out of it.[18] Ten years earlier, in 1923, he was already urging action on the authorities in London and New Delhi, but neither the India Office nor the Viceroy of the day seemed to share his view of the importance of broadcasting in India: 'There is neither vision nor recognition of the immense potentialities of broadcasting', he wrote angrily in his diary; 'no ethical or moral appreciation; just commercialism. It is an unparalleled opportunity for service to India, but they have let the chance go.'[19] 'If broadcasting had been taken seriously in 1924', he wrote after the war, 'subsequent events in India might have been very different.'[20] When a request for help did at last come from the Viceroy, Lord Willingdon, in 1934, it was Lionel Fielden, a senior and much respected member of the Talks Department, whom Reith chose for the job which he himself had been briefly tempted to take. Similarly he sent Gerald Beadle, who later became Director of BBC Television, to Durban in South Africa in 1924 to be the local station's first superintendent. Beadle, basing himself on his experience there, was to make an important contribution to the thinking that went into the creation of the Empire Service.

The Colonial Conference of 1927 left the BBC in an awkward dilemma. Reith and Eckersley were eager to get on with building an experimental short wave station at Daventry and to proceed urgently with the necessary research. The project had been agreed in principle by the Post Office the year before, but the question of finance remained unresolved. Reith, predictably, reacted with a show of surprise and disappointment to a somewhat discouraging letter from Sir Evelyn Murray of the GPO, written shortly after the end of the Colonial Conference. Murray authorised the BBC to go ahead with building the transmitter, but he was unequivocal about who should foot the bill. He did not think the corporation could expect the Exchequer to contribute and knew of no reason why the work should be a charge on the taxpayer. The resources of the BBC, he felt, should be sufficient to cover the cost of experimental work 'which the corporation might reasonably be expected to undertake'.[21] Reith returned to the charge on 11 July saying he still could not see why the home listener should pay for empire broadcasting since its chief value would be to the empire.[22] Leo Amery, the Secretary of State for the Colonies, was not quite so discouraging as Murray. In answer to a question in the House of Commons he confirmed the Colonial Office view that 'the service would be very widely appreciated in the colonies'. However, he said, it would be premature to ask the colonies for contributions until completion of the experimental work. But he did not for a moment anticipate that 'dependencies

will show reluctance when the time comes to share the expenses involved'.[23]
That was to prove an over-optimistic statement, and it did not help Reith to
solve the immediate problem. Finally, on 28 June, Reith, clearly anxious to
bring the time-wasting to an end, wrote to Murray that he was taking steps to
push ahead with the experiments. 'In a year or so', he wrote, 'we should be in
a much better position to formulate a proper basis for empire broadcasting.'[24]
He made no mention of money, but the argument with the Post Office and
the Government's unhelpful attitude were to prove a foretaste of what was to
come. So was Reith's decision to go ahead regardless, taken in the private
knowledge that though Colonial Office officials had prevailed on the Colonial
Secretary to bring pressure to bear on the Postmaster General, this had been
of no avail.

One reason for Reith's sense of urgency was the activities of Gerald Marcuse. Against bitter opposition from the BBC Marcuse, who enjoyed strong
public and parliamentary support and was skilled at catching the attention of
the press, was licensed by the GPO on 1 September 1927 to transmit speech
and music on short wave for a period of six months. In explanation of the
Post Office decision Murray had argued that it would be politically embarrass-
ing to reject Marcuse's application. There would be glowing accounts in the
press and a strong demand from the Wireless Association to be given a
concession. Far better, he advised, for the BBC to take Marcuse and his
experiment under its wing, as this would undermine the strength of the
demand and the BBC's position would be safeguarded. 'I daresay you are right
in thinking his experiments are of no particular use', Murray wrote to Reith,
'but he will probably distribute a very different version to his supporters.'[25]
Finally Reith gave up, reassured no doubt by the fact that the Postmaster
General had made it clear to Marcuse and his supporters that he held out no
hope that a licence to transmit regular programmes to the dominions and
colonies would be granted to anyone other than the BBC. Marcuse duly
started his broadcasts on 11 September 1927. The Post Office had limited his
transmissions to a maximum of two hours a day at a power not exceeding
one kilowatt. He continued to operate almost daily until the end of August
1928, rather longer than had originally been intended, but Eckersley's fears
about the possible damaging effect on the BBC's own prospects proved unfounded. A few days before the Marcuse broadcasts started the BBC had itself
been formally authorised to start experimental transmissions, but these were
not to take place from Daventry as Eckersley had originally proposed. To
save time the BBC decided to hire an adapted short wave radio telephony
transmitter from Marconi's at Chelmsford, using an aerial slung between
already existing masts. The original aerial provided an all-round service as
opposed to a narrow directional 'beam', and power output was eight to ten
kilowatts. The first transmission, using the call sign G5SW, took place on 11
November 1927 in the form of an outside broadcast of the Armistice Day

Cenotaph Service – a reflection of the strong belief in the binding power of the shared experience of great national events which pervaded BBC thinking at the time and was to inspire much subsequent empire broadcasting.

Behind the scenes a great deal of discussion had been going on in the higher reaches of the BBC about the ultimate purpose of the new venture and who the programmes should seek to reach. Gerald Beadle, who by that time had returned from his stint in Durban to become BBC Station Director at Belfast, saw that purpose as 'maintaining a consolidated British Empire'.[26] Eckersley spoke along similar lines of 'Empire consolidation by wireless'.[27] Beadle, his horizons widened by his experience in South Africa, saw the commonwealth of English-speaking peoples as 'the greatest political and moral stronghold in the world'. He regarded communism and nascent nationalism in the empire as a grave threat to civilisation. That threat could be averted, he felt, if the commonwealth could be held together. 'Some consolidating influence is necessary', he wrote in a paper he drafted for Reith, 'and it needs to be an influence which reaches every man, woman and child. The influence needed is not propaganda in the ordinary sense of the term. It is a means of inter-course which will bring about familiarity with the everyday affairs of the empire.' For Beadle broadcasting was the obvious way of disseminating that influence. 'It cannot fail to stimulate and keep alive a keen interest in the affairs of the empire and it will, to a very large extent, prevent the imperial ideal from being swamped by local nationalism.'

A different, more cautious note was struck by Major C.F. Atkinson, the BBC's Foreign Director. In a paper roughly contemporary with Beadle's, he pointed out that programmes, though meant for the empire, would be audible the world over and not merely by listeners of British stock. Indirect propaganda suggesting a united British front against the foreigner would be inadmissible. Moreover the spoken matter would be in the same language as that spoken in the United States, and Americans would be quick to resent any suggestion that the British Empire and British ideas could be identified with the English language. Atkinson was frankly critical of Beadle's ideas. They were no doubt relevant to very pro-British colonies like Natal, but what about India and French Canada, he asked. It would be politically disastrous, in his view, 'to set up a partial organisation consisting of, so to say, the British-minded sections'. English, for him, was a sectional language with a sectional bias, 'definitely addressed to a political unit that does not include half the people speaking the language, and does include many to whom the language is unacceptable – besides enormous masses of people in India, Africa and elsewhere ethnically alien to the European culture to whom neither music nor word is intelligible'.[28] The point was a shrewd and realistic one, though in the climate of the period it was overridden by the greater potency of the imperial idea. It was not until the Second World War, and indeed well after

it, that it was to be fully grasped, and then only under the impetus of the
break-up of the empire, of Macmillan's 'wind of change', and of the spreading
acceptance of English as an international language.

There were other more practical problems which exercised the minds of the
planners, though today their solution is taken for granted. Gerald Beadle had
pointed to the fact that to reach audiences throughout the empire at suitable
local listening times the proposed service would have to be on the air very
nearly twenty-four hours out of twenty-four. The cost would be prohibitive.
Carpendale, in the same vein, had drawn the attention of the Colonial Conference to the difficulties raised by time differences, particularly in Asia, the
Far East and Australasia. 'Are they (the dominions and colonies) going to
consider setting up transmitting stations to hear London programmes in the
middle of the night?' he asked. 'Or would they request us to put on a brass
band at six in the morning?'[29] Carpendale automatically assumed that for a
brass band to be broadcast at six in the morning would require the band to
perform live in the studio at that early hour. Eckersley, on the other hand,
had already perceived the answer, in the shape of what he called 'bottled
programmes' – in other words recordings made for immediate use without
prior processing. But, as Edward Pawley, the historian of BBC Engineering,
has pointed out, recording was a relatively late starter among broadcasting
techniques and no really practical recording equipment was available until
1930.[30] Even then, as has been seen, it was far from reliable and reproduction
quality was doubtful. Nonetheless those who were applying their minds to
the problem were clearly not unhopeful of solving it even at that early stage.
Atkinson saw another possible way of making use of 'bottled programmes'.
'The bottled stuff can be sent from place to place,' he wrote, 'if so why radiate
it (and spoil it) when it can be sent by air or mail unspoilt to the rebroadcaster.
There is nothing burningly topical about a symphony.'[31] Thus was born the
idea which later became the BBC Transcription Service, with a massive output
in 1980 of over 500 hours of recorded programmes, bringing the best of BBC
Radio to local audiences in 100 countries. Financial cuts imposed by the
Government in 1981 reduced the annual output to 350 hours.

However, the central technical issue at the time concerned reception and
not recording. It is clear that in the early stages neither Eckersley, nor, for
that matter, Reith himself, envisaged that more than a handful of enthusiastic
radio amateurs would listen to the service direct from London. Their scheme
had a certain grandeur. They conceived the Empire Service as a system of
'scientifically organised relaying posts'[32] throughout the empire. This pre-
supposed a readiness on the part of dominion and colonial governments to
set up special transmitters on their territory to relay the London programmes.
Eckersley did not believe that a service could be guaranteed to what he termed
'the lonely listener in the bush'. Although he accepted that the Chelmsford
experimental station existed partly for such listeners, he took the view that

'we must consider him (the lonely listener) for, say, five years more,' presumably while the system of imperial links was being set up. Until he left the BBC for personal reasons in 1929, he continued to see the future service as mainly providing a radio link which would transport the programme in an acceptable form to the re-broadcaster, but by 1929 it had become clear from the response from overseas that the 'lonely listener in the bush' was far more important than had been imagined. The author of an internal memorandum of June 1929 was unequivocal on that point:

Contrary to our original expectation, all correspondence and other evidence go to show that it is the direct listener who most needs, most profits by and most consistently follows the G5SW transmissions ... The principal function of G5SW, if and when stabilised as a programme station, must be to serve the individual direct listener, local relay being of course possible and on occasions most desirable, but in no way the ruling consideration of the service.[33]

While the debate continued inside the BBC, external pressure for something to happen was mounting. Another Colonial Conference was in the offing, and the Post Office had reported to Reith that the Colonial Secretary, Lord Passfield, viewed matters with increasing impatience. Two years had elapsed since the conference of 1927 had enthusiastically endorsed the idea of empire broadcasting, even if the Government had been less than forthcoming on the subject of money. Though experimental broadcasts had been going ahead, there was still no sign of a more permanent service. Passfield was clearly worried that there would be protests at the apparent lack of progress and he asked the BBC to prepare a paper for the conference outlining the results of the experiment and setting out its views about the kind of service it wished to propose, how much it would cost and how the cost could be met.[34]

The BBC paper, when it emerged two months later, proved a sober and realistic document. By that time the BBC felt itself to be in a serious quandary. It was footing the bill for the Chelmsford experiment and every indication it had so far received from Whitehall suggested that however much the Post Office and the Colonial Office might support the project, that support was unlikely to be translated into hard cash. 'We shall never get money from the Colonial Office', Carpendale had written gloomily.[35] The exchange of programmes with the colonies and particularly the dominions was never likely to reach a scale which would make it possible to argue that the British home listener was deriving a substantial direct benefit from the scheme. 'We don't want their stuff', Carpendale wrote bluntly, 'and to a great extent they don't want ours.'[36] He went on to argue that to put out good popular programmes all round the dominions and the colonies to compete with what the dominion broadcasting stations were already providing would cost more than the BBC could afford, and more than the dominions would ever be prepared to pay for until the 'beam' system provided perfect reception. That was not likely to happen soon. About all that remained of the original scheme, Carpendale

concluded, was some consideration for the 'lonely listener'. The technical
advice, moreover, was that the existing Marconi transmitter and its aerial at
Chelmsford were not adequate. The transmitter was too much of a 'lash up'
and was unreliable, and for the purposes of transmitting programmes for
relaying by overseas stations rather than direct listening it was essential to
use a 'beam' – in other words a directional aerial – and not the makeshift
omnidirectional aerial which had been accepted as the best possible compromise at the start of the experiment. The BBC's Chief Accountant had written on
22 August 1929: 'I do not feel that we are justified in continuing a fairly
expensive service for a few scattered individuals over the world. I do not think
we should be justified in adopting this policy except as a result of considerable
pressure on the part of the Colonial Office'.[37] Eckersley, moreover, had
reaffirmed his view that the signal from Chelmsford 'cannot be regarded in
any way as a service as we consider service in this country'.[38]

These were the considerations that guided the drafters of the BBC memorandum. The corporation must not appear too keen, whatever its private
feelings, nor must it underplay the difficulties. If, after taking account of all
the reservations set out in the memorandum, the Government still insisted
that the service was wanted, the BBC would be better placed to insist that the
Government must pay. So the memorandum, while stating that it was now
possible to predict to some extent where reception would be good, at what
time and on what wavelengths, made it clear that the science of short wave
broadcasting had not yet been fully mastered. Though it accepted that G5SW
could now be heard almost all over the world, it was reluctant to express
anything more than very guarded optimism on the major technical issue:
'Under all reserves as to quality and regularity', it stated with a great show of
caution, 'something like a service is now possible given the requisite technical
conditions at both ends.'[39]

The memorandum was equally tentative on the subject of listener reaction.
There was not much direct evidence as to whether such a service was genuinely
desired, it said, but such evidence as was available suggested that the demand
was not confined to radio amateurs and did not just arise from the ephemeral
appeal of novelty. It came from genuine listeners, and their numbers could be
expected to rise when a more permanent service was introduced which did
not confine itself to relaying the home programmes but could adapt its timing
and contents to the needs of its listeners.

The memorandum is interesting for the insight it provides into the BBC's
view of its intended audience and its attitude towards those others who, while
not part of the intended audience, might nonetheless be expected to eaves-
drop. The target audience was quite unequivocally white and British.

The exclusion of people of other colours is justified – at least at present – by the fact
that the field of appeal of European-type programmes is substantially limited to
Europeans and also by the fact that, in proportion as native populations develop an

interest in broadcasting, the local service [in the colony concerned] will provide the natives with programmes of their own type.

British subjects living under other flags – that is to say not in British dominions or colonies – were thought to present a problem: 'There might be troublesome political implications in the idea that a broadcasting service may address itself frankly and directly to its co-nationals and sympathisers living under another flag.'

The memorandum noted that short wave stations were springing up everywhere, some under the control of governments. Their objectives seemed to be twofold: to keep in touch with outlying nationals, and to provide a world presentation of the national viewpoint in terms of national culture. It observed that neither of these two objectives was illegitimate but that the boundary between culture and tendentious propaganda was indefinite.

For the British Empire the principle of abstaining from direct address to co-nationals (living under other flags) is probably important owing to its worldwide contacts and in particular to its situation vis-à-vis the United States. That country contains not only the vast bulk (some 1,100,000) of all British whites living under other flags, but is itself the largest English-speaking nation in the world ... On the other hand, the British Empire is presumably entitled no less than others to diffuse its ideas and its culture, and it is not impossible to conceive of a situation in which deliberate recourse to propaganda broadcasting might become desirable.

By the time the memorandum came to be prepared the BBC appeared to have taken a major step forward in resolving the conflict it had identified between the needs of the more developed dominions and those of the colonies. The dominions, already well provided with radio services, would not require routine daily programmes, but they would want to participate through radio relays in the great ceremonies and events of the empire. On the other hand, broadcasting in the colonies was less well developed. There was a need for a service from London which could be relayed *in toto*. This would also meet the requirements of the 'lonely listener in the bush'. The latter would be particularly interested in news. The BBC had so far not been allowed to feature news bulletins in its experimental broadcasts from Chelmsford because of objections from the Fleet Street news agencies, which saw the worldwide broadcasting of news as a threat to their wire services and an infringement of their copyright.

While not going into details about the types of programmes to be included, the BBC was clear on one point: 'The routine programmes designed to serve listeners in the colonies should be composed somewhat differently from the standard European programme and should consist essentially of news, with entertainment and home contacts built round it.' 'Sentimental' items would be included, such as the chimes of Big Ben. This did not mean that home programmes could not find their way into the schedules, particularly if they were transmitted at a time which happened to be suitable for the colonies.

This would have the advantage of cutting costs. But they would have to be selected specially with the overseas listener in mind, not relayed automatically.

It is clear that the drafters of the memorandum felt unable to predict with any certainty the likely evolution of inter-continental broadcasting at a time when local services were often themselves at a very early stage of development. The memorandum envisaged the possibility that local broadcasting in the colonies might take on the job of serving the native population while whites listened to the distant station of their own homeland. On the other hand, even where good quality local broadcasting was available, the habit of listening direct to distant parts of the world might become general. However, there was not enough hard evidence on which to base any firm conclusions. Decisions about what immediate steps to take would have to be *a priori* and speculative.

The BBC planners seem to have made a brave first attempt at dealing with the time-zone problem. In looking at their proposals it is important to remember that they were venturing into the unknown with no previous experience to guide them. Moreover the lavish provision of transmitters, directional aerials and frequencies available to the international broadcasters of today was beyond their wildest dreams. They were planning on the basis of very limited means, and even more limited knowledge. To meet the needs of different types of audiences with different requirements and living in different time zones they envisaged four different programme segments transmitted at four different times every twenty-four hours, each designed to suit the requirements of a particular area. First there would be a 'colonial' programme largely intended for the African colonies. This would be broadcast in the afternoon and would be partly, but only partly, made up of material shared with home listeners. Then there would be a programme for South Africa which would consist largely of a straight relay of the evening home programme, though there was talk of a possible special news bulletin in Afrikaans. An 'Australasian' programme would be transmitted in the morning, but since this would take place before the day's home broadcasting had started it would have to be 'specially performed'. The same would be true of the 'Canadian' programme, which, the memorandum noted, would involve night staff and special terms for performers since it would have to be transmitted in the small hours. The assumption throughout was that peak local listening time was in the evening. Breakfast-time broadcasting was still a thing of the future.

The memorandum was candid about the technical provision which would be required for such a service. To reach all parts of the empire under varying conditions of light and darkness would require at least two frequencies fairly widely spaced apart, one below twenty metres and the other above thirty metres. The Chelmsford plant would not suffice. A new station would be needed, and the BBC engineers saw this as eventually expanding to four or five directional aerial systems beaming programmes to different parts of the empire. This would ensure much better audibility than the existing omni-directional aerial at Chelmsford. But the BBC refrained from making the building of such a station a condition for going ahead with the service. With commendable restraint the engineers advised that not enough experience had been built up to justify the heavy expenditure involved. Much land would be needed for aerials. The equipment would be costly and at the present rate of technical progress might soon become obsolescent. So they recommended temporarily setting up a more modest station, operating on two frequencies instead of the single one at Chelmsford and with an omni-directional aerial. Daventry would be the likeliest site. After five years, they said, it should be possible to specify the equipment required for a permanent station.

In conclusion the BBC made three major points. In the first it set out the classic case for being entrusted with the responsibility for the new service:

It has been assumed throughout that an Empire Service, if called for, would be placed executively in the hands of the BBC, as no new body, whether of public service or commercial constitution, would be able to provide the service at lower cost, since such a body would not have the benefit of BBC general programme expenditure, not to mention its experience and organisation.

In the second point, the BBC sounded a note of caution: 'While optimism as to the eventual popularity and effectiveness of an empire broadcasting service is justified, the work of the immediate future would be one of pioneering.' There would be difficulties, disappointments and criticism. The BBC would need the support of the dominion and colonial authorities concerned. The third point, predictably, concerned money. The BBC made it clear that 'the responsibility of deciding whether a service is required ... must clearly be left entirely to those whom it concerns'. 'As home listeners cannot listen to the short wave stations, it does not appear that any part of the expense of the "outgoing service" can equitably be charged to them.'

Immediate official reaction to the BBC memorandum seemed encouraging as far as it went. Passfield was impressed by its merits, though he added that the project was 'not free from difficulties'.[40] The Post Office, in its own comments to the Colonial Office, endorsed the BBC view that British listeners should not have to pay. The countries which would benefit should pay, the Post Office averred. The Colonial Office seemed to agree. A meeting of officials representing the various ministries concerned was called to clear away any difficulties before the Colonial Conference met. The India Office, which had unaccountably been left out of the previous consultations, was included, but not the Foreign Office. Reith attended personally. It soon became clear that the main purpose of the meeting was to find objections to every possible solution to the financial problem. No one wanted to pay. Thus it was pointed out that in any scheme requiring listeners to pay a licence fee it would not be possible to charge foreign listeners. Moreover, so far as India and the colonies were concerned, it was felt not to be right to charge the cost of the service to the general revenue of each colony because the service would mainly benefit whites whereas general revenue was largely derived from taxes paid by natives, who were not among the intended audience. As to white listeners, it would be difficult to collect licence fees from many of them because they lived in small, scattered and isolated communities. The Dominions Office representative said there was practically no prospect of obtaining a financial contribution from dominion governments. The Treasury representative seems to have said nothing, even when asked point blank by Reith why the service could not be paid out of the large sum (£400,000) which the Treasury retained annually from the broadcast licence fee income. 'Let the Treasury say how much it would be prepared to make available', Reith proposed. The response, if there was any, was not recorded.[41]

The meeting ended inconclusively with a request to the BBC to produce a cheaper scheme confined to transmitting news, gramophone records and existing home programmes. It is true that all the ministries concerned placed on record their whole-hearted support for the idea of empire broadcasting and their anxiety that it should go ahead. Reith might have felt mildly encouraged by this, but he was too much of a realist to be deceived. The meeting had annoyed him.

We are likely to be let down all round [he wrote to Atkinson]. In fact we have been already. Or perhaps it might be better put that we are likely to be left with the baby to carry because we are too decent to let the infant drown. Apart from ordinary instincts of humanity, we realise that it might have a great career in front of it.[42]

But he was resolved to stick to his guns: 'We will not be put upon', he wrote, 'other people have got to do something, including, in my opinion, refunding us for the past.'

Neither the Colonial Conference, which met on 30 June 1930, nor the Dominions Conference which followed soon after, gave Reith any cause for going back on his gloomy appraisal of the prospects. The BBC scheme had been duly scaled down and its cost nearly halved. The Post Office representative felt able to say that if the colonial governments supported the scheme and said they were prepared to contribute something towards the cost, he thought the Colonial Secretary and the Postmaster General between them might be able to persuade the Treasury to provide the means to make a start. However, though warm support was once again expressed, it soon became clear that the colonies would not countenance meeting even part of the cost out of ordinary revenue. The only possible source of funds, in their view, was from a colonial licence fee, which had yet to be instituted. It was unlikely that this would produce funds for some time, and then not on a sufficient scale to cover the full cost. So, though the colonial governors expressed their unanimous and enthusiastic appreciation for the BBC's help, and the reduced scheme was agreed, the question of where funds were to be found to make a start was left in the air.[43]

The outcome of the Dominions Conference was even more discouraging. Harold Bishop, the Assistant Chief Engineer, described the proceedings as 'unsatisfactory and silly'.[44] The meeting had had nothing constructive to propose about financing. The composition of the Committee on Communications was hardly calculated to fill Reith with confidence. Though chaired by the Prime Minister of New Zealand, most of its members were Post Office telecommunications specialists and accountants. South Africa, for instance, was represented by its Commissioner for Inland Revenue and its Commissioner for Pensions, and Australia by the Government's Financial Adviser and the accountant from the High Commissioner's office in London. It was hardly the kind of body that could be expected to take a broad, long-term view on a matter of this kind, and it did not. It began by turning down the BBC's reduced scheme which had been agreed by the colonies. Reith returned with a modified and slightly cheaper version of the original BBC proposal, but though this was eventually agreed and the now customary lip-service was paid once again to the idea of empire broadcasting, the conference stalled on the question of finance, claiming it needed further information before it could determine if the technical and financial difficulties could be overcome. As a first step it invited the BBC to get in touch with dominion broadcasting organisations to ascertain their views as to the value to them of such a service and their readiness to make a contribution to the cost in return for the right to relay.[45] In other words the dominion governments were not themselves going to contribute anything. The Treasury, for its part, had make it clear that it was 'far from satisfied that a case has been made out for committing the British Exchequer to the proposed expenditure'.

The BBC proposals had thus been neatly and deliberately kicked into touch. Reith moved immediately to try to break the deadlock. Broadcasting organisations in the dominions were urgently contacted, as the conference had requested, but Reith made it clear to the Post Office and the Colonial Office that little practical result was to be expected. The BBC had regular contacts with dominion radio stations and knew full well that there was no large scale demand for a programme service from Britain other than the occasional relaying of major events and ceremonies. The Australian Broadcasting Company's reply, when it came, confirmed this. High quality reception was essential, it said, if the interest of listeners was to be maintained beyond the novelty stage, and this could not be achieved. There was no interest in a broadcast news service, only in occasional relays.[46] Writing simultaneously to the Post Office and the Colonial Office, Reith emphasised once more that there was a real and steady demand for the service from the colonies and that there was a need for Britain to be able to hold its own in the face of developing foreign competition. The mother country had a direct responsibility towards the colonies which no longer existed towards the self-governing dominions, who in any case had their own broadcasting services. He urged both government departments to agree to make a start with a service to the colonies without waiting for what was bound to be a negative or at best non-committal response from the dominions. Enough benefits would accrue to Britain itself, including the stimulation of commonwealth trade, to justify the British Government in financing the operation.[47]

What followed was predictable, and indeed Reith himself had predicted it. In a conversation with Sir Samuel Wilson, the Permanent Under Secretary at the Colonial Office, Reith established that that ministry, for its part, had no money, and neither had the colonies themselves. Revenue might be expected in due course from the proposed colonial radio licence fee, but not until the service had been in operation for some time.[48] In the meantime, Wilson had drawn a blank with the Treasury. 'I can get very little out of them', he wrote to Reith, 'except that there is not the slightest chance of the Chancellor agreeing to a special vote for the amount we require.'[49] Then came the expected question: Would Reith not agree to the BBC priming the pump? No, said Reith. If the worst came to the worst he would of course go back to the Board of Governors, but he held out no hope that the Board would reverse its view that the British listener should not be asked to foot the bill. Finally, as Britain moved into the financial crisis of the summer of 1931, Wilson wrote to Reith in terms which left no room for hope: 'Our efforts to get the Treasury to agree to help us in initiating a colonial scheme have fallen through, and in view of the present financial situation, my Secretary of State is not prepared to press them any further.' The only hope, Wilson said to Reith, lay in 'some arrangement with you'.[50]

Reith's disappointment was profound: 'Few things are more important from the point of view of the spirit of British culture, British information and British propaganda', he wrote to Wilson in reply. 'Moreover it is a consolidating element within the empire, which in these days one cannot ignore. We are behind every other country of any size in this matter.'[51] Publicly he refused to believe that the Treasury could not be prevailed upon to reconsider its decision. But privately he had already accepted the inevitable. After a conversation with Sir Samuel Wilson in May 1931 he noted in his diary that 'the scheme may drop altogether' and commented bitterly: 'It is tragic that so important a matter should be allowed to drop for lack of £22,000 a year, but it is typical of the way in which this country is run.' But in a handwritten footnote of a later date he added: 'Actually, however, I was quite determined that it should not do so and that if the Government maintained their unhelpful, feeble attitude the BBC should do the whole thing on its own.'[52]

As Britain plunged deep into financial and political trouble, and despite the fact that the BBC itself was expected to make its own contribution to the cuts in national expenditure which were being called for by the Government, the Board of Governors agreed to Reith's recommendation that the BBC should go it alone.[53] Reith must have smiled wrily on receiving Wilson's letter of appreciation: 'I am awfully glad to hear this', Wilson wrote, 'and I would like to offer you my best congratulations on your decision ... I am sure it is sound and that you will never regret it.'[54] Reith thought it right to remind Wilson in his reply that, at the recent Colonial Conference, the colonial governors had undertaken to introduce a colonial radio licence fee system and to contribute its proceeds to the cost of running the service. Perhaps the Colonial Office should write to them to make sure the undertaking was not forgotten. In the meantime the Board of Governors resolved on 28 October 'to proceed with the erection of a high power transmitting station for empire purposes,'[55] the site of the station to be Daventry, where External Services transmitters operate to this day. The die was cast.

2
The Empire Service

Seen in the light of present day experience it is hard to imagine how Reith and his colleagues can have hoped that the early broadcasts of the Empire Service would make a major and immediate impact. Practically no funds had been made available for programme purposes, and leaving aside the news and the introductory addresses by Whitley and Reith most of the first day's programme offerings consisted of music either on gramophone records or relayed from the national networks. There was a good deal of dance music which was the staple of broadcasting at the time, mostly relayed live from dance halls and hotels up and down the country. There were some light classics, a piano recital on records by the French pianist Alfred Cortot, and chamber music by Mozart, Mendelssohn and Arenski. Each of the five two-hour transmissions into which the day was divided included a talk. E.M. Forster reviewed new books in one transmission, the cartoonist David Low addressed himself 'To one of my so-called victims' in another, and Vernon Bartlett, recently recruited on to the staff to give talks on foreign affairs, spoke about 'The world and ourselves'. Captain C.G. Graves who had been Assistant Director of Programmes since 1929 and whom Reith had placed in charge of the Empire Service, recalled in 1937 that there was no undue confidence within the BBC that the service would take hold, even though the experimental broadcasts of the last five years from Chelmsford suggested that the demand was there. According to Graves, Noel Ashbridge, who had succeeded Eckersley as Chief Engineer in 1929, had been very guarded about the prospects when they first discussed them shortly after Graves's appointment, despite the fact that Ashbridge had always been among the most positive advocates of the project. Indeed he had argued strongly for the service to start on a substantial scale if it was to have any chance of establishing itself. 'Looking at the programmes for that day and subsequent days', Graves wrote in 1937, 'I blush, but you must remember that all we had to spend on them was £10 a week.'[1]

It is well to bear in mind, however, that the element of expectation and novelty must have acted as a powerful incentive for prospective listeners. The fact of being able to listen to London over vast distances was clearly an exciting prospect not just in a technical sense but because of the strength of the spirit of empire which was still at large. Broadcasting, too, was still a relatively new thing. In the older dominions it was not as far advanced as in Britain and large areas outside the main centres of population received no service. Most of the colonies had no radio services at all. As to programming, it was still unsophisticated by modern standards. A high proportion of the daily diet took the form of music, much of it light, popular stuff, referred to disparagingly by those who thought broadcasting ought to be more ambitious as 'restaurant-type music'. But to the contemporary mind even dance music was capable of being invested with a civilising mission. In a pamphlet published at the time and much disliked by Reith, Sir Harry Brittain conveyed something of the climate of the time.

There is something magnificently romantic in the thought that men on trek in the desert or jungle will be able, by switching a little lever, to listen to the dance bands of sophisticated civilisation. I have known many of these lonely pioneers who are seeking something "beyond the ranges". Despite their years of wandering they nearly all have a nostalgia for home. I have known men in the wild places of northern Canada read any trashy novel that mentioned Piccadilly or the Strand ... How much more disturbing to that spirit of nostalgia will be the sounds of the Britain they love! Imagine the men in the heart of an African desert hearing the frantic applause at a vaudeville item in the Palladium.

What undoubtedly helped to give the service a flying start was King George v's eventual acceptance of the BBC's suggestion that he should broadcast to the country and to the empire on Christmas Day 1932. The idea clearly took some years to gain the approval of the Palace. Reith first broached the possibility with Lord Stamfordham, the King's Private Secretary, in 1927, and the matter was touched on again on a number of occasions in subsequent years. The King, of course, was occasionally heard on the air, but this was invariably in the context of state occasions which he was called upon to address. One such occasion was the opening of the Naval Conference in January 1930. The event, including the King's speech, was widely relayed all over the world. On that occasion, Reith proudly noted, the Savoy Hill control room was 'the radio centre of the world, hundreds of transmitters depended on it'.[2] The King was said to have been delighted with the result. However there was no response when the BBC's Chairman, J.H. Whitley, suggested to the King that he might open the Empire Service transmitters, and it was not until October 1932 that Reith succeeded in bringing matters to a head with Sir Clive Wigram, who had succeeded Stamfordham as Private Secretary. Wigram, though sympathetic, was none too happy about the prospects. 'He said he had had two sleepless nights about it', wrote Reith in his diary, 'and was it a religious service. Eventually he said he was in favour of it, but that he found the King difficult to manage. The King was frequently saying he was too modern.'[3] After several exchanges of letters and telephone calls the matter was finally settled as Reith wished and an announcement was issued by the Palace on 24 November.

The broadcast itself came as the climax of the Christmas Day empire link-up and was carried on all domestic and empire transmitters. 'An anxious afternoon for all concerned in the BBC', Reith wrote. 'So many things that might go wrong. The complications and delicacies of timing and switching and relaying from one part of the world to another. Nothing went wrong. All excellent. It was a triumph for him [the King] and for BBC engineers and programme planners.'[4] On Reith's instructions the King was announced at the microphone by Admiral Carpendale, Reith's deputy. 'The King was evidently quite moved and spoke more personally and effectively than I had ever heard him. It was quite extraordinary how quickly replies came from the various parts of the empire. One of the most impressive things was the sound of Niagara.' More important, in the long term, was the new, more direct and more personal channel of contact which had been introduced in the relationship between monarch and people, both at home and abroad. Such a development was entirely in line with Reith's view of the ultimate purpose of the Empire Service. 'The King was delighted with the whole affair', Wigram reported to Reith. Gerald Cock, the pioneer of BBC outside broadcasts, who was in charge of the arrangements for the King's broadcast at Sandringham, received a pair of gold links with the King's monogram on them. 'He evidently had quite an interesting time, the King being in very good form', Reith noted in his diary.[5] Reith glowed with satisfaction at what had been achieved:

It was the most spectacular success in BBC history so far. The King had been heard all over the world with surprising clarity. Only in New Zealand were parts of the speech inaudible owing to atmospherics. It was sensationally starred in foreign countries; the *New York Times* in large type: 'Distant Lands Thrill to His "God Bless You"'; two thousand leading articles were counted in Broadcasting House.[6]

The King was 'very pleased and much moved' with the bound volume of letters received from all over the empire which Reith sent to him through Wigram. The French writer André Siegfried, a perceptive observer of national character, described the effect of a later broadcast by King George v, his Jubilee address to the empire in 1935, in terms equally applicable to that first Christmas Day message:

I heard in Canada King George v at the time of his Jubilee address his people over the radio. Each individual heard his voice and had the feeling of being in his presence. He no longer seemed a symbol, something cold, abstract; he was a human being speaking to human beings. And what was he saying? Just what could best touch all these men, attached, in accordance with their traditions, to a liberal conception of life.

Whatever the truth about the effect of the King's first broadcast to the empire and the attendant world-wide publicity on the subsequent success of the new service, it was certainly considerable and was thought to have been at the time. According to Graves the broadcast was widely regarded overseas as an Empire Station programme whereas it had been planned long before it became known publicly that the Empire Service would be on the air. It set the standard for the new service and it was imperative, Graves felt, to retain the interest thus aroused. At all events the size of the BBC's mail bag from abroad made it clear beyond any doubt that the service could be heard and that it was meeting a genuine demand, not just from radio amateurs but from ordinary listeners. In the first year 11,250 letters were received, 13,500 in 1934 and over 25,000 in 1935. Significantly, though the trend was later reversed, between sixty and sixty-five per cent of those letters came from the United States. By May 1934 Ashbridge was able to tell Reith that 300-400 letters were being received from America every week. This was in itself an interesting comment on the fears which had earlier been expressed about possible adverse American reactions to a service which identified the English language with the British Empire and British ideas. Though there was some heart searching inside the BBC about this unexpected predominance of American listening, the explanation was not hard to find: with a population of 125 million at the time the United States represented by far the largest single concentration of English speaking people in the world, four times as numerous as the population of British stock in the whole of the British Empire, which was the intended audience. It had a commercial broadcasting system which catered largely for a mass audience, and with at least a million radio sets capable of receiving short wave signals it had a larger potential audience for foreign broadcasts than any other country in the world.

Graves started with a staff of four – himself, Malcolm Frost and two secretaries. He was joined shortly after from Manchester by J.B. Clark, who was to have a long and distinguished career in the External Services, of which he was the Director for thirteen years. Despite the slender resources available the scale of the service from the start was considerably more substantial than the scheme which had been put forward by Reith at the Colonial Conference in 1930. The four daily transmissions set out in the BBC's Memorandum of 1930 had been increased to five. The daily broadcast time had been raised from under eight hours to ten. Whereas the proposals discussed at the Colonial Conference had been intended primarily to serve the colonies, the service as it actually emerged placed as much emphasis on the older dominions and did not ignore the interests of British listeners in foreign countries. It was in effect an embryo World Service.

The earliest transmission scheme as it was introduced on 19 December 1932 was based on the assumption, soon to be proved faulty, that it was possible to beam programmes exclusively to particular regions of the world and that only listeners in the intended target area would be able to hear them. Thus the first transmission of the day, from 9.30 to 11.30 am, was designated for Australia and New Zealand. The second, from 2.30 to 4.30 pm, was intended for India; the third, from 6.00 to 8.00 pm, for East and Southern Africa, and the fourth, from 8.30 to 10.30 pm, for West Africa. Canada and the West Indies were served by a fifth, overnight transmission scheduled from 1.00 to 3.00 am.

However two facts soon became apparent. The first was that short wave broadcasting could not select one regional audience to the exclusion of all others. Cross-listening was inevitable. For instance it emerged that listeners in Western Australia and the West Indies found that the Indian transmission, though not intended for them, was easier to receive in their area, while the evening transmission to West Africa was found to be more audible in New Zealand in the morning than the transmission intended for Australasia. The second fact to emerge was that though it was originally assumed that most listening was done in the evening, as normally happened in Britain, short wave listeners were in fact prepared to tune in at other times if an audible signal was available. The first of these two lessons was to have particularly far-reaching effects. It strengthened the BBC's resolve to speak only with one voice. Whatever regional emphasis was placed on any particular programme it could never be at the expense of overall consistency since it had to be assumed that it was likely to be heard almost anywhere. Thus not only did it come naturally to the BBC, as a matter of fundamental policy, to deal with its listeners with unwavering honesty, but it was also made imperative by the technical characteristics of short wave broadcasting. Such considerations became crucially important on the introduction of foreign language broad-casting in 1938, when Reith resolutely opposed any suggestion that the approach to news broadcasting should be any different in the foreign services from what had become well established practice in the Empire Service or that the Arab world should be treated differently from Latin-America. The BBC applied these principles to a unique degree among external broadcasters, and the source of its later effectiveness and reputation is to be found in those early decisions born both of principle and of practical necessity.

Such thoughts, however, were far from the minds of Graves and Ashbridge in those first few months of the Empire Service. 'What I need is £sd.',[7] Graves wrote to Ashbridge only a few weeks after the start of the service. By that he meant 'a programme allowance which does give me a chance of putting on exclusive and decent quality programmes, particularly OBS'.* But he then went on to argue that it was not worth asking for more until and unless there could be a certainty that reception would be good enough to justify pro-gramme expenditure roughly equivalent to the funds allotted to the average regional station at home. Giving programmes financial priority over technical improvements at that stage would be placing the cart before the horse. As an engineer Ashbridge could not disagree. He took the view that 'the perform-ance of the station is somewhat better than was anticipated during the design period',[8] but he admitted that the excellent propagation conditions which prevailed during the tests preceding the official opening of the service had given an excessively rosy impression of what was to be expected. Conditions had then worsened and there had been complaints of poor reception from

*Outside Broadcasts.

some areas. By and large, however, the individual listener, whose interests were paramount in the minds of Graves and Ashbridge, appeared to be better satisfied than dominion radio stations, which required a consistently reliable signal of high quality which would enable them to schedule relays of London broadcasts long in advance. This they were not getting, particularly in New Zealand and to some extent in Australia. They looked on the Empire Service as a potential source of free programmes of high quality to help eke out their own slender resources. As Ashbridge pointed out in a note to Reith, the exaggerated publicity given to the new Daventry station, which had been described as the most modern in the world, had led to unrealistic expectations. If colonial and other broadcasters want to relay the Empire Service, Ashbridge wrote, 'we shall be only too pleased', but that was not the primary objective, which was to serve individual listeners.[9] Technically speaking the two requirements were in conflict, since point-to-point communication, necessary to achieve the highest quality for rebroadcasting purposes, required highly directional aerials and a narrow beam. This was incompatible with the BBC's stated objective, which was to provide a broadcast service for all parts of the empire.

Ashbridge was aware that invidious comparisons were being made with the performance of other stations and set out to put the record straight, as many of his successors have had to do down the years in answer to generalised complaints of poor reception. The French station 'Radio Coloniale', broadcasting from Pontoise, had received high praise for audibility but was said by Ashbridge to be a little better than Daventry in South Africa and Western Canada, while elsewhere 'we are reported better'.[10] The German short wave station at Zeesen, which was rapidly to become the BBC's main competitor, evidently operated on a series of relatively narrow beams directed at the strategically important areas selected by the German Government for political reasons. Within its limited service area it undoubtedly provided a stronger signal than Daventry. The Dutch station at Huizen, while providing a signal of about the same strength as the BBC in its main target areas in the Dutch East Indies and the Caribbean, enjoyed better audibility than the BBC in India. As for the American stations at Pittsburgh and Schenectady, their performance was thought by Ashbridge to be roughly on a par with the BBC's.

The answer to the audibility problem lay in the first place in the aerial design at Daventry. The two Standard Telephones and Cables transmitters installed at the new station in 1932 were capable of supplying a power output of ten to fifteen kilowatts. This was regarded as very substantial at the time and was described as 'high power'. It was certainly as high as any existing short wave transmitter anywhere in the world, though the Germans were soon to start the power race when they began to re-equip their station at Zeesen with fifty kilowatt transmitters in 1934. Experiments with new aerial arrangements at Daventry began within a few weeks of the start of the Empire

Service and a much improved performance was obtained within six months by using somewhat crude, locally improvised installations on higher masts which were available on the site. By 1935 the whole system had been successfully redesigned to comprise twenty-five aerials, fourteen of which were equipped with reversible reflectors. This aerial complex was designed to cover the six short wave broadcasting wave bands and to work on the twelve wavelengths assigned to the BBC at that time.[11] It was a far cry from the rudimentary installation at Chelmsford on which the experiments had begun in 1927, with its one omnidirectional aerial, its eight to ten kilowatt transmitter and its single frequency.

In the meantime Graves and Ashbridge were analysing the voluminous correspondence received from all over the world for indications of listeners' tastes and interests and to test the acceptability to the audience of the transmission pattern introduced at the start. Within a few months Graves had succeeded in securing a programme allowance of £100 a week, still a paltry amount by the standards of domestic broadcasting, but by the end of 1933 this had been doubled to £200. After only three months and in response to a large number of requests from listeners, two hours had been added to the afternoon transmission to India. A further two and a half hours were added by the end of June 1933, making a daily total of fourteen and a half hours. The decision had also been taken to cease to describe each transmission by the name of the region of the globe for which it was intended. This was logical in view of the substantial evidence of cross-listening. 'One period of transmission', the BBC Year-Book* stated in 1934, 'can cater coincidently for apparently different needs in widely separated countries, and at the same time provide an evening programme for a third country.'[12] Transmissions were henceforth to be referred to as 'Transmissions I to V', and there were some changes in the pattern as well as increases. For instance it was found impossible because of propagation difficulties to give Australia and New Zealand a reasonable service at the time originally chosen and it was decided that the only way to deal with the problem was to alter the time of the broadcasts according to the seasons. A new band of broadcasts was introduced at midday and the two evening transmissions intended for different parts of Africa were placed end to end to form a single block of four and a half hours.

At the end of the first eighteen months Graves and Ashbridge stood back to take stock. On the programme side news had shown itself to be the most popular single item, particularly with isolated listeners without immediate access to other sources of information. However Empire News, Graves felt, needed to be separated from Home News and to have its own staff. Outside broadcasts of sport and public occasions had been very welcome too. So had light classics, popular and dance music, jazz and variety. On the other hand

*The title of this publication varies over the years. We have used the correct style for each year.

talks had had a mixed reception. Shortage of resources had compelled the Empire Service planners to confine the talks output largely to what was available in the home networks, and as Graves put it, 'Talks of a general character which are acceptable to home listeners are not usually of a type that appeals overseas.'[13] There was a need for special empire talks and speakers: 'The method of presentation should be different – simpler and never academic.' In effect Graves was making the case for his own programme department, and he was soon to get it, at least in embryo. 'It has been definitely proved', he wrote, 'that in order to achieve satisfactory listening overseas, the employment of a different technique from that used in this country is desirable.' What was needed, he said, were two extra staff to work under him, one to deal with music and the other with outside broadcasts, talks, variety and drama. They would be partly concerned with commissioning 'exclusive' empire programmes and partly with the adaptation and presentation of suitable home programmes. In the talks field their main objective would be to promote closer understanding between the peoples of the commonwealth.

All this was modest enough by today's standards, but it was a beginning and pointed the way to future developments. It was certainly not too much in view of the objective which Graves had set himself. It was essential, he said, to raise the empire programmes to the level of the home services in order to maintain a position in world broadcasting in keeping with the prestige of the BBC and of Britain. He stressed the growing importance of foreign competition in the English language, more particularly though by no means exclusively from Germany. A new dimension was quietly being introduced into the picture. The *BBC Annual 1935* put it this way:

> The Empire Service, though in a real sense domestic to the British Commonwealth of Nations, has the further mission of putting the British outlook – not meaning thereby propaganda but simple presentation – on the immaterial map of the world that is being created by the short wave stations of the various countries. France, Germany and Italy ... all possess short wave service through which to address the whole world, and the British Commonwealth, both as community and as idea, cannot but take its turn on the platform.[14]

Almost imperceptibly, and without departing from the original objectives of the Empire Service, the BBC was beginning to move towards a broader conception of its role in the world, one which involved the dissemination of British views and British values not just within the empire but to a wider public which was beginning to be exposed to the growing propaganda effort of Germany and Italy. Already the BBC was being made aware that in the colonies and in India its audience was not confined to British expatriates but included a growing number of educated 'natives'. This was due to the creation of broadcasting stations in increasing numbers in the colonies and to the development of what was then known as wireless exchanges – in other words wired rediffusion systems – in major population centres in the colonies.

Direct relays were at the same time being increasingly supplemented by the use on the local air of recorded programmes made available by the BBC. Malcolm Frost, who had been sent on a tour of the empire at the end of 1932, reported that there would be a greater readiness to relay the Empire Service if it offered programmes of higher quality. Frost himself was a strong advocate of supplying 'bottled' BBC programmes to would-be rebroadcasters in the empire. The unreliability of short waves as a means of communication would be overcome and individual stations would be able to schedule BBC programmes when it suited them and to repeat them if they wished as often as they liked. He had taken a first sample selection of programmes with him on his tour and these had gone down well wherever he went. The selection included 'Songs from the Shows', British musical comedy successes, with the Wireless Chorus and the BBC Orchestra, *Postman's Knock*, a musical comedy by Claude Hulbert; a dramatised biography of Christopher Wren, a vaudeville programme with the BBC Dance Orchestra, and a programme of traditional Scottish music including pipe bands. Graves reported that the New Zealand Broadcasting Board had taken the first batch and would take at least one such programme each week if a regular supply could be arranged. Similar reactions came from Australia, South Africa, India, Ceylon, Kenya and Southern Rhodesia. By the end of 1934 a second sample selection of music, drama and talks had been issued and widely ordered by overseas stations, and J.B. Clark was describing this new activity as 'a valuable supplement to the direct Empire Service'.[15]

It is curious to note, however, that Graves, although appreciating the value of transcriptions, appeared to give them a low priority. Late in 1934 he was recommending to Reith that 'at the end of this year we should stop this recorded programme work'.[16] He was supported by J.B. Clark. As they saw it, reception was improving, live relaying by overseas stations was on the increase as a result, and the need for a supply of recordings of high quality was on the decline. Money was needed elsewhere: 'I don't think we should be spending money on this sort of business', Graves wrote to Reith. Fortunately, wiser counsels prevailed and the BBC Transcription Service was allowed eventually to grow to its present status as the biggest manufacturer and distributor of high-quality recorded radio programmes in the world – one of the glories of the External Services and a powerful means of cultural projection for Britain.

By the end of the second year of the Empire Service Graves had obtained much of what he had said he needed. An Empire Orchestra of twenty-one players had been formed in response to the marked preference of listeners for live as against recorded music. Special contracts were negotiated with the Musicians' Union to allow for live late-night and early-morning transmissions for which other orchestras were not available. Daily broadcast output was up to sixteen hours from the original ten. The staff increases requested by Graves had been agreed and in particular an Empire News Editor, J.C.S. Macgregor, had been appointed in September 1934 with a staff of three sub-editors – the forerunner of the External Services News Department of today, with its staff of over 100 journalists and its daily output of 250 news programmes. Henceforth Empire News bulletins would be separately prepared with the particular needs of the world-wide audience in mind.[17]

There were plenty of causes for satisfaction at the end of that second year. The number of listeners' letters was continuing to rise and there were unmistakable signs that the audience itself was growing. So was the amount of relaying by overseas stations. Graves might feel, as he did, that the BBC was hardly able to keep up with foreign short wave developments and that the years of delay had cost Britain a lot, but a great deal had been achieved in a remarkably short time and the vision and tenacity of Reith and his colleagues had been amply rewarded. BBC programmes were being systematically and ever more widely disseminated all over the empire and close working relations had been built up with the new colonial and dominion broadcasting organisations. The increased resources had enabled J.B. Clark, who had now assumed the function of Empire Service Director under Graves as Director of Empire and Foreign Services, to step up the number of outside broadcasts of public events of particular interest to the empire as a whole or to particular dominions or colonies. Special programmes and messages were regularly broadcast on the National Days of the various dominions. Major events which featured prominently in the schedules and were widely relayed overseas included for instance the opening by the King of the new South Africa House in Trafalgar Square and of the Mersey Tunnel, the service to mark Anzac Day, the Falklands Islands Centenary, the inauguration of the England to India telephone service and of the new England to Australia air mail service, and the launching of the *Queen Mary* and of the Orient liner *Orion*, this last by means of a 'wireless impulse' from Australia triggered by the Duke of Gloucester. The Cup Final, the Derby, the Oxford and Cambridge Boat Race, test matches, Wimbledon and the Davis Cup, the Armistice Day ceremony at the Cenotaph in Whitehall, Trooping the Colour and the Aldershot Tattoo all became regular programme fixtures enabling audiences throughout the empire to share a common experience through the medium of radio.

Every event of this kind [the BBC *Year-Book 1934* proudly proclaimed] has been broadcast throughout the empire since last December. By means of electrical recordings a reproduction has invariably been given to all zones whose programme hours do not coincide with the times of the actual broadcasts. No form of programme has given greater satisfaction.[18]

The culmination of this first phase in the history of the Empire Service came with King George V's Jubilee in May 1935. It was an event made for the Empire Service since it drew towards the centre of gravity of the empire with a powerful emotional force the thoughts and loyalties of English-speaking people all over the world. All the major events – the service of thanksgiving at St Paul's, the ceremony in Westminister Hall, the navy, army and air force reviews – received extensive coverage. The climax came with the King's own broadcast on 6 May. From all accounts reception was generally very good. Reuters reported from Australia that Australians remained up throughout the night or rose early to hear the King's broadcast. The Australian Broadcasting Commission cabled that there was 'tremendous enthusiasm' in Australia. From Canada it was reported that 'loyal Canadians from coast to coast and up to the furthermost northern outposts listened in and were deeply affected by the King's voice'. Reactions from other parts of the empire were on similar lines. Relays were not confined to the empire. Many American stations carried the broadcast. So did stations in Buenos Aires, Rosario and Montevideo, and from Paris Reuters reported: 'Thousands listened at cafes. Every cafe on the Boulevard Montparnasse tuned in and vast crowds paused from the day's work to sit silently listening to the loudspeakers at the little tables out in the warm May sunshine.'

More poignantly the King's death only eight months later was another occasion when broadcasting was able to draw the empire together in a common experience. The *BBC Annual 1936* described how listeners all over the world had been enabled to be 'present' in London and Windsor and spoke of 'a real sense of imperial unity at a time when it was most needed'.[19]

Graves had also been keen to foster the injection of more programmes from the dominions into the Empire Service. He had always seen the service essentially as a system of programme exchange: 'One of the ultimate objectives of empire broadcasting', the 1934 *Year-Book* stated, 'is an exchange of programmes between the dominions and colonies and this country.' One of the first such ventures was a relayed commentary on the scene from the top of Table Mountain, 'Four thousand feet above Cape Town', transmitted on 6 March 1933. It had been arranged and carried out by the Africa Broadcasting Company, the forerunner of the South African Broadcasting Corporation, whose Johannesburg station director provided the commentary, preceded by a short talk by the Governor-General of South Africa. Empire Day also provided a suitable opportunity for bringing in contributions from overseas. The 1933 programme, broadcast on 24 May and entitled 'News of Home', was prepared by the BBC and reflected life in Britain, but in subsequent years dominions took it in turns to produce an appropriate broadcast. Graves's ambition was to see a substantial increase in the number of programmes from the empire transmitted in the BBC's home services. He thought this would help to dispel the suspicions of the dominions that the BBC was only interested in a one-way flow. In a paper of November 1934 rather grandly headed 'Imperial Policy' he complained bitterly that he was making no headway with the home programme planners in this respect. Many of his successors were to make the same point.

On the other hand, with its handful of staff and its limited financial resources the Empire Service was bound to remain largely dependent on the home services for its more costly and spectacular broadcasts. Although empire themes tended to get dragged into almost every aspect of broadcasting – or at least so it seemed to some – the schedules were not short of musical events of the highest quality which any service would have been proud to broadcast and which had nothing even remotely to do with the empire. Most if not all were simultaneous relays of home programmes. Promenade and other concerts were regularly broadcast, and so were opera performances from Covent Garden and Sadler's Wells, this despite the fact that, as the *BBC Annual 1936* put it,

The technical limitations in propagation on short waves call for the special adaptation of performances of music, speech and sound effects. Programmes designed for the home audience and simultaneously radiated from Daventry cannot be adapted exclusively to the requirements of the short wave service. A measured pace of speech, a directness of approach, a clear background in dramatic productions and a steady level of modulation in music of all kinds have proved of value in promoting intelligibility at the receiving end.[20]

The BBC's Chief Engineer, Sir Noel Ashbridge, would have heartily endorsed these words. He was forthright in his views on programmes and argued against transmitting most kinds of music except the very light and familiar. He was equally opposed to the broadcasting of most plays, of 'quick, slapstick vaudeville', of long talks, complicated features and poetry readings. He was also bluntly critical of Empire Service announcers:

I have heard them in action a good deal [he wrote in 1937] and although they attempt to be 'friendly', I don't think they are at all convincing. There is far too much of the 'motor salesman' or 'hotel receptionist' and not enough confidence. I would suggest using considerably older men with a good deal of experience of the world and public speaking behind them, with strong voices and a strict avoidance of modern accent.[21]

However Ashbridge's more direct concern was with the technical performance of the Daventry station and the policy decisions to be made about its future development. In spite of the frequent inadequacy of the signal for relaying purposes he advised against spending money on adding a narrow-beam facility to the Daventry installation. The BBC was in the broadcasting, not narrow-casting business. 'I think it is most essential that we should develop the broadcasting service as highly as possible, and that in no case should a relayed service be allowed to drown it at the expense of the isolated listener.[22] 'Quite agree', noted Reith in his own hand in the margin.

Ideally, Ashbridge wrote, an omni-directional aerial system was best for the kind of world-wide service the BBC was trying to provide. But such a system was incapable of producing enough power to be effective. Operating a series of broadly directional aerials was inevitable if the BBC's signal was to be competitive with that of its strongest rivals. This applied more specifically to the German station at Zeesen, which he and Graves saw as a direct threat to British influence. Ashbridge had heard that the Germans were embarking on the installation of transmitters of much increased power at Zeesen: 'I imagine that they are determined to be the paramount station on short wave, whatever they spend, in order to spread their propaganda.'[23] Ashbridge would have liked to dispose of aerials suitable for all wavelengths in all directions so as to be able to broadcast to the whole empire day and night, but this would be costly and would have to be achieved gradually. In the meantime a third and much more powerful transmitter would be installed at Daventry in eighteen months to two years' time. Graves and Ashbridge were anxious that Reith should be fully aware of the threat presented by German competition: 'Norman* in after lunch', Reith noted in his diary on 28 August, 'and stayed to hear Ashbridge and Graves talking about the Empire Service, which I believe we must develop much more quickly, and intensively, because of competition in other countries, particularly Germany'.[24]

Reith had recently written to Sir Philip Cunliffe-Lister, the Colonial Secretary of the day, to raise again the question of financial contributions from the colonies. He also wanted to stress the need for a more rapid development of local broadcasting and rediffusion in the colonies.[25] He had received no reply. The question of colonial licence fees had clearly not been pressed very hard by the Colonial Office, and only one Governor, Sir Arnold Hodson, first in Sierra Leone and then in the Gold Coast, had come forward of his own accord with a small token contribution. This led Graves to observe wrily: 'I really think that an official letter should be sent to the Secretary of State, suggesting that every six months Sir Arnold Hodson should be moved to another colony.'[26]

Reith now wrote again to Cunliffe-Lister, this time more pressingly. He set out for him the full alarming details of the growing German and Italian external broadcasting menace. Not only were the Germans re-equipping Zeesen, the Italians too were building new transmitters in preparation for stepping up their overseas services. Both were now broadcasting not just in their own language for the benefit of their own expatriate nationals, but also in a number of others including English. Their programmes were frankly propagandist in character.

It is possible for the German station to use a more concentrated type of beam transmission [Reith warned the Colonial Secretary] than we can employ at Daventry, having regard to the wide geographical areas which our service must cover. This means that in certain areas where the danger of foreign political influence through these channels may exist (for example in mandated territories in Africa) and other big

---

* R. C. Norman, the BBC's Chairman, brother of Sir Montagu Norman, Governor of the Bank of England.

centres of population lying in the paths of the German beams, the transmission in question can be picked up with the utmost facility. News bulletins, which we have reason to believe are prepared in the German Ministry of Propaganda, are read at fixed times in English and other languages.[27]

The BBC was holding its own, Reith said, but everything possible must be done to widen the dissemination of British programmes. Funds were needed to make Daventry more technically competitive, and colonial governors should be urged to speed up the development of broadcasting and rediffusion facilities in the colonies so that the Empire Service could be more widely distributed.

Reith was only partially successful. Not for the first time he emerged with expressions of moral support but no firm financial commitment from the Government. Graves had ended his major paper on the Empire Service of April 1934 by saying that it could be argued that the limit of expenditure from existing funds had been reached. The BBC would need new funds if there was to be further development. However, Graves wrote, 'The political importance of empire broadcasting should now be sufficiently realised for the Treasury to consider it reasonable if the BBC were to suggest that a small proportion of the enormous sums annually appropriated [by the Treasury] from licences be handed over for the development of the Empire Service.'[28] That was a device which had already been considered in 1931, and it met with no greater success this time. However Reith did get something: at a meeting at Broadcasting House on 14 February 1935, he and the BBC's Chairman, R.C. Norman, spoke to the Postmaster General about the needs of the Empire Service. The Post Office minute of the meeting stated that the BBC was thinking of a further capital investment of £180,000 at Daventry and of increased running costs of £80,000 per annum. The Postmaster General, who by that time was Sir Kingsley Wood, a future Chancellor of the Exchequer, expressed his warm support and full approval for the BBC's plans. However he felt that in view of the financial implications the Treasury should be consulted. This was duly done on 21 February when Sir Warren Fisher, on behalf of the Treasury, endorsed the BBC's proposals and undertook that 'due regard would be paid to this commitment in any future financial adjustments'.[29] It was better than nothing.

In the person of Malcolm MacDonald Reith was shortly to be dealing with a new and more imaginative Colonial Secretary, and one with a keen interest in broadcasting. Reith went to lunch with him on 19 September armed with a detailed brief on the competition the BBC was now up against. It quoted a report in *The Times* of the previous day stating that 'there is an Arabic broadcast from the Bari station which daily serves up to Arabic listeners virulent attacks on Great Britain and British policy in the Middle East'. The German broadcasts, Reith told MacDonald, were confined almost entirely to giving the world a favourable impression of conditions of all kinds in Nazi

Germany. They were full of news of the Nazi Party Congress at Nuremberg. They could not be said to be specifically anti-British in character, but, Reith's briefing notes made clear, 'there has on occasion been definite distortion of British and other events, with interpretations of them favourable to Nazi ideals'. They were 'carefully edited and efficiently delivered in clear English, but the manner of delivery and composition is naive'. As for the Italian broadcasts from Bari, while definitely subversive, they were badly compiled and inefficiently read. Reith told MacDonald that he expected an increase in sensational news items and in statements based on mere rumour as the international situation developed. The BBC's role, in his view, was not to engage in direct contradiction but to 'help in stifling rumour and sensation by the presentation of fully authoritative and carefully reported news'.[30] The international climate in Europe and elsewhere was indeed fast deteriorating. Germany had repudiated the disarmament clauses in the Treaty of Versailles and reintroduced compulsory military service earlier in the year. The Saar had been reintegrated with Germany following a plebiscite in January, and the infamous Nuremberg Laws outlawing the Jews were introduced just as Reith and MacDonald were due to meet. Only two weeks later Mussolini invaded Abyssinia.

It was against this sombre background that in October 1935, at MacDonald's request, the BBC submitted a major 'Memorandum on Broadcasting and the Colonial Empire'.[31] Copies were not only sent to the Colonial Secretary and the Postmaster General, as protocol required, but also to the Prime Minister, Stanley Baldwin, the King's Private Secretary, Sir Clive Wigram, the Treasury, the Broadcasting Committee chaired by Lord Ullswater which was in the process of carrying out the periodic review of broadcasting prior to the renewal of the charter, and to all colonial governors. Its preamble is worth quoting for its forthright and resolute tone:

Broadcasting itself is new; it is so potent an influence that its development should not be hindered by precedents and susceptibilities, nor by considerations of financial stringencies. Already other countries have followed our lead and are securing to themselves that which their short wave services were designed to secure, the interest and gratitude of empire communities. From this more serious consequences – commercial and political – may follow. There is no time to be lost.

The memorandum went on to point out that Britain would have been ahead of other countries had there not been endless delays in the late twenties and early thirties, and it continued:

The time has come for consideration to be given to definite, comprehensive action throughout the colonial empire to the end that the Daventry service should cover the empire satisfactorily, that colonies should be equipped to receive the Daventry service (a proposition quite distinct from the encouragement of direct listening by individuals), providing themselves with central receiving apparatus with a view to the Daventry service being relayed (in whole or in part according to local resources); that the necessary arrangements for relay throughout the colonies should be made either by the wireless exchange system or by local transmitters, and that broadcasting be institutionalised and treated as an organic interest in the Colonial Office and in all colonies.

'The terms in which individual and collective appreciation of the service has been expressed', the memorandum stated, 'leave no doubt as to the immense contribution it can make to the solidarity of the empire.' It made the important new point that with a white population of only 200,000 out of a total of sixty million in the colonial empire as a whole any colonial broadcasting service must be 'designed to appeal to the natives as well as to whites'. However the Empire Service itself was 'essentially British in character' and was therefore likely to appeal in the first place to the 'white' population in the colonies. The BBC did not consider that it would ever be practicable to cater from Daventry for purely 'native' interests in language and music. However, the memorandum went on,

Broadcasting provides a far reaching means of promoting unity of speech and culture, and the development of native resources will lead to a wider audience for programmes western in type. This is born out in the case of the operation of wireless exchanges in West Africa, where it is understood that a large proportion of subscribers are native.

The BBC's thinking about its role in international broadcasting was only slowly moving away from the original concept of the Empire Service. The idea of helping to hold the empire together by means of radio remained paramount in Reith's mind. To the extent that a wider public, including non-whites, was becoming accepted as a legitimate and even desirable potential audience, this was due in part to the growing body of evidence suggesting that you could not pick and choose your listeners and that non-whites were listening whether or not they were intended to. But more importantly it was due to the growing realisation that in the threatening international climate of the mid-thirties the new use to which Germany and Italy were putting short wave radio must soon compel the BBC itself to think afresh about what it was trying to do and for whom. Reith himself was very much a man of his times in his central preoccupation with empire. It was natural that when originally thinking of ways in which the new medium of short wave broadcasting could be put to use in the public interest his first thought should have been for kith and kin overseas. It is to his eternal credit that he had the imagination and flexibility of mind to realise that the new situation called for a new approach. He was no slower than the majority of his contemporaries in grasping the sinister reality of the German menace, and probably more clear-sighted than most. He understood certainly not later than 1935 that if Britain was to make its voice heard effectively in the world, broadcasting in English only was not enough. Other languages would have to be introduced.

In the meantime there were those inside the BBC who were already champ-

ing at the bit and becoming increasingly critical of the performance of the
Empire Service and of the approach of its planners. Lionel Fielden, whom
Reith had sent to India at the viceroy's request to develop Indian broadcasting, was particularly scathing. There was too much 'restaurant'-type music,
he wrote. British listeners were getting bored, and the service was 'not within
miles of catching the ear of the young students of India, who are certainly the
most important audience with which it has to deal in that part of the world'.
England, he wrote, was projecting the worst of its culture. The cure he offered
was radical. The word 'empire' should be left severely alone. So should the
'sentimental twaddle about Big Ben'. Instead the BBC should:

concentrate on giving the world the best of England's writers, poets, musicians,
engineers, actors, playwrights, philosophers, etc. This surely is the best propaganda
that any nation could do for itself. If it [the Empire Service] is really intended to be, as
I suppose it must inevitably be, a world service of the first importance reflecting
England's attitude and culture, then surely it must be put over with tremendous drive
and imagination.

To his way of thinking these two qualities were not strongly represented in
the Empire Department at the time.[32]

Fielden was not alone in his views. Felix Greene, the BBC's representative
in North America who had been a close associate of Fielden in the Talks
Department, thought likewise and said so in a memorandum timed to coincide
with Fielden's. Greene felt that programmes were 'flabby and uninspired' and
bore little relation to the needs or tastes of listeners in distant lands. To think
that the weaknesses of the service were due to shortage of money was gravely
mistaken. There was a total failure in London to grasp the extent to which the
service was in need of overhaul. Administrative skills were more conspicuous
at the top than creative flair, and the service had now outgrown the personal
capacities of those in charge. He went on to recommend the creation of a more
expert and professional Transcription Service, the seconding of staff from
the dominions and India to the Empire Service to increase audience awareness
and the creation of a Monitoring Service: 'To know immediately and precisely
what is being said by Rome and Germany to our empire and colonial
listeners will become of immediate importance', he wrote prophetically.[33]

Reith saw Greene's and Fielden's memoranda and minuted them back to
Graves in his own hand: 'This is serious, isn't it? – even discounting Fielden's
pessimism and G's desire for a new job.' Graves was not convinced. Reith
had hinted that he agreed to some extent with Greene and Fielden that there
was more 'organising' and 'administrative' ability than 'creative' talent in the
top layer of the Empire Department, but Graves, who was by now Controller
of Programmes, loyally defended his subordinates and particularly J.B.
Clark, who was clearly the main target: 'I am quite confident that he is the
best man in the corporation for this important work', he wrote.[34] On an
earlier occasion he had described him as 'that rare combination, a man

possessing creative as well as administrative ability' and had expressed his
certainty that Clark would ultimately become 'one of the leading men in the
corporation', as indeed he did.[35] 'They are of the sophisticated type', Graves
wrote of Greene and Fielden, 'and Fielden's judgement in particular is based
on his own conception of the highest standards of broadcasting.' These, he
argued, were not necessarily right for colonial and dominion listeners.

To force the pace with highbrow programmes is the wrong way to go about it.
Much that is unsuitable for home listeners will always be necessary in empire programmes. We shall be making the greatest mistake if we overtly show signs of wishing
to be educative, and if we are blatant in our projection of this country.

And he took the opportunity to complain that the Empire Service had
always been regarded as a Cinderella of broadcasting and it was high time
that it should be realised that to work for the Empire Department was just as
important as to work for any other department in the corporation.

However Greene and Fielden were not entirely alone. Others were lending
support to the view that all was not well. Malcolm Frost in particular wrote
a long critical analysis based on a detailed study of all the evidence available.
His essential conclusion was that there was not much point in broadcasting
to the dominions programmes of a type that listeners could get from their
own local stations with much greater clarity. Famous orchestras, choirs,
soloists of international repute, famous personalities – Lloyd George and
Churchill were frequently asked for – more outstanding programmes from
the home services were what was required. Frost quoted an 'intelligent and
widely cultured man in Saskatchewan' who wrote:

I am not surprised that the majority of letters which you receive commend your
programmes because the only people, in so far as I can discover, that listen to them
are English, and I can well appreciate how enjoyable they must be to them. If you
merely want a select audience comprised of those who think everything from home is
wonderful, no matter how mediocre it may actually be, your present programme
schedules will fit the bill. On the other hand if the Empire Broadcasting Service is
intended to be a link in the chain binding the empire, you must make an effort to get
the attention of those who normally have little interest in what England is thinking
and doing, and who are prone to pass judgements on what they hear coming over the
air.[36]

Even Ashbridge shared the mood of disquiet. In the early days, he wrote
privately and in confidence to Reith, the service had been intended to cater
essentially for the lonely British expatriate. It transmitted simple programmes
in which sentimentality bulked fairly large. It had been modified a good deal
over the years, and he was beginning to wonder whether it wasn't now falling
between two stools: 'Are we catering for the sophisticated listener or for the
remote planter and farmer?'[37]

As for Felix Greene he returned to the charge a few months later over the failure of the Empire Service, as he saw it, to reflect in any way other than in news the Austrian Anschluss crisis of March 1938. 'What influence did this tremendous event have upon our own service to the peoples of our empire?' he wrote from New York. 'Almost none whatever. With people throughout our dominions and colonies turning to the BBC for authoritative interpretations of events we continued for all the world as if nothing had happened.'[38] He quoted a Canadian broadcasting official as saying:

News and information – that is what every Canadian wanted from London, and you went on with your quartettes (*sic*). We had to take the commentaries from Europe broadcast by the United States companies. We don't want our news from London and Europe via the United States.

On March 14th [Greene wrote scathingly] at the time when America (and Canada) was listening to an account of Hitler's arrival in Vienna we were presenting to our listeners in the empire 'Stars of the Cabaret World'. When, later, American listeners heard a very informative and dispassionate account of the day's momentous events from Berlin, our transmitters were sending to the ends of the earth 'Old Folks at Home – a series of popular melodies'.

In Greene's view this showed a grave failure on the BBC's part to meet the responsibilities and requirements of an international broadcasting service: 'The authority and reputation of the BBC will be impaired in North America and, I have no doubt, throughout the world.'

This was one of those classic head-on confrontations which have periodically enlivened the history of the BBC and are the almost inevitable preliminary to change. To be fair, particularly at this distance in time, it is well to remember that the practice of instant comment and analysis, of which some complain that there is now too much, was then unknown. There were considerable inhibitions on the discussion of live and controversial issues. Immediate comment was still actively discouraged. Answering questions from the Ullswater Committee in the summer of 1935 R.W.A. Leeper, the Head of the Foreign Office News Department, recalled one occasion when, according to him, the BBC had caused the Foreign Office some embarrassment. This occurred when Germany left the League of Nations and the Disarmament Conference in October 1933. On the very same night Vernon Bartlett, in one of his periodic broadcasts on international affairs, had given his own interpretation of that event. It had been wrong, Leeper held, that the minds of millions of listeners should be influenced in one direction before there had been any time for the Government to make a statement in the House of Commons.[39] He went on to say that this was the only occasion in his recollection when such a thing had happened and that generally speaking, 'BBC officials do their best to avoid causing embarrassment to our own Government and giving offence to any foreign government.'[40] But times were moving fast and broadcasting practice had to move with them. What had been intended as a leisurely 'home' service for empire listeners, proceeding at a stately pace and in a preordained manner, was now being called upon to react more flexibly to the demand created by the quickening pace of international events. It was the end of an era and the start of a new one, far more momentous and far more dramatic, in which the BBC, like the nation, had ultimately to rise to the supreme challenge of war.

3
Clouds of War

As soon as the potential for reaching audiences beyond national frontiers in their own language was appreciated, efforts were made at an international level to lay down rules about what was and what was not permissible. There were debates on the subject within the International Broadcasting Union, which Reith had helped to found in the mid-twenties and whose Secretary-General, Arthur Burrows, was a former BBC man.[1] These debates led in due course to a resolution, passed by the council of the union at its meeting in Madrid on 13 May 1933, which described matter broadcast to foreign audiences to which exception was taken by the recipient country as 'propagande inadmissible'. However the resolution had no standing in international law, even though it was binding on the broadcasting organisations which formed the union's membership. Non-members, in any case, were not affected.

The League of Nations was addressing itself to the same problem at about the same time, and in September 1931 it requested its members to seek ways of using radio 'to create better mutual understanding between peoples'.[2] An international committee of experts was set up to draft an international broadcasting convention, and a special League of Nations conference met in Geneva in 1936 to consider the experts' report. This led to the banning of broadcast material 'which, to the detriment of good international understanding, is of such a character as to incite the population of any territory to acts incompatible with the internal order or the security of a territory of a High Contracting Party'.[3] Aggressive propaganda, deliberate misstatements and incitements to war and insurrection were also outlawed.

The convention had little effect except on those already disposed to observe it. In any case the two chief culprits, Germany and Italy, were not among the signatories, and no international resolutions on a matter such as radio propaganda was going to inhibit them when they were prepared to act in breach of international conventions and agreements on far more crucial matters.

There is no conclusive evidence to show whether the initiative for suggesting that Britain should respond to the German and Italian radio menace in languages other than English came from the BBC or from the British Government. Certainly no such thought would ever have occurred to either had it not been for the growing Axis effort. Conducting propaganda by radio was not thought to be a proper activity for the BBC to engage in, and as will emerge later there were considerable reservations at a high level inside the corporation over the very principle of broadcasting in foreign languages even if the material broadcast was free of propaganda.

In his verbal evidence to the Ullswater Committee given in the summer of 1935, Rex Leeper, then Head of the Foreign Office News Department, and 'an early prophet of the Nazi menace',[4] claimed that the use of foreign languages 'was a matter we brought to his [Reith's] attention a long time ago before he had any idea of doing it'. 'Some of our ministers in South America said it would be extremely useful', he stated, 'if there were broadcasts in Spanish on British cultural subjects – nothing whatever to do with politics; and at the time the BBC said they could not do it'.[5] Reith, who was in the habit of scribbling his own terse comments in the margin of documents that passed across his desk, wrote 'Nonsense' at this point.

For his part Reith has stated in his autobiography under the heading 'Broadcasting in foreign languages':

I had tried periodically and urgently for three years to have this matter taken seriously. Almost every month brought news of extensions of activity in totalitarian lands. Now in the summer of 1937, after several months of desultory talks, the Cabinet at last got the matter on its agenda.[6]

The first mention of the subject in Reith's diary occurs in mid-March 1935: 'I dined in the House of Commons with a party arranged by Geoffrey Lloyd', he wrote, 'I told them about the Empire Service and the possible extension of that to cover transmissions in foreign languages, that is the general dissemination of English culture similar to what some countries are already doing.'[7] The wording of that entry suggests that the subject had already been under discussion for some time and that Reith, an experienced and forceful lobbyist, was using the opportunity of the Westminster dinner to arouse the interest and support of MPs. Sadly his diary does not tell us how his audience reacted.

However it was not long before he was to get an opportunity to air the subject more formally. The Ullswater Committee was sitting throughout the summer of 1935 and Reith was called before it to give verbal evidence on a number of occasions. So far as external broadcasting was concerned he had three objectives in mind. The first was that the Empire Service, which had not so far been formally authorised in terms of the charter, should receive the committee's *imprimatur*. The second was that the serious financial implications should be recognised. Reith was still smarting at the Government's failure to make proper financial provision for the Empire Service, and Ullswater provided an ideal opportunity to get a formal recommendation by an independent official review body on the record. The third aim was that the corporation should be encouraged to broadcast in foreign languages. In his verbal evidence to the committee Reith laid great stress on German compe-

tition, particularly in languages other than German, and on the lavishness of
German funding. What the Nazi Government was after, Reith said, was
'creating good will towards Germany and encouraging German trade'. 'They
go almost any length to create good will', he told the committee, 'We so far
have done nothing to combat this.' Reith then posed the question 'whether
we should not – some of us feel strongly that we should – start now to do
something by way of projection of British culture in other languages, as so
many countries are now doing'.[8]

Reith told the committee that the German broadcasts from Zeesen received
a subsidy of £3,000,000 from the German Government. 'Where do they get
all this money from?' Lord Ullswater enquired incredulously. 'They cannot
pay their debts!' Reith, never slow to spot an opening replied: 'Presumably in
the same way as the Treasury gets contributions from the BBC – by levies.'
Reith then proceeded to illustrate the high priority which the Germans, unlike
the British, were giving to their short wave operations: 'The sort of thing they
do which would lend colour to such a figure', he said, 'is the turning out of
the Berlin Philharmonic Orchestra in the middle of the night to play to parts
of the British Empire – that shows how serious they are.' Again an expression
of disbelief from the Chairman, Lord Ullswater: 'When you say they turn out
the Berlin Philharmonic Orchestra you mean they keep them sitting up?'
Reith confirmed that this was so.[9]

Simultaneously Reith was lobbying the Colonial Office. In the 'Memorandum on Broadcasting and the Colonial Empire' prepared at Malcolm Mac-
Donald's request he managed to slip in a reference to foreign languages: 'A
strong broadcasting service to and within the empire is not the end of the
matter', the Memorandum stated. 'The projection of England in foreign
languages and to other countries is outside the scope of this memorandum.
But sooner or later it must be undertaken; and the sooner the better.'[10]

In the end, and with the strong support of the Colonial Office, the BBC
obtained what it wanted from Ullswater: 'We recommend', the report stated,
'that the Empire Service should be expressly authorised in the new charter
and that the additional funds required for its development should be provided
by the corporation from its increased licence receipts.' The following paragraph was perhaps not quite as firmly worded as Reith might have wished:
'In the interest of British prestige and influence in world affairs', it stated, 'we
think that the appropriate use of languages other than English should be
encouraged.'[11] The note of urgency was distinctly muted, but at least it was
on the record.

Within the BBC itself no time was lost in setting up a committee to study
the implications of Ullswater and to make recommendations. Its findings
were finalised on 18 May 1936, two months after Hitler's remilitarisation of
the Rhineland. Only a few days before, Addis Ababa had been occupied by
the Italian Army and Ethiopia annexed by Italy. The committee's report,

originally drafted by J.B. Clark, was subsequently revised by Graves, who by that time had moved up to become Controller of Programmes, and by Sir Stephen Tallents, who had recently joined the BBC from the Empire Marketing Board as Controller of Public Relations. It divided the foreign languages in which the BBC suggested it might start broadcasting into three categories in descending order of priority. At the top were three languages described as 'primarily foreign' and chosen because it was thought they would have prestige and influence value. They were Spanish and Portuguese for Latin-America – languages in which Germany, Italy, France and Holland were already broadcasting – and Arabic, in which the main contender was Italy.

The second group of languages consisted of German, French and Dutch. Oddly, as it seems in retrospect, particularly in the case of German, the intention was not to broadcast primarily to the populations of Germany, France and Holland but to their colonial or former colonial peoples. In the case of German for instance the main declared target was the former German territories in East and South West Africa. The report commented that broadcasting in these languages could not be expected to have any prestige or influence value comparable to the first group and that it 'might be open to greater misunderstanding'. Finally certain languages like Afrikaans, French for Canada, Tamil for Malaya, Swahili and half a dozen unspecified Indian vernaculars were suggested as a much lower priority.[12]

The report made clear that while there would be little difficulty in devising a round-the-clock plan for transmitting news bulletins in the relevant languages at convenient local times, no such plan could be implemented except in the case of Spanish, Portuguese and French for Canada until the projected extension of the Daventry station was completed in 1937. An earlier injection of foreign bulletins to areas other than the western hemisphere would mean dislocating the existing programme service in English. Graves and Clark were strongly opposed to this.

Their attitude was understandable. Between them they were the architects of the Empire Service. It was their creature and they were intensely dedicated to it and to its purposes. But their misgivings went further than a mere question of dislocation of schedules and diversion of resources. They were concerned about the fundamental wisdom of embarking on foreign language broadcasting at all. Felix Greene had written from New York shortly after the publication of the Ullswater Report to express grave doubts about the effect on American opinion of implementing the Ullswater recommendation on foreign languages.[13] These doubts were shared by Alan Dudley, then in charge of the British Library of Information in New York and thus in close touch with many Americans who took an interest in British affairs. Dudley quoted an editorial from the *Indianapolis Star*:

Other countries are engaged in radio propaganda using several languages to deceive their supposed listeners. Great Britain is perhaps the only country on the globe, with the exception of the United States, not broadcasting political propaganda in a foreign tongue. It is unfortunate that this great civilising agent has been so grossly abused by the world's dictatorships. An opportunity for mutual understanding and culture has been perverted by the tools of greed and oppression.[14]

Dudley, backed by Greene, feared that if the BBC itself took up foreign language broadcasts it would be suspected of propagandist intentions. This might in turn damage the credit and impair the prestige of the Empire Service itself.[15]

Graves and Clark were clearly sympathetic to this argument, particularly as they had become intensely aware of the value attached by listeners to the credibility of the Empire Service bulletins.

The BBC has set itself without any qualifications to present the news in the empire bulletins truthfully, impartially and objectively. During the tense international situation of the past year the authority and impersonality of the Empire Station's news bulletins has been widely and spontaneously recognised, notably by individual listeners in America and by a number of American newspapers.[16]

This was not an asset to be thrown away lightly.

Reith himself, though convinced, on all the evidence, that Britain could not stay out of the race, appears to have been anxious to be seen to pay due heed to the misgivings of his subordinates. On a number of occasions he went out of his way to ensure that their views were properly reflected. To Herbert Morrison, who had written in June 1936 to ask if the BBC had ever considered broadcasting news in German and Italian,[17] he replied that the matter was under discussion but that it involved a danger to the BBC's reputation.

It is more in Britain's interest – and also a subtle form of propaganda from the British point of view – to avoid any action that might lead to listeners who have turned to British bulletins as a reliable source of information to think that we too were joining in the babel of broadcast nationalist propaganda.[18]

Morrison was not impressed. If the general standard of BBC news is maintained, he argued, the broadcasting of news in French, German and Italian would be desirable. 'It is really a terrible tragedy that millions of people abroad are receiving no impartial British news.'[19]

A poll of British diplomatic posts abroad carried out by the Foreign Office and the Dominions Office in the autumn of 1936 produced mixed results. British missions in the Arab world were unanimous in supporting the introduction of Arabic broadcasts. The British legation in Jeddah reflected the widely held view that far from arousing suspicions of propaganda intentions, a reliable service would disarm such suspicions. It was true that the Italian broadcasts were widely received, but the average Arab listener was convinced that the broadcasts amounted to pure propaganda and in consequence their influence was much diminished. There would be surprise in the Arab world, the legation reported, if Britain neglected to join in. King Abdul Aziz received news at Riyadh daily (and by a portable wireless set when travelling): 'It is credibly reported that nowadays he employs a special official charged with the duty of noting down the news and conveying it to his royal master.' 'Arabs are insatiable in their appetite for news', reported the British minister in the Yemen, and went on to quote two 'prominent personages' as having asked why Britain did not broadcast in Arabic like the Italians. The Frontier Officer at San'ā, Captain B.W. Seager, wrote:

There are four PHILCO wireless receiving sets in the Yemen. These are owned by (1) the King, (2) Qadhi Abdullah el Amri, (3) Qadhi Muhammad Raghib Bey, and (4) Seiyid Ali ibn el Wazir. None of these gentlemen knows English. As a consequence, night after night they listen in to the Rome broadcast in Arabic.

From Cairo, on the other hand, came the warning that, 'the use of the air for propaganda by the Italians has given foreign broadcasts a bad name, and any tendency of this sort in the British wireless would be very detrimental to its popularity in Egypt. Its strength would lie in its reliability as news.' In this Cairo was echoing the view expressed from Jeddah that, 'the absence of attempts to vie with the Italians in currying favour with the Arabs and a resolute abstention from following the Italian lead in disseminating news of a tendentious kind would eventually be repaid by the trust of the Arab listener.'

There were similar expressions of support for the introduction of broadcasts in Spanish from most British missions in Latin-America. 'The steady propaganda of the German view of European affairs needs some corrective', wrote the British minister in Caracas, 'and the objective standpoint of the empire news bulletins would supply this'. Like his colleagues in Montevideo and Buenos Aires he felt that English-language broadcasts did not reach a wide enough circle to be effective. The British Embassy in Buenos Aires discounted the risk to the BBC's reputation. Tendentious material defeated its own object, it stated: 'Sooner or later the more intelligent classes of any given community realise its nature and pay little attention to it, and eventually this knowledge is bound to percolate to less discriminating listeners.' 'Truthful factual bulletins will in a very short time receive due credit.' As for the British Minister in Lima his verdict was succinct: 'It is high time the empire entered the market.' The need for an increased British effort was confirmed by Felix Greene, the BBC's New York representative, who was sent on a tour of South America to report on the impact of Axis propaganda.

Opinion in the dominions was a good deal less favourable. Harding, the Permanent Under-Secretary at the Dominions Office, told Graves that on balance he tended to share Felix Greene's misgivings. The introduction of foreign languages 'would weaken the effectiveness of the service in empire countries'. The British High Commissioners in Australia, Canada and South Africa all stressed the need to keep any foreign language transmissions completely separate from the Empire Service itself. There was a fundamental conflict, the High Commission in Canberra felt, between the idea of 'enhancing British prestige and influence in world affairs' and the objective of the Empire Service, which was to provide a link for the British family of nations. Pretoria advised against introducing Afrikaans on the grounds that it would be regarded as amounting to 'imperialism' and 'anti republicanism'. Ottawa argued against introducing French as part of the Empire Service because it would upset English-speaking listeners. It should be on a separate frequency if anywhere.[20]

A clear division of opinion – and interests – had thus emerged between the Foreign Office and the Dominions Office, itself broadly supported by the Colonial Office, though like the India Office the Colonial Office was in favour of introducing Arabic because of its responsibilities in the Middle East.

Within the Foreign Office Rex Leeper, with the support of Sir Robert Vansittart, the Permanent Under-Secretary, was at the time the main driving force behind moves not just to alert the nation at home to the threat of war arising from Hitler's ambitions but to make Britain's policies better known abroad. Foreign language broadcasting was one of the instruments available for the purpose, and broadcasting in Arabic, in his view, should be given the most urgent priority. His mind and Reith's were moving in the same direction. 'Europe is at this time in a tremendous state', Reith told a conference of the Empire Press Union in May 1937. 'Every mutilated division of it looks to England for information and courage.'[21] But he felt bound to say that 'the Empire Service was efficient, but nothing like sufficient'.[22] The Foreign Office, for its part, seeking to meet possible objections to the introduction of Arabic broadcasting, argued that,

Any failure on our part to present our case properly in the Near East is not only a temptation to Italy to exploit our difficulties among people who have little or no access to the real facts of the situation, but also tends to undo the effect of our rearmament in a part of the world where our interests are very vitally concerned ... We have no intention of imitating the methods of the Bari broadcasts. Our object is solely to maintain a reliable service of British news and see to it that false or malicious reports are not left unchallenged.[23]

BBC opinion, on the other hand, was deeply divided, with Reith himself in favour of BBC involvement – supported by Ashbridge – but 'concerned that the department of the BBC from which the greatest support might have been expected was strongly opposed to it'.[24] Indeed arrayed against the whole idea Reith had to contend not only with J.B. Clark and his immediate subordinates in the Empire Service but also with Graves, now Controller, Programmes for the BBC as a whole and a possible future Director-General.

That opposition is clearly reflected in the record of the protracted and at times confused series of exchanges on the subject between the BBC and the British Government extending throughout most of 1937, much to the irritation of Leeper, who wanted to get on with it and regarded the BBC attitude as

'foolish ... One would think from the BBC attitude that there was no international crisis at all.'[25] Reith himself showed great fairness and loyalty to his
anxious and reluctant subordinates. He concentrated his powers of persuasion and his tactical skills on securing the necessary guarantees of editorial
independence and financial support from a government which was now
clearly in a hurry to get things started but uncertain about how to get what it
wanted.

The Foreign Office itself was under heavy pressure from the Foreign Secretary, who in turn was under pressure from the Prime Minister, Neville
Chamberlain.[26] By the middle of 1937, frustrated by what Leeper termed BBC
'haggling', it was seriously considering taking on the responsibility for running Arabic broadcasts itself, and plans were being drawn up for building a
medium wave transmitter in Cyprus which would be operated under Foreign
Office control. In the meantime the news output of the Palestine broadcasting
service would be strengthened, and A.S. Calvert, an Arabist from the Con-
sular Service, was dispatched to Jerusalem for that purpose in September
1937. 'It would be a new departure to pay the BBC to send out political
broadcasts,' the Foreign Office explained; the BBC's reputation for impartiality and independence would suffer 'by saying what the Government told
them to say'.[27]

Graves and Clark did not discourage this move. Since it was assumed –
wrongly as it turned out – that most of those who listened to the Italian
broadcasts in Arabic got their signal from the medium wave transmitter at
Bari, the British response, they argued, should also be on medium wave since
otherwise it would not be competing for the attention of the same listeners.
Since the BBC had no medium wave transmitter capable of reaching the area,
they said, there was no point in its taking on Arabic broadcasting at all. Let
the Foreign Office provide the bulletins itself if it wanted them.[28] Graves
himself told Leeper he thought the Foreign Office's Cyprus plan was the right
decision since what the Foreign Office clearly had in mind was 'a much more
strictly propagandist business than we had been talking about'.[29]

Graves and his colleagues clearly saw in the Foreign Office's decision to go
it alone in Arabic an opportunity for the BBC to bow out of foreign language
broadcasting altogether. As has been seen, the Foreign Office had been keen
on the BBC starting broadcasts in Spanish and Portuguese to Latin-America.
Indeed at one stage it seemed as if it intended the broadcasts to Latin-America
as a cover to conceal the 'anti-Italian' intention behind the proposed Arabic
broadcasts.

In the case of South America [a BBC internal paper argued] there is no question of
combatting propaganda likely to undermine the security of definite units of the empire.
It is a suggestion that the BBC should broadcast in a non-English language ... to
non-empire countries, as a competitor with foreign broadcasts in the same field ...
The reduction of the problem to one of broadcasts in Spanish and Portuguese only

has materially altered the whole question of principle; and it is perhaps not putting it too strongly to suggest that what the Foreign Office wish is to use the BBC as a counter in the diplomatic game.

The paper then reiterated the central preoccupation of its authors: 'The BBC short wave service today enjoys a position unique in the world. Alone among the broadcasting countries of any importance England speaks to the world in its own language only.'

It was the *Indianapolis Star's* argument all over again. 'The Empire Service is directed to English-speaking members of the empire, and its moral right to do so is beyond question. This unique standing the BBC would forfeit by any excursion, even the smallest, into the field of foreign languages.' The paper went on to ask whether it was worth sacrificing that position for the sake of two languages. And would the number remain at two? Would there not be pressure for more in due course? 'Once the principle was admitted, broadcasts in foreign languages might well grow into a burden which the corporation might find it hard to bear and which would seriously hamper it in its more legitimate tasks.'[30]

It was time the argument was brought to an end, and new information made available from the Middle East fortuitously helped in the process. Both the BBC and the Foreign Office had hitherto assumed that most of the listening to the Italian broadcasts in Arabic which was the source of all the trouble was on medium wave from the transmitter at Bari, in the heel of Italy. However a survey carried out by the British authorities in Palestine now revealed that this was not so,[31] and this was later confirmed from Cairo, Baghdad and Kuwait. Contrary to previous impressions a large percentage of radio sets in Arab hands were capable of receiving broadcasts on short wave. In fact what most Arabs were listening to was Rome on short wave, not Bari on medium wave. The case for a Foreign Office-run medium wave transmitter was thereby much weakened. Leeper in any case was having difficulty in obtaining Treasury support for the necessary expenditure. To cover both the coastal areas of the eastern Mediterranean and the more distant parts of the Arab world would require both medium wave and short wave facilities in Cyprus, and this was ruled out by the Cabinet Sub-Committee on grounds of expense. An attempt to interest the Government of India in taking on Arabic broadcasting in view of India's special responsibilities in the Persian Gulf came to nothing. In a note dated 1 October to his Controllers, Reith observed: 'The whole thing seems to be muddled. India has rejected Arabic. The Foreign Office can't make up its mind about Cyprus.'[32] But he then went on to break the news that 'Daventry for Arabic is definitely in the picture again.' The wheel had turned full circle.

It is at this point that Reith himself appears to have taken the matter back into his own hands, and as happened in the case of the Empire Service in 1931 his intervention was decisive. The issue was not easy to resolve. There were grave internal divisions inside the BBC, not just among senior executives, but within the Board of Governors itself. However it would have been uncharacteristic of Reith if he had not resolved to make sure the BBC ended up with the exclusive responsibility for running foreign language broadcasting. Whatever the doubts of his staff he himself had been convinced all along that the BBC could not stay aloof, and he had the gravest misgivings about the proposed Foreign Office Cyprus operation. The Foreign Office might be able to produce a news service of a sort, but they were not professional broadcasters and Reith knew that they would have difficulty in providing sustaining programmes. Besides, he was profoundly sceptical of the effectiveness of propaganda, to which he was opposed as a matter of principle. At the same time he respected the reservations of Graves, Clark and others, which he understood full well, and was determined to get the best bargain possible, thus meeting at least some of these reservations. He was clearly not unaware that he was in a strong bargaining position, sensing, as he did, that the Government was increasingly impatient for an early start to be made with Arabic broadcasts and that the Foreign Office's own alternative scheme was running into the sands. So by the time he and the BBC's Chairman, R.C. Norman, accompanied by Graves and Ashbridge,[33] appeared before the Government's Arabic Broadcasting Sub-Committee on 4 October 1937, he felt able to lay down his terms in characteristically forthright manner.

Reith's own account of the meeting in his autobiography is marked by his customary terseness:

Six conditions were set out by Norman and me: (1) foreign language services must not prejudice the Empire Service; (2) if they were to be done by or from this country it should be by the BBC; (3) it should be done on a considerable scale; (4) people would not listen to news alone; sustaining programmes were necessary; (5) special finance would be required; (6) the BBC should have the same freedom *vis-à-vis* Government departments as in the home service. The BBC was already in touch with the Foreign Office on matters which concerned them; this contact would be greatly increased if foreign language services were instituted; but the BBC must be responsible.[34]

On these conditions, Reith said, the BBC would be willing to take on broadcasting in Arabic, Spanish and Portuguese.

Not surprisingly much of the subsequent discussion turned on Reith's last condition. His diary entry for that date is beguilingly brief:

The Chairman spoke first then me and what I said pretty well finished the matter though I had Graves give all his objections. Various questions asked. To my surprise Leeper of the Foreign Office said I had more or less set all his doubts at rest – the Foreign Office wanting to run Arabic on their own from Cyprus. I made it clear that we would require finance and independence.[35]

The official minutes, however, make it quite clear that Leeper had by no means given up the Cyprus idea even if he held slender hopes for it and that the argument was a good deal tougher and more significant for the future of external broadcasting than Reith suggests. The Chairman, Sir Kingsley Wood, began by wondering whether the BBC would be able to take up a sufficiently strong attitude to foreign broadcasts prejudicial to British interests. A government station, he thought, would deal with such controversies more vigorously. Reith was in no doubt that the BBC could do the job adequately but 'in its own way'. In his view there was no problem over dealing with matters of fact. If the Foreign Office was not satisfied in particular cases and wanted something broadcast which the BBC did not like or for which it did not wish to take responsibility, then the Government could use its constitutional prerogative and require the BBC to transmit an official statement, making it clear on the air that this was done on Government instructions. But, Reith warned, 'this was not to be commended'.[36]

It was Leeper who brought matters to a head. While recognising, as Reith had noted, that the BBC had gone a long way to meet the apprehensions of the Foreign Office, he felt that news in Arabic should be dealt with differently from news in Spanish and Portuguese for Latin-America. Foreign Office thinking was at last coming out into the open, and it was in quite fundamental conflict with the BBC's attitude. For Reith consistency was profoundly important and the key to credibility. Audiences in Latin-America, Leeper argued, were westernised and sophisticated. All that was required for them was a translation of the well-balanced world news bulletins broadcast in English in the Empire Service. For the Arab world a different approach was needed. There should be careful selection and omission – selection of those items of news which it was in the interest of Great Britain to broadcast to the widest possible audience, and omission of items which the Foreign Office might think it inadvisable to disseminate. Leeper described this process as 'an innocent form of propaganda but propaganda nonetheless'. He thought that instances would often arise in practice 'where the Foreign Office would consider it essential to put across "propaganda" of this nature which the BBC quite properly from their own standpoint might view with considerable reluctance as inconsistent with the standards of impartiality and objectivity they have hitherto so consistently maintained.' Leeper made it clear that this was a point of cardinal importance for the Foreign Office, and he added for good measure that he thought local Arab news could be done better from the Near East than from London. It was a further argument in favour of a Foreign Office-run station on the spot. Norman, unaccountably, seemed disposed to be amenable to Foreign Office desires, but Reith was having none of it. The BBC, he conceded might have to show more elasticity and perhaps pay more heed to Foreign Office views in the case of Arabic, but on the central issue he was categorical:

The effect of a news service carried out by the BBC in any language would be based on telling the truth. Prestige depended on truthful and comprehensive broadcasts.

People should feel that because they have heard a statement on the British wireless it was correct; and conversely that if it was not included in the British broadcasts it was incorrect.

He was profoundly reluctant to accept that Arabic should be treated as *sui generis*. That might seem desirable now, he said, but the same problem might arise elsewhere in the future. Better to entrust the BBC with all foreign language broadcasting. It would then be able to meet these difficulties wherever and whenever they occurred. As for the proposed Foreign Office station in Cyprus, it would stand out as what it would undoubtedly be, an *ad hoc* British propaganda station. In the end it would prove counterproductive.[37]

As Reith rightly noted at the time, he won the day, but the conflict of attitudes which the minutes reflect was not finally resolved for all that. In the immediate aftermath of the meeting it became clear that Leeper, for his part, interpreted what had been agreed very differently from Reith and Graves. Graves, in a note setting out his own understanding, stated that,

It is definitely agreed that we are to have the same degree of freedom and responsibility as we have in the Empire and Home Services. The FO don't want direct contradictions. They want us to operate in the way we always said we should – no cooking of news, no direct taking up of inaccuracies, but just plain true statements.[38]

Leeper's version was quite other. The matter came up over the divided loyalties of the man appointed to be the first Arabic Editor, A.S. Calvert, who had returned from Jerusalem. In a conversation which J.B. Clark reported to Graves, Calvert told Clark that the Foreign Office readily dropped the idea of a station in Cyprus in the light of the BBC's willingness to undertake the Arabic Service, on the understanding that someone from the Foreign Office would be put in charge of it. 'Some people in the Foreign Office', Clark reported, 'seem to think Calvert is in some measure subject to Foreign Office as well as BBC discipline.'[39] Reith himself interviewed Calvert, who reluctantly accepted that in a case of total disagreement with the Foreign Office the BBC view would have to prevail. Reith told Calvert that it was up to him to see to it that the situation did not arise, but he made it clear he was far from happy with the situation.[40] Leeper, for his part, agreed with Graves that Calvert, having been seconded to the BBC, 'has only one master to serve'.[41] But he was anxious that Calvert's new masters 'should let him keep in the closest contact with his old'. He seemed to assume that because he had made the point at the meeting of the Kingsley Wood Committee that the Arabic bulletins should be 'something quite special' and 'quite apart' from the BBC's other services this had been agreed, whereas Reith, on all the evidence, had strongly demurred.

A fudged 'gentleman's agreement' was eventually reached which half satisfied the Foreign Office while meeting the BBC's main objections, but it left

Clark with the delicate task of dealing with Calvert. Clark, on that occasion, was not disposed to beat about the bush: 'The selection of news', he acknowledged in a formal note to Calvert, 'is of great importance and needs an expert knowledge of an audience and a background.' He recognised the need to increase the amount of news of specific interest to Arabs. But, he stated unambiguously,

> The omission of unwelcome facts of news and the consequent suppression of truth runs counter to the corporation's policy laid down by appropriate authority. If external bodies wish the corporation to modify an established policy, under which I have been directed to guide our new services, suitable representations should be made in an appropriate manner.[42]

It was the classic statement of the BBC's stand, which holds good to this day. It is to J.B. Clark's eternal credit that at this crucial stage, when even Reith seemed inclined to steer clear of confrontation with Whitehall and to deal with problems as they arose, he spoke out clearly and unequivocally. That he should have done so was heavy with consequences for the future.

There were to be one or two more hiccups before the way was at last clear. An attempt by Anthony Eden, then Foreign Secretary, to secure a written agreement between the Foreign Office and the BBC setting out the rights and responsibilities of each side came to nothing. The British preference for blurred edges prevailed. At the end of October, as a formal announcement of the start of foreign language broadcasting was being drafted, the Postmaster General, Major Tryon, greatly angered Reith by prematurely stating in the House of Commons that the Government had 'decided' that the BBC should undertake broadcasts in 'certain foreign languages'.[43] 'It was of course most unfortunate that any statement should have been made in those terms,' Reith wrote later. 'It would prejudice the new service before it began; it was of cardinal importance that it should be known that this was a BBC and not a Government service. For the BBC would be trusted where the Government might not be.'[44] As the facts emerged, Tryon had made the statement on his own initiative when put on the spot by Herbert Morrison who felt the Government was being dilatory over introducing broadcasts in French, German and Italian, a matter Morrison had raised with Reith some time before. Reith was with difficulty dissuaded by Kingsley Wood from putting out a correcting statement. Matters were put right on 1 November by Sir John Simon, Chancellor of the Exchequer, speaking in the debate on the King's Speech on behalf of the Prime Minister. The BBC had been looking at the possibility of introducing foreign language broadcasting for some time, Simon said, and following Ullswater it had made it clear that it would respond speedily to a Government request to make a start. That request had now been made.

I should like to make it clear that, in this new service, the corporation will have the same full responsibilities and duties as are set forth in the charter in relation to their existing services. His Majesty's Government are satisfied that the corporation are to be relied upon to maintain in this new service the same high standard which is characteristic of their Home and their Empire Services.[45]

It was a statement with which Reith had every reason to be well pleased. He had been consulted in advance about its wording, and it gave him everything he wanted. The BBC was now on firm ground. He recorded with pride that Warren Fisher of the Treasury had told him that,

Our not being made to have a written agreement with respect to the Foreign Office on foreign language broadcasts was a great tribute to us – me especially. Eden had wanted something definite but the Cabinet minute referred only to a gentleman's agreement between Vansittart and myself.[46]

He had also been assured by the Postmaster General that the proportion of the licence revenue payable to the BBC would be reviewed to take account not only of the development of television, which had just started, but also of the running costs of the new services and of the investment in necessary new short wave transmitters at Daventry. 'Almost the whole evening on the phone about arrangements for foreign languages which I said would start in four weeks',[47] he noted in his diary after Simon's Commons statement. As it turned out this proved over-optimistic. In fact the Arabic Service transmitted its first bulletin eight weeks later, on 3 January 1938. Another two months elapsed before the inauguration of the Latin-American Service on 14 and 15 March. The first Arabic bulletin provided a stark illustration of the distance which still separated Leeper and the BBC on the issue of what was proper news for the BBC to broadcast to the Arab world. It included a report of the execution by the British authorities of a Palestinian Arab found guilty of carrying a gun. Leeper regarded this as a flagrant departure from what he thought had been agreed: 'Straight news', he wrote, 'must not be interpreted as including news which can do us harm with the people we are addressing.'[48] What he did not say, perhaps because he was not aware of it, was that the news of the execution had already been broadcast in the Empire Service without causing a ripple. Nor did he at that stage appear to appreciate the danger to the BBC's credibility of omitting uncomfortable items of news which other hostile radio stations might be making much of. It was a lesson which Whitehall was to learn the hard way in the first two years of the war. Though in the end the divergence of view between Leeper and the BBC was superficially patched up and arrangements were made for regular consultations to enable the Foreign Office to put its point of view on controversial items, the 'gentleman's agreement' could not conceal altogether the fundamental difference in approach between the BBC and the Foreign Office. J.B. Clark, for his part, refused to accept that there could be any basic difference, 'except in small degree',[49] between the Arabic news and the news broadcast in the Latin-American Service. That was to remain the BBC's attitude throughout the war, and indeed right through to the present day.

4
The Politics of Propaganda

Like the British nation as a whole the BBC was in many respects ill-prepared for the demands which the war was to make on it. Hitler and Goebbels had long ago thought through the role which radio was to play in the coming conflict. 'In war words are acts', Hitler had written in *Mein Kampf*. Churchill, in contrast, believed that war must be won by deeds, not words. As far back as 1933, in conversation with Hermann Rauschning, Hitler had laid stress on psychological dislocation of the enemy as a necessary preliminary stage to military offensive, just as heavy artillery bombardment in the First World War had softened up the forward positions of the opposing army as a preliminary to the infantry assault: 'Our strategy is to destroy the enemy from within, to conquer him through himself. Mental confusion, contradiction of feelings, indecision, panic – these are our weapons.'[1]

The German Ministry of Propaganda saw radio as its chief instrument, and Ewald Banse, Professor of Military Science at Brunswick Technical College, was writing in 1934:

It is essential to attack the enemy nation in its weak spot, to undermine, crush, break down its resistance, and convince it that it is being deceived, misled and brought to destruction by its own government ... The originally well-knit fabric of the enemy nation must be gradually disintegrated, broken down, rotted, so that it falls to pieces like a fungus when one treads on it in a wood.[2]

The British on the other hand showed little taste for thinking of this kind. As a nation they regarded propaganda as suspect and were instinctively averse to the deliberate perversion of truth as a policy to be publicly adopted by Government in the pursuit of national ends. Neither Churchill nor Eden had much interest in propaganda. Some Whitehall officials like Rex Leeper may at an early stage have seen radio as a useful weapon, but they were in a minority. Later, during the war, the talented and resourceful British practitioners of 'black' radio broadcasting showed themselves well able to outmatch Goebbels in the use of deceit and fabrication.[3] But whereas such methods were central to the Nazi scheme of things and ideologically respectable, British 'black' broadcasting, whatever its effectiveness – and it had its undoubted successes – was never more than a fringe activity. The British took

to it with as much flair and gusto as they did to other forms of irregular
warfare. It was a useful temporary expedient, it was fun, and it appealed to
the British taste for cloak-and-dagger activities and deception, but it grew in
shallow soil and did not survive the circumstances which led to its use.

On the other hand the British had one considerable advantage. They had
not succumbed to the mystique of radio, as the Germans did. In Britain radio
was held to be a service to the public, as well as an art, even if a minor one,
and not an instrument of state. That was the sense of the arrangements made
to define the relationship between the broadcasters, the Government, Parliament and the nation at large under the BBC's first charter.

This meant that although confusion reigned in Britain during the last years
of peace over what role broadcasting should play in wartime and what degree
of autonomy, if any, it should retain, and although the debate on these
questions continued well into the third year of the war, that very confusion,
inefficient though it may now appear, may paradoxically have ensured that
the British made a more effective use of radio in the end. In the main the
British held on grimly, if a little shakily at times, to the notion that ultimately
no effective propaganda policy can in the modern world be based on lies. It
was the very opposite of the Goebbels doctrine, and Britain emerged from
the wartime conflict between the two concepts of propaganda the decisive
winner. The victory was a moral one and it arose not from superior means
and greater technical skills but from superior principles. Such a policy seemed
the only possible one for a democratic nation fighting against tyranny, but it
also brought long-term dividends. Nonetheless, it remains remarkable that it
was adopted from the outset, all the more so as the temptation to play down
the disasters of the first three years of the war must at times have seemed
overwhelming. On the other hand, as one British participant put it, 'One
knew perfectly well that if we lost the war, if there was a German invasion,
we'd all be shot anyway. So why not tell the truth. Whereas if we held out and
the tide turned, the fact that we told the truth would mean that the Germans
would believe us, as indeed they did.'[4] The BBC itself, by its steadfast and
consistent attachment to the truth, often against considerable pressure and in
spite of the irritation it caused and the attacks it attracted, played a decisive
role, not just in securing that moral victory, but in winning for Britain the
gratitude and respect of those it had addressed throughout the war.

But if this was indeed the BBC's finest hour – just as it was the nation's – it
was not achieved by design and was largely the outcome of hasty improvisa-
tion. Despite repeated pleas to the Government the BBC's place in the state at
war was not recognised until well into the second year of the war. There was
no overall plan for the development of foreign language services, and in the
early stages new services were introduced piecemeal, usually at very short
notice and more often than not in response to events rather than in anticipa-
tion of them. Transmitters, studio facilities and office accommodation were

woefully inadequate to keep pace with the rapid expansion of services which took place at the Government's request in the first two or three years of the war, and the stresses and strains which this produced led to a near breakdown in the BBC's administration which was among the reasons for the replacement of F. W. Ogilvie as Director-General, Reith's successor, in January 1942.[5]

If the BBC can be claimed to have to some extent 'missed the boat' in the early stages of the war, the blame must largely rest with the Government of the day, whose attitude reflected faithfully the reluctance of the British people as a whole to face the reality of the imminence of war. That attitude was also reflected at a senior level inside the BBC. However once the internal BBC argument on this issue had been settled – those who had opposed foreign language broadcasting loyally accepted the decision once it was made – Reith made clear to the Government the BBC's readiness to meet official requests. No such requests were received during the months that followed the introduction of the Arabic and Latin-American Services early in 1938. It was only as the Czech crisis gathered momentum in September of that year and as the danger of an outbreak of hostilities became more apparent that J. B. Clark, by then Director of Overseas Services, was officially warned that he might be called upon to arrange at short notice for news bulletins to be broadcast in German. Steps were taken to gather together the names and addresses of people with the necessary qualifications who could be called upon if necessary, but there was no positive indication from the Foreign Office that the service was likely to be needed and the arrangements were not tested in advance.

It was not until Tuesday 27 September, two days before the Munich Conference itself, that the BBC was asked to provide facilities that very night to transmit German, Italian and French language versions of a broadcast to the nation which the Prime Minister, Neville Chamberlain, was due to make at 8 pm.[6] The Foreign Office undertook to provide speakers and translations but later that day it transpired that it would be unable to do so in the case of French and German. At 6 pm that night the Foreign Office asked if the BBC could provide news bulletins as well as the translations of the Prime Minister's broadcast. A frantic search for German and French translators and announcers ensued. J. B. Clark tracked down G. Walter Goetz, the German artist who was drawing cartoons for the *Daily Express*, at a cocktail party and sent him post haste to Broadcasting House to do the German version. The Hon. Francis Rennell Rodd, later Lord Rennell, undertook the Italian version, having served as an intelligence officer in Italy during the First World War and later worked in the British Embassy in Rome. Duncan Grinnell-Milne, a BBC announcer, read the French version. The English text of the Prime Minister's speech, broadcast at 8 pm, was reaching the translators page by page between 8.15 and 8.30 pm and each page was translated as it came in and broadcast while the remainder of the speech was still being translated. A BBC internal report afterwards commented that 'there had been inevitable delays and stumblings by the announcers, which caused unfavourable comment in many quarters and spoilt the effectiveness of Mr Chamberlain's speech. But in view of the difficulties under which the work was carried out this was excusable.'[7]

The first broadcasts were transmitted on all BBC wavelengths and replaced normal scheduled programmes on medium wave intended for British listeners at home. They were also carried on short wave on all Empire Service frequencies, where, as with the home services, they replaced advertised programmes. The Prime Minister's address in English was reported to have made a particularly big impression in the United States, where President Roosevelt heard it in the course of a Cabinet meeting at the White House. The news bulletins on that day also included translations of an appeal by Mrs Roosevelt, which had been suppressed in Germany, and of the replies to it from France, Britain and Czechoslovakia. The following day, 28 September, they included the text of an appeal to Hitler by President Roosevelt himself and of King George VI's proclamation calling up naval reservists and Marines.

Daily broadcasts in all three languages continued thereafter throughout the period of the Munich crisis, though the number of transmitters used was gradually reduced. Some regional medium wave transmitters inside the United Kingdom, including the London regional station, continued to carry the three foreign language bulletins for some time, though this seems to have led to remarkably few protests from home listeners whose normal programmes had been disrupted. A few wrote or telephoned to say they thought there was something wrong with their sets as they kept getting foreign languages instead of English. One understandably confused listener complained angrily: 'I consider it against public policy to allow the Germans and Italians to take over radio at 7 pm. They are both against the British.'

The decision to continue the French, German and Italian bulletins was made on a day-to-day basis after the crisis had passed, until after about a month the BBC and the Foreign Office agreed that the new services should be maintained indefinitely. There was little evidence at first that they were being heard by those for whom they were intended. Little correspondence was received, though there was a certain amount of criticism of delivery at the microphone and of the quality of translation. There were also complaints from Germany that the timing of the BBC German bulletin coincided with a news bulletin on the German home service. The German authorities at that stage made no attempt to control listening, as they were later to do with mounting severity, and there was no jamming. Early in 1939, when the BBC German transmission was extended to half an hour, indications began to be received that they were having 'a profound effect'. Hitler threatened retaliation, and Dr Hesse, the Director of DNB, the German official news agency, on a visit to London, told a Foreign Office contact that the BBC broadcasts were proving a growing irritant to increasing numbers of Germans who were not necessarily Nazi sympathisers. He had been asked to raise the matter by the German Ministry of Propaganda. The Foreign Office official concerned, Charles Peake, observed that 'it seemed odd that if the news given were resented in Germany that it should be increasingly listened to'. Dr Hesse had no answer to that.[8] For their part, Foreign Office sources in Germany were unanimously in favour of going on.[9]

The BBC itself was far from satisfied with its own performance.

The French and Italian bulletins were more satisfactory than the German from the start [an internal post-mortem noted] but there was great difficulty in achieving in all three languages the high standard attained in the Arabic and Latin-American Services, though improvement was gradually made. Some thirty people, all strongly recommended and apparently qualified, were made use of, but few proved to be satisfactory, either as announcers or translators.[10]

The Munich crisis proved an important broadcasting landmark in another respect: it was the first major international crisis in which radio fully came into its own as a prime source of news. An editorial in the *Listener* observed afterwards that 'broadcasting emerged from the crisis as one of the determining factors'.[11] There was a fifty per cent increase in the time allotted to news in the Empire Service. Programme plans were freely adjusted and bulletins extended to up to thirty-five minutes to cater for the world-wide hunger for news and comment. Reuters agreed on 12 September to lift its ban on the rebroadcasting of BBC English language bulletins overseas, more particularly in Australia, and on 28 September leave to rebroadcast was extended to the United States, where the Mutual Broadcasting System seized its chance and for a few days was able to give BBC Empire Service bulletins coast-to-coast coverage in its network of affiliated stations. But it was too good to last. In Australia press interests protested vehemently. Reuters eventually withdrew permission to relay on 3 October. It was not restored until after the outbreak of war.

Much was learned by the BBC from the experience of Munich. The crisis drove home the importance of broadcasting news at frequent intervals in times of international tension. In the Empire Service the bulletins became the most important element in the programme to the world-wide audience anxiously following the development of events in Europe: 'The calm voice of the BBC announcer evoked special comment from abroad, in contrast to the excited accents of the American announcers and the extreme anti-Czechoslovakian propaganda from Germany.'[12]

Beyond the words spoken a more subtle message was being conveyed over the airwaves by the contrasting styles of the leading protagonists:

Those who listened to the broadcasts of Herr Hitler's speeches at Nuremberg and Berlin [the *Listener* observed] could have been left under no misunderstanding of the atmosphere in which the German attitude to the international problem was evolving. By contrast nothing could have been more effective in clarifying our own minds and

simplifying our emotions than the tone of voice of Mr Chamberlain's own broadcast
... What a contrast in broadcasting techniques – between the fiery oration delivered
in the *Sportspalast* before cheering masses of followers and the calm talk from the
quiet room in Downing Street addressed to small groups of listeners round the family
hearth.[13]

Already the truth was being established that no amount of ranting on the
radio could turn a bad cause into a good one and that the power of an idea
was not dependent on strident and repetitive presentation, as Hitler and
Goebbels believed.

For the moment, however, more practical matters loomed larger in the
preoccupations of both the Government and the top management of the BBC.
The whole issue of the role of broadcasting and of the position of the BBC in
wartime had been raised by Reith as far back as 1934. He had spoken to Sir
Maurice Hankey, the Secretary to the Cabinet, who had advised him to get in
touch with Major-General J.G. Dill, then Director of Military Operations
and Intelligence at the War Office. There had been a meeting. Prickly, pessimistic and contemptuous of Whitehall as he was, Reith had been pleasantly
surprised: 'I had not reckoned on meeting such a one as Dill', he wrote, 'I was
attracted by him personally, but it was the complete understanding and
confidence he showed at that first meeting which most impressed me.'[14]

Reith appointed Ashbridge, the Controller of Engineering, and two others
to represent him in the detailed discussions to come. The practical issues
concerned the security of BBC buildings and transmitters and how to maintain
broadcasting in the face of the heavy air raids which, it was anticipated,
would immediately follow the outbreak of hostilities. There was a lot of
detailed planning to do and the BBC got on with it vigorously and with
foresight under Reith's overall direction. On the question of the BBC's role in
wartime, Dill's initial reaction had been encouraging: 'He said he fully realised
the importance of broadcasting,' Reith noted; it was 'sheer nonsense for
anyone to talk of its suppression in war; it would have an immensely important part to play'.[15] Wing Commander E.J. Hodsoll of the Home Office Air
Raid Precautions Department, who was one of the officials involved with
Dill, did not believe that the Government should take over the BBC on the
outbreak of war: 'After thinking over this matter a good deal and discussing
it with various people,' he wrote, 'my own opinion is strongly that it would be
better if the BBC were left as they are, though naturally there would be
extremely close liaison between the Government and the BBC officials.'[16]

That was in 1934. By the time of the Munich crisis four years later, however,
the question had still not been settled. After an initial setback at the hands of
Kingsley Wood, who seems to have thought it possible to discuss the role of
broadcasting in war without the BBC being involved, Reith had managed to
get himself invited to be a member of a sub-committee of the Committee of

Imperial Defence charged with working out the details of the setting up of a Ministry of Information on the outbreak of war. Other members of the sub-committee included Sir Robert Vansittart, the Permanent Secretary at the Foreign Office, Sir Warren Fisher, the Permanent Secretary of the Treasury, as well as Sir John Dill. Reith was deeply shocked when at the first meeting the Foreign Office representative suggested that the proposed ministry should be accommodated at the Foreign Office and that the Foreign Office Press Section should form its nucleus: 'I rarely heard anything so monstrous,' Reith wrote in his diary. 'It seemed unbelievable. Everybody appeared surprised.'[17] The suggestion was not adopted. Much groundwork was done in the ensuing years on such matters as wartime censorship arrangements, which were amicably resolved, but the question of the BBC's relations with the proposed ministry remained undecided.

On one point Reith had already made his own priorities clear. In a paper on 'The Position of the BBC in War' which he sent to the Postmaster General, Major Tryon, at his request in July 1935, he laid emphasis with great percipience on what he felt should be the prime role of the broadcasters in wartime: most people who had given the matter any thought saw this as being the maintenance of the morale of the civil population. Reith saw it differently. For him what mattered most was integrity: 'It is essential that the responsibility and reliability of the BBC's News Service should be established beyond doubt', he wrote, 'even though in practice accuracy could not amount to more than the nearest approach to absolute truth permitted by the overriding war conditions, including censorship.'[18]

Reith himself had been offered the Director-Generalship of the Ministry of Information but had declined. Instead he suggested Sir Stephen Tallents, who had been in charge of public relations at the GPO and Chairman of the Empire Marketing Board before joining the BBC as Controller of Public Relations in 1935. Tallents was duly chosen as Director-General Designate and started work in October 1936, though he did not become Director-General when the ministry came into existence and instead was put in charge of the BBC's Overseas Services in 1940. But in 1938 he was at the centre of the planning for the new ministry, and his presence there reflected the intention that the BBC should work hand-in-glove with the ministry once war started. A BBC man was best placed to work out the details of how the two bodies might cooperate. Indeed Tallents was the forerunner of the many BBC officials who at various times during the war occupied positions in the Ministry of Information where they dealt on behalf of the ministry with broadcasting matters which brought them into daily contact with their former colleagues at Broadcasting House. Some, like Lindsay Wellington and A.P. Ryan, occupied key positions at different times during the war in both organisations.[19]

In May 1938 the Committee of Imperial Defence had approved a recommendation that as the ministry would have responsibility for censorship

control over the programmes of the BBC the ultimate responsibility for broadcasting, which in more normal times was vested in the Postmaster General,
should be transferred to the Minister of Information for the duration. It was
assumed at that stage that the Board of Governors of the BBC would 'go out
of commission during the period of complete Government control'.[20] Curiously it seems to have been felt that the members of the board 'would be
anxious to take up other work more immediately concerned with the war
effort'. In any case a simplified channel of command would be required in
wartime and a Board of Governors would get in the way. Tallents proposed
that the existing Board of Governors should be replaced by a board consisting
of only two members, a Chairman and a Vice-Chairman. The Director-
General of the BBC and his Deputy should be appointed to these two positions
and combine their executive functions with those of Governors:

> It is assumed to be intended [Tallents wrote] that the BBC should retain in war time
> so much of its normal independence as is compatible with the censorship by the
> ministry of all relevant broadcast programmes . . . No doubt in practice the corporation
> would collaborate readily with the Minister of Information, but his operation of a
> censorship would inevitably impose upon him a wider responsibility for BBC pro-
> grammes than the Postmaster General accepts in time of peace.[21]

It was important, Tallents urged, that the relationship should be clearly
defined.

Reith, for his part, appears to have been quite happy with what was
proposed. No doubt there would be problems when the time came to go over
to wartime arrangements, but at least the BBC would remain a separate entity
and with a strong Director-General its independence would be safeguarded
within the limits of what was practical under wartime conditions. The
Director-General would be responsible to the Minister of Information 'on a
level with, but in no way subordinate to the ministry's Director-General. He
would in part of his work be subject to guidance and direction, but while
conforming to Government policies, he would be given great latitude in
execution. 'In the rest,' Reith wrote, 'he would be a free agent'.[22]

With Reith in charge it might have been so. He would have brought to such
an arrangement the benefit of his skill and experience as well as the weight of
his personal authority. He had in any case contributed a great deal to Government thinking on the role of broadcasting in war and to the necessary
contingency planning. But with his departure for Imperial Airways in June
1938 the BBC found itself increasingly at loggerheads with the Government
over a large range of issues. 'The basic trouble', as Asa Briggs has put it,
'leaving on one side the unexpected character of the war itself, was that both
the BBC and the Government had gone into the war uncertain of what their
future relationship would be.'[23]

This fundamental uncertainty was epitomised in the handling of the question of the composition and role of the Board of Governors in wartime, and

indeed of whether there should be an independent board at all. Surprisingly, individual Governors had not been told of the agreement negotiated by Reith with Sir Thomas Gardiner, of the Post Office, early in 1938, under which their services would be dispensed with in wartime. When told what was intended during the Munich crisis, they appeared to acquiesce in their own proposed demise. However they were clearly incensed at not having been consulted and returned to the matter with great vigour in June 1939. One of their number, Sir Ian Fraser, raised it formally with his colleagues. The representations they then made to Downing Street centred on the argument that even though it might be thought right to reduce their numbers it would be quite wrong to merge the functions of Governors with those of the Director-General and his Deputy, as had been agreed by Reith. What was important in their eyes was that whatever limitations to the BBC's independence might turn out to be necessary in wartime, that independence must remain a fact and be seen so to remain. The board was the corporation, it was the embodiment of the BBC's unique status, and its continued existence was the only guarantee that the BBC would not become, in effect, an offshoot of the Government: 'The total eclipse of the independence of the corporation', they stated, 'would be widely re-garded as a serious blow to liberty, and would create difficulties for the Government before the public opinion in the country.'[24]

These arguments clearly caused second thoughts, and a compromise was worked out which, it was hoped, would be acceptable to the BBC. The Chairman, Sir Allan Powell, and the Vice-Chairman, C.H.G. Millis, would remain in office and between them would consititute the full board. The Director-General and his Deputy would continue in their purely executive functions. However the formula did not get an easy passage. The Prime Minister's belated explanation to the House of Commons that the reduction in the number of Governors had been made 'in order to ensure the smooth and swift operation of the broadcasting system under war conditions'[25] did not go down well with the Opposition, and some of the Governors who by then had received their notice made public their profound disquiet and their resentment at the underhand way in which their future had been disposed of. The new arrangement, wrote one of their members, the historian H.A.L. Fisher, in a letter to The Times, had only been agreed as a result of energetic protests by Governors. They accepted it, Fisher said, as a temporary wartime measure, but 'it would not have occurred to them to suggest it, having regard to the general interest of the listening public'.[26]

Eventually the decision was to be reversed by Duff Cooper, as Minister of Information, but not until April 1941. Two of the former Governors, Sir Ian Fraser and Dr J.J. Mallon, the Warden of Toynbee Hall, were then re-appointed. They were joined by two new members, Lady Violet Bonham Carter and A.H. Mann, the former editor of the Yorkshire Post. A few months later Harold Nicolson, who had been Parliamentary Private Secretary to Duff Cooper, was appointed to bring the board to its full complement. It was, in Asa Briggs's words, 'probably a more able and lively team than any before them'.[27] They remained in office until after the end of the war. Determined and independent-minded in their various ways, they were able to resume even in wartime the crucial role of the board in defending the freedom of the broadcasters and shielding them from undue pressures. Their presence undoubtedly had a beneficient effect on the relationship between the Government and the BBC. It ensured that the BBC was recognised as something other than an arm of Government and was treated as such, in spite of Churchill's own strong prejudice against it. The man who had the vision to bring about this change was not Duff Cooper, who took the decision to bring the board back to its full pre-war strength, but his successor after July 1941, Brendan Bracken, one of Churchill's closest confidants.

Before this could happen, however, the BBC had to face one more major challenge to that very autonomy the newly restored board thought it had been appointed to embody. To understand the nature of that challenge it is necessary at this point to digress and to dwell for a moment on the many vicissitudes through which the BBC's relationship with the Government passed during the first two years of the war.

As the war clouds gathered in the early summer of 1939, the BBC could be forgiven for not being clear about what that relationship would be once war broke out. The Ministry of Information was being put together in the confident expectation that war was inevitable. Senior staff were being appointed, but few, if any, had any knowledge or experience of broadcasting – or for that matter information and propaganda. Following the decision in January 1939 that Sir Stephen Tallents should be asked to withdraw as Director-General Designate,[28] two appointments had been made in quick succession to replace him. The first was Sir Ernest Fass, the Public Trustee, who was soon compelled to resign because of ill health. The second was Lord Perth, a diplomat, former Secretary-General to the League of Nations and former Ambassador in Rome. Perth himself had no knowledge of or interest in propaganda. He was replaced shortly after the outbreak of war by Sir Findlater Stewart, the Permanent Secretary at the India Office, 'a typical civil servant', as Lionel Fielden, who had just returned from India, described him: 'For propaganda you needed a Beaverbrook, a Reith, a Priestley, a Coward – surely not a civil servant.'[29] A.P. Waterfield, the Deputy Director-General, was no better qualified, and neither was Sir Kenneth Lee, who briefly held the post of Director of Radio – swiftly modified to 'Director of Radio Relations' on representations being made by the BBC, which felt that the title implied a greater degree of authority over broadcasting than it was prepared to accept. Lee had been Chairman of the firm of Tootal Broadhurst. Lionel Fielden himself had been considered for the job, but, as Waterfield told him, Lee had been preferred precisely because he had no experience of broadcasting: 'We don't want any friction, you see', Waterfield explained.[30] Sir Robert Bruce Lockhart, who was later to become Director-General of the Political Warfare Executive, commented at the time on seeing a list of the staff of the new ministry in *The Times* that 'the personnel is unbelievably poor'.[31]

Sir Kenneth Lee himself succeeded Findlater Stewart as Director-General in November 1939, but even he lasted only a few months. He was replaced by Frank Pick, who had been Deputy Chairman of London Transport. He in turn made way in December 1940 to Walter Monckton, whose Deputy was to be Cyril Radcliffe, later Lord Radcliffe, the distinguished judge. Though Radcliffe in particular was an exceptionally able man, it was not until Brendan Bracken's appointment as Minister of Information in July 1941 that any headway was made in sorting out the internal chaos in the ministry itself and in bringing to an end the inter-departmental rivalries which frustrated its efforts. Neither Lord Macmillan, the first wartime minister, nor Reith, who succeeded him, nor Duff Cooper, who followed after Reith's brief and un-happy period of office, proved either able or willing to take the steps necessary to disperse the organisational fog which hung over Malet Street, the head-quarters of the ministry. Nor could they obtain for it the powers they felt it required if it was properly to do the job for which it had been created. 'I get horribly depressed from time to time by the burden of this ministry', Monck-ton wrote in despair. 'There is so much to do, and with all his great and good qualities my master [Duff Cooper] is very hard to get to the point of drastic action or to take great interest in a concrete form.'[32]

In June 1941 he and Radcliffe finally spelt out for Duff Cooper what was wrong with the way the ministry was operating. There was no unity of command, they said. The British Council was not under the minister's control, and neither was the BBC, 'in spite of a vague right of control over it which it has proved impossible to render administratively effective'. The ministry should have the authority necessary to handle the issue of official news by direction, and to control its form, timing and treatment. At present, they said, the ministry had no positive function. Representatives of other government departments operated inside the ministry but not under its control, each dealing separately with its own news, so that there was no control or coordi-nated direction of any kind. The Government could not be said to have a policy in regard to news. The policy was to have no policy and to live from hand to mouth. One person should be able, on his own authority, and at his own risk, to decide what news should be issued and when.

The present system results in news being held up while the question of its release is considered by one or more other departments whose primary function is not the handling of news. Security considerations cannot always be the final consideration ... There must be occasions when you should risk adding to the enemy's knowledge because of the advantage of speaking up on your own side.

And they went on to conclude that, 'There is widespread dissatisfaction at the moment [with our news and propaganda] and it is largely justified. We have been slower than the Germans in handling news; we have been less decisive and prompt in propaganda.'[33]

A.P. Ryan, who at the time was Home Adviser to the BBC, was even more forthright. In a paper written for Monckton at about the same time he said that the Ministry of Information was 'a sop to Cerberus'. 'The history of animal management contains no more dismal record of failure.'[34] It irritated the press, the public and Parliament were unimpressed by its performance, its relations with the BBC were not happy, and it had not won the affection of the Cabinet. Lip service was paid to the importance of propaganda in wartime,

But behind the scenes, in the lobbies, in the committee rooms and in clubs, the spirit of scepticism is vocal ... Statesmen, civil servants and leaders in the fighting services cannot openly say that news is a nuisance and propaganda a cheapjack charlatan game. They know that compulsory censorship is impractical. Hence the setting up of the Ministry of Information and the omission to define its functions and to endow it with recognised authority.

In their own paper Monckton and Radcliffe drew the obvious parallel: 'The Germans', they wrote, 'despite their huge preponderance in men and material, have never relaxed their attention to propaganda. Far less can we afford to do so.'

For the BBC the main problem was to persuade the armed services to release news early enough to get the British version of the facts out before the Germans could publish theirs. News editors wanted enough detail to disprove the exaggerated and often wholly invented German stories. Programme staff, in the Overseas Services in particular, wanted the armed services to cooperate in making speakers available who had taken part in successful operations. The services were deeply reluctant to abandon their normal routine, which called for next-of-kin to be informed before details of an engagement were released. The Admiralty went as far as to suggest at one stage that details of naval losses should be broadcast only once a week. But since these details were available to the press they automatically became available to the rest of the world and the Germans had them anyway and made them available to William Joyce – 'Lord Haw-Haw' – for his propaganda broadcasts to Britain from Radio Hamburg. These broadcasts had caused a mounting argument in Britain about whether they should be answered point by point. Ministers and Whitehall officials feared that Haw-Haw was only too readily believed and was thus having a bad effect on the morale of the nation: 'My hostess's servants "listen in" to Haw-Haw', a titled lady wrote to Tallents, 'and one of them remarked the other day that there was probably something in what he said'. She feared there must be 'thousands of people who, like those maids, listen to him daily and find themselves influenced by his malicious lies'.[35] Much of what Haw-Haw said was, of course, pure fabrication, but it had a certain insinuating quality and dwelt insistently on what Robert Silvey, the Head of the BBC's Audience Research Department, called 'undeniable social evils in this country'. Silvey was later able to show conclusively, in a report dated March 1940 and based on a mass survey of listeners, that the alarm was quite unfounded. But the argument about answering back enabled Ogilvie, in a series of letters to relevant ministers and top officials, to make some telling points. One result of the growth of radio as a source of information, he argued, was to make the world increasingly a single place. It was becoming impracticable to isolate particular sections of it.

News is what listeners principally look for at present from China to Peru [he wrote]. It is on its news service that the prestige of any station (and country) finally depends, and the Haw-Haw question makes it all the more important that the BBC's news service should be allowed to maintain its standards of truthfulness and speed. It will be a very bad day for this country if people at home and abroad begin to say: 'The BBC seems to be keeping back unpleasant news. What is the British Government trying to hide?'[36]

Ogilvie's letters were not entirely without effect. From Monckton, then Director-General of the Press and Censorship Bureau at the Ministry of Information, he received an encouraging reply:

We simply must hammer home your main point – full and prompt news. Slowness conjures up a picture of reluctant extraction of teeth. Suppression in modern conditions fails save in the few exceptional cases ... But if we are prompt and candid our news service will be trusted and the reputation, for instance, of the BBC will be enhanced for all purposes.

It was easier said than done. In a secret and carefully documented paper sent to Sir Kenneth Lee of the Ministry of Information on 25 March 1940, Ogilvie listed a large number of occasions when information had been released too late, with disastrous consequences for the British case.[37] The Nazi propaganda machine had seized its opportunity and got its own highly coloured version out first, gaining for it a credibility it did not deserve.

Perhaps the most telling example was the case of the German air raid on the British naval base at Scapa Flow, in the Orkneys, on Saturday 16 March 1940. The raid took place just before 8 pm, and the German Radio began broadcasting its own account of it at 3.40 am the next morning in its English service to North America. It first claimed that the Luftwaffe had damaged three battleships and a cruiser. Later in the day it broadcast a highly dramatised description of the raid, complete with sound effects, claiming hits on HMS *Hood*, *Repulse* and *Renown*. By the 19th the German version had been picked up by the American press and widely disseminated throughout the United States. The number of ships claimed to have been hit had grown. The *New York Times* carried the headline 'Scapa Flow loss put at six warships', and its leading article stated that the Germans had won 'the most important victory of air power over naval power since the outbreak of war'. The Germans, it said, had succeeded in making Scapa Flow untenable.[38] Other American papers took a similar line.

Yet none of this was true. The Admiralty had rung the BBC at 7 am on the morning after the raid with a request that the news be withheld until the relatives of the casualties had been informed. It did not issue a communiqué until midday on the 17th, sixteen hours after the raid and over eight hours after the first German broadcast to America claiming heavy British naval losses. That communiqué, which contained the barest details, was broadcast in the BBC news bulletin at 1 pm. Later Chamberlain told the House of Commons that the raid had been a failure. Not more than twenty bombs had been dropped. There had been minor damage to only one ship, and no capital ships or other military objectives had been hit. Yet a suggestion by the BBC that American correspondents in Britain, including Ed Murrow of CBS, should be allowed to go to Scapa Flow to see for themselves was turned down. The London *Evening Standard* backed the BBC's case:

> The old saying that a lie gets half way round the world before truth has time to get its boots on should be hung up in the offices of every government department. Delay and suppression encourage rumour. And rumour will run errands for Dr Goebbels but never work for us. Sealed lips are as dangerous as careless talk.[39]

Ogilvie drew the attention of the Government to many other failures of cooperation by the armed services which in his view had been damaging to the national interest. On 19 February 1940, for instance, CBS had carried coast-to-coast an interview with the captain of the German prison ship *Altmark*, but a BBC request for an interview with the captain of the destroyer *Cossack*, which had freed the British merchant seamen held on board the *Altmark*, was turned down by the Admiralty. On 3 March 1940 NBC carried a talk by Grand Admiral Raeder justifying the sinking of neutral and allied shipping. The BBC recorded the broadcast and played it back to senior officials at the Ministry of Information. All agreed that a quick answer was required but much to their bafflement they were unable to get the Admiralty to agree to put up an official spokesman of comparable standing. In the end Admiral Sir Roger Keyes, long ago retired, agreed on his own responsibility to do the job but then fell ill and was unable to broadcast.

The Air Ministry was no better. Once again a top German military figure had been interviewed by one of the American networks and had received wide publicity all over the United States. This time it was Lieutenant General Ernst Udet, the First World War air ace, who was now the chief of the technical department of the German Air Ministry. He was interviewed by William Shirer, the CBS correspondent in Berlin. The BBC sought the help of the Air Ministry in arranging for an RAF speaker of comparable calibre but failed.

Ogilvie put it to the Government that the great issues at stake demanded 'a real change of outlook'. The 'direct and sustained cooperation of the

Government' was necessary. Without it, Ogilvie argued, 'the country's broad-casting service cannot become a fully effective instrument of war'.

It seems essential [he wrote] that the Service Departments should take most earnest account of the outstanding opportunities for victory or defeat in the world's mind which the radio commands; that even such honourable reluctances as spring from a desire to reserve statements for a first hearing by Parliament, to spare the feelings of the bereaved or to preserve the traditional reticence of serving officers and men, may in the national interest have to yield to the paramount necessity of so declaring the British case that it may catch the ear of the world before the enemy has had time to forestall and distort it.[40]

It did not prove easy to wean the official mind from its traditional caution and secretiveness. Even when there were successes to report, British accounts tended to be less full and circumstantial than the enemy's and fell short of maximum effectiveness. This was a criticism which was widely voiced over-seas, particularly in the United States. The German Radio made a prompter and more effective use of eye witness accounts than the BBC was allowed to do. Well-wishers abroad were asking for more. The RAF raid on Sylt imme-diately after the Luftwaffe's own abortive raid on Scapa Flow was a case in point. It was an undoubted success and news of it was, for once, released ahead of the Germans. However the Air Ministry would not allow pilots who had flown on the raid to appear at the microphone until forty-eight hours after the raid, even though they had been photographed for the press and had made short statements for publication almost immediately. Only one officer was eventually allowed to broadcast, and as a result had to spend twelve hours at Broadcasting House to do six different interviews for different programmes.

A.P. Ryan, ever a trenchant and outspoken critic, commented bitterly on the decision taken in April 1941, on the joint advice of Eden and Wavell, to withhold the news of the British landings in Greece. The official reason given was that 'no excuse must be given to the Germans to invade Greece'. Ryan was incensed. 'Is it seriously argued', he wrote, 'that they [the Germans] would have put forward or held back the date of their invasion to fit in with the issue by the British of a communiqué giving information about our troops which was already common knowledge all over the world?'

The Germans, in fact, had not waited. They gave as their reason for invading Greece the fact that the British were there first. They themselves had been putting out the news of the British landings to the world as soon as they happened. The BBC, in its services to Yugoslavia in Serbian and Slovene, for instance, was not allowed to tell Britain's new ally what it had already learnt from the common enemy. 'Why should Serbians listen to the BBC?' Ryan asked. The situation, he felt, was 'positively farcical'. Belief in British news had been gravely undermined to no good purpose, and the public all over the world encouraged to listen to the German Radio. No news, Ryan felt, should be withheld at any time unless its publication could be shown – and shown to the satisfaction of a patriotic layman – to help the enemy. 'Whether we in this country like it or not', he wrote, 'when a fact is published anywhere in the world, it will within a space of time to be measured in minutes rather than hours be known all over the world!'[41] It took time for the lesson to sink into the official mind.

The Ministry of Information was not the only governmental organisation involved, and a good deal of confusion arose in the early stages from the often conflicting directives which emerged from different warring Whitehall bodies, all claiming a right to dictate what was to be said or not said at the microphone. In the very earliest stages in broadcasting in European languages after Munich a system of informal liaison on policy matters developed between the BBC and the relevant desks at the Foreign Office. Leonard Miall, who joined the embryo German Service early in 1939 to be the editor of the first German language news commentaries – or 'Sonderberichte' – remembers those liaison meetings at the Foreign Office as agreeable and relaxed occasions. He quickly got onto terms of friendly cooperation with his opposite numbers.

As to policy guidance, 'the situation was slightly odd because the official policy was still appeasement but the Foreign Office was against it'.[42] Soon, however, the control of propaganda to enemy countries passed to a specialised committee presided over by Sir Campbell Stuart, a Canadian who had been involved in official propaganda under Northcliffe in the First World War. This developed into a fully fledged department, the Department for Enemy Propaganda, at the outbreak of hostilities. It was housed at first at Electra House on the Embankment in London and became known as Department EH. Later it moved to the indoor riding school building at Woburn Abbey in Bedfordshire and became known as 'Country Headquarters' or simply 'The Country', its location being a military secret, as indeed was that of the buildings from which the BBC itself was sending its foreign broadcasts. Woburn guided not only the 'white' broadcasting of the BBC but also Sefton Delmer's 'black' radio operation – stations using deception and pretending to broadcast from German soil – the designing and dropping of leaflets and other cloak-and-dagger forms of psychological warfare.

At the outbreak of war few if any inside the BBC had any awareness of the existence of this organisation. Miall was merely told that from now on he would no longer be dealing with the relevant Foreign Office desk but would receive his directives from this new, shadowy and top secret body. He would not even deal with it directly. There would be a go-between, and this would be A.P. Ryan, who had been appointed BBC Liaison Officer with Department EH. Ryan would relay instructions from the anonymous cloak-and-dagger experts in 'The Country'. 'One wasn't allowed to know where "The Country" was', Miall recalls, 'It was just referred to as "The Country" '. But he felt that the new arrangement was far less satisfactory than the informal relationship he had managed to build up with the Foreign Office.[43] In due course, however, matters improved, particularly after the creation of the Political Warfare Executive in the autumn of 1941 and the bringing of those of its sections dealing with 'white' broadcasting under the same roof as the BBC European Service at Bush House.

It is hard to make much sense of the many twists and turns in the Government's handling of the control of propaganda to enemy and enemy-occupied countries during the first two years of the war except in terms of successive and usually unsatisfactory compromises between the conflicting aspirations and interests of Whitehall departments and their ministers. Reith's bitter comment about the frustrations of his own period of office says it all: 'What would Dr Goebbels have thought of it all?' he wrote; 'I had been hailed as his opposite number, counterpart, arch-enemy. How he would have laughed – if he could have believed a tenth of what was happening here; at any rate it would have been a nice bed-time story for him, in almost daily instalments.'[44]

With Reith's departure from the ministry in May 1940, coinciding as it did with the German victory in the West and the coming to power of Churchill, a drastic reorganisation now took place, but this itself generated further difficulties. The Ministry of Economic Warfare under Hugh Dalton assumed responsibility for all political warfare activities in the German-occupied continent of Europe. 'Now set Europe ablaze!' Churchill had told Dalton.[45] Dalton's authority extended over subversion and sabotage, which were the responsibility of the newly-formed Special Operations Executive – SOE – but it also took in propaganda in all its forms, both 'black' and 'white'. Control of Electra House – or 'The Country'– thus passed for a time to the Ministry of Economic Warfare, though it was Rex Leeper, the Head of the Foreign Office Political Intelligence Department, who was appointed to be its new Director in succession to Sir Campbell Stuart. Leeper formally worked for Hugh Dalton, but the Foreign Office retained the last word on propaganda policy. As Germany overran Europe responsibility for propaganda to the countries the Germans had occupied was automatically transferred from the Ministry of Information to Leeper and his organisation. No procedure could have been better calculated to produce chaos and dissension. To quote Sir Robert Bruce Lockhart, who was eventually called in to tidy up the mess, 'there was more political warfare on the home front than against the enemy'.[46]

The first attempt at sorting out the muddle in the spring of 1941 did not go nearly far enough and merely replaced one set of problems by another. Since Duff Cooper, the Minister of Information, was 'at loggerheads' with his colleague Hugh Dalton, 'the right and obvious course', Bruce Lockhart felt, 'was to put all propaganda, as distinct from information services and publicity, under one minister, but in a coalition the right course in smaller matters may cause serious conflict in bigger matters, and an unsatisfactory comprom-

ise becomes the only solution'.[47] After much wrangling in Cabinet the compromise emerged: since the Cabinet could not agree on one single minister,
three ministers would be collectively responsible, acting as a ministerial committee, but none would be in a position to overrule the others. Eden would be
in the chair. The others would be Dalton and Duff Cooper. Bruce Lockhart
was asked to chair a committee of officials which would do the actual work
and which eventually became the Political Warfare Executive or PWE. It
included Brigadier Sir Dallas Brooks, who became Bruce Lockhart's deputy,
and Rex Leeper. Sir Orme Sargent, a senior Foreign Office official whom
Bruce Lockhart consulted about whether or not to accept, advised against it:
'His view – and it was mine too – was that I was being produced like a rabbit
out of a conjurer's hat in order to provide an easy and temporary solution to
a silly ministerial squabble.'[48] Eventually however, under pressure from
Beaverbrook, who was a personal friend as well as his former employer on
the *Evening Standard*, he accepted, though with great reluctance. He thus
became the nearest thing to a propaganda chief that Britain ever achieved in
the Second World War.

He could not have been more different from Goebbels. A cultured, civilised
Scot and a Catholic with a deep devotion to his native country, he was also a
bon viveur and a big spender with a tendency to get into debt. He had been
successively Malayan rubber planter, diplomat in Russia, secret agent, journalist for the Beaverbrook Press and prolific writer. At the time of his
appointment to head the Political Warfare Executive he was the British
Diplomatic Representative with the Czech Government in exile. Benes and
Masaryk were his close friends. A fluent Russian and Czech speaker, he had
been acting British Consul-General in Moscow during the First World War.
Having returned to Britain after the break in diplomatic relations between
Britain and the new Soviet Government he had been sent back to Moscow as
semi-official British representative. The western policy of intervention, to
which he was opposed, had led in September 1918 to his arrest and imprisonment in the Kremlin. He was released a few weeks later and exchanged for
Maxim Litvinov under arrangements negotiated, oddly enough, by the young
Rex Leeper whose superior he was now to become. He played an important
role while in Moscow in persuading Trotsky to allow the Czech Legion a safe
passage home. His lifelong affection for the Czech people, to whom he
broadcast regularly in their own language for many years after the war,
stemmed from that episode.

However, far more important for the BBC's future in the long run than
Bruce Lockhart's appointment was the almost simultaneous arrival on the
scene of Brendan Bracken, Churchill's protégé, as Minister of Information in
succession to Duff Cooper. Even though, as it turned out, he proved an
inspired appointment, he too, like Bruce Lockhart, showed great reluctance
in accepting the job. 'An unquiet cemetery' was how he described the ministry,

and there was some justice in the remark. It had been a graveyard of ministerial reputations. In the end it took 'a mixture of blandishment and firm-
ness'[49] on the part of Churchill, aided by Beaverbrook, to persuade him to
set aside his misgivings. In succeeding where others had so signally failed, he
was undoubtedly helped by the support which Churchill had pledged to give
him as part of the deal. But fundamentally it was his unique personality and
range of talents which carried him through. Harman Grisewood, whose
position as Assistant Controller of the European Services of the BBC placed
him in a privileged vantage point, judged him to be quite exceptional: 'The
most accessible minister, and the most forceful' was how he described him;
'Decisive, not very like the average, run-of-the-mill politician.'[50]

Bracken set about the task of reforming his own ministry with gusto.
Impatient of bureaucracy, keen to get rid of the dead wood accumulated over
the first two years of its existence, he went through the Malet Street headquarters 'like a dose of salts'.[51] Monckton, the Director-General, had at an
early stage expressed a desire for a change: he did not think much of the new
arrangement for shared ministerial responsibility and had no stomach for the
battles which he rightly foresaw as inevitable. Bracken quietly let him go on
extended leave of absence to other temporary assignments. On taking over
Bracken had found the document which Monckton and Radcliffe had drawn
up, setting out what needed to be done to make the ministry effective, and
saw no reason to dispute their diagnosis. He made Radcliffe Director-General
before the year was out, and, with such a supremely able man in charge of
day-to-day business, he was left free to concentrate on recovering for it the
powers it had lost – or never been given. In Bruce Lockhart – 'inquisitive,
gregarious and kindly', as Bracken's biographer has described him[52] – he had
a diplomat with a difference, resplendent in winter in his Russian fur coat,
who would know how to handle the talented but touchy and uncompliant
BBC people at Bush House as well as the cloak-and-dagger warriors at
Woburn.

There was little chance that Bracken and Dalton would hit it off, and
Dalton himself described their relationship as 'often stormy',[53] but eventually
the problem solved itself. Dalton's power lay in his strong political base in
the Labour Party. So long as he was at the Ministry of Economic Warfare
Churchill would not risk stirring trouble with his coalition partners by seeking
to remove propaganda to Europe from his jurisdiction, however desirable
such a move might have been in practice. But early in 1942 Dalton was
promoted to the Board of Trade. The way was clear. Dalton's successor at
the Ministry of Economic Warfare, Selborne, was no match for Bracken, who
lost no time in persuading Churchill and Eden that the Ministry of Economic
Warfare was *de trop* in the management of propaganda. Henceforth two
ministers only would be involved: Eden, as Foreign Secretary, would have
the last word on propaganda policy, and the Minister of Information would

be in charge of day-to-day implementation and administration. So far as
'white' broadcasting to enemy and enemy-occupied countries was concerned,
the BBC European Service, while remaining an integral part of an autonomous
BBC, would receive its guidance on propaganda policy from Bruce Lockhart's
Political Warfare Executive. It was not the perfect solution, since there was
still a division of responsibility between the PWE and the Ministry of Information and between Eden and Bracken. But it was made to work. Certainly
it was infinitely better than the bickering triumvirate Bracken had found on
arrival.

One of Bracken's major tasks at the outset was to bring about an improvement in the unhappy relationship between the BBC and those parts of the
Government machine with which it had to deal. The BBC was in danger of
becoming an Aunt Sally for all the frustrations of ministers, politicians and
service chiefs, principally on account of the almost uniformly gloomy nature
of the news it was disseminating during the first two or three years of the war.
A good deal of the criticism it was having to face was ill-informed. Some of
it was baseless. Much of it should have been directed at others, since it
concerned news items, the substance and often the wording of which had
been derived from official sources and vetted by the Government departments
concerned. One of the worse cases was the coverage of the Norwegian campaign. The BBC came under heavy fire for the picture it had given of events,
but it was entirely dependent on what the armed services were prepared to
say. It was not told when the decision was taken to withdraw from Norway,
although newspaper editors had known about it for two or three days,[54] and
Noel Newsome, the European News Editor, complained bitterly that his
department had been deliberately fed with misleading information in order
to 'throw dust in the eyes of the enemy'. The impression had been created
that the campaign would be carried on. 'I cannot but resent most strongly',
Newsome wrote, 'that we were used as a blind tool.'[55]

This kind of complaint cut little ice with ministers, who blamed the BBC
because it was the most obvious scapegoat. Reith himself, sitting in the
Cabinet as Minister of Transport during Duff Cooper's period of office as
Minister of Information, was gloomily aware of the intensity of ministerial
discontent: 'Churchill spoke with great bitterness', he wrote. The Prime
Minister referred to the BBC as 'an enemy within the gates, continually causing
trouble, doing more harm than good'.[56]

Reith himself had sought to mend matters during his brief period of office
as Minister of Information, but Chamberlain had warned him against unduly
exploiting his unique knowledge of the corporation. In any case he found
Ogilvie unresponsive if not defensive. Clashes and ructions continued and
were particularly frequent during the period when Frank Pick was briefly
Director-General of the Ministry of Information under Duff Cooper in 1940.
According to Ivone Kirkpatrick, who was working in the ministry at the time,

'no more disastrous appointment could have been conceived'. Pick, who had made his name with London Transport and had introduced good design into the Tube, found his new job totally bewildering and applied to it 'an ignorant and aggressive mind'. 'No man', Kirkpatrick wrote, 'could have shown more resolution in propounding and pushing through truly calamitous ideas.'[57]

Kirkpatrick resigned in disgust shortly after, but Ogilvie had no such alternative and had to withstand the onslaught of Pick's ill-informed criticism. Pick's tone was usually peremptory if not downright offensive: Was the BBC 'carrying out any propaganda abroad which is worth anything?' he enquired of Ogilvie through Wellington in September 1940.[58] Two months later he was suggesting to Ogilvie that the Government would end up taking over the BBC, such was its low opinion of it. Ogilvie responded sharply, challenging Pick all the way and describing his attitude as 'wholly mistaken and inefficient'.[59] But the criticism continued.

In the end a committee presided over by Sir Kingsley Wood came up with the proposal that the Government should appoint two official 'Advisers' to sit with the BBC to help strengthen the machinery by which the Ministry of Information's directives on news and propaganda were transmitted to the broadcasters and, in effect, to supervise their implementation. The first Adviser, on the home side, would be the ubiquitous A.P. Ryan, who knew the BBC well from the inside. The other would be Ivone Kirkpatrick, who came originally from the Foreign Office and had earlier spent some time at the Ministry of Information. He would advise on matters pertaining to foreign policy and overseas broadcasting. Both would be on the staff of the Ministry of Information.

Not surprisingly the BBC did not take kindly to the idea. It was too much like a veiled take-over, even though the corporation was given the right to appeal to the minister against the 'advice' given if it disagreed with it. It saw the appointment of the two men as leading inevitably to interference in its normal editorial processes and cutting across established channels of control. Duff Cooper, however, invoked wartime necessity. The Advisers, he said, would represent 'the minister's wartime suzerainty in the broadcasting field'. They would 'keep the BBC informed of any forthcoming developments in Government policy and in the trend of public affairs which are, in his [the Adviser's] opinion likely to affect the BBC in the discharge of its functions'.[60] The Governors, who were restored to their full numbers at about that time, were not easily mollified. To them the so-called Advisers seemed more like supervisors, and on 6 May 1941 Powell, their Chairman, wrote to Duff Cooper that the Governors 'would find great difficulty in accepting the draft [of the proposed terms of reference] as it stands'.

The Governors [Powell wrote] have undertaken to accept your advice on matters affecting the national war effort, and while recognising the need for some terms of reference for the Advisers, they hope that the undertaking which they gave you may be accepted in the spirit in which it was given. They cannot believe that it is either necessary or likely to make for efficiency in day-to-day working that the Advisers' functions should include elaborate provision for the oversight of the Governors' doings and those of the Director-General in order to ensure that they are as good as their word.[61]

The argument about the precise definition of the role of the Advisers was only part of a broader debate between the Government and the BBC. Its central underlying theme was the real extent of the BBC's independence and the functions of the Governors. Monckton had notified Ogilvie of the Cabinet's decision to appoint the two Advisers at the end of December 1940, and Ogilvie had immediately pointed out to him that unless the role of the proposed Advisers was 'very carefully defined', 'it might obviously invalidate the position of the Governors'.[62] Both Kirkpatrick and Ryan were appointed and took office before the matter of their terms of reference had been resolved, the first in February and the second in March. By June, though there had been much correspondence betweeen the BBC and the ministry in the intervening weeks, there was still no agreement. Duff Cooper managed to attend a meeting of the Board of Governors on 12 June without raising the subject. He apologised to Powell a few days later, saying that he had been unavoidably called away and that had he been able to stay he would have said as follows:

On all matters of national policy connected with the war effort it is my desire that the two Advisers shall represent the views of His Majesty's Government and that if for any reason the Director-General of the BBC is unable to accept the advice that is so given to him, he shall refer the matter to the Minister of Information, whose decision shall be final.

He added that he did not think that any problem should arise over finding a form of words to embody the principle.[63] Powell responded by pointing out that it was ultimately for the Governors to decide whether advice was acceptable or not, not for the Director-General. He invited Duff Cooper to attend the meeting of the board on 10 July.

By this time, however, matters were coming to a head. On joining the Governors at Broadcasting House that day Duff Cooper told them that the Cabinet had decided that his ministry should take full editorial control of the BBC and that it would be responsible both for initiative and censorship. He had been instructed by the Cabinet to carry the Board of Governors with him 'so far as possible'. He complained that the arrangements in regard to the Advisers were not working well and that he had been told of twenty instances when there had been failure on the BBC's part to carry out the ministry's directives. He further suggested that the Director-General of the BBC should become a member of the staff of the ministry in order to get over the difficulties.[64]

Not surprisingly the Governors were completely taken aback. They were unable to find evidence of the failures mentioned by Duff Cooper. They were assured by Ryan, the Home Adviser, that there had been none. They reminded Duff Cooper that he had himself acknowledged not so long ago that much of the blame lay on the ministry's side: too many people at different levels in the ministry took it upon themselves to give instructions to BBC staff. Instances were given. A special board meeting was called for the following week, which Duff Cooper was once again invited to attend. On arrival he was told by Powell that 'Governors were anxious to cooperate in every way in the work of the ministry, but that they were unanimously of the opinion that the proposal in question would be unworkable and would therefore be unacceptable to the corporation'.[65] Much discussion then followed about what should be done to extract both sides from the *impasse*. Duff Cooper acknowledged that on further enquiry inside the ministry he had found that the instances when the BBC was alleged to have failed to carry out the ministry's instructions were fewer than he had thought. Monckton had told him of only two, and they both turned out to have taken place the previous year, before the Advisers had been appointed. However Duff Cooper had another shot in his locker, or so he thought: a series of talks by J.B. Priestley was currently being broadcast on the Overseas Service. Why had the ministry not been told? It should have been. It had been, Ogilvie retorted. Monckton himself had cleared it.[66]

Fortuitously or not, the very next day Duff Cooper, much relieved, was shunted off to Singapore and replaced by Brendan Bracken, who lost no time in reassuring the Governors about his intentions. The Cabinet directive appeared to have been set aside. Attending a BBC board meeting for the first time on 24 August, Bracken said he saw 'no difficulty at all in working in cooperation with them on the basis of the existing arrangements'. While some parts of the charter were necessarily in cold storage during wartime, he was satisfied that it was 'undesirable in the national interest for the BBC to be taken over by the Government' and that 'the more freedom the corporation could have in the conduct of its affairs the better it could serve the national interest'.[67] On the subject of the two Advisers he produced an unexpected proposal, which was adopted in due course: he did not think it was satisfactory that two permanent officials not on the corporation's staff should be in a position to give directions to the corporation which it must carry out. Why not take them on the BBC's staff while at the same time letting them keep a rank in the Ministry?

A later statement by Bracken in the House of Commons publicly confirmed what he had said to the Governors:

> The Governors act as trustees to the public and Parliament for the maintenance of the integrity and high standards of British broadcasting. They have always recognised that in wartime it is necessary and right that the government should control the policy of the BBC in matters affecting the war effort, the publication of news and the conduct of propaganda. Subject to this measure of control the Governors, in addition to their

responsibility as trustees, remain in charge of the administration and technical services
of the corporation and the moneys voted to it by this House.[68]

The restoration of the board and the ministerial reaffirmation of its constitutional status may have passed relatively unnoticed in the dark circumstances
of 1941, but it brought to an end the confusion which had prevailed from the
very start of hostilities. For the European Service in particular it meant that
in the running battle with Whitehall departments support was at hand when
needed. The BBC owed much to Bracken. He appears to have grasped instinctively what it was that made it the effective instrument it became during the
war and seems to have been determined, in spite of Churchill's known disap-
proval, to ensure that it was in a position to operate at its best. But that was
to mean a measure of ruthlessness in dealing with two major issues, the
question of the Director-Generalship of the BBC and the organisation of the
Overseas Services. In both cases he made sure he got his way.

5
People, Policies and Control

When Reith had been asked by the Board of Governors for his advice on who should succeed him he had expressed a preference for Cecil Graves and had warned the Governors that he thought Ogilvie unsuitable. The board had not heeded his warning and it can fairly be said that by 1941 Reith was being proved right. A distinguished and highly civilised academic, Ogilvie was a totally unknown quantity when he was appointed. There had been great surprise among BBC staff at the board's choice: 'A nobody chosen to succeed this enormously great figure who had just vanished into a cloud',[1] is how one contemporary described it. It was a sad anti-climax. Though Ogilvie fought hard to retain as much as possible of the BBC's independence and to gain recognition from the Government of the BBC's place in the nation at war, he could not dominate the situation as Reith had done. The administrative machine which he had inherited from peacetime began to show signs of strain, and he found himself overwhelmed by the task of coping with the massive expansion of overseas broadcasting and with the financial, technical and administrative problems to which it gave rise. The organisation which Reith had left behind in 1938 was as a small family business compared with what it had become by the end of 1941. Between the beginning of the war and 31 December 1941 staff numbers had more than doubled. Ogilvie himself acknowledged that he had no experience of business management and no interest in it. A large part of his problem, as even Duff Cooper helplessly acknowledged, lay in the Government's failure to provide the means for the expansion which it had itself required. But the BBC management was itself not up to the task. There were substantial overspendings, and the Treasury was becoming increasingly restive. Gerald Beadle, the West Regional Director, had taken over the administrative controllership in London on an acting basis in the autumn of 1940 and had quickly concluded that the BBC's internal management was in a chaotic condition.

Matters came to a head in the summer of 1941. The state of the BBC's finances had become a subject of public comment and concern. There had been a criticism in the House of Commons of the deplorable working conditions and overcrowding at Bush House, where the bulk of the European

Services had moved in March 1941 – for reasons of security Bush House could not be publicly mentioned by name, even in the House of Commons, and Philip Noel Baker, who had taken up the cudgels on behalf of the broadcasters, referred to it as 'the Black Hole of Tooting Bec'. The ambitious plan for a triple expansion of overseas broadcasting drawn up at the request of the Government and agreed in January 1941 had had to be substantially scaled down and deferred because of the apparent impossibility of providing the required buildings. All this led Bracken to take drastic action. He turned to Robert Foot, the General Manager of the Gas, Light and Coke Company and a man with a reputation for business efficiency, and asked him to go and spend three months with the BBC as 'General Adviser on wartime organisa-tion'. Foot accepted, though with the greatest reluctance. He arrived at Broadcasting House on 1 November 1941 and soon concluded that the BBC was drifting nearer and nearer to control by the Government because its internal organisation was not sufficiently strong and efficient to enable it to manage its own affairs. That inevitably meant increasing Treasury inter-ference.

On 27 January 1942, less than three months after Foot's arrival, Ogilvie 'resigned', or rather was asked to retire. Though the formal decision was taken by the Board of Governors, its instigator was undoubtedly Bracken, though he firmly denied any involvement. Harold Nicolson, a Governor at the time, noted with regret in his diary: 'I'm sure this is right, as Ogilvie is too noble a character for rough war work. Yet I mind deeply in a way. This clever, high-minded man being pushed aside. I hate it, but I agree.'[2] It was a sad epitaph.

Ogilvie was replaced by a diarchy, Foot sharing the Director-Generalship with Cecil Graves, the most senior and conservative member of the BBC 'old guard' and founder of the Empire Service. Though the move was seen by the press as a victory for the Ministry of Information and as one more nail in the coffin of BBC independence, the truth, as it emerged, was quite other. The Governors who had been installed in April 1941 were in any case not the kind of people would have agreed to being 'treated merely as figure-heads', as one of their more outspoken members, Lady Violet Bonham Carter, put it at the time. To quote Asa Briggs, once Bracken had taken over there was no question of 'taking over the BBC'. Confrontation gave way to cooperation.[3]

As Bracken proceeded with his programme of radical reforms there remained one further item on his BBC agenda. This was the organisation of the Overseas Services. Rapid growth in the early stages of the war had produced its own problems. As has been seen, the first bulletins in foreign languages had been made the responsibility of the Director of the Empire Service, J.B. Clark. All that was thought necessary at the time was to add a small separate news unit to prepare bulletins for translation. The BBC's original intention appears to have been that this new unit should operate in harness with Empire News and very much in the same spirit.[4] There was a great determination on Clark's part that foreign language news bulletins should remain free of the taint of propaganda – as Empire News bulletins had been from the start – and there was much suspicion of Foreign Office intentions.

As to the foreign announcer/translators, they were grouped together in a pool and operated under the eye of a team of language supervisors and switch censors – linguists of British nationality and known dependability whose job was to ensure both accuracy of translation and a faithful reading of the text at the microphone. Their chief was a suave and gifted linguist married to a Hungarian, V. Duckworth Barker, more generally known as 'Ducky B'. Individual foreign language services did not exist as such and had no separate identity except as groups of translators, though they fairly quickly acquired one. Much of the broadcast output consisted of news bulletins, though news talks began to make their appearance early in 1939, starting with the German Service. Problems of coordination between the output of news and news talks on the one hand and the rest of the programme output on the other did not begin to appear until 1940 with the rapid expansion in daily airtime and the consequent increase in opportunities for a wider variety of programme formats. But thereafter a situation was rapidly reached in which, as Kirkpatrick put it,

Talks and features staff could put out anything they pleased without regard to the opinion or output of the News Editors. Worse still, News Editors were not in a position to criticise the translation of their own bulletins since the translators were responsible only to Salt [the Director of European Services] and could decline to receive instructions or criticism from the News Editors.[5]

Thus Hugh Carleton Greene, the German News Editor, and Darsie Gillie, his counterpart for the bulletins in French, did not acquire responsibility for the programme output other than news and news talks until 1941. They worked to Noel Newsome, the European News Editor, while the various small units of foreign language staff dealing with Features and other programmes came under the European Productions Manager, Gibson Parker, himself one of the subordinates of J.S.A.Salt, the Director of European Services.

Salt's own appointment, which dated from 19 July 1940, was part of a wider reorganisation reflecting the growing importance of overseas broadcasting within the BBC as a whole. Sir Stephen Tallents had been appointed Controller (Overseas) in May 1940, with J.B. Clark as his Deputy. A separate European News Department had been in existence since before the beginning of the war under Noel Newsome, operating under the overall direction of the Overseas News Editor, A.E. Barker.

The wider reorganisation of the summer of 1940 involved the creation of four divisions: the European Services under Salt, and the Empire, Latin-

American and Near Eastern Services, each under its own Director. R.A. Rendall, C.A.L. Cliffe and S. Hillelson were the first holders of those posts. However this organisational pattern was far from conducive to a proper coordination of output in each language. On the contrary it proved divisive and a source of tension and internal strife. Nowhere was this more so than in the European Services, as Kirkpatrick noted. Salt, despite his title, had no control over the most important part of the output, news and commentaries. Though he had an overall responsibility for planning, intelligence, scheduling, programme operations and presentation, and controlled the pool of foreign announcers and programme assistants, his editorial functions were confined to what came after the news bulletins and news talks. The latter were the responsibility first of Leonard Miall, whose functions as Editor of the German 'Sonderberichte' had been expanded to take in news talks in other languages, and later of Alan Bullock as European News Talks Editor working to Newsome. No coordinating machinery existed, and geographical dispersion made the problem even worse. While the bulk of the German news and news talks staffs were at Maida Vale in the winter of 1941, for instance, the German Features Department under Walter Rilla, a well-known pre-Hitler German film star, was at Bedford College in Regents Park and remained there for some months after the rest of the German staff had moved to Bush House.[6] The same was true for some time of Jacques Duchesne and his colleagues of 'Les Français parlent aux Français', and one of them Jean Oberlé, recalls that the scripts of some of the programmes were written in Regents Park, sitting on the grass.[7]

To these difficulties had to be added more fundamental differences of approach. Salt, an old BBC man of pre-war vintage – he had been Programme Director in Manchester before coming up to London to join the Overseas Services as Deputy Director of Intelligence – was, like Clark and Tallents, deeply resistant to governmental direction. This inevitably brought him into frequent conflict with the Foreign Office, the Ministry of Information and Electra House. He was himself only too conscious of the drawbacks of the existing scheme of things. 'The present system', he wrote to Tallents in December 1940, 'gives rise to certain difficulties in coordination and complicates our relations with the Ministry of Information and other government departments.'[8] He proceeded to table a whole series of proposals for reorganisation involving the creation of a number of regional services or groups of services, each with its own news, talks and programme sections, working under the overall direction of a Service Organiser, thus, as he saw it, resolving the problem of editorial coordination. All his projected reorganisation had one point in common: news and news talks in the European Services would become his responsibility and he would thus assume total control over the whole of the broadcast output of the European Services.

Salt's proposals did not meet with universal support. For one thing they appear to have been overambitious and caused J.B. Clark to write to Tallents that 'the European staff is being developed on inflated and ill-controlled lines', even though he supported Salt's overall approach.[9] Graves himself thought highly of Salt's ability but did not see him as a good organiser. But much more serious in many ways were the misgivings in Whitehall at the prospect that news and commentaries would come under Salt. The Foreign Office and Electra House saw them as the sharp end of the output, as indeed they were, and did not relish the prospect of having to work through Salt, whom they regarded as uncooperative, as was indeed also the case with Tallents and Clark. Kirkpatrick himself, now Foreign Adviser to the BBC, was strongly opposed to the Salt scheme and argued that the key to improving the effectiveness of the European Services was to create a central direction of propaganda.

The discussions over Salt's proposals inevitably leaked and this led to growing internal tensions and uncertainty. The news staff saw Salt's move as a take-over bid leading to the break-up of the overseas news organisation. As one of them put it, Salt 'wanted to collect the lot'.[10] Eventually the grumblings about the alleged reluctance of the BBC European staff at Bush House to take their instructions from the psychological warfare people at Woburn brought matters to a head. There was, as Harman Grisewood, who became Assistant Controller of the European Services, has pointed out, something of a power struggle between the two, in which Woburn 'wanted to dominate and direct the BBC's services in detail. The "black" operators developed their own psychology, which was aggressive and superior. The Bush House people were defensive and suspicious.'[11] At Bracken's level it was clear that there was a need to produce within the Overseas Services a pattern of organisation which would roughly coincide with the area of activity of PWE – in other words a European Service under a single command, responding more willingly to PWE's directives than was felt to have been the case in the past. This was what Kirkpatrick was strongly urging on Bracken. Moreover, with the completion of Hitler's conquest of Europe and the German invasion of Russia a new situation had been created. It seemed to Kirkpatrick that the BBC would have an important role to play in rallying European resistance to the Germans and that a radical reorganisation of the European Services was required. 'In particular', Kirkpatrick wrote, 'the European Services should be detached and converted into an independent organisation'. [12] In any case by that time the scale of the BBC's European operations had become such as to fully justify splitting the Overseas Services into two separate parts – one broadcasting to Europe and the other to the rest of the world.

The change came on 9 October 1941 when Ogilvie, as Director-General, announced that a new European division would be created, with Kirkpatrick as Controller. Tallents had been about to promulgate his own reorganisation, embodying Salt's ideas, when Bracken, prompted by Kirkpatrick, prevailed on Sir Alan Powell, the BBC Chairman, to remove Tallents and to accept the scheme put forward by Kirkpatrick. Tallents, though offered an alternative appointment inside the BBC, refused it and left the corporation to take charge of fuel rationing. He had hoped eventually to succeed Ogilvie as Director-General and had acted as Ogilvie's deputy on the many occasions when Cecil Graves was absent through ill health. But by then the odds against him had clearly become too great. Salt was posted off to be number two to the BBC's representative in the United States, Lindsay Wellington, whom he was later to succeed.[13] A.P. Ryan, the BBC's Home Adviser, became Controller (News Coordination) in yet another move in his complicated journeyings across the uncertain wartime boundaries between officialdom and broadcasting.

It would have been surprising if such a major and controversial series of moves had taken place without leaving behind it a trail of ill-feeling and apprehension. There was particular resentment among Tallents' closest colleagues about the way his removal had been engineered, even though Tallents, relative newcomer to the BBC that he was and a man who had already had a distinguished and at times eventful career behind him when he came to Broadcasting House, had never truly succeeded in winning over the 'old guard'.[14] On the other hand it was he who had presided over the rapid growth of overseas broadcasting in 1940 and 1941, and this had been a substantial achievement, the many criticisms notwithstanding. As to his deputy, J.B. Clark, it was at first suggested by Bracken that Kirkpatrick as a newcomer would need a deputy who was well versed in the BBC's ways and that Clark would be the ideal man. Ryan could go to the Overseas Services.[15] The BBC resisted this notion and Harman Grisewood was appointed instead. Clark became Controller of the newly separated Overseas Services, on a level with Kirkpatrick.

A great deal of the animus over the reorganisation was inevitably directed at Kirkpatrick, who was seen as a wily and threatening intruder who had 'intrigued' his way into the Controllership of the European Services and had been instrumental in getting rid of Salt and Tallents. There was an element of truth in this view, though there are indications that Bruce Lockhart was opposed to his appointment and only acquiesced to it on being advised privately that 'it would be unwise to begin straight away with an attack on Kirkpatrick and the FO would view any attempt to oust him (from the BBC European Service) with displeasure'.[16] At all events the initiative for Kirkpatrick's appointment clearly came from the Government rather than from the BBC and the BBC Governors merely endorsed it. Many people, not surprisingly, saw this as a sign that the Foreign Office was in effect taking over the European Service. It was also a sign, ominous to some, that the old school of pre-war BBC officials was on its way out.

Kirkpatrick's first move on taking over, apart from dismantling the complicated structure set up by Salt and bringing all output in each language, including news, under one single editor, was immediately to seek to clarify for the staff the relationship between the European Service and the Government's policy-making apparatus.

The European Division [he announced] will derive its policy instruction, through its Controller, from the Government's new Political Warfare Executive, which is responsible to the Ministry of Information and the Ministry of Economic Warfare. This institution will be translated into broadcasting terms by the Director of Propaganda (the new title proposed for Newsome, the European News Editor) and conveyed to the staff in his directives and by other means.[17]

The almost military directness of this promulgation and the implied total subjugation of the European Services to Government direction may have seemed to confirm the worst fears of those who saw Kirkpatrick as a mere instrument of the ministerial will. Indeed it was in line with the views Kirkpatrick had expressed a year or more earlier about the need for closer control of the BBC at a time when Electra House was complaining bitterly about its inability to get its way. But as it happened things turned out rather differently. In the first place Kirkpatrick was never able to achieve the degree of centralised control which he had aimed for when he first took over. Broadcasting is by its nature peculiarly resistant to rigid central direction, particularly if the talents of those at the creative end of the operation are to be given full scope. Moreover having introduced a regional structure in place of the functional one he had inherited from Salt he soon found that strong personalities like Greene, Gillie or Macdonald of the Polish Service would go their own way when entrusted with major responsibilites, and he was wise enough to realise that it was best to give them their head since they were pre-eminently well qualified and able men. As he wrote to Bruce Lockhart towards the end of 1941, a year's experience in the BBC had taught him that the best men should be free to act without too many restraints.[18]

But more important, the roles had now been reversed. From gamekeeper Kirkpatrick became almost overnight a poacher. Once settled in the Controller's chair he soon showed that he intended to be his own master and that his loyalties now belonged to the BBC. His friends and former colleagues in the Foreign Office found him in no way disposed to fall in with their desire to bend the broadcasting operation to their purposes, while his new charges at Bush House discovered in him the best defender of their independence and integrity that they could have wished for. He dealt with pressures even from the highest level of government with the utmost robustness. He had revealed something of his methods to Bruce Lockhart during a visit to the French Service in July 1941:

When French broadcasts began [Bruce Lockhart noted in his diary] the announcer made a strong attack on Vichy for surrendering Indochina to the Japs. Language very similar to that in our leaflet. I asked Kirk how he had managed to get the FO permission when I had failed. He replied that he had not, but on the contrary he had chanced his hand. When I said I should use this tomorrow to point a moral to the FO he begged me not to, saying all that would happen would be that FO would exert greater control over him.[19]

Both Kirkpatrick, and in his absence Grisewood, were frequently exposed to pressures not just from the Foreign Office but also from the two other ministries forming the triumvirate, often operating quite outside the normal and recognised PWE channels. Each ministry tended to think it could pick up the telephone and make demands of the BBC which conflicted with established policy, and according to Grisewood frequently did.[20] Kirkpatrick steadfastly rejected such requests, invoking when necessary the aid of Bracken, by whom he knew that he would invariably be supported. He dealt equally firmly with the PWE regional section heads whom he met regularly. He would go through their written directives to the BBC, crossing out without hesitation what he thought was undesirable, brooking no argument and challenging them to take the matter further up. As Grisewood put it, 'he was quick-witted and sure-footed like a mountain animal, with a good head for heights and well used to rough weather'.[21]

The manner of Grisewood's own appointment as Kirkpatrick's deputy was unpropitious to say the least. He was Assistant Director of Programme Planning at Broadcasting House when he was told he had been chosen. The appointment came as a total surprise to him. He felt it wise to admit to Kirkpatrick, whom he found formidable when he met him at close quarters for the first time, that he had none of the more obvious qualifications for the job. Even if he had, Kirkpatrick told him unhelpfully, there wasn't a job there for him to do. 'I asked him why then had an appointment been made,' Grisewood recalls; 'I thought you'd know that', Kirkpatrick answered sharply. He, Kirkpatrick, had never wanted an assistant and had never asked for one. It was the BBC which had insisted on having one of its own men as number two. It was not a good start, but the two men soon got onto terms, though Grisewood remembers spending his first week in office reading the novels of Stendhal.[22]

Kirkpatrick was not a man in the traditional diplomatic mould, even though he was later to rise to the very top of his profession.[23] An Irish Catholic educated at Downside – Grisewood, as it happened, was also a Catholic, but an Ampleforth man – he had been severely wounded in the First World War and had joined the Diplomatic Service soon after. He had retained in middle age, in his whole manner and approach, the soldierly characteristics of his youth. 'He won his points by attack rather than by persuasion. Military brusqueries came easier to him than urbanity', Grisewood recalls.[24] Bruce Lockhart described him as 'always at his best in a crisis', 'quick, decisive', and a man 'not afraid of responsibilities'.[25] Others described him more irreverently as a 'clever, aggressive, cocky little man'.[26] He had spent five years as First Secretary at the British Embassy in Berlin between 1933 and 1938. Unlike Sir Neville Henderson, who was Ambassador at the time, but like such as Rex Leeper, he had been one of those most opposed to the official policy of appeasement and had seen clearly that Hitler was hell-bent for

1 Sir John Reith in 1938

2 Royal visit to the Overseas Services, July 1940: the King and Queen talking to Michael Barkway, Empire News Editor. On the right is F. W. Ogilvie, Director-General, and in the background Sir Stephen Tallents, Controller (Overseas).

3 The Council Chamber at Broadcasting House after the landmine explosion in December 1940. The portrait of Reith hangs in the same position today. European Services translators worked in the Council Chamber at the time.

4 From left to right: Ivone Kirkpatrick (Controller, European Services), Noel Newsome (Director of European Broadcasts) and R.W. Foot (Joint Director-General), looking at a portrait of Princess Natalie Bagration by Marek Zulawski, of the Polish Service, at an exhibition of works by members of the European Services in 1942.

5 J.B. Clark in 1945.

6 The Monitoring Service, Caversham: Report Writers' midnight conference, 1945.

7 The French Service Newsroom in wartime: from left to right: Olive Hunter, secretary, Darsie Gillie, French Editor, Dan Sturge Moore and Blair Brennan.

8 The German Service: farewell dinner given to Hugh Carleton Greene in 1946 on his departure for Germany. (Left to right, standing) Christopher Dilke, Robert Lucas (Robert Ehrenzweig), Marius Goring, Fritz Wendhausen, Edmund Wolff, Martin Esslin, Heinrich Fischer, Peter Illing. (Sitting) Lindley Fraser, Julius Gellner, Hugh Carleton Greene, George Gretton, Hans Buxbaum and Walter Hertner.

9 'Colonello Buena Sera', Colonel Stevens, one of the best-known voices in the wartime Italian Service.

10 Sir Ian Jacob in 1950.

11 The Atlantic Relay Station under construction on Ascension Island, 1965.

12 George Bennett, Head of the African Service, Abdullahi Haji, of the Somali Service, and a Somali listener.

13 A recent Soviet poster attacking the BBC and the *Daily Telegraph*; The caption reads: 'See how dirty and how fake are the canards from this lake.' On the sail: 'The Soviet threat!'

14 Pope John Paul in conversation with Jan Krok-Paszkowski, Polish Programme Organiser at the time, and his wife at the Vatican, 1978.

15 'That's the end of the foreign news, and now to hear the domestic news you can switch over to the BBC Radio.' A cartoon published in an Iranian newspaper in October 1978.

16 'Psst! Señor ... What does the BBC say?' A cartoon published in *La Prensa* of Buenos Aires on 17 April 1982, during the Falklands crisis.

conquest and war. He knew Germany, the German language and the German leaders well, and this placed him in a position of unique authority not just within the European Service but also vis-à-vis those in Whitehall and elsewhere who sought to manipulate it. 'A master of intransigence', as Grisewood called him, he put his experience of a wider and tougher world to good use in strengthening his new command rather than subjugating it.[27] As a direct result the European Services were able to operate in a climate of far greater security than might otherwise have been the case. This was reinforced when Kirkpatrick was invited by Bruce Lockhart to become a member of the Executive Committee of PWE, a gesture intended to dispel the suspicions of the BBC by giving its top official inside the European Services a say in the formation of propaganda policy at the highest level.

Other factors were at play which had an equal bearing on the situation. Although the BBC, especially in its overseas services, regarded itself as 'bound by silken cords' which, to quote Sir Alan Powell, the Chairman of the Board of Governors, could sometimes feel like 'chains of iron',[28] and although the corporation felt itself to be 'under orders',[29] the tradition of independence so strongly fostered by Reith – often to the acute irritation of outsiders – was by now too deeply rooted not to survive intact into the war. At working level there was no doubt or argument about the ultimate purpose of the broadcasting operation: it was the winning of the war. Nor was there any argument about the Government's right to issue directives on matters connected with the war effort. The Government had assumed that right as part of its wartime emergency powers, and the BBC had willingly accepted that it was so.

However although the theory was that the Government was responsible for policy and the BBC for implementation, in practice the position was a good deal less simple. Those who emerged as the senior editorial figures in the European and Overseas Services did not regard their role as merely that of cyphers blindly carrying out Government directives. The editorial staff thought of themselves primarily as broadcasting professionals in their own right, not as servants of the Government, and they brought to the task of disseminating the truth and propagating the values for which the war was being fought an element of personal commitment which was incompatible with the slavish observance of directives emanating from outside. They insisted on their right to argue about the wisdom of particular directives and in many cases contributed to the framing of policy in cooperation with their opposite numbers in PWE or the Ministry of Information. They defended fiercely what they regarded as their prerogatives as broadcasters when unduly harrassed by 'self-appointed advisers and mentors',[30] particularly as they found themselves not infrequently exposed to conflicting pressures from different bodies. The former peacetime Editor of the *Radio Times*, Maurice Gorham, for instance, who was now in charge of the North American Service,

saw to it that full use was made of the advice of the various government
departments he dealt with but 'without giving them undue temptation to
interfere'. Sigmar Hillelson, a former Director of Intelligence in the Sudan
who became Director of the Near Eastern Service, put the position succinctly:
'Let the man at the wheel be told where to go', he wrote to J.B. Clark, 'but let
him take responsibility for the manner of his driving. If he fails to get there he
will have to stand the racket.' But he saw no harm and considerable advantage
in exchanges of views with Government departments 'even if our opposite
numbers are (as so often happens) badly briefed on the elementary facts'.[31]
J.B. Clark, himself the watchful guardian of the BBC's interests over so many
years, formulated the ground rules with great precision:

> The only matters to be submitted to outside authorities [he wrote] would be points
> that were doubtful in the opinion of [BBC] policy scrutineers who might go up the
> internal ladder for advice in the first place. In the absence of overriding policy
> considerations, as distinct from personal opinions, disclosed by such external refer-
> ences, the acceptance or rejection of the advice would remain subject to the corpora-
> tion's discretion in the light of our considered policy.

He then went on to explain why he regarded it as essential that these rules
should be adhered to:

> I naturally do not wish to be boot-faced about this; circumstances will naturally
> temper action. But both Controller, News Coordination [A.P. Ryan] and ourselves
> have recently experienced cases in which purely personal opinions of individuals (in
> Government departments) not founded on real policy have been inconsistent with our
> considered policy or otherwise unacceptable.[32]

Much the same attitude guided people like Hugh Carleton Greene and
Darsie Gillie, in charge, respectively, of the big and all-important German
and French Services. In Greene's case relations with PWE were made a great
deal easier by the fact that he got on well with the PWE German Section Head,
R.H.S. Crossman, a pre-war Oxford don and fluent German speaker, with
whom he formed a lasting friendship. Crossman had joined the Ministry of
Information at the outbreak of war before going on to be a leading if
controversial member of the Woburn establishment under Leeper. Even
before the war started he had been one of those recruited by Leonard Miall
to contribute to the output of 'Sonderberichte'. He continued to contribute
after the war broke out, and when an early morning programme for German
workers was started in the spring of 1940 under the editorship of Patrick
Gordon Walker, he was one of those who contributed to it. His good relations
with Greene made the drawing up of directives for the German Service a
collaborative affair rather than an act of authority by PWE. 'We saw very
much eye to eye', Greene recalls.[33] The German Service, like others, worked
within a series of weekly directives. Every Friday night there would be a
policy meeting at the old indoor riding school at Woburn Abbey, chaired by

Crossman. Greene would travel down, usually accompanied by Lindley Fraser, who as well as being the German Service's chief commentator, was also its liaison officer with PWE. A former Professor of Economics at Aberdeen University, he had once greatly amused King George VI during a royal visit to the European Service by telling him, in answer to a question, that his pre-war job was 'trying to teach economy to Aberdonians'.[34]

Those weekly meetings at Woburn were pleasant, convivial occasions. It was not just that they provided a welcome opportunity to escape for one night from the London bombing. There would be a good dinner and plenty of beer. The mood would be cheerful, and the directive for the following week would be hammered out after dinner. Relations were further improved by the institution of cricket matches between a PWE side and 'The Bushmen', in which Greene kept wicket for his side.[35] But as Greene has pointed out the news was no respecter of directives, particularly weekly ones. The day-to-day requirements of coverage inevitably made it necessary to depart from what had been agreed the previous Friday night if comment was going to take account of the latest developments. 'This', Greene says cryptically, 'was not always appreciated by the Government.'[36]

The relationship was further eased when Bruce Lockhart, against heavy opposition from the Woburn organisation, succeeded in February 1942 in moving the PWE staff concerned with providing guidance and directives to the 'white' broadcasters of the BBC back from 'The Country' to Bush House, under the same roof as the European Service. Only the secret activities of PWE – those concerned with 'black' broadcasting and other hush-hush forms of subversion – remained at Woburn. Rex Leeper, who had been personally responsible for building up the Woburn organisation and bringing together its team of propaganda experts, strongly resisted the move. 'He insisted that propaganda and political warfare were more effectively conducted from the country, where there was time for thinking and planning.'[37] Bruce Lockhart saw instead the great advantage of bringing the policy makers and the broadcasters together and he was strongly supported by Eden and Bracken. Leeper had to give way and resigned shortly afterwards to become British Ambassador to the Greek Government.

In all the dealings which the BBC had with the Government's policy-making bodies one consideration always came uppermost. This was the safeguarding of its credibility, which it regarded even then as its greatest asset. The Government had made a decision of principle right at the start that 'all British information should be truthful and objective'.[38] That had been Reith's view from the earliest days. The BBC itself would have added that British information should also be as fast, detailed and objective as the needs of military security allowed, and, as had been seen, that there must be occasions when even considerations of security should not be allowed to prevail when a

greater advantage was to be derived from disclosure. The full significance of
that decision of principle may not at times have seemed to the hard-pressed
news editors of the BBC to have been fully grasped in Whitehall. Nonetheless
there was a whole world of difference between the occasionally timid and
short-sighted approach to the release of news adopted by British officialdom
and the blatant lies and distortions to which the Germans resorted. As Lindley
Fraser put it in his book *Propaganda*,

> By 1939 or 1940 the world had seen clearly enough that on a long-run basis lying
> propaganda will defeat its own ends; even if each particular lie deceives ninety-five per
> cent of the audience, yet the five per cent who are not taken in, who from their own
> experience know it to be a lie, will from then on be hostile or distrustful, and the larger
> the number of lies the more completely disillusioned will the audience become.[39]

He quoted as an example the French communiqués during the German *Blitz-
krieg* against France in May and June 1940, which in their attempt to put a
brave face on disaster and to conceal its full magnitude became totally
discredited with the French public. Moreover whereas in Germany full powers
had been given to an elaborate and lavishly staffed centralised propaganda
machine directed by one man, in Britain the balance of pressures went in the
opposite direction. It was not just that there was no real propaganda 'su-
premo' to match Goebbels. Britain's inability to produce one and to give him
the sort of powers that some thought necessary was itself revealing. British
propaganda was the product of untidy intellectual argument among small
groups of free men who were agreed on principles and objectives but not
necessarily on means. About the need to tell the truth they were ultimately at
one, even when the truth was unpleasant, so that, as one news editor put it,
'if a battleship was sunk we raced to the microphone to get it in before the
Germans'. Such stories were quite intentionally placed at the top of the
bulletin because they were the most important news of the day. Because they
were disasters for the allied cause, they would in any case be luridly headlined
by German propaganda.[40]

Credibility also depended on the professional authority of BBC news. 'It
was soon learned', wrote Tom Beachcroft, 'that the wider the audience the
greater the need for watchfulness and accuracy. Innocent slips of facts, or
faults in balance or proportion, took on the gravest implications.'[41] Much
effort was deployed by Bush House news editors in persuading their PWE
opposite numbers, who attended daily service meetings, that the BBC could
not broadcast unattributable stories of doubtful veracity derived from secret
sources without endangering its reputation as a source of news.[42] Conversely
the BBC was only too aware, as it kept having to point out, that once a story
had been carried by one of the news agencies there was no point in hoping
that by keeping it out of BBC bulletins it was possible to prevent it from
getting known. Hugh Greene quotes as an example an incident which took
place in 1942 when Sir George Franckenstein, who had been Austrian Ambas-

sador in London, called on Churchill after lunch one day to present him formally with a silver tea caddy. Churchill had lunched well and in his reply, which was fulsome, made an unwise reference to the gallant efforts made by the allied armies and airforces 'in order that Austria may be free'. The story came through on one of the news agencies. Hugh Greene saw it and decided to carry it in the German news. However, as he recalls, the liaison officer at the Foreign Office rang up in a great state to ask for the story to be suppressed. The Allies, he said, were still discussing the future of Austria. They had not yet decided whether Austria would be free. Greene pointed out that the story was on the agency tapes and must therefore be regarded as being out. 'I'm sorry, old boy', he told his contact; 'it's about to go out in a few minutes in our next German bulletin, so Austria will have to be free, won't it!'[43]

Accuracy and comprehensiveness were two of the pillars on which the wartime reputation of BBC news was built. A third was consistency. The same truth must be told to everyone. There could be no question of broadcasting different versions of what was taking place to different audiences in different languages, as the Germans did in the mistaken belief that they would not be caught out – or that if they were it was a matter of no importance. As suspicion of propaganda grew, so there was an increasing tendency for listeners who were able to do so to tune in to broadcasts not aimed at them. This was true even of American correspondents based in London who would listen to what the BBC was saying to Europe or to its own audiences at home rather than to what it was saying to America. In central Europe many potential listeners spoke and understood more than one language. A knowledge of German was fairly widespread, as was also the case with French, though to a lesser extent. In the Middle East and North Africa, English and French and sometimes both were commonly understood by the educated classes as well as Arabic. So was Greek, for instance, in the Levant. Although in the European Services each major service – the French, the Germans, the Poles – had its own newsroom and news editor, the material from which it made up its bulletins was originally compiled by the Bush House Centre Desk under its Editor, Noel Newsome. The Centre Desk had full access to all available news sources, including monitoring of enemy and neutral broadcasts, and functioned in complete independence from any PWE policy directives, its policy being to provide an objective and reliable account of events as they unfolded, applying the normal criteria of responsible journalism.[44]

The regional newsrooms enjoyed considerable freedom in the arrangement of their bulletins and even in the wording of individual stories, so that a story as it was broadcast in German, for instance, could be markedly different in wording, though not in substance, from the Centre Desk original. 'Practically every news story was rewritten in German,' Hugh Carleton Greene recalls. In any case neither he, as Head of the German Service, nor Darsie Gillie, in charge of the French Service, were admirers of the output of the Centre Desk.

Of the ten or so members of staff manning the desk not more than two or at the most three had been professional journalists before joining the BBC at or after the outbreak of war. Donald Edwards, who became European News Editor in 1943, recalls being brought in as Assistant Editor from the *Daily Telegraph* in 1940, to bolster up the European News Room with his professional expertise. He had been working as a night sub-editor, mainly on the foreign side, and was normally responsible for putting the *Daily Telegraph*'s front page to bed. He was thus able to bring his skills at quick, last minute editing to bear on the preparation of Bush House news. He himself was well aware that Centre Desk stories were often capable of improvement, and he introduced the practice of giving a general distribution throughout the whole of the European Services to stories written in the German news room for broadcasting in German only. This was also true at times for stories written, for instance, in the Polish newsroom.[45]

However there could be no question of foreign language bulletins departing from commonly accepted editorial principles, partly because those principles were never in doubt in anyone's mind but partly also because no bulletin could be broadcast without first being checked and stamped by the Policy Editor of the day – one of the Centre Desk seniors – so that whatever variations of treatment might arise from regional rewriting, consistency of approach was always safeguarded in the end. It was a question of central control and keynote-setting on the one hand and local flexibility on the other. The system inevitably generated tensions between the centre and the regions, but as Tom Beachcroft put it in a 1946 essay on British broadcasting:

> The sources of knowledge and of news were immense; but any form of rigid control would have caused hopeless delays. It was the fundamental principle of objectivity, and the long experience of craftsmanship in pursuing this, that now achieved expression on a vast scale. In the end it was repeated acts of individual skill and judgement that created this authenticity; but these acts all sprang from one central intention.[46]

No account of Bush House news in wartime can be complete without a portrait of its Editor, Noel Newsome. Like Donald Edwards he had come from the *Daily Telegraph*, but he had acquired much of his early journalistic experience in Malaya rather than in Europe, of which he was largely ignorant. He had what one of his colleagues described as a Churchillian desire to play a big part in winning the war. He showed a bulldog-like determination, a confidence and an energy which made him invaluable during the darkest days of the war in 1940 and 1941. At his two daily meetings he gave a strong lead on the main subjects for comment, and this was embodied in his daily written directives, which became legendary. In due course, in the spring of 1941, he took to broadcasting himself regularly in the English Service to Europe under the pseudonym of 'The Man in the Street'. A collection of these talks was published just after the war under that title. They were full blooded, forthright, polemical and combative – the very opposite of the cool, analytical approach normally associated with BBC commentators. Some thought them rather left-wing. He paid little heed to PWE directives and indeed was not wholly approved of by PWE. In effect he was fighting his own war.

Although his qualities were widely acknowledged, there were many inside the European Services who took issue with his approach and with his directives, which as the war progressed were increasingly ignored by the more powerful service heads. Grisewood saw him as almost the incarnation of nineteenth-century isolationist Britain, an old-fashioned English radical for whom 'all Europe was variously enslaved to the Pope and other corrupt and despicable authorities'. He tended to look on foreigners as lesser people, and England's role, as he saw it, was to 'tell the foreigners, groaning under their tyrannies, the good news that England was the land of the free, where the flame of liberty burned bright, and the military power of Britain would soon show itself again as the liberator'.[47] It mattered little to him, as it did a great deal to heads of services such as Greene, Gillie or Macdonald, that such attitudes might be out of place in addressing audiences with their own attitudes and sensitivities. Consequently his influence declined in the larger and more powerful services. In his conflicts with the regional 'barons' he was bound in the end to have to yield to deeper knowledge and longer experience of particular countries. As one of his contemporaries put it he did not understand the susceptibilities of Europeans and gloried in the fact. However it was to Greene, Gillie and their like that Kirkpatrick and Grisewood tended in the end to give their support, and in any case Newsome was enough of a politician to know when not to press his point.[48] Newsome's value had been at its greatest in the darkest days of the war. Like Churchill but on a smaller stage he had been the dogged inspirer of the will to fight on. As the tide turned his qualities ceased to be quite so essential and by 1944 he saw his future elsewhere. He was seconded to SHAEF after 'D' Day and eventually moved to the newly liberated Radio Luxemburg.

High level issues such as these – and the in-fighting at the top – had little bearing on the day-to-day concerns of the rank-and-file programme staff, whose interest was focused on the immediate requirements of their job – not to speak of the internal politics of their own service and of the practical problems of living in wartime London. The dramatic circumstances of 1940 had conspired to assemble in Bush House a remarkable polyglot community, unique in its diversity and in its range of talents and experience. Many of its members were exiles of considerable distinction in their own fields and the jobs they did in the BBC were often well below their real capacities in the worlds from which they came. Many, too, had their own political views and allegiances and felt deeply involved in the often tragic fate of their own countries, where they had left friends and relatives. They included stage and film directors, actors, artists, writers, academics from many disciplines, schoolmasters, as well as a fair sprinkling of journalists. They tended inevitably to work in relatively self-contained groups of one nationality, living a life of their own and deeply committed to the task of communicating with their particular target audience. Most had little awareness of what went on beyond the confines of their own service. Most, also, were new to the arts of radio, often even to those of journalism, but they took to them with zest and in some cases brilliance. They readily absorbed the ethos of public service broadcasting as it had been developed by Reith. Indeed they gave it new life and vigour precisely because the majority of them were newcomers and in a sense pioneers. Increasingly caught up in the heady excitement of the new role they were discovering for themselves, they developed a sense of professional mission and a dedication to the job which remain characteristic of the External Services to this day. Morale was high: 'You were devoted to a cause in which you believed entirely without qualification', Leo Shepley remembers.[49] Hours were long, many worked late into the night or on the 'dawn shifts', sleeping in makeshift dormitories – or, like Kirkpatrick, on the office table.[50]

At the same time a lively social life went on almost as an integral part of professional activities. There was a well-developed sense of fun and comradeship, and as much broadcasting business was probably conducted in 'Studio Finch' – as a now defunct pub in the Strand was affectionately known – as in the studios and offices of Bush House across the road. It was the place for relaxing and chewing the cud after the end of the evening transmission. Many remember those times as some of the best years of their lives, and Harman Grisewood dates the birth of what he calls the *esprit* of Bush House to those years.[51] As Leo Shepley put it, Bush House in wartime was 'a sort of extraordinary encapsulated place in which we lived for nothing else but the war of words'.[52] Alan Bullock remembers it as 'the shadowy world of Europe', which you entered when you stepped out of the real world of the streets of wartime London into the overcrowded basement studios from which the voices of hope and freedom went out into the night to the unknown waiting millions on the other side of the Channel.[53]

6
The Wartime Expansion

In retrospect the sudden growth of overseas broadcasting following the outbreak of war can be seen to have been almost as important an event in the history of the BBC as the growth of television was to prove ten or fifteen years later. Up to 1939 the BBC had developed smoothly and gradually within a strong unitary framework and the focus of its activities had been essentially domestic. For all but one of its first seventeen years it had been under the dominating influence of Reith. Its total staff in 1937, the year before the start of foreign language broadcasting, was only about 3,500 and it was still possible for the Director-General to know personally a high proportion of the programme staff. By the middle of 1941 staff numbers had risen to nearly nine thousand. In the overseas services alone programme staff increased from 103 in 1939 to 1,472 in 1941. Such a large increase in one particular sector of activity – and a new one at that – was bound to have a profound effect on the character of the organisation as a whole.

Even though with the introduction of the Empire Service in 1932 the BBC had begun to venture into the international field it retained an essentially domestic, not to say provincial character. That venture had not taken it out of the safe, familiar world in which the Empire figured, so to speak, as part of England's back yard. Senior BBC officials might travel to the far-flung outposts, but they remained on British or British-controlled soil throughout, and a kind of cultural insularity pervaded the whole organisation, as indeed it pervaded most of the country. In this context Europe seemed far more remote than Australia or Canada.

Moreover many of those who were now in senior positions had joined the BBC in its early pioneering days. Some had come in with Reith right at the start. Not a few had served as officers in the First World War and continued to use their military rank. They were rightly proud of the institution they had created, of its high standards and of its independence. They were 'the Regulars', as Kirkpatrick was fond of saying, and their reaction to the influx of new blood which came in with the war was not unlike the reaction of the old regular army when faced with a similar experience. What had been a carefully protected, almost cocooned profession was suddenly opened to an onrush of gifted amateurs who rapidly became professionals in their own right. Old ways and the old self-sufficiency were swept aside as solutions to the problems of swift expansion had to be improvised and fresh minds addressed themselves to the new task of speaking to foreign audiences, devised new programme forms and reacted to the dramatic circumstances in the midst of which they were operating.

In the field of news and news presentation the impact of new blood was to be particularly great. It was 1930 before the BBC took over from Reuters the production of its own news bulletins and 1934 before it took on a professional journalist, R.T. Clark, to look after foreign news. J.C.S. Macgregor, who was the BBC's News Editor at the time, was a former Edinburgh announcer, and neither he nor any other member of his staff had any professional experience of journalism. In that same year Macgregor became the first Empire News Editor, but it was not until February 1938 that a professional journalist was appointed to the overseas services. This was A.E. Barker, a son of Professor Ernest Barker, who was recruited to edit the news bulletins of the nascent foreign language services by Cecil Graves over a lunch at the Athenaeum. Barker had served for a number of years as a foreign correspondent for *The Times* in Warsaw, where he had known Rex Leeper, then at the British Embassy there, and Darsie Gillie, the *Morning Post* correspondent. All saw clearly the growing threat presented by Hitler. Barker returned to London to become *The Times* Diplomatic Correspondent and was once again in contact with Rex Leeper, now Head of the Foreign Office News Department and the foremost advocate of 'psychological rearmament', whose anti-appeasement views he shared.[1]

By the outbreak of war BBC news had become increasingly professional in its handling of the growing volume of major international stories which came crowding in. The Munich crisis had provided not only a challenge to the rapidly developing skills of the small editorial staff, but also overwhelming evidence of the importance of news. The BBC was deservedly applauded for the calm tone and objectivity of the Empire Service bulletins. Even so, as late as 1940, out of an editorial staff of a dozen or so in the European News Department, only three or four including the Editor and his Deputy were professionals with previous experience of newspaper work. The youthful Michael Barkway, who succeeded J.C.S. Macgregor as Empire News Editor when the latter was promoted to be Empire Service Director, had joined BBC news straight from Cambridge in 1934 and had never worked on a paper. Neither had Troughton, the man who replaced him when he was temporarily seconded to the League of Nations just before the war: 'A delightful Irish colonial civil servant' was how he was described by A.E. Barker.[2]

By 1942, however, all three of the BBC's central newsrooms were in the hands of experienced professionals: Bernard Moore, who had covered League of Nations affairs in Geneva for the *Daily Herald*, was now in charge of

Empire News. The formidable Noel Newsome had come over from the foreign desk of the *Daily Telegraph* in the opening days of the war in Poland to run European news. Other former Fleet Street men followed in his wake: Hugh Carleton Greene, who as *Daily Telegraph* correspondent, had been expelled from Germany shortly before the war and had then gone on to report the war from Poland and France, came into the BBC in October 1940 as German News Editor. Darsie Gillie, who had gone on from Poland to Paris to work for the *Manchester Guardian* and had then had a brief spell in the RAF, became French News Editor in the summer of 1940. Donald Edwards, who succeeded Noel Newsome as European News Editor in 1943, also came from the *Daily Telegraph*.[3]

Apart from the Latin-American and Arabic Services, the early foreign broadcasts consisted almost entirely of news, supplemented from January 1939 in the case of the German transmissions by short daily commentaries setting out the British attitude on international issues – the 'Sonderberichte' – in the production of which first Ralph Murray and then on a more permanent basis, Leonard Miall and Maurice Latey were involved. These were in fact the first news commentaries ever broadcast by the BBC, and Latey recalls that, apart from Miall's informal contacts with the Foreign Office, they were very largely left to work out for themselves what line they should take. In particular when Hitler made his first peace offer after Poland had been overrun Latey himself wrote a 'Sonderbericht' rejecting the offer without consulting or referring the matter up for guidance. The *News Chronicle* picked up the story, made more piquant by the fact that it was some time before the Government itself reacted. Far from being reprimanded for his initiative, Latey was congratulated.[4]

In those months that preceded the outbreak of war, shortage of transmitter time precluded anything more substantial than brief transmissions in each language. The Foreign Office in any case was showing no signs of wanting a quick expansion. The British Embassy in Warsaw, for instance, advised against the introduction of Polish broadcasts only a few weeks before the outbreak of war on the grounds that it might upset the Poles, who had 'an efficient and unbiassed service of their own'.[5]

By the beginning of the war, though the German and Arabic broadcasts had been increased to one hour a day and the French and Italian to half an hour, only two new foreign languages had been added to the original six: these were Spanish and Portuguese for Spain and Portugal, which were introduced at Foreign Office request on 4 June 1939, fifteen months after the inception of the service to Latin America.[6] At this stage the possibility of a massive development of foreign language broadcasting in the event of war had clearly not been envisaged and there were still grave reservations on the subject inside the BBC. Cecil Graves, for instance, in a conversation with Lord Perth, the Director-General of the Ministry of Information, on 6 July 1939, expressed the view that it was necessary to give 'very careful thought' to the implications of an extension of foreign language broadcasting 'because of a risk of reprisals, German listeners feeling we were propaganding [*sic*], etc.',[7] while on the first day of the German invasion of Poland, Maurice Latey was prevented from broadcasting a programme in German which made use of recordings of Hitler's speeches, carefully collected by the BBC, to contrast Hitler's past pledges to Poland with the aggression of which he was now guilty. Latey was firmly told that this was not something you could do to a foreign head of state.[8] The programme was authorised once war had been declared by Britain, but the incident provides a good illustration of the reluctance felt in many quarters to depart from peacetime practices and of the anxiety to avoid provocation. The climate of the times is epitomised in one of its more melancholy and bizarre aspects by the proposal which was put to the Director-General, apparently quite seriously, that the BBC should broadcast to Germany, as a token of Britain's peaceful intentions, the sound of the nightingale in Bagley Woods, one of the broadcasting stunts of the time. Harman Grisewood, who tells this story, does not go on to say whether this was ever done, but he recalls several meetings with Ogilvie at the time: 'He talked gravely and sadly about the Germans but did not, I felt, see the situation in its truly horrible proportions. He was still very much concerned with the issue of whether war could be averted.'[9]

However the entry of German troops in Prague on 15 March and the denouncing by Hitler only a few days later of Germany's non-aggression pact with Poland did have their effect. It was not just that news commentaries in German were introduced, at Foreign Office request, to provide a means of warning German public opinion more plainly that Britain would fight if Poland was attacked. The number of German bulletins was also increased, bringing the total daily transmissions up to forty-five minutes on 16 April. Another bulletin in French was added, though it does not seem to have been thought appropriate to raise the output of news in Italian to the same level: broadcasting in Italian continued to be confined to only one daily bulletin until the outbreak of war. Nor does it appear to have been felt desirable to start broadcasting to Czechoslovakia. That had to wait until the outbreak of hostilities. Certainly the British, at that stage, were in no mood to seek to match the German effort. Nor were they in a position to do so.

However there was one field in which they showed early signs of taking a lead. This was the monitoring of foreign broadcasts, and it is interesting that throughout the war they made far more use of it as a source of news and intelligence than did the Germans. Even though the German Foreign Ministry carried out a certain amount of monitoring its activities in this field were disapproved of by Goebbels, who regarded them as treasonable. British beginnings were slow and tentative. In the earliest stages, starting in the summer of 1937, the Foreign Office itself listened desultorily to Italian broadcasts in Arabic and to German broadcasts from Zeesen largely to acquire evidence of the kind of material the Axis stations were putting out. When the BBC started its own broadcasts in foreign languages it took over from the Foreign Office though without recruiting specialised staff. Monitoring was part of the duties of foreign broadcasting staff and was carried out when time could be spared from other duties. There was also some home monitoring by individual members of staff, and Leonard Miall, editing the German Service news commentaries, was doing his own amateur monitoring of Zeesen from Broadcasting House. Others were involved too, the Royal Institute of International Affairs, for instance, which was carrying out some monitoring of German and Italian domestic bulletins and analysing trends. But though Felix Greene, for one, recognised as early as 1937 that 'to know immediately and precisely what is being said by Rome and Germany to our empire and colonial listeners will become of immediate importance,'[10] the Foreign Office itself showed no signs in the year immediately prior to the outbreak of war of wishing either to take over monitoring or to encourage it on any scale, and the BBC found itself having to reduce the amount of listening and to confine the transcription of selected broadcasts to a weekly document. It was not until the summer of 1939 that the embryo Ministry of Information formally asked the BBC to undertake wartime monitoring, and then only on a far more limited scale than the BBC had recommended. It was symptomatic of the growing importance of the propaganda war and of the increasing realisation that the study of what the enemy was saying would bring rich dividends that by February 1940 the workload of the Monitoring Service had so increased that it had practically reached the level originally recommended by the BBC.

By that time the Monitoring Service had become a separate department. From the start on 26 August 1939 it operated from Wood Norton, a country estate on an attractive hillside overlooking the Avon near Evesham which had belonged to the exiled Duke of Orléans. A wooden hut housing the receivers and a set of aerials had been erected by the engineers at the top of a 300-foot hill behind the Orléans mansion. In the earliest days, recordings of incoming broadcasts were made in the hut on wax cylinders, and monitors themselves scrambled up the hill several times a day – and night as well – to collect the cylinders in wicker baskets. These primitive arrangements were gradually improved, and a teleprinter link was established with London to transmit the raw material to the editorial bureau which was being organised by Malcolm Frost, the Head of the Overseas Intelligence Department. By October 1941 the *Daily Digest* produced in London from the material monitored at Wood Norton was averaging 100,000 words. A shorter daily summary of 3 or 4,000 words, the Monitoring Report, gave the highlights of the material included in the *Digest*, while a research section was producing a weekly analysis and specialised studies on aspects of broadcast propaganda. Nearly 250 bulletins in thirty languages were being monitored each day and the staff had grown to about 500. To quote Asa Briggs, 'as the war went on through its many contrasting phases the monitors watched it all, catching its immediacy, its intricacy, its subplots and its surprises'.[11]

It is one of the more intriguing features of the early days at Wood Norton that monitoring attracted an unusual number of people of talent who were later to rise to high positions in their chosen field. They included academics like William Empson, the future art historian Ernest Gombrich, a future publisher George Weidenfeld, the poet Geoffrey Grigson, a future Head of BBC Radio Drama and world authority on the twentieth century theatre, Martin Esslin, and Anatol Goldberg, who, though a Russian, joined the Monitoring Service on account of his knowledge of Spanish and in later years, as Chief Commentator in the East European Service, became the BBC's best known voice in the Soviet Union.

It took a few days for the irresistible nature of the German onslaught on Poland to be fully appreciated and for British opinion to realise that Poland was about to be sealed off from any contact with the outside world. From now on it would stand sorely in need of the one commodity which Britain at least could provide in the absence of practical military assistance: news of the progress of the war elsewhere. Konrad Syrop, then the London correspondent of the Polish liberal newspaper *Kurjer Polski*, remembers running into the Polish Press Attaché in Portland Place shortly before the outbreak of war and being told that the BBC was planning to start broadcasts in Polish. The BBC was looking for suitable staff and he agreed to let his name be put forward. He was asked to come in for a voice test at eleven o'clock in the morning on what turned out to be the day Britain declared war on Germany, Sunday, 3 September. The voice test was inevitably delayed because everyone wanted to listen to the Prime Minister's broadcast to the nation, and there was a further delay caused by the first air raid warning of the war. However Syrop was duly taken on together with two others. On the 6th there was a dry run to initiate the newcomers, who had never broadcast before in their lives, to the mysteries of BBC news and studio procedures, and on the 7th the first Polish bulletin went out from a studio in Broadcasting House, preceded by an announcement in English and an introduction by the Polish Ambassador, Count Raczynski.[12] The news it had to give could not have been encouraging to the few listeners who managed to pick it up. For the Poles the night was setting in, as it had already done for the Czechs, and from then on only the BBC would be providing that ray of hope of which so many were to speak afterwards. Czech listeners heard their first bulletin from London the next day, preceded by a message from the Foreign Minister of the Czech Government in exile, Jan Masaryk.

By the end of 1939 broadcasts in German had been increased to one and a half hours a day, providing news bulletins and talks at intervals throughout the day and evening; Italian broadcasts had risen to one and a quarter hours a day and broadcasts in French to one hour a day. Daily bulletins of fifteen minutes each were also introduced by the end of September 1939 in the languages of those countries of Central and South East Europe where it was thought most important that German influence should be countered. Broadcasts in Hungarian had started even earlier than Polish, on 5 September. Broadcasts in Rumanian and Serbo-Croat began on 30 September. Turkish followed on 20 November as part of the Near East Service, which was also responsible for broadcasts in Arabic. The introduction of a Bulgarian bulletin had to wait until the following February.

Only four months after the outbreak of war the BBC had therefore added seven new languages to the existing nine, which included Afrikaans for South Africa, introduced on a once-a-week basis in May 1939 as part of the Empire Service and increased to two bulletins a day by the end of the year. The Arabic Service was by then well established and included light entertainment by leading Arab artistes recorded in Cairo, talks by eminent scholars, Koranic readings by readers of high repute and English lessons. The Latin American Service had been expanded to three hours every night in July 1939. It too included not just news but appropriate music, features, talks by visitors from Latin America to Britain, programmes on the national days of the various Latin American Republics as well as news commentaries.

As for the Empire Service, it now included fourteen news programmes every twenty-four hours as well as topical talks, thus moving further in the direction first advocated by Felix Greene in 1938.[13] The use of transmitters had been adjusted so as to give the Empire Service the widest possible coverage at all times of the day and night, though the service still fell well short of continuous broadcasting twenty-four hours out of twenty-four. In August a special English Service to Europe had been introduced, made up of a selection of items from the Home and Empire Services 'likely to be of appeal to continental listeners'.[14] The major decisions about overseas broadcasting policy so far as news was concerned had been taken and the scene was set for the climactic events of 1940, which in turn were to lead to the massive expansion of which today's External Services are the heirs.

Before 1938 the BBC's engineers, in their forward planning, had concentrated on providing the Empire Service with the transmitter resources and aerial systems required to give the service worldwide coverage for as high a proportion of the twenty-four hours as possible. In achieving even this limited objective they were handicapped by shortage of funds, a situation which was to recur throughout the post-war period. At the start of the war the BBC disposed of nine short wave transmitters, all of them at Daventry, of which only five were of a power comparable with the more numerous senders available to the Germans at Zeesen. Rapid expansion of programme hours was therefore out of the question without a corresponding increase in transmitters, for which a lead time of eighteen months to two years had to be assumed. It was not until February 1941 that a new station at Rampisham, in Dorset, was opened equipped with four Marconi transmitters of the latest design, each with a power of one hundred kilowatts. With its fifteen masts and twenty-nine aerial arrays, the station was able to provide full world coverage and was mainly intended for reception beyond the confines of Europe.

In the meantime the BBC's engineers had acquired a new Marconi transmitter originally intended for a foreign government and had installed it at the existing medium wave site at Start Point in Devon in January 1940. They had also converted the existing medium wave transmitter at Start Point for short wave use in daytime, thus providing an embryo alternative short wave station should Daventry be put out of commission by enemy air attacks. Another medium wave transmitter, at Clevedon near Bristol, was similarly converted for short wave use in September 1940 and four modern Marconi transmitters were added on the Daventry site. By the end of 1940 the BBC's engineers had succeeded by one device or another in nearly doubling the number of transmitters available when the war broke out. It was a remarkable achievement, but it fell far short of what would be required to accommodate the triple expansion of programme output which the Ministry of Information asked the BBC to consider at the end of 1940. For that, the BBC said eighteen new short wave transmitters would be needed in three groups of six. The go-ahead for this major development was eventually given and the three stations were duly completed in 1943. Two were built within about a mile of each other at Skelton, near Penrith in Cumbria and the other at Woofferton near Ludlow in Shropshire. The Skelton installations were equipped with six Marconi and six STC transmitters, while the Woofferton station was given six American RCA fifty kilowatt transmitters. By November 1943, when the STC transmitters became operational at Skelton, the BBC disposed of the impressive total of forty-three short wave transmitters in the United Kingdom.

So far as much of Europe was concerned, however, short wave transmissions were not enough. Only the longer short wave bands were suitable for the shorter distances involved in broadcasting to Western Europe. In any case few potential listeners at that time had access to short wave receivers. To reach a majority of listeners it was essential to provide a medium wave service, at any rate in the evening. An additional complication was that before the outbreak of war the RAF had insisted that medium frequencies could only be used on synchronised groups of transmitters in order to avoid enemy aircraft using individual transmitters as navigational beacons. This had meant, among other things, that at the outbreak of war, the BBC had had for a time to reduce its domestic services to a single network.

Neither the French, nor, more important, the Germans took this wise precaution. Apart from anything else it meant that throughout the war no BBC service was ever completely interrupted through damage to transmitters,

since listeners were always able to continue listening to a more distant transmitter on the same frequency. German transmissions on the other hand, were
frequently lost as a result of air raids.

At the beginning of the war the European Service was using one medium
frequency, 1149 kHz, on a synchronised transmission from three sites, Brook-
mans Park, near Hatfield in Hertfordshire, Moorside Edge, five miles west of
Huddersfield, and Westerglen near Falkirk in Stirlingshire. In October 1939
the much more powerful long wave transmitter at Droitwich was converted
for use on medium wave and joined the 1149 kHz synchronised group. A
further regional transmitter, at Washford, on the Bristol Channel, joined the
group in November 1939. In the meantime experiments were being carried
out on a new type of aerial at Start Point. A crucial advantage of the new
design was that it made it impossible for enemy aircraft to use the station as
a navigational beacon. The success of the experiment led the BBC engineers to
install a similar system at Droitwich, which in February 1940 began to operate
alone on 1149 kHz while the regional medium wave transmitters originally
used on that frequency shifted to another, 804 kHz. In October 1940 a further
medium frequency was brought into service for European coverage purposes,
using the Start Point transmitter. This meant that by the end of 1940 the
European Service disposed of three separate medium frequencies, thus making it possible to transmit three different foreign language programme streams
simultaneously.

At the same time the BBC was re-equipping existing sites with new and
more high-powered medium wave transmitters. Thus by March 1941 Brook-
mans Park and Moorside Edge had been re-equipped with 150 kW transmitters for use by the European Services, while at Droitwich two new transmitters
were coupled together to provide a single unit capable of delivering a power
of 400 kW, very high for those days. It came into operation in February 1941.

In the meantime work was proceeding on the designing of a very high-
power long wave transmitter for use at a site in eastern England and capable
of providing an effective all-day signal throughout northern Germany and as
far east as Berlin. The station was eventually built at Ottringham, near Spurn
Head in the East Riding of Yorkshire, and came into service in February
1943. It consisted of four 200 kilowatt Marconi transmitters capable of
operating both on long and medium wave. It was designed in such a way as
to make it possible for the transmitters to operate singly or in groups of two,
three or four, so that with all the transmitters radiating on one frequency it
could attain a power of 800 kilowatt, thus making it the most powerful
broadcasting station of its time.

A further powerful medium wave transmitter, in which Churchill, who
regarded it as a kind of secret weapon in the propaganda war, took a strong
personal interest, was built at Crowborough in Sussex in 1942. Known by the
code name 'Aspidistra', it was intended for use by Woburn's 'black' broad-

casters. The BBC was able to make use of it when it was not required by PWE for its own purposes. Made up of three transmitters capable of operating together on one frequency and delivering a total power of 500 kilowatt, it made a valuable addition to the BBC's transmitting facilities.

Thus the initial advantage enjoyed by the Germans at the outbreak of war, had been largely wiped out by the end of 1943 and the BBC's engineers were able, with increasing effectiveness, to provide the broadcasters with the technical means to achieve that domination of Europe which Goebbels himself was eventually compelled to acknowledge.[15]

In 1940 much of this was still to come. Nonetheless by the end of the year the BBC was broadcasting in thirty-four languages of which no fewer than twenty-five had been added since the war began. Seventy-eight news bulletins, amounting to 250,000 words, were being broadcast each day and transmission time in foreign languages had more than trebled, from forty-four hours a week at the outbreak of war to 145 by the end of 1940. The services in French, German and Italian in particular had been substantially increased. Largest in size at that stage was the French Service, with three hours of programme time each day, including six news bulletins. Next came the German Service, with two and a half hours on the air each day, including eight news bulletins. As for the Italian Service, by August 1940 it had been increased from only one daily bulletin at the outbreak of the war to two hours a day.

The introduction of broadcasts in new languages roughly followed the course of events in northern and western Europe during that fateful year. However, the invasion of Finland by the Soviet Union in November 1939 does not seem to have been thought a sufficient reason for starting broadcasts in Finnish, which were not introduced until 18 March 1940, a week after Finland had been compelled to make peace. A Swedish bulletin had been introduced a month earlier. Danish and Norwegian bulletins were first broadcast on the day of the German invasion of those two countries. To start with, Danish listeners were given only a brief news summary within the Norwegian period, but this was increased to a daily five-minute bulletin a few days later and a full fifteen-minute period was introduced in May. The Norwegian Service started with a daily ten-minute bulletin, but the Norwegian period was soon raised by degrees to nearly an hour a day. Daily bulletins in Dutch were introduced in April, almost exactly a month to the day before the German invasion of the Low Countries, and by the end of the year a start had been made with broadcasting in Flemish and French for Belgium, Luxembourg dialect, Icelandic, Albanian, Maltese, Persian, Hindi and Burmese. The Belgian audience received bulletins in Flemish and French on alternate nights, the Albanians a daily five-minute bulletin, the Persians a fifteen-minute bulletin four nights a week, the Icelanders and Maltese a weekly newsletter and the Burmese a fortnightly newsletter. All were to be substantially increased in the course of the following year.[16]

At the same time, under the talented leadership of R.A. Rendall, who had returned from Palestine to take charge of the Empire Service, that service was itself undergoing a rapid and quite radical transformation. When it was first introduced in 1932 it had been assumed that each separate daily transmission would be received only in the region of the globe for which it was intended. This had soon been shown to be a fallacy. As the months went by there had been mounting evidence that listeners all over the world were prepared to tune in at almost any time of the day provided the signal was audible, regardless of whether or not it was intended for them. As a result the various daily transmissions had been redesignated by numbers rather than by the description of the region to which each was beamed. Following the outbreak of war it became clear that this approach needed to be modified. By 1941 Rendall was able to claim that the service could now more justly be described as a 'world service', but he also set out as his aim to try to reconcile the demand for a round-the-clock news service available the world over, with the need for programmes of special interest to listeners in particular parts of the world. There was special concern at that time with speaking specifically to audiences in America, which, while still formally neutral, was increasingly crucial to Britain's ability to survive. Rendall saw the aim of the service as being to provide 'a vivid picture of the people of Britain at war' and 'letting the people speak for themselves and so for their country'.[17] By 1941 he had added four hours a day to the service's time on the air, which was now nearly twenty-one hours a day. Four main component branches had been established, the North American, African, Eastern and Pacific services, each under a Director working to Rendall. Each sought to serve the primary audience defined by its title while at the same time not overlooking the many secondary audiences which might be tuning in elsewhere in the world.

Although the initiative for proposing new developments in the foreign language field was clearly recognised as lying with the Ministry of Information and the Foreign Office, the BBC contributed its own views on priorities. The debate was not always smooth, particularly as the ministry tended to be irritatingly wayward and capricious in its requests and at times impatient of BBC objections, however well-founded. Matters were eased to some extent by the presence on temporary secondment in the key position of Director of Radio Relations at the ministry in 1940 of Lindsay Wellington, the BBC's former Assistant Controller of Programmes, but his task was not made easier by the absence of coordination within the machinery of government itself. Much confusion arose from the overlapping of functions and the rivalries between the numerous ministries and other official bodies which regarded themselves as entitled to a voice in the formulation of overseas broadcasting policy. There were arguments not only about the conflicting claims of different languages but about the time of day at which the broadcasts should take place, with the Ministry of Information often insisting on times unsuitable for the intended audience or which would involve displacing existing broadcasts in other languages which it had itself asked for. Momentary shifts in Government priorities and even the personal whims of ministers presented the BBC with practical problems which could only be resolved by confronting ministry officials and even ministers themselves with the hard facts. Thus in September 1940, as the London blitz was getting underway, the BBC was faced with an angry complaint from the Foreign Secretary, Lord Halifax, that there had been 'too much interference lately with the foreign broadcasts of the BBC.'[18] Halifax's intervention had been prompted by a communication from the British Ambassador in Lisbon, who had received many complaints from Portuguese listeners following a change in the timing of the Portuguese transmission. This change was a consequence of a more general but momentary reduction in the volume of broadcasting to Europe which took place on 19 September 1940. The BBC had reluctantly had to reduce its European output from two networks to one on account of the dispersal of BBC operations to the provinces ordered by the Government to avoid disruption by enemy bombing.[19] All this had to be explained to Halifax by Ogilvie, who afterwards described the whole episode as 'a ridiculous and tiresome misunderstanding'.[20] Halifax duly apologised, but the incident was symptomatic of the confusion which reigned in the Government machine and of the pressures the BBC was having to contend with. It also illustrated the readiness with which the BBC was blamed even when, as in this case, it was not at fault and was merely carrying out Government directives.

At the working level, J. B. Clark, Assistant Controller (Overseas), the most experienced of the senior BBC officials involved, and the one least inclined to take kindly to excessive and unreasonable government interference, was attempting to persuade Ministry of Information officials that it was unwise to make constant changes in the timing of broadcasts: 'It is most undesirable', he wrote, 'for us to regard revision of schedules as a game which can be played daily or weekly.'[21] Listeners had an aversion to complex 'shuffling', as the complaints from Portugal had shown, and there had been others. 'Effective broadcasting depends on the inculcation of listening habits', ministry officials were told at a meeting on 15 October: 'Any change, however well "trailed", is bound to lose us a proportion of the audience.'[22] Ministry officials took the point, though complaining that they found the BBC uncooperative, but they were themselves harrassed by ministers who had no time for such practical details.

Shortage of transmitters was not the only problem. Suitably qualified staff had to be found. Although many refugees from Germany, Austria, Italy and the occupied countries had found their way to London, not many could meet the BBC's complex requirements, as J.B. Clark had noted at the time of Munich. They had to speak adequate English as well as their own language, they had to be highly literate and capable of translating accurately and fast, they had to have a natural flair for the subject matter they were dealing with, to be capable of working against a deadline, and to have a reasonable broadcasting voice. Not all accents were acceptable. In the early stages it was felt that German Jews would not be suitable because they would be instantly recognised as such by the audience in Germany. Above all, the BBC was anxious not to give hostile critics any grounds for charges that the BBC's foreign language services were run by emigrés and were pursuing emigré rather than British objectives. Thus in the German Service all news commentaries were broadcast by speakers of impeccable British ancestry,[23] though most features were written by staff of German – and frequently Jewish – origin. Similarly in the Italian Service the most notable commentator was Colonel Stevens, a former Assistant Military Attaché at the British Embassy in Rome. His name became a by-word in Italy, where he was known as 'Colonello Buona Sera', from the opening words of greeting he invariably used on the air. Born of a Neapolitan mother and an English father, Stevens spoke English with a slightly foreign intonation and Italian with a distinct Neapolitan accent with English overtones. With his paternal, benevolent approach reinforced by the prestige of his military rank, he became immensely popular with his increasingly wide Italian following, particularly during the first three years of the war, before the Italian capitulation. But although he was an excellent broadcaster he never wrote his own scripts, which were drafted for him by an Italian Jewish journalist from Trieste, Aldo Cassuto. Cassuto had been a ghost writer for the editor of the Trieste newspaper *Il Piccolo* and, with no ambition to go to the microphone himself – and indeed no talent as a broadcaster – was the ideal partner for Stevens.[24]

It was rare that foreign broadcasters employed by the BBC became broadcasting personalities, regularly addressing their compatriots and purporting to speak for themselves. The major exception was the French Service, where an outstandingly talented group of Frenchmen of disparate origins led by Jacques Duchesne – by his real name Michel Saint-Denis, the theatre producer – broadcast every night for four years a programme whose title 'Les Français parlent aux Français', was indicative of its special character. There a virtue was made of the fact that the participants were themselves Frenchmen, speaking to their compatriots in their own right. It was a unique example of the BBC giving its head to a group of expatriates who nonetheless were operating under BBC direction, however loose, succeeding in a remarkable way in fusing together their own distinctive Frenchness and their dedication to the objectives which they shared with their hosts.

However, with exiled governments assembling in London in the early summer of 1940, the British Government and the BBC were faced with requests for time on the air to enable them to speak direct to their compatriots quite separately from what the BBC might itself be broadcasting in their own languages. Some indeed attempted to obtain control over all broadcasts to their countries. The formulas which were eventually adopted varied considerably from country to country, and quite apart from the time set aside for officially arranged broadcasts, close contact was maintained between the BBC services concerned and officials of the various exiled governments, who in many cases attended regular service meetings. However in no case did the British Government agree to hand over all responsibility for broadcasting to any particular country to the foreign authorities concerned in London. The BBC itself insisted that notwithstanding the cooperation it sought to achieve with foreign governments in London, it must remain master in its own house and free to accept or reject advice as it saw fit.

Relations between the BBC and some exiled foreign governments were frequently stormy, since the specific interests of these governments and British policies did not always coincide. In the case of the French Service, although some of the French staff personally supported de Gaulle and had his approval in working for the BBC – Jean Marin and Jean Oberlé were two cases in point – others did not. Some indeed, like Pierre Bourdan, were personally strongly opposed to de Gaulle though equally if not even more hostile to Pétain. So far as de Gaulle himself was concerned, it was understood that the French team 'would keep in close touch with us, and this is in fact what happened a good part of the time ... for as long as the interests of Great Britain and the Free French remained identical. Later there were to be crises during which the propagandists involved in "Les Français parlent aux Français" did not side with us.' But General de Gaulle did add that 'the talent and the efficacy of this group left us in no doubt that we should give them every possible support.' De Gaulle was shrewd enough to realise that in the field of propaganda as in others, the British, 'while quite genuinely anxious to assist in every way the spread of the influence of de Gaulle and the Free French in France, were also doing so in their own interest and were determined to remain in overall control.'[25]

Although the broadcasts made in the free time set aside for foreign governments were not strictly speaking subject to British policy directives those making them were never given complete *carte-blanche* to say whatever they wished. They were required throughout to submit scripts either to the Foreign Office or to the relevant BBC officials acting in their capacity as censors, who were entitled to impose cuts and modifications. Prime Ministers were no exception to the rule. Even General de Gaulle had to submit to what must have seemed to him a humiliating requirement, though he makes no mention of it in his *Mémoires*, stating instead that 'It goes without saying that as far as I personally was concerned I never accepted any kind of supervision or even any foreign advice on what I had to say to France.'[26] Nonetheless there was at least one instance when Darsie Gillie, the French Editor, acting as policy censor, thought it right, after much agonising, to require a particular sentence to be removed from one of General de Gaulle's broadcasts. The Free French

Headquarters at Carlton Gardens strongly objected but eventually had to bow to Gillie's demand and the broadcast duly went ahead without the offending sentence.[27]

The Free French were allotted first one and later two five-minute periods each day for their own free use. These daily broadcasts formed part of the same period as the BBC's own French transmissions but were separately announced, first with the words *'Liberté, Egalité, Fraternité'*, later changed to *'Honneur et Patrie'*. There then followed the words: *'Voici le porte-parole des Français Libres'*. This too was modified as the Free French changed the form of words by which they described themselves, first to *'La France Libre'* and later *'La France Combattante'*. In the case of broadcasts by General de Gaulle himself the announcement would run: *'Honneur et Patrie – Voici le Général de Gaulle'*, a form of words which, when spoken at the microphone in suitably solemn tones, conveyed to the audience something of the awe-inspiring nature of the occasion, and of the speaker. After his first two broadcasts of 18 and 19 June, the General broadcast again on the 22, 23, 24, 26, 27 and 28 June. Thereafter his appearances at the microphone became less frequent and he chose to speak only on major occasions. The regular – and anonymous – spokesman of the Free French in 'Honneur et Patrie' was almost from the start Maurice Schumann, a young Second Lieutenant who had been a journalist and had made his way to London in the dark days of June 1940 to continue the struggle. With his nightly appearances his voice became as well known in France as Alistair Cooke's is in Britain. His role, first in making known the existence and activities of the Free French and later in stirring the depths of French pride and fanning the will to resist cannot be overestimated. It is worth noting that the audience in France made no distinction between 'Honneur et Patrie' and the BBC's own broadcasts. They were all 'Gaullist'.

Even though there were periodic difficulties with the Free French over 'Honneur et Patrie' – for a brief period at the end of 1942, when the Allies made a momentary deal with Admiral Darlan in Algiers, the Free French refused to avail themselves of their free time – relations with the Polish Government in exile turned out to be far more difficult, at least in the early stages. After Poland had been overrun by the German armies the French Government had made broadcasting facilities available to General Sikorski's Government in exile for a daily programme to Poland – 'Radio Polskie' – which was under exclusive Polish control. When France collapsed and Sikorski's Government sought refuge in Britain, it tried in vain to obtain a similar arrangement with the British. It was late in 1941 before the Ministry of Information finally acceded to the Polish Government's request for 'free time' and the title 'Radio Polskie' was heard again on the air. Even then the conditions imposed on the Poles were a good deal more stringent than for the Free French, and there were frequent clashes as they sought to influence the BBC Polish Service's editorial policies and pressed for more time on the air for

themselves. Major bones of contention were future policy towards Germany
and the Soviet Union and Polish territorial claims in Eastern Europe.[28] In
the circumstances and given the conflicting susceptibilities of other allies like
Czechoslovakia and the Soviet Union the British Government thought it wise
to act with extreme caution and to keep the London Poles under tight control.
Polish Government speakers were required to submit scripts in advance for
policy vetting and were discouraged from touching on issues concerning the
post-war settlement in Eastern Europe. BBC switch censors had strict instructions from Kirkpatrick to cut off the 'Radio Polskie' transmissions instantly
in cases of major deviations from the agreed script.[29]

Arguments over such matters so envenomed relations that the BBC's Polish
Editor, Michael Winch, finally had to be moved in an effort to restore
relations.[30] His successor, Gregory Macdonald, came from the European
News Department but had had a long and intimate connection with Poland
before the war. A graduate of the School of Slavonic Studies and a Catholic,
he first went to Poland as a journalist in 1927. He was one of the few people
in Britain with a close knowledge of the country and its culture and politics
– Darsie Gillie was another – and he proved an altogether more understanding
partner in the dialogue between the BBC and the Polish Government in
London than either Winch or particularly Newsome had been. It was not in
Newsome's intellectual make-up to be particularly sympathetic to the London
Poles, whom he regarded as 'feudal reactionaries'.[31] He tended to look on
the Soviet Union through rose-tinted spectacles and took the view that Polish
internal resistance and the Polish Home Army were fictions created by the
London emigrés and did not in fact exist. It took the Warsaw rising to persuade
him that he was wrong.[32] Macdonald handled his Polish Ministry of Information contacts – a Polish liaison officer, Count Balinski, attended the Polish
Service weekly meetings – with tact and sympathy, seeking, wherever possible
to avoid confrontations wounding to Polish *amour-propre* without on the
other hand yielding anything on essentials.[33]

Surprisingly, even though Newsome, for his part, was personally a good
deal more sympathetic to the Czechs than to the Poles, the Czechoslovak
Government in exile, which was not fully recognised by the British Government until mid 1941, was not granted 'free time' until much later, in March
1943. On the other hand there had been close and continuing contact between
the Czech authorities in London and the BBC Czech Service. The Czechs,
understandably, would have preferred to have all broadcasting in Czech –
and Slovak – under their own control but soon realised that this was one
point on which the British would not yield. Once they were granted free time
– which incidentally they had not asked for – they enjoyed a good deal more
latitude in saying what they wished than the Poles. Their own spokesmen, of
whom Jan Masaryk became the most famous and the most effective, talked
freely about postwar Europe in ways which were denied to their Polish
colleagues.

As for the Dutch Government in exile, after initial discussions in June 1940 in which the Dutch authorities in London put forward a relatively ambitious scheme for a programme of their own which would include entertainment as well as talks, the Ministry of Information fairly rapidly agreed to a daily fifteen-minute transmission which became known as 'Radio Oranje' and was duly inaugurated on 28 July 1940 by Queen Wilhelmina in person. Admittedly this was less than the Dutch had asked for, but it was soon increased to thirty minutes, and a further fifteen minutes were added in 1944 to enable the Dutch Government to broadcast to the East Indies.

In contrast the Belgian audience seems not to have been thought worthy of special attention, at least in the early stages. This may have been in part because it could be claimed that the BBC was already broadcasting in both the languages spoken in Belgium. Such an argument would not have cut any ice in Belgium itself and the BBC was well aware of it. A limited BBC operation in French and Flemish on alternate nights eventually got underway towards the end of September 1940. Given the title 'Radio Belgique' – or in Flemish 'Radio Belgie' – it was run in the case of the transmissions in French by Victor de Laveleye, the man who later invented the 'V' campaign and a future Belgian Minister of Justice, and in the case of the transmissions in Flemish by Nand Geersens, better known to his audience as Jan Moedwil. It was not until February 1943 that the Belgian Government in exile was allowed a fifteen-minute slot of its own, known as 'Radiodiffusion Nationale Belge'. This was broadcast on four nights a week, two in French and two in Flemish. A month later it was raised to two fifteen-minute transmissions daily, one in each language, but the official Belgian broadcasts disappeared after the liberation of Belgium in September 1944.

The case of Norway is in many respects quite unique among the countries overrun by the Germans in 1940. The Norwegian Service – together with an embryo Danish Service – had started in a small way with a daily news bulletin at only a few hours notice on the day Germany had invaded Norway and Denmark. By 1943 it was broadcasting one and a half hours a day and continued to do so until the end of the war in Europe. Its early days were marked by strenuous efforts on the part of members of the management of the Norwegian State Broadcasting Authority who had made their way to London to secure complete control over broadcasting in Norwegian from London. The Ministry of Information, which was dealing simultaneously with similar Dutch requests, was not keen to let the Norwegians have their way and the BBC was resistant to any scheme that might diminish its own control over what went out on the air. Both were in favour of granting the Norwegian Government in exile free time, while the main broadcasting effort in Norwegian would remain in the hands of the BBC. However, the Norwegians themselves, in the end, opted for a different solution which was eventually adopted. Rather than accept free time, they proposed that the former

Head of the Norwegian Radio's News Department, Toralv Øksnevad, who
had arrived in London, together with two other members of the staff of
Norwegian Radio, should be seconded to the BBC while continuing to be paid
by the Norwegian Government. They would work as BBC staff members
under BBC direction. The arrangement was unique in that it ensured maximum
cooperation between the BBC and the Norwegian authorities in London while
not in any way impinging on the BBC's ultimate editorial control over what
was transmitted. Both sides were clearly satisfied with the arrangement, which
continued to operate smoothly right up to the end of the war.

During the summer of 1940 issues of high policy such as these were the subject
of many discussions and much correspondence with the Ministry of Information. But there were other, more practical and immediate problems to
wrestle with as the BBC strove to meet the Government's requests for expansion. Room had been found in Broadcasting House, then without its postwar
extension, for the staff manning the first, limited foreign broadcasting operation, and more room was made available for the early expansions by the
dispersal of domestic programme departments to locations in the depths of
the English countryside as a precaution against bombing. Nonetheless the
pace of expansion was such that soon every available space at Broadcasting
House was occupied by offices. Even the Council Chamber was taken over.
There the translators of the smaller services worked under the stern and
imperious gaze of Reith, whose portrait stared down at them from above the
fireplace. Security accommodation had been provided in the lower ground
floor and basement to allow broadcasting to continue when air raids were in
progress. Emergency studios had been installed and an alternative control
room, replacing the one on the top floor of the building, had been set up in
the lower depths, within earshot of the underground trains of the Bakerloo
Line. Staff worked above ground in the daytime but would go down into the
basement at night when the sirens went. Makeshift dormitory accommodation had been provided in the Concert Hall, which was held to be relatively
safe, and a washing line with blankets hung over it separated the men's section
from the women's. Noel Newsome, the European News Editor, would often
retire there, wearing a Malay sarong, a habit acquired in his early days in the
East.
  Before the war few people worked in Broadcasting House outside office
hours. Now a whole new breed of broadcasters haunted the corridors at
night, hurrying to the studios for the late night or early morning transmissions
to Europe, manning the Empire and European News Rooms or working
overnight on editing the digest of what had been said on the latest broadcasts
from Rome, Berlin or Paris.[34]
  Outside, the entrance to Broadcasting House was protected by a wall of
sandbags and guarded by armed and helmeted sentries; while on the roof the

BBC's own air raid wardens looked out for enemy aircraft and falling bombs. In October 1940, as German air raids over London increased in severity, Ogilvie, the Director-General, reported to the Overseas Board that he had raised the question of two armoured cars from the War Office for use by BBC staff who had to make night journeys through the streets of London while the air raids were in progress.[35]

By that time, on 15 October, Broadcasting House had received its first direct hit, from a delayed action bomb which exploded shortly after 9.00 pm. Bruce Belfrage was reading the 'Nine o'clock News' on the Home Service when the explosion took place. Listeners heard a dull thud, there was 'a slight pause, a whispered "are you all right?"' and Bruce Belfrage went on reading the news as if nothing had happened.[36] Just at the same time, in a nearby studio, another news reader, Carl Brinitzer, was in the process of broadcasting a German news bulletin. He too carried on without detectable signs of alarm, and even the most attentive listener in Germany would not have known what had just happened.

The bomb had crashed through the outer wall on the seventh floor of the building on the Portland Place side, skidded through an opening in the wall of the inner studio tower, fallen two floors down and come to rest in the Music Library on the fifth floor. It had done so much damage on the way that it was not immediately realised that it had not yet exploded. It was some minutes before it was found and evacuation ordered. The French Service team of 'Les Français parlent aux Français' who had been at work in the Broadcasting House Chapel, which was in fact a studio designed for religious broadcasting, got out just in time to get down to the basement and carry on with their programme from one of the emergency studios there, which had been set up in a former ladies' lavatory. Others were also rushing downstairs taking with them recordings to ensure continuity of transmission. The area in the immediate vicinity of the bomb was occupied by members of the editorial staff of the Monitoring Service, not all of whom immediately dropped what they were doing. Seven people were killed when the bomb finally exploded, of whom four belonged to the Monitoring Service.[37] Some were killed trying to push the bomb outside.

A great deal of damage was done by the blast and many studios were wrecked. However, emergency repairs were rapidly put in hand by the engineers, who performed miracles of ingenuity in sorting out the tangles of broken wires and reconnecting essential circuitry. Broadcasting continued without the public either at home or overseas becoming aware that Broadcasting House had sustained a direct hit.

Just such an eventuality had long been foreseen, and arrangements had been made by the BBC's engineers to provide stand-by studios should Broadcasting House be put out of action. These were located in a disused skating rink at Maida Vale in west London. Surmounted by a large glass roof, the building was hardly calculated to inspire a sense of security during air raids. Nonetheless an armoured car stood almost permanently outside Broadcasting House at night, ready to transport programme staff at breakneck speed to Maida Vale should the need arise.[38]

The occasion duly came on Sunday 8 December 1940, when a huge land-mine drifted down into Portland Place onto a lamp post and exploded there shortly before 11.00 pm, killing a policeman and setting a car on fire. The massive explosion shook the whole building and did extensive damage, start-ing a number of fires and causing flooding in the security operational areas in the basement. Once again staff behaved with exemplary composure. All that listeners in Europe would have been aware of was a ten-second break in transmission. George Foa, who was reading the 10.45 pm Italian News when the bomb went off, apologised briefly for the interruption and resumed his reading of the bulletin without giving his listeners any clue as to what had just occurred. Behind the scenes the damage was being quickly assessed and urgent steps were immediately taken to transfer the European operation to Maida Vale. By 11.45 pm, less than an hour later, the Maida Vale Studios had been taken over and staff were at work there, ready to transmit the 11.45 pm English News bulletin. Only a Norwegian bulletin was lost, but as the Overseas Board minutes recorded, 'Mr Bye apologised in Norwegian for its absence and promised the usual early morning Norwegian bulletin.' This was duly broadcast at the advertised time, together with the rest of the sequence of 'dawn' bulletins in other European languages.[39]

Much of the European Service spent the rest of that winter encamped at Maida Vale. Josephine Gaman, a secretary with the German Service, remem-bers the accommodation as 'a series of hot, overcrowded underground cells'. She worked for Patrick Gordon Walker, the future Labour Foreign Secretary, and two others in a room which was later bombed and in which six others, including Leonard Miall and the rest of his German Talks Unit, had to be fitted in. 'There were not enough desks for us all. Telephones were inadequate, lines were always engaged, there were no listening facilities, and recording studios could only be booked with great difficulty. It was almost impossible to write talks in these conditions. The odd administrator from Broadcasting House used to come over periodically to try and get us to conform to BBC rules and receive complaints, but we were left pretty much to ourselves.'[40]

In spite of this and of the fact that the large studio had been used as a repository and was full of old furniture, elaborate and ambitious productions were undertaken. Leo Shepley, at that time working for European Intelli-gence, used to take part in Italian features. The producer was George Foa, who was an expert on Italian opera and was inclined to make liberal use of recorded sound effects to heighten the drama. Shepley recalls one feature about the Italian invasion of Abyssinia which included a plentiful use of the recorded sound of exploding bombs. There were air raids every night at the time and a watchman on the roof would phone down to the studio whenever enemy planes were overhead. The cast would then take refuge in the control cubicle, which had a slightly more substantial ceiling. On the night in question, there had been so many interruptions from air raid alerts that those taking part voted to carry on regardless of danger. The programme was being recorded down the line to Broadcasting House, and immediately after one of the recorded bombing effects had been played lights began flashing on the control panel. It was Broadcasting House on the line enquiring whether Maida Vale had been hit. The recording engineers had mistaken the recording for the sound of the real thing coming over live on the studio microphones.[41]

In the meantime parts of the Overseas Services had been dispersed to Wood Norton. Many of the home programme departments had gone there at the outbreak of war, and staff lived in billets at Evesham, travelling to and from work in two double-decker buses acquired for the purpose, or cycling along the banks of the Avon. The canteen was in an adapted cow shed, studios had been set up in converted stables, and the Monitoring Service, also based there, was quartered in huts newly put up on the hillside. They were joined in September 1940 by the Arabic, Turkish, Spanish, Portuguese and Latin American Services. A strangely assorted international community grew up there made up of drama producers, musicians, the actors of the BBC Drama Repertory Company, which was born there, the polyglot world of foreign monitors and broadcasters and the engineers and studio technicians who kept the show on the road. Later, after the bombing of Broadcasting House, the Empire News and Presentation staff moved to the area as well, though to another country house in the vicinity, Abbey Manor.

These moves were to be of relatively short duration. By early December 1940 Duff Cooper, the Minister of Information, was pressing for the early return of all overseas departments to London with the exception of the Monitoring Service, which needed to be in the country for technical reasons. Government policy on dispersal had changed, and meanwhile complaints about working conditions at Maida Vale had prompted the BBC to suggest that Duff Cooper should be asked to come and look the place over for himself on the occasion of a visit to the French Service.[42] He duly came on 30 January 1941, and the outcome was further pressure from the ministry for new accommodation to be found.[43]

Despite impressions to the contrary the BBC had not been idle in its search, but it was still suffering from the failure of the Government to give the Overseas Services – and for that matter broadcasting as a whole – the kind of priority which was needed to secure London office buildings of a suitable kind in the face of the intense pressure on available accommodation. The problem was not made easier by the special nature of the BBC's requirements. What it needed was office buildings with basements which could be made secure from bombing and where broadcasting could carry on regardless of air raids. Two such buildings were eventually found. The first was Bush House, where the BBC was able to secure a lodgement in the south-east wing and the centre block.[44] The second was 200 Oxford Street, the former Peter Robinson department store.

Built in the late twenties by an American entrepreneur, Irving T. Bush, Bush House had not only an imposing appearance but, what was far more important, extensive lower ground and basement floors. However despite the vulnerability of Maida Vale to enemy bombing, no immediate move turned out to be possible. There were delays over the building of a blast wall intended to make the basement of the south-east wing more secure, and the aid of Reith, by then Minister of Works, had to be invoked to get matters speeded up.[45] By the time the move took place on 17 March 1941, the building was far from ready for use as a broadcasting centre. Some of the staff had to spend a week or so working from hotel bedrooms at the Waldorf Hotel, across the road. Others were parked for a time in the nearby Public Trustee building.

The early days at Bush House were not auspicious. The lower ground and basement areas in the south-east wing, where the European News Department and the studios were located, were so overcrowded as to be unsalubrious. Bruce Lockhart, who went down to have a look in July, found working conditions 'terrible'. 'Forty to fifty feet below ground, no air-conditioning, too little space and very indifferent ventilation.'[46] The studios were still in the process of being built, and only three were ready on the day of the move, of which two were no more than tiny cubicles. There was no disc-playing equipment and to provide an emergency power supply the engineers had to make do with a $3\frac{1}{2}$ horse power air-cooled engine.[47] Four studios had originally been envisaged, but with continuous expansion it soon became clear that this would not be sufficient and by the end of the war the number had been increased to fifteen.[48] Working conditions did eventually improve, though not before they had been denounced by Philip Noel Baker in a House of Commons debate as just one more proof that the Government was failing to take the needs of propaganda, 'especially through wireless', sufficiently seriously. It took the direct intervention of PWE with Brendan Bracken to get things moving. PWE itself moved into Bush House in February 1942.

PWE, of course, was to disappear at the end of the war, but the BBC European Service settled in Bush House permanently, and in a strange way the building, with its maze of shabby corridors and overcrowded offices, became the embodiment of its traditions and of its spirit. After the war, as more accommodation became available in various parts of the building, services which had had to be dispersed in a number of other locations both in London and outside were gradually brought together in Bush House, and by 1958 the whole of the broadcasting operation was at last brought under one roof and remains there to this day.

Number 200 Oxford Street was acquired in March 1941 to accommodate the Empire Service and other non-European services, then dispersed for the most part at Wood Norton and Abbey Manor. It, too, had ample space below ground to house studios and technical areas. Some of the studios were so far below street level that the periodic sound of the Central Line trains of the London underground entering the nearby Oxford Street tube station was clearly audible as a distant rumble and was picked up by the studio microphones, to be transmitted to all parts of the globe. The office accommodation was austere. The ceilings were very high and the huge open floor space of the old department store had been broken up into smaller offices and cubicles by brick partitions which, with few exceptions, reached well short of the ceiling. The effect created was that of a series of loose boxes or stables. Noise naturally rose from each cubicle and merged with other noises as it reached the top of the dividing walls. 'Typewriters, telephone bells, telex machines, footsteps reverberating in narrow passages, the sound of secretaries receiving dictation and the murmur of ordinary conversation produced a strange cacophony that at once had the blessed effect of mildly sedating the tenants and offering a perpetual challenge to mental concentration.'[49]

There were to be other direct hits or near misses on buildings occupied by the Overseas Services. Maida Vale was severely damaged in one of the last raids of the Blitz early in May 1941 and a member of the German Service, E.O.G. Lewald, who was on emergency stand-by duty, was killed there that night. Bedford College, in Regents Park, which had also been taken over by the BBC and where the Headquarters of the Overseas Services had their offices for some time, was also hit and partially destroyed at that time though without loss of life. A 'V' bomb exploded outside Bush House in July 1944, causing many casualties.

In the meantime Wood Norton, a relatively safe haven in the heart of the Worcestershire countryside, was gradually being emptied of its international population, and more particularly of the Monitoring Service, which was moved to Caversham Park, near Reading, its present location, in April 1943. The real reason for the decision to move from Wood Norton could not be revealed at the time because of security considerations, but it stemmed from the Government's concern, in the summer of 1941, that London might become untenable through enemy action. The possibility that the development of a German nuclear bomb might be imminent and that such a weapon might be used against London was being treated very seriously. The Monitoring Service had so expanded by that time that insufficient room was now left at Wood Norton for it to be used as an alternative broadcasting centre in case of need. The Monitoring Service therefore had to go elsewhere. In the end, the threat never materialised, but the decision to move, taken without consultation and made known to the staff in August 1941, gave rise to a grave internal crisis. Richard Marriott, who had been in charge of the Monitoring Service since June 1940, and Oliver Whitley, his Chief Monitoring Supervisor

at Wood Norton, both highly dedicated and efficient officials, strongly questioned the wisdom of the move. They did not object to moving out of Wood
Norton in principle, but they held that while Wood Norton was not an ideal
site for a monitoring station, the proposed new location at Caversham Park
was worse from a technical standpoint. Marriott strongly felt that no move
should take place until an alternative had been found which made possible a
very substantial improvement in the quality of reception of foreign stations.
Moreover unresolved anxieties had been caused among the Monitoring staff
at Wood Norton over such practical matters as housing and financial arrangements at Caversham.

Marriott and Whitley were incensed by the insensitive handling of the
situation by Ogilvie, who persisted in taking the view that orders were orders,
particularly in wartime, and that they should be carried out without question,
this despite the serious doubts expressed by his deputy, Cecil Graves, and
representations by J.B. Clark. Matters were not improved when Ogilvie went
down to Wood Norton to address the Monitoring staff. By that time Marriott
and Whitley, who had been joined by John Shankland, the Head of the
Monitoring Service's 'Y' Unit, had decided to resign.[50] Ogilvie refused to
allow them to be present at the staff meeting he came down to address.
However monitors are by profession highly trained in reporting accurately
what they hear, and their account of Ogilvie's address led Marriott and
Whitley to accuse him of having misrepresented their reasons for resigning.
Fired with a burning sense of injustice, Whitley wrote a memo to all the
members of the Board of Governors telling them what he thought of the
Director-General's conduct. He was immediately instructed to hand in his
pass and his bicycle and to leave without working out his notice period. It
was not till later that he discovered that his memo had not been delivered to
its addressees at the time. Lady Violet Bonham Carter and Harold Nicolson
got their copies months later and promptly wrote to Whitley expressing the
hope that he would return to the BBC after the war. Shankland left in
December 1941 and Marriott and Whitley a month later. Marriott joined the
RAF while both Shankland and Whitley joined the Navy. Shankland was later
killed in action.[51]

The incident, coming as it did at a point when doubts about Ogilvie's
ability to hold down his job were becoming increasingly widely shared,
accelerated his downfall.

At this point it is necessary to return to the central theme of the expansion of
the Overseas Services, since the issue of the move of the Monitoring Service
was merely one symptom in a crisis which had been steadily building up.
Its cause was the mounting evidence that the BBC's pre-war administrative
machine was no longer up to the task of dealing with the extraordinary
demands made upon it by the very rapid growth of the overseas broadcasting

operation during the first two years of the war. As has already been seen,[52] by the beginning of 1941 the BBC had more than trebled its output in foreign languages as compared with the position at the outbreak of war. Four networks were now operating and enough transmitters were becoming available to provide simultaneous services at peak listening times in any particular part of the world both in English and in the relevant local language. All transmissions were now divided into fifteen-minute blocks, and the BBC, mainly due to the need to satisfy the exacting requirements of the American Networks, which were rebroadcasting a growing number of BBC programmes, had learned the virtues of very precise timing, largely ignored before the war.[53] This practice had been extended to all networks, and this now made it possible for transmitters to be switched simultaneously from one network to another at agreed transmitter junctions, thus ensuring both the fullest possible use of each transmitter and the best possible signal quality in each area. This system, which is now taken for granted, was pioneered by Tom Chalmers, who was then in charge of Empire Services presentation. Already twenty-three countries were rebroadcasting BBC news bulletins.

The first indication that the Government itself had even more ambitious ideas came in November 1940 when Lindsay Wellington, speaking on behalf of the Ministry of Information, told the BBC of the ministry's 'active desire' to treble the overseas broadcasting effort, more particularly in foreign languages, and asked for a long range programme of development to be prepared.[54] The BBC, he said, was not at this stage to regard the financial and technical implications as limiting factors. The implication was that the political will would be forthcoming and that the money would be found.

For the BBC, struggling as it had been with the consequences of the Government's failure in the past to match its requests with the necessary practical support, this was welcome news. By mid-January a major paper was in draft which Ogilvie sent to Walter Monckton on 16 January 1941. The Ministry was warned that 'the fullest priorities would be required in the matter of cash, men and materials' and that 'a powerful direction would be required from the Cabinet'.[55]

The BBC's detailed proposals fully matched in their scope the spirit of the directive received from the ministry. The 'World Service', as it was now being referred to, including not just the English language services but also those in 'empire languages', would be more than doubled. New languages would be introduced, which would include two Chinese dialects, Tamil, Malay, Singalese, Bengali, Gujerati, Mahrati, Thai, Swahili and Hausa, most of them on a once-a-week basis to start with. The daily output of the Latin-American Service would grow from four to eleven and a half hours. The Near East Service – in Arabic, Turkish and Persian – would expand to six hours a day. But it was in broadcasting in European languages that the most massive expansion was proposed. The French and German Services, the BBC recommended, should become almost continuous throughout the day and night. Broadcasting to Italy should be raised to fourteen hours a day. To meet the technical requirements of the new services, eighteen new high-power short wave transmitters would have to be added to those already in use. There would also be a need for further medium wave and long wave transmitters.[56] The existing staff of approximately 1,800 would increase to 3,500. The additional cost involved in implementing these proposals was estimated at £2,100,000 per annum, and in addition a capital sum of £2,300,000 would be required to meet the cost of new transmitters, studios and office accommodation.

The proposals were agreed by the Ministry of Information and duly submitted to the Treasury, which gave its financial approval on 9 May 1941.[57] So far, in all the circumstances, matters seemed to be proceeding smoothly, and the BBC's engineers were already placing orders for the first batch of new transmitters. However, perhaps not surprisingly given wartime shortages of every kind, the eventual fate of the expansion programme did not live up to this auspicious beginning.

The question of accommodation proved the major stumbling block. The existing buildings available to the BBC simply could not accommodate the increased numbers needed to staff the proposed expanded output. For a time a radical solution was envisaged. A 'broadcasting factory' would have to be built on a 'green fields' site, and a preference was expressed by the Home Defence Executive under Sir Findlater Stewart for a location outside the area of immediate danger in London but within easy reach of the capital. The site eventually chosen was Aldenham House, the present home of Haberdashers Askes School, in Hertfordshire. Six new programme operational buildings would have to be put up there, and a total population of some 6,500 people, if families were included, would have to be provided with living accommodation in the area. As the full implications came to light, it became increasingly obvious that the original estimates were hopelessly inadequate. The capital cost of the total programme had more than doubled on account of the proposed Aldenham development, and by September 1941 the annual increased revenue required had escalated to nearly £4,000,000.

By this stage the whole scheme was in serious trouble. Already in June there were indications that the Government was not going to give the 'triple expansion' project the degree of priority which the BBC thought necessary. To Ogilvie's request for help, Monckton had replied a trifle testily that it was 'useless to expect the Cabinet to give unspecified priorities to an unspecified extent in unspecified commodities'.[58] By September, J.B. Clark was telling his immediate subordinates that 'the priority situation in regard to building of all kinds is in a parlous state'.[59] Moreover the increases in capital and running costs now so greatly exceeded the figures of which preliminary warning had been given to the ministry that there was a serious danger that the future of the plan itself would be jeopardised.

To give the Ministry of Information its due, it fought hard to preserve as much of the BBC's original plan as possible, but it was now confronted with a general government directive ordering a drastic national cut-back in all building programmes due to acute shortages both of manpower and materials. Monckton himself, writing to Ogilvie, reported that he had taken a very strong line in support of the BBC. The transmitter programme was safe, he said, but there would have to be other reductions in the capital programme, though a limited expansion of broadcasting would still be possible.[60] Ogilvie confessed that it was the BBC's feeling that 'under present conditions it would be unrealistic to proceed on the assumption that expansion of this magnitude was a practical proposition'.[61]

He was right. Though it was eventually agreed in December 1941 that the BBC should purchase Aldenham House, the grandiose idea of moving the whole of the Overseas Services there and housing them in purpose-built accommodation was abandoned. The house became the home of the Latin-American Service for ten years. The Near Eastern Service and Empire News were also there for a time before rejoining the bulk of the Overseas Service at 200 Oxford Street.

Though the BBC had undoubtedly made its own contribution to the collapse of the 'Triple Expansion' project in its original form, the Ministry of Information's initial request for proposals was clearly over-optimistic. A paper for the Board of Governors, written in April 1941 at the point at which the board had reverted to its full pre-war membership, commented bitterly that 'outside the Ministry of Information, with which the BBC works in close cooperation, there is still insufficient recognition of broadcasting as a vital part of the national war effort, and there is no ready machinery of government for measuring broadcasting against other national claims and deciding between them'.[62]

The BBC at that time was repeatedly stung into justifying itself against criticisms levelled at its alleged failure, for instance, to provide adequate accommodation for its expanded Overseas Services. Thus the Chairman of the Governors, Sir Alan Powell, writing to Duff Cooper in July after complaints of bad conditions at Bush House, said the BBC could not accept criticisms of its own handling of the matter. It had tried everywhere to obtain secure accommodation which was essential if broadcasting was to continue uninterrupted during air raids. However government departments had themselves occupied much of the available office space in London at a stage when the Overseas Services were much smaller. 'Up to now', he complained, 'the matter has been treated in a piecemeal and makeshift fashion.'[63]

The BBC was equally forthright when it came to responding to criticisms of alleged lack of foresight in planning for the building of new transmitters for the Overseas Services: 'The whole initiative and pressure in the matter of the provision of new stations and transmitters before and since the war', Governors were told by Ashbridge, the Controller (Engineering), 'has been taken by the BBC, and they have been met month after month with delays and adjournments.'[64] Nonetheless Ashbridge was able to point out that even though the Axis powers might now dispose of more short wave transmitters than the BBC, the aggregate power of the BBC's own short wave transmitters was now superior by a substantial amount. It would become even more so when the eighteen new transmitters agreed under the expansion scheme were completed.[65]

The truth was, as Duff Cooper himself admitted to the BBC Governors at his last meeting with them on 17 July 1941, that he had not succeeded in persuading his senior colleagues in the Cabinet – and more specially Churchill himself – of the importance of broadcasting to the war effort.[66] It was a failure of which the Governors were only too well aware.

Despite these vicissitudes substantial increases in broadcasting had been achieved by the end of 1941. The number of languages had been raised from thirty-two to forty, and weekly output hours had increased by about sixty per cent, from 145 to 231. An hour a day had been added to the French Service, and nearly two hours to the German Service. The Latin-American Service had been increased by fifty per cent and the Arabic Service by almost as much. A start had been made with weekly newsletters in Standard Chinese, Cantonese, Bengali, Tamil, Gujerati, Mahrati, Sinhala and Malay. A daily fifteen-minute transmission in Thai had been introduced on 27 April 1941. However, none of the recommended African languages came into use until well after the war, in 1957, at the start of decolonisation in Africa.

Development continued throughout the rest of the war. By the end of 1942 total broadcast hours were double what they had been at the beginning of the year, and the number of languages in which Britain was speaking to the world had risen to forty-five, of which twenty-two were European. At its peak in 1944 the French Service was broadcasting to France for six and a half hours a day, the German Service for over five hours and the Italian Service for over four. The major objectives of 'triple expansion' were therefore never quite achieved. 'Double expansion' would be nearer the mark for most of the larger services like the German, French, Italian and Arabic. But some services, like the Latin-American, the Polish and the Hungarian were in fact broadcasting more than three times as much at the end of the war as they were at the end of 1940. Broadcasting in Japanese started in July 1943, and for a while, there were limited broadcasts in Hokkien, a Chinese dialect widely spoken in South East Asia, in Icelandic, and in Luxemburgish. Special transmissions in French and Dutch for South East Asia made their appearance in 1944, and for a few weeks in April/May 1941 the BBC even ran special transmissions for Switzerland.

Altogether, by the end of the war in Europe, the BBC was broadcasting a grand total of over 850 hours a week in its Overseas Services if the separate programme for British Forces overseas is included. It was speaking to the world in forty-five languages. With Germany's foreign broadcasting system eliminated it had become the largest international broadcasting organisation in the world, a position it was to retain until the early fifties, when the United States and the USSR overtook it and rapidly drew ahead. But that is another story.

7
Voices of Hope and Freedom

As Asa Briggs has written, the history of the French Service in the Second World War is 'the most remarkable of all the stories' of British wartime broadcasting.[1] It has about it a heroic quality which stems partly from the tragic predicament in which France found itself after the collapse of June 1940, and partly from the fact that the service became associated with the whole idea of resistance inside France, with all that this implied in terms of danger, of courage and of suffering. In practical terms it played a key role in the struggle to persuade Frenchmen to turn their backs on the fatalism and despair engendered by defeat and in due course to resume the fight. It provided a message of hope at a time when all was darkness and grew to form an integral part of the history of wartime France. Its real history starts not with the beginning of broadcasting in French in September 1938, nor even with the outbreak of war, but with the collapse of France, the arrival of de Gaulle in London, and the almost simultaneous coming together in the BBC of a small, disparate group of Frenchmen who had made the personal decision not to accept their country's defeat and, through broadcasting, to make their own contribution to its eventual liberation.

There had already been some evidence during the period of the phoney war that the BBC news bulletins were finding a small interested audience. The fact was commented on by the French press, which compared the BBC favourably with Paris Radio. There were the beginnings of cooperation between the BBC and French Radio early in 1940, and the French sent one of their best known commercial broadcasters, Jean Antoine, to London to report on the British war effort. All this came to an end when the Germans broke through to the Channel coast in May 1940 and cable communication with Paris was lost. At this point Antoine's successor, Jean Masson, proposed a new quarter-hour evening programme in French, to be transmitted on BBC wavelengths, to maintain contact between Britain and France. The programme, called 'Ici la France', was given a peak placing at 8.15 pm and inaugurated on 19 June, the day after General de Gaulle's first famous broadcast appeal to the French people, by M. Charles Corbin, the French Ambassador in London. It was later increased to thirty minutes. Masson, who had earlier been instrumental in bringing the Queen to the microphone to broadcast to the women of France, enlisted the help of a number of other Frenchmen, including Yves Morvan, a young Breton journalist working for the Havas news agency, who under the assumed name of Jean Marin was to become one of the best known voices on the BBC's wartime French Service.[2] However the Armistice quickly brought to an end the official French Radio participation in 'Ici la France'. Masson was recalled to France. Both he and Antoine later worked for Vichy Radio. 'Ici la France' lingered on for a short time but it had been overtaken by events and more specifically by the advent of de Gaulle.

During those dark days of June and July 1940 Cecilia Reeves, then Senior Talks Assistant in the French Service, was endeavouring to get together a team of French broadcasters to handle the necessary expansion of the service. Amongst others she consulted Peter Pooley, the creator of 'Radio Newsreel' in the Empire Service, and it was Pooley, who had a wide knowledge of the theatre, who told her about Michel Saint-Denis. Saint-Denis came from a theatrical family and was himself a stage director. He had been a liaison officer with the BEF and was at the time at Weymouth awaiting repatriation to France. He had worked in the theatre in London before the war and had run a training school for actors in Islington. He had heard one of General de Gaulle's broadcasts and found himself in sympathy with the General's call for continued resistance, though not with the General himself: 'I decided that with the British, whom I already knew, I would fight for the liberation of France, but without the Cross of Lorraine.'[3]

Having been demobilised from the French Army he thought of joining the British Army and was in fact offered a British commission, but his talk with Cecilia Reeves at Broadcasting House persuaded him that he could make a more useful contribution through broadcasting and he accepted the task of leading the still non-existent French team. Cecilia Reeves managed to persuade the BBC authorities that he was the right man for the job and, as she recalls, 'He joined us immediately, so that our daily meetings were further enriched, and there was an immediate sympathy between him and Darsie Gillie.'[4]

Gillie himself had been recruited only a short time before by Arthur Barker, whom he had known in Warsaw, and was now editing the French news. Later, when Kirkpatrick reorganised the European Service on a regional basis late in 1941, he became Head of the French Service as a whole. He turned out to have been an inspired choice for what was perhaps the most complex and politically sensitive job in Bush House at the time. As well as being a highly experienced journalist with a profound knowledge of Europe and particularly France, he was a man of deep culture and a classical scholar. As such he commanded great respect with the French staff. Though naturally reserved he had a hidden fund of humour which also endeared him to his team. But above all he was a man of conscience and scruple. 'He would wrestle with himself over difficult decisions of policy, pacing up and down the corridor, body swaying, kicking the partitions as he passed, trying to think things through.'[5] No better person could have been found to lead the unruly, argumentative French staff and to obtain of them a willing acceptance of the fact that while they spoke as Frenchmen they must still perforce abide by rules which were of British making.

Saint-Denis's own strength lay in his talent as an *animateur*. He took to radio as if he had done nothing else all his life. Neither a journalist nor a man with strong political views of his own, he was the one member of the French staff who most clearly appreciated the extent of Pétain's following in France and the reasons for it. He had on the other hand a burning commitment to the liberation of France and a deep concern for, and understanding of his audience. As Tangye Lean wrote at the time, 'With a message to give and enough theatrical experience to invent original ways of giving it, half an hour's propaganda became more exciting in his hands than any other programme I have ever heard. Neither content nor means of presentation gave the listener a chance to switch off. Themes were attacked from all angles, angrily, wittily, musically, in dialogue.'[6]

Saint-Denis made clear from the outset the conditions on which he was prepared to work for the BBC. His team would of course work in every way for an allied victory. But it would genuinely have to be a case of Frenchmen talking to Frenchmen, in their own words and with their own thoughts: 'It must be taken for granted,' he said, 'that you can never put pressure on us to broadcast material to France which is in the British interest if it is not equally in the interest of France.' The principle was agreed, and Saint-Denis acknowledged handsomely after the war that 'this undertaking was strictly observed by the English'.[7]

Gillie himself fully shared Saint-Denis's view of the position of the French team. He realised that there would be bound to be occasions when Saint-Denis and his colleagues should be allowed to speak in their own right, responsibly but nonetheless independently of British official policy. One such occasion was Field Marshal Smuts's controversial speech to the Parliamentary Association of the British Empire in November 1943. In that speech Smuts spoke disparagingly of France's post-war prospects, contrasting the French with the Germans, whose qualities he extolled. Not surprisingly the speech caused great affront in the French Service at Bush House, and much more widely in pro-French circles in London. Saint-Denis urged that it was not enough for de Gaulle's official spokesman to rebut Smuts's views in 'Honneur et Patrie'. If the BBC's own French programme was to carry any credibility with its audience in France it must be seen to react as Frenchmen would expect it to react. The BBC, Saint-Denis argued, must show that it allows its French staff the freedom to speak out as Frenchmen on such a matter. Characteristically Gillie agreed and in fact sharpened what Saint-Denis was proposing to say.[8]

Once recruited Saint-Denis set about forming his team. Before the war he had been accustomed to working with groups of actors, but they were groups with a difference. *La Compagnie des Quinze*, which he directed in the thirties, did not just comprise people who could only act. 'They could sing, draw, design and make costumes and accessories, even improvise scenarios, write, or compose music.' He went about the problem of selecting his staff in the same spirit. His original team of six included Jean Oberlé, a painter who was in London as a war correspondent – 'the last of the *boulevardiers*', as Saint-Denis described him – Jean Marin, who had already started broadcasting commentaries to France; Jacques Brunius, a film scriptwriter who had been working with Cavalcanti and who broadcast as Jacques Borel; Edouard Mesens, a musician brought in by Brunius; Maurice van Moppès, an illustrator who had worked for the French satirical magazine *Crapouillot* and was a friend of Oberlé – it was he who was the author of most of the slogans and ditties which became such a feature of the French Service; Pierre Lefèvre, an actor who had been a pupil of Saint-Denis and became Chief Announcer; and Pierre Bourdan, a journalist who worked for the French news agency in London. By his real name Pierre Maillaud he had been passed on to Cecilia Reeves by the Ministry of Information, and though he had never broadcast before, his first script, analysing the consequences of the armistice terms imposed on France by the Germans, was 'a brilliant five-minute text in cold, clear unemotional language'.[9] With Jean Marin he rapidly became one of the best known commentators on the French Service, a steady, rational voice never seeking to conceal the gravity of events but always pleading convincingly the cause of hope and patience. Saint-Denis himself broadcast as Jacques Duchesne and became commonly known as such.

Duchesne's team would not have been Frenchmen if they had not argued vehemently among themselves from the outset about their objectives. What emerged in the end might seem obvious in retrospect, but as Duchesne put it, 'it provoked violent discussions during the most difficult and therefore most exhilarating period of the war – the winter of 1940-1'.[10] The liberation of France was the first and over-riding aim. On that they were all agreed. That meant doing everything possible to weaken the enemy and to encourage a spirit of resistance and hope among the French population. Opposition to Vichy, which stood for collaboration with the enemy, also went without saying. They rejected the armistice as an act of betrayal and the result of a political *coup d'état*. A first issue which caused much agonising was whether or not Marshal Pétain should be attacked on the air. Bourdan, who was deeply hostile to Pétain – as indeed also to de Gaulle – had done so in his first broadcast commentary. This had aroused unfavourable reactions among the French community in London. It was argued by many who were by no means defeatist or pro-Vichy that Pétain was held in such respect by the majority of Frenchmen at the time that it would be unwise to attack him in person. This became one of the fundamental directives of the French Service, which remained in force throughout the war, though Pétain's policies and his ministers were fair game.

The first fruit of the coming together of Duchesne and his companions was a weekly programme called 'Les Trois Amis'. While working for BBC Foreign Liaison earlier in the war Cecilia Reeves had had much to do with American correspondents in London and had admired the three-point discussions with CBS mounted every week between its correspondents in Berlin, Paris and London. The discussion format, she felt, would suit the French, who were naturally argumentative. With a trio as talented at Duchesne, Bourdan and Oberlé – the *enfant terrible* of the service – there were definite possibilities: 'What we had in mind', Oberlé recalled afterwards,'was three friends chatting together in a relaxed manner. We had to be three to be able both to agree and to argue with each other. Pierre Bourdan would contribute his clear logic and his peremptory tone, softened by friendship; Jacques Duchesne his common sense and his balanced outlook. Then there had to be a fool. I was chosen for that role. A fool or rather someone who doesn't understand, a chap who needs convincing, the eternal man in the street who keeps saying: "That's all very well, but how will it all end?" Naturally at first I protested vigorously but Duchesne talked me into it: "You've got the best part", he used to say. "In the theatre you'd get all the applause." '[11]

Duchesne wanted to be in a position to say things which would 'echo the pessimism with which Frenchmen all too naturally viewed the future at that time'. Instead of repeating *ad nauseam* 'We're going to win the war', the proposed programme format would enable a pessimist, usually Oberlé, to say: 'Things aren't too good, are they. Come on, it's true, we're going to lose, aren't we. Admit it.' The others would then argue cogently that however bad things might look there were good grounds for hope in the long run. The discussion would be dictated straight onto the typewriter by the three men crowded with two secretaries in Duchesne's tiny office at Broadcasting House – 'like the Marx Brothers' box in *A Night at the Opera*'.[12] Afterwards, in Tangye Lean's words, 'It came out with such speed and precision that one imagined an Olympian calm surrounding the mechanics of the performance. But a minute or two before the studio clock hand had reached half past eight, in shirt sleeves at a table, "Les Trois Amis" would still be rehearsing their long conversation. Jacques Duchesne would be arguing heatedly with Jean Oberlé.' Was this the script or a private political argument, one wondered. As the clock hand reached its destination, however, the picture altered. A gesture was enough to make everyone respond exactly. But easily, even gaily – the only strained face now would be Jacques Duchesne's as he prepared to announce: '*Aujourd'hui, quatre cent cinquième jour de la lutte du peuple français pour sa libération!*'[13]

'Les Trois Amis' started on a weekly basis on 18 July 1940. It was joined on 1 September by another weekly programme, 'La petite Académie', which had its origins in the fact that the Germans had occupied the hallowed premises of the French Academy. Intended as light relief and offering the team plenty of opportunities for their very special brand of wit, it took the form of meetings of an imaginary academy whose purpose was to revise the French dictionary in imitation of the proceedings of its real life elder sister, but concentrating on words like 'armistice' whose meaning had been changed by events or twisted by Vichy or German propaganda. Jacques Brunius played the part of the President, Oberlé was the *Rapporteur*, Duchesne the *Archiviste* and Maurice van Moppès the *Secretaire Perpetuel*, accompanied later by the dog Musso, played by Pierre Lefèvre and introduced to enable the team to poke fun at Mussolini.

Both these weekly programmes were grouped, together with others, under the overall title 'Les Français parlent aux Français', making up a daily thirty-minute period which was broadcast each night at peak listening time from 6 September 1940 until 22 October 1944 without interruption. It also included the news commentaries of such as Jean Marin and Pierre Bourdan, contributions by visiting French and other personalities, with songs, ditties and slogans inserted at intervals to lighten the mix and provide variety and entertainment. Derision, expressed in witty, epigrammatic style, became one of the most effective weapons used by 'Les Français parlent aux Français'. It started with Oberlé's slogan, first broadcast on 29 July 1940: '*J'aime mieux voir les anglais chex eux que les allemands chez nous.*' Shortly after, the programme launched a ditty based on a catchy popular tune of the thirties which was used in a jingle advertising a well known brand of tonic. The tune was all the rage just before the war. The words, which were a comment on the German-run Paris radio, caught on immediately, and the tune could be hummed or whistled with impunity:

> Radio Paris ment,
> Radio Paris ment,
> Radio Paris est allemand

Many others – hundreds in fact – followed over the next few years, the product of Van Moppès's prolific imagination, injecting an element of gaiety and high spirits into the nightly programme and prompting laughter at the expense of the Vichy authorities and the German occupying forces at a time when there were few grounds for cheerfulness. The songs and slogans were recorded at weekly sessions at the Maida Vale studios. Francis Chagrin, who also arranged the music, would conduct a scratch orchestra made up of some of the most brilliant musicians in London, and Jean Oberlé and van Moppès would sing or speak the words.[14] It was part of the extraordinary spirit of those days that even at the height of the blitz this small group of Frenchmen whom strange circumstances had brought together in London would meet each week in a former skating rink and there, incongruously, would conjure up wit and laughter of a kind which one would more normally expect to find in small cabarets on the Paris Left Bank.

Letters from French listeners began to reach the BBC towards the end of September 1940, and though the largest numbers tended to come from the unoccupied zone and there was an interruption when the Germans completed their occupation of France in November 1942, they continued to reach London in sufficient numbers to give the programme staff a clear idea of the preoccupations and attitudes of the audience. A weekly programme in which letters were read out and answered on the air, 'Courrier de France', was introduced on 3 January 1941 and was presented by Jacques Brunius. Cecilia Reeves insisted that all questions dealt with in the programme should be genuine, much against Duchesne's original inclination, though he later acknowledged that she had been right. One woman listener wrote to say she had always assumed that the programme was a skilful piece of propaganda until she heard her own letter read out at the microphone. Later the programme also included extracts from the clandestine press.

Thirty-five letters had arrived from France addressed to the BBC by the end of September 1940, of which the first was addressed to Pierre Bourdan: 'If you could only see us listening to your broadcasts', the writer, a woman from Paris, said. 'That's all we live for now. No one believes the news broadcast by "their" radio or published in "their" newspapers. Everyone, I tell you, everyone has only one wish: to be liberated by England and by General de Gaulle.'[15] There is very little evidence that more than a handful of French listeners heard de Gaulle's now famous first broadcast appeal of 18 June 1940. Cecilia Reeves who lived in France for many years after the war, as did Darsie Gillie, whom she later married, states that it was twenty years before either of them met a Frenchman who had. By the end of the year, however, there were growing indications both from letters and from reports from other sources that the BBC's French broadcasts had made a major breakthrough and that the role and activities of General de Gaulle were becoming widely known. Early in 1941 a Breton recently arrived in England reported listening to a broadcast by General de Gaulle in a small restaurant in the presence of German soldiers, and another witness, also from Brittany, reported that ordinary people were listening to the BBC without even bothering to close their doors.[16] In Paris, the correspondent of the Spanish newspaper *Ya* described in a dispatch to his paper in October 1940 how he had heard what he called 'a veritable pandemonium of British radios pouring through balconies, windows and patios',[17] while a Swedish journalist similarly reported that 'One can often hear General de Gaulle's voice through open windows in French houses, and hundred of thousands of French people already know his voice.'[18] These were early days, of course, and penalties for listening to the BBC were to be increased in due course. The Germans, who were curiously tolerant in the early stages, soon began to confiscate radio receivers, and Vichy acknowledged the growing influence of the BBC by banning public listening to foreign stations which indulged in what it called '*une propagande anti-nationale*'. Jamming of the medium wave transmission seems to have been a more effective deterrent than penalties, even though it was never completely successful, to judge by the evidence of massive listening which became available after the liberation. As André Philip, the French socialist politician, told Tangye Lean after he had made good his escape to England, 'The underground resistance movement was built up by the BBC. In the first six months, the first year even, it was everything. You can't imagine how we depended on it. We needed help from outside and the BBC gave that help.'[19] He spoke, of course, for a minority at that stage. The collapse of France had left the majority of French people in a mood of deep despair and disillusionment. 'They lied to us' was an expression which occurred again and again in everyday conversation, and there was deep and understandable scepticism on the part of many about everything that was heard on the radio:

> People listen to London [a correspondent wrote a few months after the armistice]. They don't know who is telling the truth. They wait. They are building up their own individual opinion. We have all been so duped by the papers and by the wireless that we don't believe in anything completely any more.[20]

The truth is that in the weeks that followed the armistice most people in France, wherever their sympathies might have been, shared the view held by Pétain and Weygand that Britain could not survive on its own and would shortly go the same way as France. Duchesne and his colleagues were not helped in their task by the decision of the British on 3 July 1940 to open fire on the French fleet at anchor at Mers el Kebir, in Algeria, which enabled Vichy and German propaganda to play on the latent Anglophobia so prevalent in some sections of French society. However Maurice Schumann, to whom fell the agonising task of voicing French reaction from London, bravely avoided recrimination and charged instead that ultimately it was Vichy which was the guilty party:

> How can you expect such a goverment, defeated because it has accepted defeat, disarmed because it has agreed to surrender its weapons, bound hand and foot by fetters it has forged with its own hands, to envisage for a single moment the possibility of resisting German demands? When Germany orders it to take up a position against England it obeys ... In England the collaborators of Hitler are safe in jail. In France they are in the government.[21]

The dismal failure of the ill-fated Anglo-French expedition to Dakar at the end of September, and with it the dashing of any hopes that the French colonial empire as a whole might opt for de Gaulle, proved another set-back for the broadcasters, but there again they resolutely refused to give way to discouragement. Bourdan instead launched a scathing attack on Governor-General Boisson, whom he accused of having been a systematic defeatist from the start. His decision to resist the Allied landings was not an act of defence against a foreign invasion of French territory, Bourdan said; it played into the hands of German strategy.

Discouraging though such developments may have been their impact appears to have been overridden in the minds of a growing number of French people by an event of much more fundamental importance: the RAF's victory over the Luftwaffe in the Battle of Britain and Hitler's failure to bring Britain to its knees, as he had promised to do. The pessimism of Pétain and Weygand were now shown to have been ill-founded. Conversely de Gaulle's own faith in the future was vindicated. On 17 August Bourdan was able to note, significantly, that, 'In Berlin, the stands from which the German crowds were due to watch the march past of Germany's victorious troops after Britain had made peace have been taken down.' No statement could have been better calculated to put heart into the numbed and despairing spirits of Frenchmen. There were rumours of the spectacular defeat of an actual German attempt at invasion, which a British businessman writing from Lisbon claimed had made 'an enormous impression', and the Swiss newspaper *Neue Züricher Zeitung* commented at the end of November that British propaganda 'would not have been effective had it not been backed up by facts which are obvious to everyone'.[22] By the end of the year BBC intelligence assessments were sufficiently confident to suggest that 'our French broadcasts have already reached a point when they could start a rising in France'.[23]

This was certainly over-optimistic, though de Gaulle's headquarters at Carlton Gardens were themselves sufficiently confident to go ahead, with British official concurrence, with a broadcast appeal by the General calling on all Frenchmen to demonstrate their feelings by remaining indoors between three and four pm on New Year's day 1941. Tangye Lean, writing shortly after, suggested that the success of this first experiment had been slight. Further calls for demonstrations on the Feast of Jeanne d'Arc on 1 May 1941, on 31 October 1941 and on May Day 1942 met with growing success, but it was not until 14 July 1942 that evidence of a massive response from the French public at large was at last forthcoming. General de Gaulle's call for demonstrations in the streets of unoccupied France to mark Bastille Day showed not only how far he had travelled since the dark days of June 1940, but also how radically the temper of a growing proportion of the French population had altered. The response was overwhelming. At the appointed hour hundreds of thousands came out into the streets of cities like Lyons and Marseilles and did as de Gaulle had bidden. In Lyons, where the Vichy police opened fire on the demonstrators, four people were killed, and de Gaulle rubbed home the lesson by issuing a call for the population to file past the graves of the victims at a set time the following Saturday. The call was obeyed.

For the French Service, and more particularly for Jacques Duchesne and his team, those first two years after the fall of France were the most testing. There had been the exhilaration of the Battle of Britain and the revelation, which came to most Frenchmen through the BBC, that Britain was not going to go down. There had been the heroic winter months of the London blitz, which had attracted admiration for British steadfastness – and commiseration too – and contributed to the growing popularity of the BBC's French staff, who were seen as being in the front line and carrying on bravely through the nightly air raids. But a whole series of grave setbacks had followed which, by restoring the myth of German invincibility, had seriously shaken French morale. The rapid conquest of Yugoslavia by the Germans, their no less rapid descent into Greece, the loss of Crete, the British defeats in Libya and the disasters in the Far East had been severe blows to French hopes of early liberation, unrealistic though these may have been. 'What France needs at the moment', said a BBC Intelligence Report in June 1942, 'is not accurate news but good news.'[24] Many Frenchmen, suffering under increasingly severe shortages of every kind, weary, disillusioned and confronted with the growing brutality of German measures of repression, were sorely tempted to give up the struggle. A railwayman writing from the occupied zone gave it as his view that to many people collaboration was beginning to look more attractive: 'What we need is a good British victory against the Boche if French opinion is to be prevented from slipping further down the dangerous slope on which it is already engaged.'[25] Another listener, writing from Normandy, put his finger on the really sore spot: 'Don't keep talking about the Second Front', he wrote. 'Do something about it instead.'[26]

During this period a heavy burden of responsibility was placed on the French Service commentators (the original group was reinforced as more Frenchmen made their perilous way to London) and on 'Les Trois Amis' in their daily task of arguing out with the audience the reasons for hope and the need for patience and fortitude. Today the texts broadcast by such as Jean Marin, Pierre Bourdan, Jacques Duchesne and Darsie Gillie himself, broadcasting as James Darcy, read movingly as remarkably honest and intelligent assessments of the position, never seeking to gloss over defeats, but at the same time never failing to place individual developments, however catastrophic, in a wider perspective and to remind listeners of positive aspects they might have overlooked. All too often in the early days Bourdan, for instance, would feel compelled to start his evening commentary with the words '*Ce soir, les nouvelles sont mauvaises*', but even on such occasions he would bring out reasons for not despairing. Realism of this kind, the frank admission that all was not well, helped powerfully to create confidence in the minds of listeners in the honesty of the broadcasters and were later to pay immense dividends.

Many other Frenchmen as well as foreigners had by then contributed to the programmes of the French Service. There were new arrivals on the staff like Paul Bouchon, Roger Chevrier, Jean-Pierre Granville, Louis Roche, a diplomat, and Jean Vacher-Desvernais, an Inspecteur des Finances, while throughout its wartime existence the service provided a forum for the views of large numbers of distinguished outside contributors. Most of the leading

Free French personalities as well as many resistance figures from France and politicians from Algiers, including Communists like Waldeck Rochet, were heard at the microphone, and there was a steady trickle of British and foreign personalities like the Spanish writer Salvador de Madariaga, the film director Cavalcanti, Emlyn Williams and Micheal MacLiammoir. One valuable addition to the pool of talent was the comedian Pierre Dac, who reached London after spending months in a Vichy prison. A contributor of exceptional value on the economic side was George Boris, who had been the secretary of the French Socialist leader Léon Blum. He held an official position in the Free French organisation and became a brilliant broadcasting analyst of the growing weakness of the German economic position. Another regular contributor, British this time, was William Pickles, who in February 1942 was put in charge of a regular early morning programme for French workers. Behind the scenes the French news was edited under the direction of Dan Sturge Moore by such as Edgar Adams, a former *Times* man with an accent which was a rich mixture of Irish and Burgundian who became an immensely popular sports broadcaster, J.G. Weightman, now one of Britain's foremost French scholars, Vyvyan Holland, Oscar Wilde's son, and Victor Mollo, a brilliant and compulsive bridge player who used to work long spells of night shifts by choice in order to play bridge in the afternoons.[27]

The most memorable single contribution to the French Service, however, was that made by Churchill himself in October 1940. By then Churchill had already become for the French a symbol of the indomitable British will to resist, and his decision to appear himself at the microphone and to speak in his own inimitable brand of French at the height of the London blitz had an electrifying effect. Duchesne was summoned to Downing Street because Churchill was unhappy about the French version of his proposed broadcast. He wanted a more personal touch, and he and Duchesne worked together for several hours to produce a French text with the right Churchillian accents. 'Don't make it sound too correct', he said to Duchesne. They lunched and dined together, and emptied a bottle of brandy in the course of the afternoon. At 8.30 pm they were both in the Whitehall War Room, ready to go ahead with the live broadcast.

Shortly before the broadcast was due to start, the map of the BBC's transmitter network in the master control room, with a coloured light showing for each transmitter, indicated that practically all the transmitters due to radiate the broadcast had been switched off because of enemy air raids. Gibson Parker, then in charge of Presentation, queried with the Chief Engineer whether there was much point in the Prime Minister going ahead. 'Let's see what happens a bit nearer the time' was the reply. Gibson Parker then watched as the red lights on the wall gradually changed to green as transmitter after transmitter opened up all over England in time for the Prime Minister's broadcast, only to return to red alert after it was over.[28]

There are many who still recall the directness and simplicity of Churchill's opening words and the almost roguish tones in which he uttered them in his characteristically Churchillian French: '*Français, prenez garde, c'est moi, Churchill, qui vous parle.*' Many, too, recall his closing words, with their stirring cadences, which left behind them a warm glow of confidence, much needed at the time:

Allons, bonne nuit, dormez bien, rassemblez vos forces pour l'aube, car l'aube viendra. Elle se lèvera, brillante pour les braves, douce pour les fidèles qui auront souffert, glorieuse sur les tombeaux des héros. Vive la France! Et vive aussi le soulèvement des braves gens de tous les pays qui cherchent leur patrimoine perdu et marchent vers les temps meilleurs.

The 'rising of decent folk everywhere' would have been premature at that stage, yet less than a year later mounting evidence of acts of sabotage and armed resistance began to emerge. German officers were being shot in the streets of Paris and provincial cities, and grisly reprisals followed. From that time on the French Service, like other services to occupied countries, became increasingly concerned with the problem of how to stimulate the will to resist while at the same time counselling caution and the avoidance of premature action. Typical of the line followed at that stage was a talk broadcast in September 1941 in which Bourdan made the point that 'insurrections, whether local and general, would not serve the interests of France. A French uprising must be a strategic act which coincides with the decisive allied offensive against Germany.' Speaking to railway workers Pickles took a similar line: 'A derailed train, a blown-up bridge may be magnificent gestures of resistance, but their value as such is seriously diminished if they lead to the loss of French lives.'

The issue was complicated by the fact that early in 1941 a major policy initiative was taken independently by the BBC European Services which was to have wide and controversial repercussions. Towards the end of 1940 a young Belgian wanted by the Germans for his role in the anti-German demonstrations in Brussels on Armistice Day had arrived in London and had told Victor de Laveleye, the BBC's Belgian programme organiser, that some practical way should be found of enabling Belgians to become collectively aware of their pro-Allied feelings. De Laveleye responded by what was to become one of the great propaganda moves of the war, though at the time neither he nor anyone else had any idea of the importance of what he was about to do. In a broadcast on 14 January 1941 intended for French-speaking Belgians, he proposed to his listeners that they should adopt the letter 'V' as a rallying emblem, a symbol of their belief in the ultimate victory of the Allies. They should go out and chalk up 'V' signs wherever they could, on walls, on doors, on the roadway.

The success of the appeal surpassed all expectations. What had been thought of in a purely Belgian context was soon shown to be having its effect

over the border in France, where the BBC's programme in French for Belgium
was clearly audible. Within days letters were received from France which
spoke of multitudes of little Vs appearing on all sides. A listener in Normandy
wrote in February that 'As soon as the Belgians gave their friends the "V" as
a rallying sign I went and chalked "V" on the walls.' He was only one of
many. The same thing happened in Holland after the BBC had broadcast a
similar appeal in its Flemish Service, where it was pointed out that 'V' stood
for *Vrijheid* – freedom.

Newsome and his deputy, Douglas Ritchie, were quick to grasp the possibilities offered by the new symbol. Newsome in any case had always been an
'activist' and a crusader in broadcasting terms and believed that radio could
and should achieve direct results in support of the armed services. Here at
last was a common theme which could be espoused by all the European
Services acting in concert.

On 22 March 1941 'Les Français parlent aux Français' devoted a special
edition of their programme to it, and the results were immediate and spectacular. Two days later an American correspondent in the unoccupied zone
wrote of anti-German inscriptions at Moulins, in central France, on such a
scale that the Germans felt compelled to impose a heavy collective penalty on
the town. There was talk of 'an avalanche of "V"'s', and a letter from
Marseilles on 27 March reported 'not a single space without "V" signs on
walls, pavements and doors'.

More widely, in France, the number of 'silent' demonstrations of opposition and patriotism, prompted by tracts and clandestine newspapers as much
as by broadcasts from London, was on the increase. On 14 July 1941, for
instance, Frenchmen and Frenchwomen used all their ingenuity to appear in
the streets wearing items of clothing and accessories making up the colours of
the tricolor. 'Never had people scrutinised each other with such care,' wrote
the author Jean Guehenno after a stroll through the streets of Paris; 'Everyone
was trying to work out how others had contrived to achieve the desired effect.
In the end this mutual attention produced a feeling of cheerful complicity.'[29]

That was one of the avowed objects of the 'V' campaign. Similar developments were taking place at about the same time in countries as far apart as
Holland and Norway, Czechoslovakia and Yugoslavia, and the omens were
sufficiently favourable to encourage Newsome and Ritchie to go ahead with
a campaign on an altogether grander scale and with objectives which could
no longer be described as psychological but were assuming an increasingly
operational character.

A BBC 'V' Committee was constituted, Ritchie produced a paper entitled
'Broadcasting as a new weapon of war' which was circulated on 4 May 1941.
The new committee first met on 26 May and endorsed Ritchie's proposals.
The aim would be 'to create a frame of mind in which our listeners will feel
themselves part of a great army', and 'to give instructions to this army that

will be good for its morale and bad for the morale of the German garrisons'. There was also a practical objective – to increase Germany's economic difficulties. There was talk of strikes, sabotage and go-slows, of hoarding of rare strategic metals important to the German armaments industry, and Ritchie's paper concluded, bravely and perhaps rashly: 'When the British Government gives the word the BBC will cause riots and demonstrations in every city in Europe.'[30]

Ritchie, as the main instigator of the campaign, began to broadcast regularly in the BBC's English Service to Europe under the pseudonym of 'Colonel Britton'. His broadcasts became the main vehicle for the 'V' campaign, and 'Colonel Britton' became as famous inside Britain as in Europe, though great care was taken not to reveal his true identity to the inquisitive British press. One of the by-products of the 'V' campaign is that it caught the imagination of the British public. Churchill himself adopted the 'V' sign, and a message from him was broadcast on the European Service on 19 July 1941 in which he described the 'V' sign as 'the symbol of the unconquerable will of the people of the occupied territories'.

A few weeks earlier, on 27 June, Ritchie had had the further brilliant idea of translating the 'V' signal into sound. The Morse version of the letter 'V' and the opening bars of Beethoven's Fifth Symphony – Beethoven's 'Victory and Freedom Symphony', as Ritchie described it – were all pressed into service. The following day the 'V' sound on drums was introduced as the station identification of all the BBC's European Services. The idea caught like wildfire and became part of the legend of wartime Europe.

Despite its obvious success, however, the 'V' campaign as such was relatively short lived. The Germans, concerned at the impact it was having, decided that the best way to neutralise it was to take it over. They hung a huge 'V' sign on the Eiffel tower, radio stations in occupied countries adopted the opening bars of Beethoven's Fifth Symphony as their own station identification, newspapers ran articles about it, and Fritzsche, the ace German radio commentator, spoke of 'V for Viktoria' as 'the old German war cry' in a talk to the German home audience. Much confusion was created and ingenious ways had to be found to get round the German countermeasures. These did have some effect, but the Germans never truly succeeded in appropriating the 'V' signal.

The real reason for the demise of the 'V' campaign is to be found elsewhere. Inside the BBC itself it had its opponents. Neither Darsie Gillie nor Hugh Carlton Greene approved of it. The French team, supported by Gillie, strongly opposed an extension of the full campaign to the French Service, though 'V' slogans were injected into the evening programme. Greene, for his part, regarded the campaign as ill-judged and likely to encourage false hopes and the taking of premature action by over-enthusiastic resisters. Others felt that a general campaign directed from the centre could not be as effective as one that took account of the special opportunities for resistance in each country.

More important, there were doubts and misgivings in official circles outside the BBC. Leeper, though not unfavourable, felt that the BBC was straying beyond its proper role. Subversion was not the BBC's business, and SOE feared that the campaign might place some of its own under-cover activities at risk. Eden, who had been consulted by Bruce Lockhart, paid tribute to 'the excellent "V" campaign conducted in the BBC transmissions' but ruled that the BBC should confine itself to 'harmless agitation' and should not encourage 'violent action'.[31]

In the meantime Ritchie's suggestion that 14 July 1941, the French National Day, should be specially marked throughout occupied Europe had run into heavy weather. Other Allied governments in London felt too much emphasis was being placed on France. Ritchie was prevailed upon to change the date to 20 July.[32]

The upshot was that soon after the creation of the Political Warfare Executive a PWE committee was created to bring under overall policy control what had in effect been a piece of BBC private enterprise. This does not appear to have been in itself an indication that either the Foreign Office or SOE wished to bring the campaign to an end. On the contrary the Foreign Office gave its backing to a BBC proposal for a major go-slow campaign which Ritchie would launch over the air and which duly started on 22 August 1941. Workers were encouraged to take practical steps to damage the German war effort. They were to lose their tools, mis-route railway wagons, cause breakdowns and muddles in offices, send letters to wrong addresses and make unnecessary phone calls. Allied leaders including Ernest Bevin took part in the broadcast campaign; the 'Tortoise Dance' from Saint Saens's Carnaval des Animaux was featured in programmes; 15th September was designated as 'Tortoise Day'.

However the fact that Ritchie was no longer able to operate on his own initiative appears to have removed the main thrust behind the campaign. Although it continued throughout the winter of 1941-2 and PWE's own 'V' committee came down firmly in favour of carrying on, Bruce Lockhart had clearly come to the conclusion that it had exhausted its usefulness. The decision to wind it up was taken by him personally on 5 May 1942 against the recommendation of his own staff supported by the Foreign Office and SOE. It was communicated to Ritchie on 8 May.[33]

In the end, successful though the 'V' campaign undoubtedly was in catching the mood of occupied Europe at a particularly difficult stage in the war, it was able to be of little real operational value. In any case the military position of the Allies at that stage did not make it possible for them to exploit its success. In that sense it was premature. In psychological no less than in strategic terms the entry first of the Soviet Union and then of the United States into the war were to have an altogether more fundamental impact.

*   *   *

In France, in any case, the situation was developing along lines of its own. On 22 June 1942 Laval had launched his call for French factory workers to volunteer to go to Germany to work in munitions factories against a promise that French prisoners of war who were agricultural workers would be released in equal numbers. Pierre Bourdan, speaking in the French Service, greeted this development with the comment that this was the first piece of good news for two weeks: 'We hadn't expected such a clear and flagrant admission of Germany's difficulties.'

From then on exposing the truth about what was euphemistically called *la relève* became one of the central themes of the French Service. *'Ne va pas en Allemagne'*, was the constantly repeated injunction, though the French team, acutely conscious as they were that it was not for them, sitting in relative safety in London, to ask their compatriots at home to risk their lives, consistently urged them to be cautious. By 5 October Henri Hauck, the former Labour Attaché at the French Embassy, was telling listeners to the early morning programme for workers that of the 150,000 volunteers called for only 17,000 had so far come forward, so that eventually *la relève* gave way to the notorious STO – *Service du Travail Obligatoire* – which was to do so much to fill the ranks of the *Maquis*. André Philip, de Gaulle's Commissioner for the Interior, dotted the 'i's in a broadcast on 1 March 1943: 'It's not a question of *relève* any more', he said, 'it is deportation pure and simple.' Detailed advice and instructions were broadcast about how to avoid or at least delay being sent to Germany, and at about that time BBC Intelligence Reports were beginning to draw attention to the important role which the working class had started to play in the resistance, particularly since the German invasion of the Soviet Union. Equally significant of the march of events was the fact that the existence of a *Maquis* in the Haute Savoie was mentioned for the first time in a broadcast on 16 March 1943.

The Allied landings in North Africa, following hard on the Eighth Army's victory at El Alamein, caused a great wave of hope and elation across the length and breadth of France. Here at last was the good news which some had almost given up hoping for. Jean Oberlé reflected the mood faithfully in a commentary broadcast on the day following the landings. Addressing himself to those in France who had advocated collaboration as the only sensible course he asked: 'Well, what do you say now? You who for two years kept saying that the British were hopeless and that the Americans would never be ready.' And to his compatriots in France he joyfully announced: 'Dawn has come at last. Allied might is now on the move. From now on nothing can stop it. Rejoice, but be calm, be patient.' It was wise advice.

Though operation 'Torch' ushered in what Churchill himself called 'the end of the beginning', for the French it was also the start of a period of confusion and discord, the first encounter since 1940 between the few who had responded to de Gaulle's appeal and the many more who had not. The

American decision to do a deal with Darlan was greeted by Duchesne's team and indeed by Gillie himself with dismay and disgust, particularly as Darlan was regarded by the London French as one of the evil geniuses of Vichy and was treated with special venom in 'Les Français parlent aux Français'.[34] At first Duchesne and his colleagues were so concerned at the likely impact of the news in France that they pleaded with Gillie to have it kept out of BBC bulletins. Gillie persuaded them that this would be going against all the BBC's principles and would destroy its credibility with its French audience.

The issue led to a crisis in the relations between the BBC and the Free French Headquarters at Carlton Gardens. Though the Foreign Office eventually allowed de Gaulle's statement dissociating himself from the Allied negotiations with the Vichy authorities in Algiers to be read at dictation speed at the microphone by Schumann, permission was withheld for two speeches by de Gaulle on the same subject to be broadcast. As a result de Gaulle's headquarters withdrew from cooperation with the French Service and, with the General's approval, Schumann decided not to avail himself of the two daily five-minute periods allotted to him. He stopped broadcasting on 25 November and did not resume his talks until after the assassination of Darlan on 24 December.[35]

Throughout this difficult period Duchesne and his colleagues, hostile as they were to Darlan and shocked by what had happened in Algiers, sought loyally and anxiously to say nothing that might interfere with the ultimate objective of defeating the Germans. To them this was more important than what Bourdan called contemptuously 'those temporary political arrangements'. Even so Duchesne, for his part, thought it right to make it clear that 'our consciences cannot be freely disposed of. We are happy with what is happening in the military sphere, but we have forgotten nothing. We remain faithful to every word which has been spoken from London, to all the principles which we have defended.' He was thus reminding his listeners that some Frenchmen at least had not waited until the end of 1942 to take up arms. Many had lost their lives because some of those who now found it opportune to join the fight had chosen at first to collaborate with the enemy.

The French Service's policy at that time led to sharp exchanges between Gillie and George Boris, speaking for de Gaulle's Headquarters in London. Boris was well aware that listeners in France made no distinction between the Free French and the BBC French Service. For that reason he found it disturbing that BBC commentaries should not be more outspoken in denouncing Allied collaboration with Darlan. He wanted the freedom to make clear Free French revulsion against Allied policy. There could be no possible cooperation with the BBC so long as that freedom was denied.

The immediate issue was disposed of by the elimination of Darlan, but the whole episode was symptomatic of the major change which was taking place in the nature of France's involvement in what had now become a global conflict. The simple, black-and-white issues of June 1940 were giving way to far more complex problems, of which unity among Frenchmen in the fight against the Germans was uppermost in the minds of Gillie and his French staff, who were aware, for instance, of the irritation caused in France by the rivalry between Giraud and de Gaulle. It was truly the end of the beginning. In France itself resistance, better organised and in close touch with de Gaulle's organisation in London, was stepping up its pressure, fuelled not just by the unmistakable signs that the Germans were now in serious difficulty but also by the growing ferocity of German reprisals and the rising rate of deportation of able-bodied Frenchmen to Germany. France as a whole was being drawn into the sphere of military operations, and Jean Marin was able to conclude a feature marking the Axis debacle in Tunisia on 7 May 1943 by recalling the words spoken by General de Gaulle in his broadcast of 18 June 1940: 'France', he said, 'had lost a battle, but she hadn't lost a war. Now, three years later that war is being won.'

Despite the stimulus of approaching victory the task confronting the French Service during the next twelve months turned out to be no less exacting than it had been during the first two years. For one thing the slowness with which the hopes aroused by the Allied successes in the Mediterranean were being realised had to be explained away, particularly as in France itself conditions were worsening dramatically. In February 1943, with the Allies closing in on Tunisia and the German surrender at Stalingrad, Duchesne could refer joyfully to 'the flood of good news' from the various battlefronts, and in August Bourdan was able to have fun at the expense of German propaganda, which had greeted the capture of Kharkov in 1941 as a major victory but now treated its recapture by the Russians as an event of no importance; but Borel, in *Courrier de France*, was showing his awareness of the darker side of the picture, as the French Service had always sought to do. He quoted a letter from a woman listener which spoke of health conditions as 'deplorable'. 'Doctors are at a complete loss', she wrote, 'faced as they are with patients who seem to be in good health one day and are dead the next. Children, adolescents and workers in factories are increasingly prone to nervous breakdowns, fainting fits, headaches and giddiness.'[36] Two hundred and fifty thousand young people had already been sent to Germany by April 1943, listeners were told, and the number of executions by the Germans was on the increase. One listener wrote: 'We're holding on, but make haste because the coming winter will be hard.'[37]

During this period one of the principal functions of the French Service was to give its audience as full a picture as possible of the growing tide of resistance inside France. Despite the spread of the clandestine press the BBC was still the main source of information about events inside France available to all, so it was from the French Service that in September 1943, for instance, French listeners heard a moving account of the funeral somewhere in France of the nine members of the crew of a Halifax bomber which had been shot down. The ceremony had been delayed because the authorities feared a demonstration.

The next day the funeral cortège set off from the village school. The oak coffins were covered with flowers, that of the aircraft's captain was covered with a large British flag which had been hastily stitched together during the night. Wreaths bore inscriptions such as 'To our liberators', 'To the defenders of liberty in the world' and 'To the heroes who fell for us'. Then came a crowd of at least 2,000 people. Many had come from as far away as twenty-five kilometres by bicycle or even on foot. At the cemetery a choir of young girls sang the Marseillaise and a slow and majestic 'God Save the King'.

At the same time the French Service was being increasingly used as a channel of communication with the French public at large for instructions and advice on operational matters. Counselling caution continued to be the underlying policy. In October, with no prospect of a second front until 1944 Bourdan, who carried great personal authority, was warning members of the resistance impatient for action not to show their hand too soon: 'By all means persevere in your action, which has now become a nightmare to the enemy', he advised, 'but avoid presenting him with an easy target'. There were other, more secure means of passing on operational instructions intended only for those in the know. These were the famous *messages personnels* which appeared with growing frequency in the French Service transmissions from 1941 onward. These were previously agreed coded signals, known only to those who had to act on them, and announcing such things as parachute drops or the arrival of agents, or triggering off military sabotage operations. Their often incongruous wording – the significance of which was not known even to the announcers who read them at the microphone – added a touch of mystery to the programme output. Sentences like *Le lapin a bu un apéritif, Mademoiselle caresse le nez de son chien* or *Jacqueline sait le latin*[38] provided opportunities for endless speculation as well as some amusement for the ordinary listener, while the rapid increase in the volume of traffic of this kind just before 'D' Day was a clear indication that something major was afoot.

Given the ambiguity in French eyes of the position of the BBC's French staff, which had first surfaced during the Darlan episode, it would have been surprising if further tensions had not developed, particularly after de Gaulle's seat of power had been transferred to Algiers. The position was all the more galling to some members of de Gaulle's administration as the transmitters of Algiers radio were not capable of reaching the whole territory of Metropolitan France and BBC transmitters were therefore essential to communication with the French public. Understandably the fact that Duchesne and his colleagues were outside the jurisdiction of the Algiers administration was a powerful irritant to some, who regarded the London team as suspect. Henri Bonnet, de

Gaulle's Commissioner for Information, said as much to Ian Black, a senior member of the French Service on an official visit to Algiers. Black noted the strong prejudice against Duchesne and his colleagues to be found in Algiers at that time. The reasons for it were not hard to find. Few of the BBC team were declared Gaullists. There was even a suggestion in *Combat*, the official Gaullist newspaper in Algiers, that they were in fact acting as British agents. This drew an impassioned rebuttal from Gillie. They had always spoken as allies of Britain, not as 'agents', he wrote to Emmanuel d'Astier, de Gaulle's Commissioner for the Interior. Their status as 'Frenchmen responsible to their consciences as Frenchmen and guardians of the interests of France' had not been tampered with. 'No attempt has been made to put pressure on any of them to say things which they did not wish to say or which they thought it would be wrong to say.'[39]

With the imminence of the second front, however, such disputes were soon set aside. Bonnet sent to London as his representative charged with sorting out the difficulties with the French service a man who had many friends in England and approached his task with tact and understanding. This was Jean-Jacques Mayoux, a former professor of English at Nancy University who sat as a delegate of the home resistance in the Algiers Consultative Assembly. He fully accepted that 'Les Français parlent aux Français' must retain its independence, but with a national uprising in the offing there was clearly a need for close consultation between the BBC and de Gaulle's administration. Agreement was rapidly reached in April 1944 for the regular attendance at French Service policy meetings of Mayoux himself, his deputy André Gillois and a representative of General Koenig, the Commander in Chief of the French Forces of the Interior.

Mayoux explained the new arrangements to the audience in France in a broadcast on 9 May. He spoke feelingly and appreciatively about the BBC and its staff and paid homage to 'the spirit of liberty and sympathetic understanding which our English friends have shown to us'. 'Les Français parlent aux Français' had been the voice of France for four years. Now it was necessary that there should be closer liaison between the BBC's French team, whose independence would be respected, and the Comité Français. Great events were in preparation, and orders from London must be addressed direct to Frenchmen in France. 'When you listen to "Les Français parlent aux Français" you will be hearing responsible voices directly reflecting decisions taken by your Government.' The principal voice was to be that of André Gillois, who had been appointed official spokesman for the French Committee of National Liberation. He was introduced on 12 May as the man who from then on would be giving directives from London. Symbolically, from now on the official spokesman would be heard as part of the programme 'Les Français parlent aux Français' rather than separately as in the past, to reflect more closely the fact that the whole of broadcasting in French from London was now focused on the build-up for the coming battle.

What passed over the air during the next few weeks conveyed a feeling of mounting expectation and excitement. Advice on a multiplicity of subjects was being offered almost daily: to town dwellers about leaving the cities wherever possible, to country dwellers about giving shelter to people from the towns; about not obeying on any account instructions from the Germans or from the hated Vichy Militia to attend at designated places, and about other ways of avoiding mass deportations; about getting to know the state of the country roads and forests in order to be able to be of help to Allied troops; about forming small groups of friends for mutual aid in emergencies, and about digging trenches as protection against air raids. There was much talk, too, of 'national insurrection', though the advisability of such a course was contested by the more sober military minds: most *Maquis*, as was to be tragically demonstrated in the Vercors, were not equipped to stand up to a full scale German attack, and premature uprisings beyond the immediate reach of Allied military assistance were therefore of doubtful wisdom.

Nonetheless to the few who were in the know the flood of *messages personnels* read over the air on the evening of 4 June could mean only one thing, though even then the Germans do not seem to have been unduly alarmed. Over seventy messages were read that evening, lasting a full twenty minutes, far more than usual, and whereas in the past most messages had been unrelated to each other, what was now being transmitted was the full set of instructions for all resistance groups to go into action in accordance with an agreed plan. Though SHAEF itself was sceptical of the effectiveness of a nationwide uprising and aware of the risks involved other considerations appear to have prevailed, in particular the need to avoid giving the Germans any indication about where the blow was to fall and whether the first landings were merely a feint, as Hitler himself continued to believe for some weeks after 'D' Day. In addition it was clearly essential to the success of the Allied invasion that there should be the maximum possible interference with the movement of German troops and supplies, as indeed did take place, though sometimes at considerable cost.[40]

The Normandy landings ushered in not just the beginning of the end of Nazi rule in Europe and the liberation of France but also the final phase of the work of the French Service in wartime. Its role in the struggle first for survival and then for victory was now almost over. On 6 June, as the Allies were consolidating their bridgehead, de Gaulle had arrived at Bush House for what turned out to be his last broadcast from London, to be greeted by Bruce Lockhart, Kirkpatrick, Duchesne and Gillois, as well as a number of American officers, whom he ignored. Oddly enough he had never met Gillois, who was introduced to him by Duchesne as 'your representative with the BBC'.[41] The General had refused to take part in the early morning sequence of 'D' Day broadcasts planned by the Allied Supreme Command, in which he had been intended to come last, after the King of Norway, the Queen of

Holland, the Grand Duchess of Luxemburg, the Prime Minister of Belgium and Eisenhower himself. There was more than protocol involved. He had been incensed by the tenor of Eisenhower's proposed 'D' Day proclamation to the peoples of Europe which, when it came to address the French, made no mention of de Gaulle and the French Committee and merely instructed the existing civil authorities to carry on. Once France had been liberated, Eisenhower proposed, the French would themselves choose their own government. De Gaulle had been told of the wording too late for any changes to be made – the leaflets were already printed – but he had protested vigorously.[42] For him this was tantamount to introducing Allied Military Government in France and he was having none of it. Moreover he found the terms of the proclamation too cautious. So he would broadcast alone, later in the day.[43] As always, he found the lofty resounding words to fit the occasion:

> The supreme battle has started ... It is not just the Battle of France, it is France's own battle ... For the sons of France, wherever and whoever they may be, the simple and sacred duty is to fight the enemy by every available means ... The instructions given by the French Government and by the French military leaders appointed for the purpose must be carried out to the letter.[44]

For listeners to the French Service what followed was not just the story of the Allied victory in Normandy and of the breakthrough to Paris and beyond. It was also the story of how France helped to liberate herself, of the triumphant freeing of city after city, and of the ecstatic welcome given to the liberators, and, in Bayeux and Isigny, to de Gaulle himself when he once more stepped on French soil on 15 June. It was essentially a French story, told by Frenchmen for Frenchmen, and through the words spoken at the microphone from the Bush House studios or recorded in the field by such as Bourdan and Lefevre it is possible to relive the excitement, the jubilation and the relief as the population of France breathlessly followed the progress of its own liberation on the 'English' radio. Even in the darkest days the French Service had never failed to tell its listeners that liberation would come. Now it was happening.

The climax came with the liberation of Paris, prematurely announced in a communiqué from the Conseil National de la Résistance broadcast over an almost inaudible makeshift transmitter inside the capital. After much heart-searching and checks with Carlton Gardens the communiqué was given wider dissemination by the French Service. According to Gillie it was the worst mistake made by the Service throughout the four years of the occupation.[45] There were to be several more days of fighting before Leclerc's First Armoured Division entered Paris and the Germans finally surrendered.

During that final tense period the London team, starved of news of the struggle in the capital, was hanging on to every word broadcast by what Duchesne called *la voix de Paris*, coming over barely audibly – a curious reversal of the roles that had been played over the preceding four years – but on 26 August the service was able to transmit in full a recording of the speech made by General de Gaulle the previous night at the liberated Paris Hotel de Ville, calling for unity and the pursuit of the war to the end. It was the culmination of de Gaulle's personal battle for recognition by the Allies – and by the French people – of the legitimacy of his claim to the leadership of a France restored to independence.

It was also the French Service's final major act in its wartime guise. Soon the team of 'Les Français parlent aux Français' dispersed and returned to France. The programme was broadcast for the last time on 22 October 1944. Its place was briefly taken by a team from the new 'Radiodiffusion Française' in Paris, sent over to broadcast from London over BBC transmitters until the damage to the French transmitter network could be repaired. Duchesne, in his last broadcast, spoke movingly of his gratitude to:

Our English friends who, having welcomed General de Gaulle, the first 'resistant of France' as he is now called, allowed us to speak to you each day. Above all we thank the Englishmen of the BBC, with whom we have been able to work in the saddest and most difficult times – and there were many of those – because they knew not only how to respect our freedom but also how to organise it.

Gillie himself left soon after to return to journalism.

Thereafter there were to be many tributes, both official and from private individuals. Over 4,000 letters were received from France by the BBC in December 1944 alone. All echoed the words used by George Bidault, then Président du Conseil National de la Résistance:

Ici Londres, les Français parlent aux Français. These were the words which in the silence of occupation, when every mouth was gagged, helped the French to surmount and overcome the lies of the enemy. Like a compass to the sailor, the wireless was to them the guide and the assurance which, at the height of the tempest, saved them from despair. It is partly, indeed largely thanks to you, dear familiar voices, that our minds stayed free while our limbs were bound.[46]

8
The BBC against Goebbels

Of all the tasks the BBC undertook during the war broadcasting to Germany was probably the most arduous and, for much of the time, the most unrewarding. There could be no relationship of friendly intimacy with the audience, no easy dialogue, no sharing of hopes and fears based on common interests and common values. There was little reaction in the shape of letters. Few Germans could have been found, at least in the early stages, who hoped for an Allied victory, and for the first two or three years of the war the BBC had little to tell its German listeners which could convince them that in the long run the war would not go Hitler's way. Like the nation as a whole it had to fight a defensive battle. But by consistently giving the German audience an accurate picture of the progress of the war and frankly reporting Britain's disasters as well as her successes it laid the foundations of that credibility which was later to pay such dividends.

That increasing numbers of Germans began to experience doubts about their country's ultimate victory can certainly be attributed in part to the effectiveness of the BBC's German broadcasts and to their growing attraction, in the final years, for an audience which, faced with the evidence, was now compelled to acknowledge that it had been misled. Ultimately, of course, the BBC's efforts would have counted for little had the tide not turned in favour of the Allies. Propaganda could not by itself win the war and was powerless against military defeat. The turning of the tide, on the other hand, led the Nazi leaders into some of their worst propaganda blunders. These were eagerly seized upon by the watchful commentators in London. Ultimately, however, their efforts to undermine the German will to fight were severely inhibited by the Allied policy of treating all Germans as equally guilty and of insisting on unconditional surrender. This made it possible for Goebbels to argue convincingly that Germany would be destroyed if it did not win the war.

Not all historians agree that this materially affected the course of the war. Ernest Bramsted, for instance, takes the view that the failure of the Allies after the First World War to live up to their wartime promises of a 'brave new world' for Germans once they had dethroned the Kaiser and established democracy, made it easy for Goebbels to denounce any Allied promises for the future as just another case of trickery. The argument was all the more effective as the carefully cultivated Nazi legend insisted that it was Allied propaganda which had been responsible for the collapse of the German home front in 1918.[1]

Early debates about the policy to be followed in broadcasting to Germany were much concerned with this issue. A.P. Ryan, for instance, was writing in March 1940 that for propaganda to Germany to be fully effective well-defined peace aims were essential. The BBC could play on a whole range of German fears, but it must be in a position to offer 'something positive'.[2] At about the same time B.E. Nicolls, the BBC's Controller (Programmes), was asking Lindsay Wellington at the Ministry of Information for 'a renewed ruling on the subject of drawing a distinction between the Nazi Government and Party and the German people'. 'There is some evidence', he wrote, 'that the distinction is regarded by the Nazis as a definite joint in their armour.' He went on to observe that there had been a tendency for the distinction which Chamberlain himself had drawn at the beginning of the war to become blurred 'owing to the pressure of the French doctrine,' according to which 'all Germans were tarred with the same brush'.[3] Wellington, however, having consulted his minister, came back with an uncompromising ruling: 'It is no longer possible to maintain this distinction', he wrote, 'the German people must be held responsible for the prolongation of the war so long as they support the present government.' As a rider, however, he added that 'nothing, of course, should be said to suggest that after an Allied victory an unjust peace settlement would be imposed on the German people'.[4]

In broad terms that was to remain British policy until the end of the war. If anything the policy hardened. Lindley Fraser, who became one of the BBC German Service's best-known voices, states in his book *Propaganda*, written after the war:

At the beginning of the war the BBC, reflecting perhaps the general trend of British public opinion, felt not merely that there was no need for bitterness towards Germans as such, but also that by stressing this point it might persuade some of them at least to join in the struggle against the common enemy. Hence the often repeated slogan in the first year of the war: 'Peace with the German people, certainly, peace with the Nazis, never.'[5]

Goebbels himself was well aware of the dangers for the Nazis of such an approach. It was, he wrote, 'an old trick of political warfare to separate a people from its government in order to deprive it of its leadership and make it defenceless'.[6] German propaganda had been adept at it. But the dramatic events of the summer and autumn of 1940 hardened British opinion and this was reflected in the tougher line taken in the commentaries of Fraser and others. The British might not dismiss altogether the existence of 'good Germans', but they regarded them increasingly as little more than 'a few courageous exceptions'.[7] German listeners were told that though it was true that there were differences of opinion in Britain on the subject, and that some people favoured a distinction being made between the Nazis and the German people as a whole, whom they regarded as 'the victims and dupes of the Nazis rather than their partners', the Government did not share this view. Germans in general, as distinct from warmongers and war criminals, 'would be treated with complete fairness after the war'. There would be no mass reprisals against a whole people.[8] But that was as far as it went. There was to be no 'blueprint' for Germany's future. Fraser, speaking on 6 December 1943, immediately after the Tehran Conference, warned: 'We shall smash your war machine, and the longer that takes the greater will be your sufferings and losses.' Once that had been achieved, Fraser added, 'We look forward to the time when you, with all other peoples in the world, may live free lives, untouched by tyranny.'[9] The Russians, for their part, were a good deal more forthcoming than the BBC was allowed to be: 'It would be ridiculous', went a statement issued by Stalin on 23 February 1943, shortly after the surrender of the German Sixth Army at Stalingrad, 'to identify Hitler's clique with the German people and the German state. History shows that Hitlers come and go, but the German people and the German state remain.' As E.K. Bramsted has commented, 'The policy of unconditional surrender and the meagre blueprint offered for a post-Nazi Germany at least made it impossible for the Germans to accuse the British authorities of unkept promises. But they also narrowed the scope of British propaganda.'[10]

As early as March 1940 A.P. Ryan had seen that 'the best target' for the BBC, 'comes from the Nazi effort to impose, both by suppression and distortion, a picture quite inconsistent with reality'.[11] Germans, he felt, knew that they were not being told the truth, therefore the BBC's first function must be to supply accurate news which must not only be true, but must also sound true. If British broadcasting was to get a hearing and win the battle against German home propaganda it must appeal by being quite different. If the British fought the Nazi radio with its own weapons, the German public would say it was a case of six of one and half a dozen of the other. Therefore, Ryan said, there must be no 'ranting'. 'Facts are stated in the British service in a crisp and business-like manner. All experience goes to show that this is the most effective way of making the voice of Britain listened to and trusted by the enemy.' The truth of that statement, Ryan felt, was to be found in the frequent references to enemy and particularly BBC broadcasts made by Hitler and other German leaders in their speeches and by the speed with which the German press and radio reacted to those broadcasts. As to talks, Ryan said, 'they must sound to the Germans as being the sincere expression of an English point of view. The fact that not all English opinion is the same need not be concealed, provided of course nothing anti-war is allowed.'[12]

In February 1940 Electra House issued a general directive to the BBC in the

form of a memorandum on broadcasts in German. This document is important for a number of reasons. In the first place it is an interesting illustration
of the kind of general guidance which the BBC could expect to receive under
wartime conditions. Secondly, although circumstances inevitably dictated
some modifications on specific points as the war progressed, the basis policy
lines it set out remained virtually unchanged throughout the war. 'The BBC's
German broadcasting', the memorandum stated, 'must aim at stimulating
doubt among the confident and at encouraging defeatism and irritation with
the regime in the apathetic. In other words it must operate by sapping, not
by frontal attacks.'[13] The main lines of attack should be that Germany
cannot win, that the Nazi regime is responsible for the war, and that the
German people are responsible for allowing themselves to be ruled by such
a government.

Playing on German fears was to be one of the main techniques to be used
– fear of defeat, of the consequences of a prolonged war, of shortages of food
and other essentials, of air attacks, of heavy casualties, and of the disintegra-
tion of family life. Broadcasts should also seek to stimulate resentment – for
instance against the luxury and privileges enjoyed by 'jacks-in-office', against
profiteering and corruption by party officials, and against preferment or
promotion for political reasons.

The memorandum gave detailed guidance on how to treat Hitler and other
party bosses in programmes. Hitler was still very popular with the mass of
German people, it said, therefore he must not be personally insulted on the
air and there must be no brutal or facetious attacks against him. On the other
hand it should be stressed that he was morally responsible for the war and its
consequences. Doubts should be instilled about his wisdom and about
whether his luck would last. Other leaders, with the exception of Goering –
also thought to have a wide following in Germany – could be treated with
less respect. Germany, it should be stressed at every opportunity, had become
isolated from the civilised community. It was suffering under a regime which
was retrograde, unbalanced and uncivilised, and it had been made to become
untrue to its own best self.

Despite its toughness the directive did suggest that German listeners need
not be left totally without hope. The kind of peace which would be acceptable
to the Allies, it said, would be better for the individual German than the
continuation of the war. It was only in the interest of the Nazis to fight on.
The directive urged that German language broadcasts should reflect 'a vigorous and manly confidence in Allied strength and capacity to win,' and an
outlook that was 'sane, healthy, balanced, civilised and in line with the best
thought of the past'.

The relationship between Electra House – and its successor body, the
Political Warfare Executive – on the one hand and the BBC on the other has
been touched on in an earlier chapter, but it is not without interest to go into

how it was intended that responsibilities should be divided between the two in the particular case of the German Service. Guidelines written by A.P. Ryan in April 1940 make it clear that Electra House would provide political guidance while the BBC was responsible for what was broadcast, invited speakers and dealt with scripts. BBC Liaison Officers, of whom Ryan was the first, were to act as a two-way channel of communication. On the one hand it was their job to keep BBC editorial staff advised of Electra House policy and to convey 'requests' and suggestions to senior BBC officials. On the other hand the BBC remained responsible for the final arrangement of the programmes and for everything connected with the broadcasting operation. It decided on the extent to which it needed to refer to Electra House on doubtful policy points, and there were strict instructions to the Liaison Officers that they were not to refer to Electra House matters within the area of responsibility of the BBC without the express authority of their BBC superiors.

In practice, as was to be expected, matters were a good deal less clear cut than these arrangements suggest. Tallents, the BBC's Overseas Controller, and Salt, the European Director, were themselves resistant to the notion that the BBC should be a mere executant, and there was plenty of room for disagreement on how the guidelines should be interpreted. Though in the early stages the absence of a senior BBC editorial figure in charge of all German output left the BBC in a weak position in its dealings with Electra House, Campbell Stuart complained bitterly of his inability to get his way, and the BBC resolutely stuck to its guns when it came to such issues as the choice of speakers. The matter came up in the case of F.A. Voigt, the former Berlin correspondent of the *Manchester Guardian*, whom Electra House wanted used as a commentator. There were misgivings in the BBC about his general approach, which was felt to be too uncompromising, and in May 1940 the BBC's Overseas Board noted that 'the BBC had the right to turn down scripts or speakers (suggested by Electra House) *from the broadcasting point of view* [author's italics] and that in any case Voigt might be ruled out because of his voice'.[14] Two weeks later it was agreed that Voigt was only to be used 'occasionally, not regularly'.[15] Relations, which were difficult in 1940 and 41, improved as time passed and became close and effective once Hugh Carleton Greene had become Head of the German Service, with R.H.S. Crossman as his counterpart in PWE. Greene gave the widest interpretation to his prerogatives and, as has been seen, was not beyond ignoring directives and acting on his own authority when he thought it right to do so.[16]

In any case he and Crossman were in broad agreement that notwithstanding overall Government policy about the guilt of the German people it was important to encourage what opposition to Hitler there was in Germany and to exploit every opportunity to sow disunity in the ranks of the enemy. So every evidence of dissent was played up, whether it was the sermons of Count Gallen, the Roman Catholic Bishop of Munster, or the activities of the 'White

Rose' group among the Munich students. This policy caused a major row inside the service when a number of the senior British staff, headed by Tangye Lean, objected to Greene's decision, endorsed by Crossman, to try and drive a wedge between the Wehrmacht and the Party following the dismissal of von Brauchitsch by Hitler in December 1941. To them the Army was just as guilty as the Party. Later, when news of the plot against Hitler's life on 20 July 1944 came through, Greene himself wrote the German bulletin story and headed it: 'Civil war has broken out in Germany.' It was the only time, he said, when he had knowingly exaggerated. He did so because he thought there was just a chance that it might encourage others to join in.

From an early stage the boundaries between PWE and the BBC European Service were a good deal less watertight than is sometimes assumed. There were many cases of staff moving from one to the other on secondment. In May 1940, for instance, Valentine Williams, a senior figure at Electra House, who had been contributing to the output of 'Sonderberichte', was temporarily transferred to the BBC to act as Associate Editor of German News. It was at Electra House's urging that the BBC set out to find a regular commentator in German to emulate the success of 'Colonel Stevens' in the Italian Service. The man eventually chosen was Lindley Fraser, who was appointed in February 1940.[17] It was also at Electra House's suggestion that towards the end of 1940 the BBC introduced a regular 'March of Time' programme under the title 'Vormarsch der Freiheit'. This in turn led to the creation of a German programme unit in addition to news and news talks.[18] Later the ideas for two of the German Service's regular wartime series, 'Kurt und Willi' and 'Frau Wernicke', also came from members of the PWE German section. 'Kurt und Willi', a dialogue between a naive secondary school teacher, who believes everything German propaganda tells him, and his cynical friend 'Willi Schimanski', a Propaganda Ministry official, who reveals to him the truth behind the propaganda, was the brainchild of a Scottish poet working for PWE, Norman Cameron. It was written by him and then put into Berlin dialect by a well-known German writer, Bruno Adler, who also worked for PWE. The part of Willi was played by the German actor Peter Illing, who later made a name for himself on the British stage, and Kurt was Kurt Wendhausen, a BBC announcer/translator who had been a well-known actor and film director in pre-Hitler Germany. The producer was Julius Gellner, a member of the BBC's German features unit, who had been director of the German theatre in Prague in the thirties. Bruno Adler also wrote 'Frau Wernicke', a monologue by a typical Berlin housewife in which she harped on the difficulties of daily life, food and other shortages, the endless RAF bombing raids and some of the other less pleasing aspects of a housewife's existence in wartime Berlin. Her part was spoken by Annemarie Haase, who later became a member of Brecht's Berliner Ensemble.[19] Both series were said to be much admired by the German Propaganda Ministry, and Goebbels himself is reported to have commented on the accurate characterisation of Willi as a Ministry of Propaganda official.

There were other programme contributions from PWE staff. R.H.S. Crossman frequently wrote the regular 'Kommentare zur Lage' while head of the PWE German section. This was an anonymous assessment of the war situation, said to come from 'authoritative circles'. Similarly Sefton Delmer, who had started taking turns as a 'Sonderbericht' writer in July 1940, had been brought up in Berlin and spoke German with a broad Berlin accent, continued to broadcast regularly for the BBC German Service even after he had moved to 'The Country' to take charge of Britain's 'black' broadcasting operations. His main contribution was a weekly broadcast showing up the fallacies and misrepresentations contained in the broadcasts of Fritzsche, the ace commentator of the German home radio.

Delmer's first broadcast ever, in any language, took place on 19 July 1940 and is an intriguing illustration of the way British broadcasters exercised their own judgement without troubling to refer to the policy makers even on a matter of major importance. On that day Hitler had made his triumphant Reichstag speech in celebration of the victory of the German armies in the West. It was the occasion he chose for making his 'final peace appeal' to the British. Delmer recalls in his autobiography that within an hour he was on the air with his reply: 'Without a moment's hesitation I turned this peace offer down.' What he proposed to say had the approval of Leonard Miall, Newsome, and Crossman for PWE, but was not referred to anyone else. Delmer addressed himself to Hitler in person:

Herr Hitler, you have on occasion in the past consulted me as to the mood of the British public. So permit me to render your Excellency this little service once again tonight. Let me tell you what we here in Britain think of this appeal of yours to what you are pleased to call our reason and common sense. Herr Führer and Reichskanzler, we hurl it right back at you, right in your evil smelling teeth . . .

William Shirer, the author of The Rise and Fall of the Third Reich, was in Berlin at the time and has described the amazement and disbelief with which Delmer's broadcast was received in official circles in Berlin. 'Can you understand those British fools?' one official exclaimed. 'To turn peace down now? They're crazy!' There was a sequel to Delmer's unauthorised rejection of Hitler's peace offer. He was violently attacked in the House of Commons by Richard Stokes, the Labour MP for Ipswich. Duff Cooper sprang to his defence and asserted that the Cabinet fully approved of what Delmer had said.[20]

The German Service offers a characteristic example of how the foreign services developed after the outbreak of war and of the human and organisational problems involved. In its early days, apart from Leonard Miall's commentators, it was not much more than a group of announcer/translators working in shifts in the 'German room' at Broadcasting House. In administrative terms they came under the authority of Duckworth Barker, the Foreign Language Supervisor, though A.E. Barker, the Overseas News Editor, was also opera-tionally concerned with staffing levels and with the availability of announcers to handle each bulletin. After the first few weeks of the war Duckworth Barker was arguing the case with A.E. Barker for an increase in establishment to fourteen rather than twelve to cope with the proposed expansion of the German Service to ninety minutes a day. Wartime working conditions made the larger number essential, he said: 'Unsatisfactory ventilation in the translating room, caused by many people sitting for several hours at a stretch in a room after the blackout seems likely to impose much greater strain than similar hours in peacetime. The risk of casualties will thereby be increased.'[21] J.B. Clark concurred.

Cramped and stuffy accommodation was not the only problem. The prewar German announcers had by then become highly professional and were jealous of the high standards they had achieved. 'Our heart is in the work. We do not look on it as an ordinary job', they wrote in February 1940 to Duckworth Barker.[22] They were protesting at the additional strain imposed on them by the need to supervise the work of new and inexperienced recruits taken on to handle the increased output. Older members were having to do double duty, checking the work of recent recruits and often having to do it all over again. The task of drawing up rotas, which they undertook themselves – another source of friction – was made more complicated, they argued, by the fact that inexperienced translators could not be left to work shifts on their own. They would have preferred to work longer hours to reduce the need for more staff but were not allowed to do so.

Matters were not improved in May 1940 by news of restrictions to be placed on enemy aliens and the prospect of possible internment. Hostile questions were being asked in Parliament which seemed specifically directed at the BBC German staff, even though practically all of them were political refugees and many were Jewish. A deputation of German announcers told Duckworth Barker they thought of themselves as 'allies in the war against Hitlerism'.[23] They were aggrieved at their peculiar position: they were doing a job of national importance, and at the same time were regarded with suspicion by the British public. The situation worsened with the collapse of the Allied front in France. Duckworth Barker spoke of a 'debacle' having been barely avoided when Boulogne fell to the Wehrmacht. There was grave anxiety among the German staff about their own future safety as refugees from Nazism. Some announcers 'professed themselves unable to work until better news came.'[24] Duckworth Barker was sympathetic and took various steps to help improve their morale, but not all BBC administrators were like him. One personnel officer took the view that 'they will have to put up with it'. For good measure he added that the problem which had arisen was 'a strong argument for employing other nationals, preferably British'. There was a risk of sabotage, he said, as well as opportunities for Fifth Column work in the event of the news getting worse still. 'I would not trust a German an inch anyhow', he added, 'I am sure they would round on us if they thought they would save their own skins by doing so.'[25] Morale was further depressed by the decision made not to allow members of the German staff anywhere near the King and Queen when they paid a visit to the Overseas Services at Broadcasting House on 16 July 1940.

The crisis passed, but some of the underlying causes of tension and resentment were not easy to dispose of. They stemmed from understandable refugee fears and from British attitudes of the time. One obvious cause of bitterness and frustration was the decision made right at the start that German staff, unlike their French colleagues, could not appear at the microphone in their own right – only as voices in features and as newsreaders – and that all commentaries had to be spoken by British voices. The reasons for this ruling were understandable in the circumstances of the time. It was important to protect the BBC against charges that it was a mere *émigré* station run by Jews and to leave German listeners in no doubt that the views they heard on the air genuinely were 'the sincere expression of an English point of view'.[26] Nonetheless a feeling among the German staff that they were being treated as second-class citizens and denied the opportunity to fight their own battle was inevitable. One former member of the German Service likened it to the feelings of Cyrano de Bergerac in the famous scene where, carefully concealed, he finds the words with which Christian woos Roxane.[27] The German Service never enjoyed the freedom and ease which were the main feature of the French Service, and such feelings persisted right to the end of the war, and indeed well beyond. They were however mitigated to some extent by the influence of Hugh Carleton Greene as Head of the Service after 1941. As in the case of Darsie Gillie with the French Service, Greene was held in great respect by the German staff as a highly experienced professional journalist with a detailed knowledge of German affairs and a natural authority which stemmed in part from a certain aloofness.[28]

The bringing together of the whole service under one roof at Bush House in 1941 and the replacement of the old functional structure created by John Salt by a 'regional' structure in which one man, Greene, was responsible for the whole output in German undoubtedly led to an improvement in efficiency. Up to that point the German Features Department created at the end of 1940 had been operating on its own at Bedford College. Headed by Walter Rilla, who had made his name as a film star and director in pre-Hitler Germany, it included Robert Ehrenzweig, who later took the name of Lucas and had been a correspondent of the *Neue Freie Presse*. With Carl Brinitzer, who later became Chief Announcer, Ehrenzweig had been the first member of the German Service to be taken on at the time of Munich; other early members of the unit were Carl Otten, an expressionist poet who had made his name as a film scriptwriter and was the author of the scenario for Pabst's celebrated film *Kameradschaft*; and Martin Esslin, a young Austrian, whose original name was Pereszlenyi who had come over from the Monitoring Service at Wood Norton and had studied at the pre-war Reinhardt Seminar.

The German Features Unit was separated from the rest of the service by more than mere geography. Organisationally it came under Salt as European Service Director and had little if any contact with either News or News Talks at Maida Vale and later at Bush House, which came under Newsome as European News Editor. Coordination was non-existent, as Kirkpatrick noted, and Rilla resisted any attempt to bring his unit's output into line.

It was problems such as this which eventually led Kirkpatrick to carry out his drastic reorganisation of the European Services along regional lines in the autumn of 1941.[29] The German Service was the first to undergo reform. Rilla was replaced almost overnight in September 1941 by Marius Goring, who had found his previous job at Electra House less than stretching and was now placed in charge of all German programme production. Rilla left to join Val Gielgud's Drama Department at Broadcasting House, and Otten, whose over-dramatic style of writing had been under fire, was removed.[30]

Electra House, and in particular Crossman, had long been critical of the standards of the German output, and this view was shared by Greene as German News Editor. An Electra House paper written in June 1941 quoted a 'responsible German critic' with long journalistic experience as saying that 'a year ago I would have given your German Service five marks out of one hundred; now I would give it forty', and it then went on to observe that this was a just estimate: 'Critics have every reason to complain that it falls so far below perfection, but they do not realise by what strenuous efforts it has been raised to even a forty per cent standard of efficiency.' Accommodation was a major problem: 'No responsible journalist', the author of the paper said, 'would undertake to produce even one copy of a daily paper if he was offered the accommodation of our German Service.' There was also an urgent need for the whole service to be housed in adjoining rooms: 'Propaganda can only be good when a genuine team spirit is created and when each section knows constantly what the other is doing.'[31]

Staff shortages were acute in key areas. The paper noted, for instance, that for a daily output of eleven news bulletins the German Editor had only four sub-editors at his disposal. This meant that when the story of Rudolf Hess's flight to Scotland broke, as the German Editor was on leave at the time and had no deputy, the bulletins in the morning and early afternoon were composed by one sub-editor. But the paper went a good deal further. It suggested – and here it was entirely in line with radical proposals which Greene himself was urging on the BBC management – that the process of news sub-editing, language supervision and translation should be merged into one; 'So long as the German staff is merely regarded as a translating unit our propaganda will remain largely a wooden translation of English into German and therefore lack vitality.' News and talks, it urged, should be composed in German, and there should be German sub-editors, with their counterparts on the talks side as well, all, naturally, working under British supervision.[32] The author of the paper accepted that 'at first sight the proposal may appear somewhat revolutionary and may be shunned owing to a fear that it would give too much influence to *émigré* Germans ... But the fact remains that without such cooperation our propaganda cannot become vital.'

With Kirkpatrick now in overall charge and with the full support of Crossman, the changes were duly introduced, though news continued to be drafted in English. Greene observed with satisfaction some weeks later that, 'We don't think anyone in the region would like to go back to the old system. The grouping of all sections of the region together, editorial, talks, translators and features has made working and editorial control very much easier. Sections are able to give one another temporary help and a much better division of labour is now possible without losing contact.'[33]

By this time the German Service was broadcasting four and a half hours a day and the consistent policy of restraint, of sticking to the truth and being frank about defeats was about to begin to pay dividends. With the German armies before Moscow Hitler had felt safe to claim on 3 October 1941 that 'the enemy lies defeated and cannot rise again'. Barely a week later his Press Chief, Otto Dietrich, in a moment of rashness which Goebbels, who earlier had himself been equally if not even more sanguine about the invasion of Russia, never allowed him to forget, announced at a press conference at the Berlin Propaganda Ministry that 'the Soviet Union is finished militarily. The English dream of a war on two fronts has definitely come to an end.'[34] 'On that day', wrote Howard K. Smith, then the CBS Berlin correspondent, in his book *Last train from Berlin*, 'German propaganda destroyed itself as an effective means of moulding opinion, spirit and morale.'[35] From then on Goebbel's propaganda apparatus turned at first imperceptibly but soon with increasing openness to the defensive, even to self-pity. The stress shifted from impending victory to the grimness of the war, the injustice of history to Germany, the absurdity of speculating on the date of victory and the need for an all-out effort on the part of the German people if the war was to be won.

Such developments were precisely what Ryan had had in mind when he had advised early in 1940 that the German Service should exploit to the full the openings offered by the exaggerated claims and the inconsistencies of German propaganda. His advice had been closely followed. Hitler's assertion after the fall of France that Britain's turn would come next was contrasted with the RAF's defensive victory over the Luftwaffe in the Battle of Britain, the deferring *sine die* of Operation Sea Lion and the failure of the Luftwaffe to bring London to its knees. The opportunities for undermining popular confidence in the claims of Nazi leaders increased as the war progressed and the Allied military potential became clear. Sefton Delmer's weekly 'Answer to Fritzsche' was one of the ways in which this sapping process was carried forward. But in no programme was it more systematically and effectively undertaken than in a regular series entitled 'Hitler answers Hitler'.

Even before the war the BBC had been quietly collecting recordings of Hitler's speeches, and the device of pointing to Hitler's broken undertakings by using conflicting extracts from his speeches had already been used once by Maurice Latey and David Graham at the outbreak of war. Martin Esslin, who found on being recruited to the German Features unit at Bedford College in January 1941 that he had very little to do, filled in the time by browsing through the library of recordings at Broadcasting House, where he happened on the collection of Hitler's speeches. He then proposed a regular programme on Hitler's broken promises in which by the appropriate juxtaposition of suitable extracts Hitler could be made to contradict himself through his own words.[36] This was particularly effective during 1941, when Hitler's promise, made at the end of 1940, that 'the year 1941 will bring the completion of the greatest victory of our history' was recalled daily on the air. German listeners were told each day that this was the 'n'th day of the year in which Hitler promised them final victory. He now only had so many days left. This technique of contrasting promise and performance was used to increasing effect as the war progressed. Thus two speeches made by Hitler at an interval of a year – the first to a huge, cheering crowd in the Berlin Sportspalast in September 1942 and the second, for the first time without a live audience, from his Headquarters in East Prussia in September 1943 – were set side by side by Martin Esslin on 30 September 1943. In the Sportspalast speech Hitler could still speak with the appearance of confidence of his strategy to bring Soviet resistance to an end: first deprive the Russians of their last great wheat-growing region, then lay hands on their last reserve of coal, and finally deny them their last source of oil. The prospect was no longer one of easy success, as it had been in earlier years, but through the sheer impact of his personal magnetism Hitler could still carry credibility with the crowds. A year later he spoke woodenly and without inflexion for only fifteen minutes without a crowd's response to lend drama to the occasion, and Russia was hardly mentioned. Esslin's script was able to pose the question 'Where has it gone, the spirit of last year? Where are the ambitious plans that only a year ago Hitler announced to the German people for this year of 1943?'[37]

The question must have been deeply disturbing to German listeners. At that juncture the German Sixth Army had long ago surrendered at Stalingrad, the Russians had recaptured Kharkov and Smolensk and were pressing forward in the Ukraine, the RAF had dropped 14,000 tons of bombs over Germany in that month alone, the remnants of the Axis armies in North Africa were in Allied prisoner of war camps and Italy was out of the war. In the occupied countries, resistance to German occupation was increasing, and the German Service was dwelling at length on the impact which American industrial production was having on the balance of military power.

Other programme formats were devised to bring home to the German audience the bankruptcy of their home propaganda. Goebbels might by now be saying in his *Thirty Articles of War*, published in millions of copies on 26 September 1943, that capitulation or bowing to the force of the enemy was inconceivable and that the German people must make a supreme effort to hold on, but what this meant for those at the front was convincingly driven home in a weekly series called 'The Letters of Corporal Hirnschal', a character modelled on Jaroslav Hasek's famous *Good Soldier Schwejk*. Brilliantly scripted by Robert Ehrenzweig, the series took the form of letters from Hirnschal written from the Eastern front to his beloved wife Amalia. Hirnschal was portrayed as robust and down to earth, 'half-naive, half-shrewd', with the native cunning of the born survivor, coping with the hardships and dangers of the war in Russia, which, as he described them, offered a sharp contrast to the bombastic claims and heroic posturings of official propaganda. With sly irony and using rich army slang he would poke bitter fun at the *Etappenschweine* (literally: base pigs) and Party parasites (*Parteibonzen*) who safely led privileged lives while their less fortunate compatriots were facing the rigours of life on the Russian front, a theme likely to find receptive ears among German listeners, with whom high Party functionaries were by now becoming increasingly unpopular.[38]

Monitoring of German internal broadcasts naturally provided an essential service to writers and commentators who needed to be constantly abreast of the twists and turns of German propaganda on the home front. Indeed by 1943 the Monitoring Service was playing a pivotal role in the war of words as a source both of news and intelligence, and its material, now exceeding a daily 100,000 words, was widely distributed among Whitehall Ministries, in the armed services and in PWE. The reading of German and neutral newspapers, of captured documents and of private letters from Germany to correspondents abroad intercepted on board neutral ships also helped to provide PWE and BBC Intelligence analysts with a picture of conditions in Germany and of the mood of the German public.

One particular development in the field of monitoring provided the German Service with an unexpected weapon which it soon put to good use. During his time as a monitor at Wood Norton Martin Esslin, on account of his command of a number of European languages, had been made a 'roving' monitor; that is to say his job was to range across the broadcasting bands – and beyond – in search of new developments rather than listening to a particular station. It was while he was searching frequencies beyond the limits of those normally used for broadcasting purposes in the summer of 1940 that he came across a German transmission at dictation-speed which on closer examination turned out to be the next day's German communiqué, which was being sent out in advance, suitably embargoed, to German-controlled newspapers and radio stations in occupied countries. Later the dictation speed transmissions were replaced by *Hellschreiber* transmissions – intended to be received by teleprinters operated by means of radio signals – on the same frequency. The Monitoring Service engineers succeeded in unscrambling the signal and with the aid of a single *Hellschreiber* machine which they had been able to procure they were now in a position to provide the startled and delighted monitors – and the German Service – with the embargoed advance texts of speeches to be given by Nazi leaders, communiqués, editorial guidance and, in due course, Goebbel's weekly articles in *Das Reich*. The latter was the greatest prize of all. It enabled the German Service to analyse and criticise the contents in advance of publication, much to the annoyance and puzzlement of Goebbels, who became convinced that a spy was at work in the Propaganda Ministry and never suspected the truth.[39]

Many other programmes addressed themselves to specialised audiences. The early morning programme for German workers has already been mentioned. There was also a programme for women, of which 'Frau Wernicke's' monologues were a part. Regular programmes were introduced at the end of 1941 and the beginning of 1942 for the German Army, Navy and Air Force. There were special programmes for Protestants, for Catholics, for peasants and for Civil Servants. But perhaps of most importance in terms of their effect on the German audience and its morale were the messages broadcast by German prisoners of war in British hands to their families in Germany.

It had been the German Service's practice from an early stage to read out the names of prisoners on the air since this provided a strong incentive for anxious relatives to tune in regularly. Messages from selected prisoners were also included, but from 1943 onwards, with hundreds of thousands of German prisoners in British camps, a nightly period of fifteen minutes was set aside for messages recorded by prisoners for their families. Evidence of the impact of these messages came in part from the letters which the families of prisoners wrote back after the broadcast. Many wrote to say that they had not heard the broadcast themselves but had been told about it by friends. Some asked whether the news was true. Gramophone requests were also played. In one case news was broadcast that a particular officer was safe and well. His relatives, who did not hear it, received ten anonymous letters telling them the good news, and there were phone calls from well-wishers from public call boxes. Some on the other hand were either brave or rash enough to sign their letters in spite of the grave penalties inflicted on anyone found guilty of listening to foreign stations.[40]

One story illustrates graphically the dilemma faced by those – and they were increasingly numerous – who braved the dangers involved in listening to the BBC. The family of one German soldier had been informed that he had been killed in action and had arranged for a Requiem Mass to be said in his memory. However shortly before the mass was due to be celebrated they heard over the BBC that he was alive. Their first reaction was to cancel the mass. But that would have meant admitting to having listened. They therefore went to the church at the appointed time. They found no one there.[41]

There is an ironical footnote to the story of these prisoner of war broadcasts. As Martin Esslin has put it the German Service served as a university for post-war German broadcasters, but not always with welcome results. A whole group of prisoners who had been trained by the BBC turned out to hold very left-wing views and after a brief spell with Hamburg Radio crossed over into East Germany. One of them, Kurt von Schnitzler, later became the leading commentator on East German television.[42] Many of the German Service's own staff had successful post-war careers. Herbert Lom, a wartime announcer, became a famous film actor. Heinrich Fischer, who had been the *Dramaturg* of the Schiffbauerdam Theatre in Berlin in the late twenties when Brecht was working with Kurt Weill on the *Threepenny Opera* and had then emigrated to Prague where he worked at the German theatre there with Julius Gellner, later became a popular figure on German television. Eberhart Schütz became Intendant of Hamburg Radio, Marius Goring became a distinguished radio actor, and Martin Esslin had a long and distinguished tenure as Head of the BBC Radio Drama Department, became a world authority on the contemporary theatre and is Professor of Drama at Stanford University, California. Hugh Carlton Greene, of course, became Director-General of the BBC in the sixties.

This list would not be complete without a mention of Thomas Mann, who after March 1941 contributed monthly talks for the German Service, recorded first from New York and later from Los Angeles. His first talk, delivered in his strong Lübeck accent, told German listeners what they could expect of him:

Deutsche Hörer! [he said, using words which were later to serve as the title of the published collection of his broadcasts] What I have to tell you from a distance has been spoken to you by other mouths. This time listen to my voice. It is the voice of a friend, a German voice, the voice of a Germany which has shown and will again show the world a face different from the frightful Medusa mask which Hitlerism has imposed. It is a warning voice. To warn you is the only service that a German like myself can now do for you.[43]

He spoke with the authentic voice of German humanism, 'with an historical authority unequalled by anyone except Winston Churchill',[44] denouncing the Nazi leaders as 'evil men, evil in the final and deepest sense of the word', reminding his listeners that 'the weapons for the enslavement of the world are the work of your hands and that Hitler and his war cannot continue without your help. Stay your hand and help no more. For the future it will be of enormous importance whether you Germans yourselves put away this man of terror or whether it has to be done from outside.' 'Germany, awake', he cried in one broadcast. 'Awake to reality, to sound reason, to yourself and the world of freedom and justice awaiting you.' Tangye Lean wrote at the time that these intensely polemical talks were 'among the finest which

European writers have produced. Mann invites comparison with Victor Hugo in exile in the Channel Islands where he wrote *Les Châtiments* in denunciation of Louis Napoleon and the disasters he brought on the French.'[45]

The warnings were without effect, for reasons which it is not the purpose of this book to analyse. Those Germans who heard them did so through heavy jamming and at increasing risk to themselves. Listening to foreign stations was banned from the day war broke out, and the severity of sentences for infringing the ban rose steadily during the first two years of the war. The view taken by the Nazi authorities of those they called 'radio criminals' was well expressed in an article in the *National Zeitung*. 'Listening to foreign stations', it said, 'lowers their [the listeners'] powers of resistance and brings about a spiritual self-mutilation no less criminal than self-mutilation by an army conscript.'[46]

Sentences were for periods of years not of ordinary imprisonment but of the harsher penal servitude. Those found guilty also lost their civil rights. Passing on what one had heard to others compounded the offence, and there were some executions. The German press and radio gave a great deal of publicity to such sentences as a warning to others. There was thus a strong disincentive to listening.

Though there was no real technical answer to jamming, every effort was made to improve the intelligibility of what came out of the studios at Bush House. Greene went to Stockholm in September 1941 to listen to the German Service under conditions not dissimilar to the ones which prevailed in Germany itself. He found that despite the severity of the jamming it was possible, though under considerable strain, to make out what was being said. He was even able to hear one of the German Service speakers addressing him personally in the middle of a dramatised programme on the sinking of a U-boat and asking: 'Are you listening to us, Hugh?' As a result of his systematic listening over a period of time a number of measures were taken: the pace of news reading was slowed down and the use of two alternating news readers was introduced; deeper voices were preferred and production techniques were simplified; in particular, elaborate dramatised documentaries were eliminated.

That listening went on in spite of jamming is certain, and there was much circumstantial evidence to prove it, though for obvious reasons less than in the case of France. The German Ministry of Propaganda's own estimate of listeners to the BBC at the end of 1940 is said to have been about one million.[47] Neutral visitors spoke of more – one to three million listening regularly – though Germans understandably kept quiet about their listening habits. On the other hand Germany was one of the countries in Western Europe with the largest number of radio sets and the Nazi authorities went on encouraging Germans to acquire receivers long after the beginning of the war. There were 16.2 million licences in 1942 in Germany, Austria and Czechoslovakia. There is little doubt that listening began to increase substantially from the moment in the autumn of 1941 when it became clear to Germans that the dramatic announcements of ever more resounding victories, preceded by fanfares of trumpets, concealed a disquieting change in the character of the war. By 1944, with the Russians pressing towards the borders of the Reich and the Western Allies streaming through France, the appetite for accurate news must have overcome the fears of increasing numbers of Germans. Lindley Fraser himself estimated the German Service's audience at that time at between ten and fifteen million daily.[48] As the Allied armies entered Germany the service was used extensively for the broadcasting of instructions to the civilian population by the Supreme Allied Commander, and those instructions were clearly heard and obeyed. Large numbers of Germans encountered when Germany finally collapsed claimed to have been regular listeners, and such commentators as Greene and Fraser discovered the extent to which they had become household names. The words of a song which was popular in Berlin cabarets immediately after the war were there to prove it:

> Dear Lindley Fraser,
> Dear Carleton Greene,
> We've often you heard
> But never you seen.

The best evidence came from the Nazi authorities themselves. The German press gave great prominence to the increasing numbers of sentences passed against 'radio criminals' after 1941. Berlin Staats Sekretär Freisler even suggested at the end of September 1941 that the public should be told that instruments existed which could detect radio sets tuned to London or Moscow. No such instruments existed and the BBC reassured its listeners that this was so.[49] Above all there was the dramatic change in the tone of German propaganda and the increasing care and precision with which it sought to deny point by point the truth of news items broadcast by the BBC. German papers openly admitted that listening was taking place. The *Flensburger Nachrichten*, for instance, commented disapprovingly in 1941 that 'some Party members are still seduced to listen to foreign broadcasts and spread them further',[50] while in September 1942 the *Danziger Vorposten* was warning that British broadcasts influenced 'even the strongest characters'.[51] In June 1942 Goering himself told Germans: 'Don't always believe what you are told. Let us refuse to accept all enemy propaganda.'[52]

Ultimately, even if the German Service was denied the role which the BBC had been able to play in France, its overwhelming victory was indisputable. Its strength lay in the respect it gained among Germans for the accuracy of its news and in what Heinrich Wiedermann called 'the sincere voices, the calmness of the speakers, the straightforward matter-of-fact tone of the commentaries, which made such an enormous contrast to the hectic shouting and the neurotic heroism of the Nazi broadcasts'.[53] Thus in January 1942 Lindley

Fraser, commenting on the disastrous course of events in the Far East and the possible fall of Singapore, admitted that, 'Many of us in Great Britain are not satisfied about the way in which our strategy in the Far East has been conducted.' Fraser indicated that a debate on the subject was due to take place shortly in the House of Commons. 'It may well be', he said, 'that by the end of the debate they [the MPs] will prove to have influenced the Government's policy, perhaps even its structure.'[54] A German prisoner of war who heard this broadcast said to himself: 'If they can admit a catastrophe so openly, they must be terribly strong.'[55] Equally important in the long run, however, was the fact that the German Service's victory over Goebbels's propaganda machine and the BBC's unchallenged reputation in Germany, painfully and patiently built up throughout the war years, enabled it to continue to exert a beneficient influence after the war and in particular to provide the blueprint for the postwar reorganisation of German broadcasting and the example which inspired a whole generation of German broadcasters.

9
Crusade in Europe

Even if the French and German Services inevitably occupy a dominant position in the history of BBC wartime broadcasting to Europe, the role of the other foreign language services forms an important element in the whole story. Everywhere in Europe broadcasts from London became the chief and sometimes the only source of reliable information on what mattered most to listeners – the progress of the war – as well as providing what so many called 'the light in the darkness', the voice that offered hope and encouraged resistance.

But just as the story of the German Service is entirely different from that of the French Service, so each of the other services to Europe assumed its own very special character, coloured by the politics, the culture and the national traits of the country concerned, by the extent of armed resistance to the Germans, the nature of the political groupings directing it, as well as by the overall requirements of British wartime policies. Not the least of the factors making for difference was the personality and outlook of the individual service editors, for this was not a mechanical operation regulated from above but one in which the interplay of people, ideas and attitudes counted for much. Many of these editors, like Shiela Grant Duff, Gregory Macdonald and Hubert Harrison, had served as newspaper or agency correspondents in the countries concerned before the war and acquired in the process not just knowledge but often also deep personal commitment. In any case they were rarely of the stuff that complaint officials are made of.

The extent to which BBC broadcasts were able to reach the mass of the population varied greatly from country to country. Holland, Belgium and even Czechoslovakia had a far higher density of radio set ownership than, for instance, Bulgaria, Greece or even Italy. In 1938 there were slightly more receivers in Czechoslovakia – just over one million – than in Italy, even though Italy's population was more than three times as large. In Yugoslavia there were about 100,000 sets, and in Greece only 23,000. In Poland the Germans made the possession of sets illegal – as it was for Jews throughout most of occupied Europe. Many Poles did not surrender their sets and kept them concealed; some listened on sets belonging to Germans billeted in their homes while their owners were out, and Polish radio mechanics employed on repairing and installing sets for the Germans took advantage of the opportunity to listen to the BBC.[1] Much news circulated by word of mouth, but more than anywhere else in occupied Europe the clandestine press became the main means of dissemination of BBC news. The number of direct listeners to the BBC Polish broadcasts was regarded in London as being very small, and those who did listen did so at great risk to themselves. According to the Polish authorities in London, thirty Poles were shot for listening to the BBC in September 1940, forty-five in January 1941 and thirty-six in April.[2]

In other countries such as Greece and Yugoslavia, for instance, though radio sets were not confiscated, those capable of receiving short wave broadcasts were required to be brought in to have the short wave facility blocked out. In Greece, too, one of the countries to suffer most grievously from Axis depredations and where there were grave shortages of fuel as well as of food and other necessities, prolonged electricity cuts were a major obstacle to radio listening since there were very few battery sets. Listening to the BBC was, of course, banned and severely punished in all occupied countries. In these circumstances it is all the more remarkable that BBC broadcasts should have had such a wide resonance and have achieved such a deep penetration.

On the part of exiled governments in London as well as some neutral governments there was acute sensitivity throughout the war to what was said on the air from London in the languages of their countries. Repeated attempts were made to influence the character of the programme output, the selection of staff and speakers, and the line to be taken on particular issues. That sensitivity inevitably extended to the Foreign Office, which was concerned with the resulting diplomatic complications, and even to the Prime Minister himself. Thus in 1944 Churchill personally issued a secret instruction that there was to be no mention on the air of EAM and ELLAS, the two Greek guerilla organisations opposed to the return of the King, without reference to him. J. B. Clark, a wise head, did not distribute the PWE circular to its twenty BBC addressees but gave instructions instead that there should be reference to himself. Not everyone concerned took the same precaution and the Prime Minister's personal involvement leaked out and caused considerable embarrassment to the Government in the House of Commons, where it was used by Aneurin Bevan as part of an attack on the Government's Greek policy.[3]

In Spain there were frequent conflicts between the British Ambassador in Madrid, Lord Templewood (the former Sir Samuel Hoare), whose main concern was to keep on good terms with Franco, and the BBC Spanish Service, which, while it was anxious to act in the national interest, was also concerned with its own credibility. Thus in 1944 Lord Templewood complained that the BBC was giving excessive prominence to the activities of exiled Spanish Republican leaders. In the view of the Foreign Office these leaders were for the most part discredited, and Spaniards were not much interested in them.[4]

C.H. Guyatt, the BBC's Spanish Editor, contested that view. There was substantial and well-documented evidence, supplied by the Madrid Embassy itself, to prove that many Spaniards, even among those holding moderately conservative views, took a genuine interest in the activities of the country's former leaders and in its political future. According to that evidence there was a large body of opinion which did not support Franco unconditionally and looked to the BBC to stand up for democratic values. Moreover American broadcasts to Spain were giving substantial coverage to what the Republican leaders were saying and doing. 'If we select or omit news on political grounds rather than on news value there is a real danger of our losing the reputation we have for reliability, impartiality and objectivity.'[5] Kirkpatrick himself had made a similar point at an earlier stage in connection with the Portuguese Service: 'Our credit would vanish if people found out that we suppressed world news to please Salazar or for the purposes of propaganda.'[6]

So far as Spain was concerned, of course, the BBC was in an awkward position, caught, as it was, between two fires. In 1941 there had been strong criticism of the Spanish Service from a different quarter: a serving member of the Monitoring Service, Ilse Barea, the wife of the Spanish Republican writer Arturo Barea, had claimed that those in charge were crypto-fascists.[7] Barea himself wrote to the *New Statesman* and the issue was also picked up by Hannen Swaffer in the *Daily Herald*.[8]

In practice 'La Voz de Londres', as the BBC's Spanish transmission was known, had an almost impossible course to steer. In Antonio Torres – by his real name R.M. Nadal – it had a brilliant commentator whose regular Sunday evening talks, vigorous, frank and pungent, had a wide following in Spain, where regular listeners referred to themselves as *bebeceros*.* So also did 'Answers to correspondents', a programme based on listeners' letters presented by Jorge Marin. Nadal's talks might not attack Franco in person nor directly criticise the Spanish regime, but they regularly took issue with the more outrageous utterances of the official Spanish press and radio, ridiculed Italian fascism and painted a picture of Hitler as 'the enemy of the European and Catholic belief in the supreme value of the individual'.[9] As Harman Grisewood pointed out, encouraging Spaniards to take a more favourable view of the Allied cause – one of the objectives of British policy – was not wholly consistent with the Foreign Office's overriding objective of keeping Spain quiet. Spain, Grisewood argued, would not be kept quiet 'by leaving matters alone, because Spain is obviously in a state of disquiet'.[10] Kirkpatrick himself pointed to another inconsistency, involved this time in the Madrid Embassy's request that the German influence on the Falange should be underlined, but that the Falange should not be directly attacked. 'Saying that there is German influence', Kirkpatrick argued, 'amounts to direct attack.'[11] Small wonder that the Spanish output was cautious in expression and conservative in tone![12]

* 'BBC people'.

Nadal had to be taken off his regular Sunday night spot for four months in December 1943 at Templewood's insistence and later refused to continue after one of his scripts had been heavily censored. There were frequent allegations, stemming from Madrid, that far from being crypto-fascists, as Ilse Barea had alleged, the Spanish staff were communists in disguise. This was hotly denied by Duckworth Barker: 'We do not employ Reds', he wrote. 'Just as many Germans assume that a native German speaker from London must certainly be a Jew, so many Spaniards regard our Spanish Service as being run by some of the least desirable émigré elements who made good their escape after the civil war.'[13] In fact three out of the four most frequent announcers were British and two of them had English names. Nonetheless in April 1942 all the Spanish staff were required to sign an undertaking that they would refrain from participation in Spanish refugee politics in Britain. Reasoning of a similar sort lay behind the ruling that Salvador de Madariaga, the distinguished exiled Spanish writer, must not broadcast direct to Spain on political matters. Madariaga broadcast regularly in Spanish to Latin-America, and his talks were repeated in the Spanish Service but with an announcement that they were 'specially written for the Latin-American Service'.[14]

At the opposite end of the spectrum the Greek and Yugoslav Services were equally beset with difficulties, though of a different kind. Both had to contend with governments in exile with which relations became at times acrimonious. In the case of Greece the auguries for harmonious relations had seemed reasonably good at the start, after the German invasion in April 1941. On 1 May 1941 the Greek Minister in London had formally handed to the BBC for safe keeping the interval signal of Athens Radio – a recording of the arcadian sound of cow and goat bells and a shepherd's flute – and the signal was used each day thereafter by the BBC Greek Service until it was returned to Athens Radio after the liberation on 5 November 1944. In Greece itself there was no doubting the anti-Axis and pro-British feelings of the mass of the population. Before the German onslaught, once the ban on the publication of Allied news had been lifted after the Italians attacked Greece in October 1940, BBC broadcasts were quoted verbatim in the Greek press and the authority of the BBC was considered as 'higher than that of Greek Government agencies'.[15]

But in London, once the Greek Government was established there, there were soon complaints from official quarters. In April 1942 the Greek Under-Secretary for Information complained that the BBC broadcasts in Greek did not reflect the directives which he understood they should be observing: 'What came out of the sausage machine did not resemble in any way what he imagined Murray [Ralph Murray, of PWE] had put into it.'[16]

The Greek Service, he claimed, was systematically denigrating the Greek Government. Some members of its staff were anti-monarchist. Moreover it was putting out to Greece items of news which, while they might be appropriate for other Balkan countries, were wholly inappropriate for Greece. He instanced the case of a declaration by the American Secretary of State, Sumner Welles, in which he had referred to 'the unhappy Bulgarians', who had been 'forced into the war against their will'. He felt that for the Greeks, who were being massacred and starved to death by a Bulgarian army of occupation, this was hardly good propaganda.[17]

Kirkpatrick responded in his usual robust manner. News to Greece, he said, must be edited on the assumption that some Greeks listened to the Empire Service or to other BBC foreign language services as well as to the Greek Service: 'Experience in almost every European country', he wrote, 'shows that if listeners who cross-listen gain the impression that we suppress in one language bulletin an item simply on propagandist grounds the effect is deplorable.'[18] He dismissed the accusation of bias out of hand. The Greek staff, he said, had no say in policy matters. It is true that at that stage there were grounds for dissatisfaction with the Greek output. The bulletins were 'very long and straggly'. Opportunities for bringing in easy references to Greece were being missed. There was a tendency to give prominence to resistance stories from other parts of Europe, such as Norway, but without linking them with stories about resistance in Greece. Greeks, the report noted, wanted meat, not hot air.[19]

Such criticisms, however, were of an essentially professional character and had little connection with the Greek Government's complaints, which were described as 'mischievous' and 'largely motivated by the wish to obtain control over the BBC's Greek broadcasts' by the Greek Editor, D.E. Noel Paton.[20]

There was probably some truth in the charge that the staff was on the whole anti-monarchist. N.F. Soteriades, an experienced former foreign correspondent who was highly regarded both by Newsome and by Kirkpatrick, certainly was, though Kirkpatrick assured Bruce Lockhart that he did not allow his political views – he was described as a 'democrat' – to interfere with his work.[21] Soteriades wrote at length to Newsome in November 1941 about the policy of the Greek Service, which he regarded as disastrous. In his view it was carrying too much material from and about the Royal Greek Government at the expense of news about the progress of the war, which was what really interested Greek listeners. Moreover by giving so much place to Greek Government pronouncements it was helping to perpetuate the fiction that the Greek King and Government had taken Greece into the war because they believed in the democratic values for which the Allies were fighting. In his view this was a gross travesty of the truth. The Greek public at home knew this and the BBC would lose the trust of its listeners.[22] Kirkpatrick commented drily that 'there is a great tendency all over Europe to reject stuff supplied by Allied governments'. 'If we could eliminate the interference of Allied governments', he wrote, 'and concentrate entirely on supplying the best and the hardest news we should have more satisfied listeners.'[23]

In the end the pressures from the Greek Government were warded off, Kirkpatrick arguing that it would be dangerous to allow it to put its own men in the service, as it would have liked to do.[24] Instead, in July 1942 it was allowed a daily ten-minute free period, but Noel Paton, looking back some time later, commented bitterly at the 'sad waste of broadcasting time' this had represented. The Greek Government, he said, had never seriously attempted to carry out its terms of reference, there had been frequent attempts to wash political linen in public and 'a high degree of irresponsibility with respect to security and policy censorship requirements'.[25] Reactions from Greece had been 'consistently unfavourable'.[26]

Later there were to be other wrangles, this time with the British Government. Churchill's decision to intervene militarily and politically in the Greek internal crisis in December 1944 had led to a major political debate in Britain and to critical reactions in the British press which were reflected in press reviews in the Greek Service. Rex Leeper, by then British Ambassador to Greece, protested angrily to London. At Westminster Churchill's Greek policy was challenged by Labour backbenchers in the House of Commons and a row developed over the Greek Service's coverage of the debate. According to Leeper it had included a comment to the effect that 'the vote of confidence is not the end for Greece. The people of England will express their real will at the next election.' Bruce Lockhart was hauled before the Cabinet to explain what had happened. It was an uncomfortable moment, but he seems to have got off fairly lightly, though he emerged 'feeling like a guilty schoolboy who has had a painful interview with his Headmaster'.[27] In fact Bruce Lockhart had agreed with J.B. Clark that the debate had been well reported. 'If anything', Bruce Lockhart wrote at the time, the coverage had been 'overfavourable to Eden', whose speech had been 'heavily covered'.[28] 'It is curious', he observed, 'how everyone near the PM believes that the BBC is a nest of Communists or of intellectual perverts.'[29]

Broadcasting to Yugoslavia, which had started in a small way in September 1939, took place in an equally charged atmosphere. There had been hurried increases in transmission time at the end of March 1941 as the political situation in Yugoslavia deteriorated, and L.S. Amery, then Secretary of State for India, had been brought to the microphone on 27 March, on account of his long and close connection with the country and of his command of the language, to make an eloquent appeal to the Yugoslav people not to be fooled by German promises and to reject the signing by the Regent, Prince Paul, of a pact with Germany. 'Will Yugoslavia sell her honour and your liberty for a German promise,' he asked. 'Will you let your people become once more a subject race?' There had been initial official reluctance to let him take such a strong line with a country which was officially neutral, but a direct call to Churchill had given him the go ahead, and there is little doubt that even if the broadcast did not in itself precipitate the *coup d'état* which brought Yugoslavia into the Allied camp it must have provided powerful moral support for those who were plotting the Regent's removal.

Some of the difficulties which subsequently developed in relation to the Yugoslav Government in exile stemmed from dissensions between the Serb, Croat and Slovene elements in the Government. A separate Slovene transmission was introduced in April 1941, and there was periodic pressure for a similar provision in Croat, which the BBC and the Foreign Office resisted 'on both practical and political grounds'.[30] The BBC was accused sweepingly of 'running a pan-Serb policy',[31] but sometimes simultaneously of being pro-Croat. Ralph Murray, the PWE official responsible for policy, took the view that Croatia had had a very fair deal. Great care had been taken to avoid undue weighting of the Serb element and to ensure that 'propaganda was always in a "Yugoslav" sense'.[32] 'We are not prepared', Murray wrote, 'to allow the British Government to be made a factor in internal Yugoslav political questions.'[33] Yet that was precisely what the various Yugoslav factions were trying to do.

Such issues paled into relative insignificance when compared with the question whether or not the British Government – and the BBC's own broadcasts – should give exclusive support to the activities of General Mihailović, the Yugoslav Minister of War and Commander-in-Chief on the ground, or recognise the growing contribution to the common struggle made by Tito's partisans. The issue first came up in June 1942, when the Yugoslav Government complained that undue publicity was being given to the partisans and Kirkpatrick gave instructions to Newsome and the regional editors concerned that those fighting the Germans and Italians in Yugoslavia should be described in general terms as 'patriots' or 'fighting forces' without any further distinction being made, thus, hopefully, avoiding the issue.[34] But soon the Yugoslav Government was complaining again, this time because a broadcast talk by a Slovene member of the Government appealing to all Slovenes to support Mihailović had been followed by a talk by Hubert Harrison, the Yugoslav Editor, in which he had stated that 'everyone who resisted the Axis, whether they belonged to the patriot forces or to the Communist partisans, was equally fighting in the common cause'.[35]

Yovanovic, the Yugoslav Prime Minister, regarded this statement as unfortunate. It would 'make people in Yugoslavia feel that Yugoslav ministers have not got the support of the British authorities when they urge people in Yugoslavia to make sacrifices in order to join or support Mihailović'.[36] The British were still vainly hoping at that stage that a reconciliation, even possibly cooperation, might be possible. There was now deep suspicion in the Yugoslav

Government that 'as a result of pressure from Moscow we [the British Government] are beginning to look on the partisans rather than on Mihailović as our main allies in Yugoslavia'.[37] There was also suspicion of Harrison personally. A former *News Chronicle* correspondent in Belgrade, he was widely known in Yugoslavia, but there were suggestions, firmly discounted by Kirkpatrick, that he was 'strongly leftist by sympathy'. One Yugoslav minister described him as a 'professional oppositionist'.[38]

In fact what Harrison had said was fully in line with official British policy, though the Foreign Office, while not disputing that this was so, pointed out that Harrison's broadcast 'was made before we had given out this line, even before we had decided on it, and to that extent was revolutionary'.[39] In future, Pierson Dixon of the Foreign Office told Murray, the internal civil war in Yugoslavia must be ignored, and broadcasts must avoid picking out the partisans for special praise. On the other hand, Dixon said, they cannot be ignored altogether. The line should be that their struggle in the parts of the country they controlled was in the same cause as Mihailović's in his area of operations. Only geography was preventing them from joining hands.[40]

It was not a very convincing brief. Nor did it succeed in resolving the matter. There was a further major dispute in February 1943 when the Yugoslav Government returned to the charge with a claim that the BBC's broadcasts to Yugoslavia were 'directed and controlled by Communist sympathisers'.[41] This time the row was provoked by a letter from Harrison to a British national working for the Yugoslav Government in which he wrote that 'We speak to the Yugoslav people, not to the Kingston House clique. If the Yugoslav people follow in the main the partisan leaders we cannot echo the Government cry that they follow Mihailović.'[42] This drew a strong protest from the Yugoslav Government and the ire of the Foreign Office.[43] Kirkpatrick once again stood up stoutly for his subordinate.[44] To Bernard Sendall, Bracken's Private Secretary, he wrote:

Unfortunately we know it to be a fact that General Mihailović is doing very little, if anything, and that active resistance is being carried out by the partisans ... I would not claim that we always deal with this extremely difficult and controversial subject in a completely blameless manner; we try to ascertain the truth through the fog of war, and, having ascertained it, speak it.[45]

Such arguments were to continue throughout 1943 and early 1944, with Kirkpatrick consistently endorsing Harrison's judgement, while the Foreign Office, for its part, was slowly moving towards full and exclusive support for Tito. By the beginning of 1944 if not before Tito's predominance had become unquestioned, and a British liaison officer with the partisans was able to report that 'listening to the BBC was regarded almost as a duty with the serious-minded partisans. It was a regular daily habit: supper, BBC, bed. Each receiving set was surrounded by a large group of eighty to a hundred.'[46] At the end one partisan general who had heard on the BBC that the war had ended told his British liaison officer, Major Ennals, that it was safe for him to go forward in his jeep. Ennals motored ahead of the advancing partisan columns, only to be greeted by German mortar and machine-gun fire. He turned about and reported back to the partisan commander, who asked indignantly: 'Don't they listen to the BBC?'[47]

As against Greece and Yugoslavia Italy, at first sight, presents a relatively straightforward picture. From June 1940 onward it was Germany's major if subordinate ally, and the objectives of the Italian Service were therefore not unlike those of the German Service. But the resemblance is deceptive. Italian popular commitment to the war was never more than ephemeral and did not recover from the early disasters suffered by the Italian Army in the Western Desert. There was growing popular resentment in Italy against the Germans due to their increasingly blatant economic exploitation and to their ill-disguised contempt for the Italians, and radical political changes were taking place under the surface of Italian life which were to come out into the open after Mussolini's downfall, when Italy, from being an enemy, became a co-belligerent.

The obstacles which had to be overcome in reaching a large audience in Italy might at first sight have seemed overwhelming. As has been seen there were relatively few radio sets, though numbers increased as the war progressed. In the main the BBC could only reach Italy on short wave, though it was estimated at the time that seventy per cent of radio sets were capable of receiving short wave signals. The Italian Service was heavily jammed and severe penalties were imposed on those who were caught listening to it. On the other hand Italian internal propaganda was so blatant and bombastic that there was a strong incentive to seek accurate news elsewhere. Moreover there was an increasingly strong undercurrent in Italian intellectual and political life which favoured western democratic values. The BBC's influence, while never quite as pervasive as it became in France, played a considerable role in encouraging this evolution and, ultimately, in helping to tip the scales against Fascism.

Much evidence of its success was unwittingly provided by Fascist leaders and by the Italian Radio itself. Ciano's diaries abound in references to what London had been saying, and there were increasingly vitriolic and abusive attacks against the BBC in general and Colonel Stevens in particular. The law against listening was tightened up. Prosecutions increased in numbers and were given wide publicity, though sentences were never as severe as in Germany. Attempts were made by the authorities to call in radio receivers in order to seal off the short wave bands, and signs of the popularity of Colonel Stevens were found by puzzled Allied troops in Sicily, who had never heard of him, in the shape of the words *Viva il Colonnello Stevens* scrawled in large letters on the walls.[48] Certainly the psychological war was won no less decisively in Italy and perhaps to greater effect than anywhere else in Europe except France.

In some respects the Italian Service's broadcasters had considerable tactical advantages over their German colleagues. Though unconditional surrender remained official British policy the Italian public was never given the impression that its guilt was inseparable from that of its leaders. On the contrary, Mussolini was carefully singled out as the chief cause of Italy's troubles, and listeners, while told that they had to bear their share of responsibility for the war to the extent that they passively condoned the existence of the Fascist regime, were given far more hope for the future than were the Germans. London became the capital of opposition to the regime and for a time the *Italia Libera* movement survived on a BBC subsidy in return for occasional talks. Italian political exiles played a far more personal role in broadcasting back to Italy than would have been conceivable in the German Service with the sole exception of Thomas Mann. Colonel Stevens himself was half Italian, and his benevolent, avuncular manner was in itself reassuring. In line with British official policy he supported the monarchy and was generally conservative in his approach to politics.[49] The emphasis was placed on decency in international relations, on the solidarity of western civilisation and on the essential fair-mindedness of the British.[50] Another commentator, John Marus, broadcasting as 'Candidus', took a far more radical line. Born in London of Italian parents he had spent much of his life in Italy, where his anti-Fascist activities had led to his being imprisoned. Shrewd, pungent and far more politically involved than Stevens, he reflected that element in Italian political life which was not only strongly anti-Fascist but also anti-monarchist and republican. His influence was to become increasingly important in the later years as Mussolini's fortunes waned and the whole temper of the Italian people changed.[51]

As one of the largest of the European Services – at its height in August 1943 it was broadcasting for four hours a day – the Italian Service was able to mount a far wider range of programmes than the average. Like the French and German Service it exploited the fictional dialogue form and used subtle irony, sarcasm and derision to discredit Mussolini and the Fascist regime and exploit the resentment felt by Italians towards their German allies. The two main regular offerings, which started early in 1941, were written by F.L.M. Shepley, who had worked in an international law office in Milan before the war, spoke fluent Italian and eventually moved to the Italian Service as Programme Organiser after spending some time with the Monitoring Service and European Intelligence. In his partnership with George Foa, the Producer, he was the political brain, steeped in detailed knowledge of the state of Italian opinion gained from the regular reading of the Italian press, obtained via Lisbon with remarkably little delay, from intercepted mail and letters from listeners which filtered through to the BBC, and from frequent listening to Rome radio.

The two programmes formed part of the main offering of the day, 'La Voce di Londra'. The first, 'Sotto Voce', was an imaginary conversation between three fictional characters, an extreme anti-Fascist, played by Paolo Treves, son of the Italian Socialist leader Claudio Treves, a moderate anti-Fascist and a 'reasonable' Fascist. The second was 'Axis Conversation' a dialogue between a German business man and a North Italian industrialist, which enabled the insensitivity and patronising benevolence of the Germans and the extent to which they were exploiting the Italians to be displayed, while the Italian would respond with subtle irony which would pass the German by but was immediately understood by the audience. The origin of the programme can be traced back to a New Year party at Shepley's lodgings in Evesham at the end of 1940, attended mainly by members of the Monitoring Service. Those present took turns to entertain the company, and among them was George Weidenfeld, who did a brilliant imitation of Mussolini delivering a speech. Weidenfeld spoke excellent Italian, but with an Austrian accent, and clearly had unsuspected gifts as a radio comedian. It was this chance event which gave Shepley the idea of 'Axis conversation', with Weidenfeld cast as the German businessman and the part of the much put-upon Italian played by Uberto Limentani, later Professor of Italian at Cambridge University.[52]

Another regular feature, this time of a more light-hearted kind, was 'L'Osteria del Buon Umore', in which five characters from different parts of Italy, some of them soldiers and speaking their regional dialects, safe in a cellar somewhere in Italy, would say what they really thought of Mussolini and the Fascist regime. The talk would be interspersed with songs and Italian guitar music. George Weidenfeld also wrote a series of programmes under the title 'Knights of the long knives' on leaders of Nazism. The first, broadcast on 7 October 1941, dealt with Goebbels and contrasted his personality as it appeared to hero-worshipping Germans with what he was really like, reminding listeners that he had once referred to the 'bastard Italian race' and that he talked of 'spiritual chastity' while burning the books of Heine, Stefan Zweig and Thomas Mann. The Italian Service transmissions were introduced with a special signature tune made up of Garibaldi and Mameli hymns with an undercurrent of Tipperary, conducted by Walter Goehr.*

From the moment Italy entered the war the policy of the service was carefully to avoid sneering at the Italians.[53] There was also to be no 'preaching', and listeners were to be given 'a sense of hopefulness'. A directive from Newsome issued on 31 March 1943 and reflecting PWE thinking, set out what was to be the main propaganda line over the next few months. There was to be a concentrated effort at undermining Germany's southern flank, timed to coincide with the final phase of the North African campaign and presaging the first strike at Europe's 'soft underbelly'. 'While Italy allows herself to be

* Mameli was a nineteenth-century poet and patriot who wrote the war song 'Fratelli d'Italia' and was killed at the age of twenty-two.

used as Hitler's pawn', Newsome wrote, 'the Allies have no choice but to smash her strength as completely as possible.' But the right course for Italians was clear: 'Italy has no obligations to Germany, who has merely exploited her resources for German ends. Mussolini's policy of alliance with Germany has not only betrayed Italian interests but has been dishonourable from the start. Italy can restore her honour by reversing it.'[54]

The Italian surrender in September 1944 and the declaration of war against Germany which followed soon after translated the arguments of that directive into fact, but they led to a curious situation, with the Political Warfare Department of the Allied Supreme Command in Italy pursuing the official policy of backing the monarchical regime of the Lieutenant of the Realm, Prince Umberto, while the BBC Italian Service was seeking to reflect the reality of the resurgent Italian political life, at least as much for its listeners in the north, where the Germans and the Fascists still held sway, as for the liberated south.

In January 1944, there had gathered together at Bari a congress of Italy's new democratic and republican forces, the Council of National Liberation, attended by all the big names of Italian politics such as the veteran liberal leader Count Sforza, the aged philosopher Benedetto Croce, and left-wing leaders like Nenni and Togliatti. The proceedings of the congress were covered by the local radio station and would not have become more widely known had not the BBC Monitoring Service picked up the Bari broadcasts and enabled the Italian Service to give them wider currency. Shepley remembers being asked by Kirkpatrick at about that time to come and see him in his office and finding there Harold Macmillan, the British Resident Minister in Algiers. He was asked to explain why the Italian Service wasn't following the same line as PWD. When he had finished Macmillan said in effect: 'Well, you know, I think that's all right. Either the Italians, when they hold a referendum, decide for a republican constitution, in which case the BBC will be shown to have been right all along. Or they don't, in which case the BBC will have been shown to be free to be wrong.'[55] In the meantime Shepley, on a visit to Rome, was being told by Prince Umberto's ADC: 'If it weren't for you, they [the Italian people] would never have known what was going on.'[56] It was a back-handed tribute, but a tribute nonetheless. Sir Noel Charles, the British Ambassador in Rome, whom Shepley also saw, was more forthcoming: he spoke of 'the almost universal listening on the part of all classes of Italians in the months which preceded liberation' and of the ability of the BBC Italian Service 'to reach classes which had always been beyond the influence of other media of British penetration'.[57] The service retained its immense prestige, he said, but it had lost the attraction of forbidden fruit. A reorientation of its policies was now needed, which would place a greater emphasis on the projection of Britain and its way of life. Already combatting Communist influence among the Italian working classes was seen as an important objective, a portent of the war of ideas which was to follow so soon after the guns had fallen silent.[58]

Poland's tragic fate in the Second World War is faithfully reflected in the history of the BBC Polish Service itself and in the frequently agonising editorial problems with which it was confronted. Almost from the start the London Radio, as it was known in Poland, had a much wider audience than merely those in Poland who were prepared to brave the German ban on listening. By the middle of the war it was also being widely listened to among Polish slave workers in Germany and elsewhere, by Polish troops in the Middle East, in Italy, in Britain, and later in north-west Europe, by Polish miners in France and Belgium, by the Polish community in London, and even as far as Kenya, where there were large settlements of Polish refugees. Shortly after the end of the lightning Polish campaign in 1939 the Polish Service had started an 'agony column' of the air which sought to help Poles scattered all over Europe and the Middle East to locate relatives, and in under a year 47,000 personal messages had been transmitted.

The Polish commitment to the destruction of Nazism was perhaps more passionate than that of any other nation, and this was as true at home, where the population was subjected to the most inhuman treatment, as it was of the hundreds of thousands of Poles who fought with the Allies at Tobruk, at Cassino, in Normandy and at Arnhem. Resistance to the Germans in Poland started early, the clandestine press flourished, sabotage spread rapidly despite the fierce reprisals, and regular communication was established at an early stage between the Polish resistance and the Polish Government in exile in London.

Because of the peculiarities of Polish psychology, as one Polish official put it, the audience did not need heartening if the war news was bad. Affected optimism which was flatly contradicted by the facts cut no ice. The audience wanted the truth, however grim, and it wanted to be assured that the fight would be pressed to a victorious conclusion regardless of setbacks and defeats.[59] The acute danger involved in listening to London also meant that presentation and entertainment value were less important. What Poles needed above all was hard information about the war which could be reproduced in the clandestine press.

As has been seen, one consequence of Poland's special predicament was the very close involvement of the Polish authorities in London in the broadcasting operation to Poland and their repeatedly expressed desire for a greater say in policy. At the regular weekly liaison meetings which started in November 1940 as well as through the Foreign Office, the Polish representatives did not just press for more time on the air. Some of the more martial members of the Polish Cabinet were urging the Polish Ministry of Information to obtain control of all broadcasting in Polish. But short of that, which the wiser

heads knew to be impossible, the Poles were asking for the contents of the
BBC's own broadcasts to be discussed with them in advance, and, when this
was refused, for an opportunity to see the texts of all BBC bulletins and for
the right to have a hand in the formulation of the service's weekly directive.[60]
This too was refused. There was much discussion about the best times for the
Polish broadcasts to go out. In this respect the Poles found Kirkpatrick
sympathetic. Grant Purves, the BBC's own Polish intelligence expert, made
the point that with very few direct listeners – the BBC estimate at the beginning
of 1943 was not much more than 1,500 in the whole of Poland – schedule
changes were less important than elsewhere. On the other hand late evening
broadcasts were of little value for direct listening because most Poles did not
have sets but went to listen with friends who had. They risked arousing the
suspicions of caretakers if their visits took place after the doors of apartment
blocks had been locked at night, and bribery was often necessary to secure
discretion.[61]

Purves agreed with the Poles about the overwhelming importance of the
clandestine press, of which there was evidence as early as November 1940,
and in due course a sequence of overnight and early morning transmissions
was arranged, with the needs of editors specially in mind, including a review
of the British press. The official broadcasts of 'Radio Polskie' had started on
1 January 1942 with a single daily fifteen minute transmission, and by the
middle of 1944 had risen to four periods amounting in all to fifty minutes out
of a total daily transmission time in Polish of two and a quarter hours. They
included not only news, which had to be based on BBC news stories, but also
talks and in particular the broadcasts of Polish leaders like General Sikorski
to their compatriots at home. There were special 'Radio Polskie' broadcasts
for the Polish armed forces and for the Polish Home Army. In addition a
good deal of the talks output in the periods reserved for the BBC, particularly
in the early morning, was supplied by the Polish authorities, though Kirkpatrick, writing to PWE in January 1942, described them as 'subject to almost
universal criticism'. The speakers, he said, were 'talking for their own benefit,
not for listeners'.[62] By the end of 1944 Gregory Macdonald, the Polish Editor,
had succeeded in cutting them down substantially and redirecting them into
'Radio Polskie's' own periods.[63]

At the end of 1941 a special scheme for transmitting operational messages
to the Polish underground by broadcasting agreed gramophone records was
introduced. The BBC was told that a Polish officer bearing the assumed name
of Peter Perkins would deliver the records to Bush House twice a day. By his
real name Lieutenant Zubrzycky, he soon became known as Lieutenant
Peterkin and became a great favourite at Bush House. A particularly sad
story is attached to these music broadcasts. The record chosen to convey to
the Polish Home Army that air operations would not be possible that day
was a sad popular tune recalling the failure of the Polish rising of 1831 – 'Z

Dymem Pozarow' ('With the smoke of fires'). The record had to be broadcast repeatedly during the first week of the Warsaw rising in August 1944 as the agreed tune could not be changed, and as ordinary Polish listeners did not know that it had an operational meaning the BBC was thought to have been particularly unfeeling.

The problems peculiar to the troubled but always courteous relationship between the Polish authorities and the BBC inevitably extended to a wide range of policy matters. Polish leaders, understandably, had little time for subtle distinctions between the Germans as a whole and those guilty of specific criminal acts. In a broadcast in June 1942 General Sikorski declared that after its defeat 'Germany will fall into a bottomless abyss', while Professor Stronski, the Polish Minister of Information, stated that 'not one German will escape without payment with interest.'[64] This went a good deal further than official British policy, and when after 'D' Day an appeal was broadcast to Poles in labour camps and in the Todt organisation to welcome anti-Nazi Germans in their underground organisations, the Polish authorities, which had not been consulted, said this was unacceptable in view of the official Polish policy of treating all Germans as guilty.[65]

Advance consultation on such matters and on the coverage of developments immediately concerning the Polish Government in exile was persistently sought by the Poles. Among the most difficult issues, particularly towards the end of the war, were those related to Poland's future frontiers, Poland's 'irrefutable rights to the sea', claims to an extended Baltic seaboard, and the ambition of the Polish Government in exile to create a 'large and powerful Polish state' after the war.[66] 'The censor', an undated secret BBC paper reported, 'is faced with exceptional difficulties in the exercise of his discretion with regard to controversial subjects'.[67] Macdonald, whose responsibility it was and who was deeply sympathetic to the Polish cause, was once accused by Newsome of giving way to the Poles too easily, but on the other hand the Poles complained bitterly that he was unduly hard on 'Radio Polskie'.

There was plenty to put his diplomatic skills to the test. The Katyn massacre, the controversy over the Curzon line and Polish relations with Russia more generally were all particularly sensitive issues on which the Poles had strong views which needed to be restrained in the interest of Britain's wartime alliance with the Soviet Union. So was the Warsaw rising on 1 August 1944 and the Soviet army's failure to respond to Polish and Allied appeals for help. The Polish Service was the first to broadcast the news of the rising on 2 August. Macdonald asked the Monitoring Service to keep an ear open in case, as he anticipated, the Home Army should succeed in coming up with its own broadcasting station. On 8 August the station, calling itself 'Blyskawica' - Polish for lightning - was located by the monitors, and thereafter the Warsaw communiqués, monitored at Caversham, were rebroadcast

in full every afternoon from London.[68] Warsaw was also communicating
with London by code, and what the rest of the world knew about the rising it
learnt largely from the BBC. The Russians did not report it until 13 August
and then played it down, and the Germans announced that it had been
crushed on 17 August, although it continued for sixty-three days, until 5
October, and cost the Poles over 150,000 dead. In the last broadcast from
Warsaw before the surrender the embattled Home Army speaker read out at
the 'Blyskawica' microphone the names of those he wished to thank for their
help during the battle; the list included Macdonald. The day after his arrival
in England on being freed from Colditz, General Bor-Komorowski, the
commander of the Polish Home Army, told Macdonald movingly: 'During
the Warsaw rising I listened to the BBC for the first time on the free soil of
Poland.'[69] To him as to many thousands of Poles the BBC had been 'the
forbidden chief instrument of hope'.[70]

Yet Macdonald, supported by Moray MacLaren, his PWE opposite number, with whom he saw eye to eye on most things, had always taken the view
that the Poles must not be given false hopes for the future. 'We could not say
that Poland's rights would be vindicated by an Allied victory.'[71] The known
facts about the Katyn massacre were reported without comment, there was
no attempt to play down the achievements of the Red Army, and the service
was circumspect in dealing with the crisis in Russo-Polish relations at the end
of 1942 and sought to curb the traditional anti-Russian sentiments of the
Poles. But the BBC did not paint a bright picture of Poland's future and when
it came to Yalta Macdonald refused to carry out the official directive that the
settlement was to be recommended to the Poles. The facts about the agreement were merely reported without comment, together with London press
reactions, by no means all of them favourable. This led to a formal complaint
by the Foreign Office and to an official enquiry which ended with Macdonald
being vindicated. At the end, when the Polish provisional government had
established itself in Warsaw and had been recognised by Britain, 'Radio
Polskie' finally closed down. The last broadcast took place on 29 June 1945.
The Poles asked to be allowed to read at the microphone the texts of all the
undertakings and treaty obligations entered into by Britain concerning the
sovereignty, independence and territorial integrity of Poland, together with
the comparable statements made by the other Allies. J.B. Clark, by
then Controller (European Services), consulted the Foreign Office, who
agreed.[72]

There are many points of similarity between the Polish and Czech wartime
broadcasting operations, but also many contrasts. After initial attempts at
wooing the population, Bohemia and Moravia were treated almost as brutally
by the Germans as was Poland. There was bitter hostility to the Germans and
to the puppet government of President Hacha and obstinate resistance to

every effort at 'germanising' the Czech lands. Systematic acts of sabotage were carried out on a large scale from an early stage and increased in intensity after the German attack against Russia. There were serious railway accidents, explosions in armaments factories, the response to the 'V' campaign and to the call for a massive 'go-slow' in industry was particularly effective, and both industrial production and communications were seriously disrupted at a time when they were vital to the German war machine on the Eastern Front. The climax came with the assassination of Heydrich in May 1942. The Germans struck back with unparalleled ferocity and brought their reprisals to a new peak of horror with the destruction of the village of Lidice in June 1942. Though Slovakia became nominally autonomous and collaborated with Hitler to the extent of sending troops to fight on the Russian front, there too resistance increased as the war progressed, culminating in the carefully planned Slovak rising of 1944, which was itself followed by German reprisals of the utmost brutality. As with Poland, therefore, there was no need for London to encourage the population to resist. Rather was it a case of having to urge caution, as was the policy elsewhere, since the response to any call for action was immediate, as was shown in 1940, when a misunderstood broadcast led to sixty workers being shot.[73]

As with Poland there was massive confiscation of radio sets and the death penalty was introduced for those caught listening to a foreign station and passing on what they had heard. Nonetheless the BBC was widely listened to: 'It is especially the London transmission which today is of tremendous importance in keeping up the spirit of the people' reported a neutral traveller who left the country in April 1941. 'It is absolutely necessary to have a message broadcast from London by President Beneš at least once every six weeks.'[74] Only a few months earlier Jan Masaryk was telling Ogilvie that he had 'almost daily evidence of how anxiously the London broadasts are listened to in our country'.[75]

Few of the kinds of problems which arose with the Polish authorities seem to have marred the cooperation between the Czech authorities in London and the BBC: 'Relations are harmonious,' a secret BBC report stated in 1943; 'The Czech Government is anxious to secure the maximum possible cooperation with the BBC. Their regular contributors produce excellent commentaries, fully in line with our policy.'[76] There were frequent talks by leading Czech figures in London including Dr Josef Stransky, the Minister of Justice, Dr Hubert Ripka, the minister responsible for information, and Dr Josef Körbel, who was charged with liaison with the BBC. President Benes himself broadcast on important occasions such as the launching of the go-slow campaign in September 1941. But the star broadcaster in the Czech Service was undoubtedly Jan Masaryk, who, as a private individual living in London at the time, had been the inaugural speaker in the Czech Service in September 1939 and had gone on to broadcast regularly throughout the war. Robert Bruce Lock-

hart recalls that he was known in Czechoslovakia as 'Honza', a character
from a Czech fairy tale called *The Tale of Honza!* In the early stages of the
war notices were posted in Prague calling on passers-by to 'Hear the Tales of
Honza tonight at 9.30.' The Germans took weeks to realise what this referred
to.[77]

In Shiela Grant Duff, who was Czech Editor in the middle years of the war
and who married Noel Newsome in July 1942, the Czech Government had a
sympathetic partner in its potentially difficult relationship with the BBC, which
had to insist that ultimately its policy direction must come from PWE. She
was succeeded by Professor R. R. Betts, who in turn was briefly succeeded in
1944 by Michael Roberts, the poet and writer. The post was then taken over
by Duckworth Barker, one of the central figures in the early development of
foreign language broadcasting.

Shiela Grant Duff, a close personal friend of Hubert Ripka before the war,
had been the Prague correspondent of the *Observer* before the war and was
deeply hostile to the policy of appeasement and committed to the interests of
Czechoslovakia. Newsome himself, as has been seen, was more favourably
disposed towards the Czechs than towards the Poles and though not a man of
the Left in the conventional sense – more a 'sturdy protestant liberal', as
Macdonald saw him – was far more inclined to believe in Soviet good
intentions in Eastern Europe than was Macdonald, whose Polish sympathies
and Roman Catholic convictions inevitably made him deeply suspicious of
them, as indeed of Beneš's rapprochement with the Russians and of the
tendency, prevalent at the time, to see the Russians as liberators.

Broadcasting to Hungary, Rumania and Bulgaria was in sharp contrast. All
three countries joined the Axis camp and fought against Britain's allies.
Hungary shared in the German attack against Yugoslavia in 1941 and, like
Rumania, subsequently sent substantial forces to fight on the Eastern Front.
Bulgaria made its own contribution by waging a pitiless campaign against
Greek and Yugoslav guerillas. In broadcasting terms all three were therefore
treated as enemy countries but there were significant differences in propaganda policy as between Rumania and Bulgaria on the one hand and Hungary
on the other. Though the services to all three countries provided straight news
and emphasised German exploitation, the growing strength of the Allies and
the inevitability of an Allied victory, broadcasts to Bulgaria, for instance,
were considerably tougher in tone than those of the Hungarian Service. There
were bitter attacks against King Boris and his supporters, and the whole
Bulgarian nation was indicted for the atrocities committed by Bulgarian
forces against the Serbs and the Greeks. There were calls for the Bulgarian
army to refuse to fight against fellow Slavs, and appeals to the people to resist
the Germans. The events of the last year of the war highlighted the fact that
both Bulgaria and Rumania lay well inside the Soviet sphere of influence, but

the ban placed on listening to the BBC suggested that even if circumstances precluded a major role for broadcasts from London they were nonetheless carefully followed. Bulgarian official hostility was highlighted by the fact that two of the BBC's speakers were condemned to death *in absentia* and that the widowed mother of one of them was put in a concentration camp.

Policy towards Hungary, clearly stemming from PWE directives, was an entirely different matter. If propaganda to Bulgaria was 'full of stern condemnation', the attitude to Hungary was one of 'gentle reproof'.[78] A BBC internal report of April 1942 noted that 'our usual zeal for political democracy is concealed from the Hungarians'. The general tone of the service at that stage was one of 'friendliness tinged with regret that Hungary had been unable to resist German pressure'.[79] There was no attempt to encourage revolt against the Horthy regime, nor any incitement to economic resistance. Whereas the Bulgarian Service included numerous talks and short comments from a wide range of speakers, comment on the Hungarian Service was largely confined to one speaker, Professor C.A. Macartney, who had had a long connection with central Europe and later became Professor of International Relations at Edinburgh University. He said of himself that he was 'not one of those who accuses Hungarian statesmen of betraying their country'.[80] As a result there were charges of 'appeasement' on a number of occasions. Kirkpatrick dismissed them as unfounded: 'Hungarian *émigrés* and their English friends', he wrote, 'will never be satisfied until we go in for abuse. In broadcasting to Hungary we must bear in mind the self-evident truth that mere abuse will not get us any further.'[81] Foreign Office anxieties arising from repeated charges against the Hungarian staff also seem to have been satisfactorily disposed of. The fact was that there was, on all the evidence, a large audience in Hungary unhampered by any restrictions on listening, and the BBC, as Kirkpatrick pointed out, had a considerable influence, to judge by the numerous references to it in the Hungarian press. Macartney himself was much appreciated by the audience for his understanding approach. On the other hand the service itself did have rather more internal problems and tensions than most. A duel between two Hungarian members of staff was barely averted by Duckworth Barker's intervention in March 1940. In a memo entitled 'Pistols and coffee' he commented that 'the incident belongs to the more picturesque sides of life in the Overseas Service'.[82] There was a tendency for the Hungarian staff to 'denounce each other and every other Hungarian in London'.[83] There were hints of corruption, resulting in two dismissals. At an early stage the service was violently attacked, as was the Rumanian Service, for being largely staffed by Jews, whose accent, it was claimed, was unacceptable to Hungarian listeners. The attack collapsed when it was discovered that the member of staff whose performance at the microphone was said to be most violently objectedto had never broadcast and was used only as a translator. Duckworth Barker, who was well placed to know, dismissed the whole affair as 'a ramp' which had been 'artificially designed to create jobs for persons able to pull string'.[84] 'Neither in official nor in private reports', J.B. Clark wrote to the Ministry of Information, 'has any evidence reached the BBC that the Hungarian Service is discredited in Hungary in the manner suggested'.[85] Later there were accusations that some members of the Hungarian staff were Nazi sympathisers, even though most of them were at least part-Jewish and one at least had been well known in pre-war Budapest as an outspokenly anti-Nazi journalist.

Broadcasting to Hungary offered an object lesson in the difficulty of formulating a convincing propaganda line capable of being sustained in the face of the political complexities confronting the audience. Hungarians complained that the BBC took no account of their fear of Communism. They needed reassurance on that score, which the BBC could not give them without upsetting Britain's Russian ally. They also pointed out that whereas the Italians were being promised a decent peace if they threw off the Fascist yoke, they themselves could not escape the invidious need to collaborate with the Axis without rendering themselves powerless to resist the Russians.

Despite all these difficulties the BBC appears to have greatly increased its following as the war progressed and as concern grew in Hungary over the rapidly deteriorating situation on the Eastern front. A Hungarian official listening to Budapest Radio in a neutral country in 1944 heard it being interrupted by a ghost voice which almost certainly originated in Moscow. His immediate comment was that the Russians would do better to interrupt the BBC Hungarian Service, since far more people listened to it.

Something akin to the dilemma facing the Hungarians also confronted the Finns. Faced with a choice of evils Finland had decided in 1941 that Russia presented a greater threat to its existence than Germany and had accordingly resumed, with German assistance, the fight which it had been compelled to abandon in March 1940. British official policy was uncompromising and required Finland to surrender unconditionally. There was no disposition in the Foreign Office to offer any explanation to the Finns of what surrender would mean, nor any assurances for the future. As Asa Briggs has pointed out, 'the BBC spent much of its time during these months [in the summer of 1944] encouraging the countries of Eastern and Central Europe – and Finland – to put their trust in the Russians',[86] but the Finns were unanimous in their determination to continue the fight for self-preservation. The BBC's Finnish Editor, Hillar Kallas, argued strongly but with little success that British policy towards Finland was mistaken. The Finns were fighting for themselves, he pointed out, not for the sake of the Germans. So long as they thought that their fate was to be left to the Russians alone they would prefer to go down fighting. But his proposal for an alternative policy involving the Western Allies as well as the Russians in the post-war settlement and offering a United Nations guarantee of independence and sovereignty for Finland after the war did not get beyond first base.[87]

Typical of the running conflict between the BBC and the Foreign Office over Finnish policy was the argument late in 1944, after Finland had been compelled to agree to a cease-fire, about whether or not the Finnish Service should broadcast a message on the occasion of the Finnish National Day. The Foreign Office argued that Finland was still technically an enemy country and in any case would be in no mood for celebration, but J.B. Clark pointed out that the Finnish Service, like others, had been broadcasting National Day messages regularly to various countries in the past, 'either in a spirit of celebration or admonishment'.[88] Eventually it was agreed that Tom O'Brien would broadcast an appropriate message on behalf of the TUC, addressed to Finnish Trade Unionists. It was to be 'of an austere character', the Foreign Office insisted. Even the proposal to mark Sibelius Week in December 1944 by broadcasts of British performances of the composer's works and a talk by Basil Cameron was carefully scrutinised from a policy angle before it was finally agreed by the Foreign Office.

No such problems arose in the case of Norway. A bad start had been made by the broadcasting by the BBC of what the Norwegians regarded as 'fake news' put out by the Admiralty and the War Office at the time of the ill-fated Norwegian campaign in 1940. This had had 'a deplorable effect on the reputation of the BBC', the Norwegians pointed out, even though they were aware – as their compatriots at home were not – that the BBC itself had been misled. For a time the London programme was looked upon as 'just another form of propaganda'.[89] The acrimonious exchanges with the Norwegian broadcasting representatives in London in the summer of 1940 had seemed to bode ill for the future of the service. At one stage in the discussions the Norwegians went as far as to say that if they could not have complete control it would be preferable not to have any broadcasting in Norwegian at all.[90] But the clouds dispersed as if by magic and both sides thereafter worked in complete harmony, with the Norwegians preferring not to take up the British offer of 'free time' and choosing instead to have their own men in the service, seconded to the BBC and under ultimate BBC policy direction.[91] Denis Winther, the Norwegian Editor, described the Norwegian section in 1943 as 'the happiest and the most harmonious in the European Service'. 'We have always retained control on everything the Norwegian Government have done', he wrote to Grisewood, 'and have never had any great difficulties with them.'[92] The BBC provided and edited the news, and the Norwegians, with their intimate knowledge of the audience, looked after the talks, though Winther stressed that they were 'always ready to carry out our line of policy'.[93] Once confidence in BBC news had been restored the audience grew rapidly: 'No propaganda works any more', wrote a Norwegian who had

escaped to America some time after the country had been overrun by the
Germans. 'Nobody reads any newspapers or listens to any radio except the
BBC.'[94] There was a sharp increase in the number of licensed receivers, for
reasons which soon became clear to the Germans, who made the possession
of a radio set illegal in April 1941. The death penalty for listening was brought
in in 1942, though without the desired effect. Norwegians responded immediately to the 'V' campaign, which caused the Quisling Minister of Propaganda to attack his compatriots for 'scribbling "V" signs everywhere'. Norwegians added 'H-7' – for Haakon the Seventh – to their 'V' signs when the
Germans attempted to neutralise the campaign by taking it over – yet further
evidence of the popularity of the King's broadcasts to his countrymen and of
the key role which the Norwegian Service played in maintaining the essential
lifeline between the Norwegian Government in London and the increasingly
active resistance movement in Norway itself.

It was much the same in Denmark: 'Never has any institution had a greater
mission than the BBC and has a mission had a greater success,' wrote a Danish
listener in March 1944; 'It has been a comfort for all European countries
under Germany's heel. Without it we should have found it very hard to hold
out.'[95] On the other hand there were dissimilarities with Norway. A legitimate
Danish Government had remained in office after the German invasion, and
the King's calm and dignified behaviour had made it possible for Danes to
accept for a time, however reluctantly, the condition of subjection in which
they found themselves. British policy in the early years was not to preach
open resistance. On the other hand the Danish Service gave full details of
the heroism shown by other oppressed people, 'particularly by the Norwegians',[96] and it gradually took a tougher line towards collaboration
with the Germans. By the summer of 1942 the policy of caution had been
abandoned and J. Christmas Møller, the Conservative leader who had been
spirited out of Denmark by SOE and became an immensely popular
broadcaster on the Danish Service, was at last given the go-ahead to take a
strong line on the air: 'Action is required of us all, of each one of us', he said.
'Not Denmark but the Danish people as such are allies ... The outcome of
this gigantic struggle concerns us all.'[97] From the end of August 1943,
following the rejection of a German ultimatum by the Danish Government,
the Danes were openly and actively at war with the Germans. Until the
liberation in May 1945 there was the same cycle of sabotage, strikes and
armed action followed by increasingly severe reprisals which was experienced
in other occupied countries. The clandestine press, fed by the BBC's broadcasts, flourished, and there was increasingly close contact between Allied
Supreme Headquarters, SOE and the BBC in London and the Danish Freedom
Council which was directing operations in Denmark, a situation which bore
a close resemblance with that which prevailed in France at about the same
time and in which broadcasting played a crucial role. Collaborationist news-

papers spoke of BBC broadcasts 'spreading poison and incitement in thousands of Danish homes', and on 29 August 1943, the day Danish resistance came out into the open, the BBC was able to broadcast a recording by a Danish resistance leader which had been smuggled out of Denmark.

In contrast the Swedish Service was speaking to an audience which, while it was predominantly anti-Nazi, was nonetheless neutral and well served by a high quality press and a dependable radio news service. Sweden may have been isolated from the West but it was not starved of reliable information. Polemical broadcasting would have been counter productive with such an audience. Consequently, though the service carried news and commentaries and talks by Swedish journalists working in London like Erik Rydbeck and Alf Martin, the correspondent of the Göteborg *Handels och Sjöfartstidning*, Sweden's most outspoken anti-Nazi newspaper, it sought to make its main impact in the cultural field and through projection of wartime Britain. One of its main achievements was a series of specially commissioned talks by eleven Nobel Prize winners, including Einstein, Thomas Mann and Lord Robert Cecil. There were also talks by such as Wickham Steed, the former editor of *The Times* and a brilliant broadcaster of the time, and Harold Nicolson. Nonetheless the service was not itself neutral. 'It was never British policy to attack Sweden's neutrality', Halvor William-Olsson, a member of the service and the producer of many of its major talks series, wrote many years later. 'Our target was the spirit of neutrality, the tendency to play down the moral issues and to present the war as a struggle among the great powers of no concern to innocent neutrals.'[98]

Moral issues, of course, were what wartime broadcasting to Europe had ultimately been about, even if, for the British, survival had been a powerful spur at the start and political expediency made its mark, here and there, at the behest of government, on what the broadcasters often saw as a crusade. If hopes of a better and juster world were kindled among countless millions among the ashes and ruins of Europe, the BBC was not the least of the influences which brought this about. Among those whom it helped to survive through the dark years there were many who would say afterwards that it had been the main one.

10
London Calling the World

Though it was in Europe, inevitably, that the war of ideas took on its most dramatic and memorable form, it had its echoes in the wider world outside. Because the war itself rapidly became a global conflict in which Britain was involved at every point, broadcasting, with its enormous reach and its still relatively unexplored potential, became a key weapon in Britain's hands. It disseminated throughout the world a truthful account of events, it nurtured and developed existing friendships, helped to strengthen the cement which bound together the peoples of the English-speaking world, and gave world-wide currency to the values in defence of which Britain had taken up arms.

While only very limited beginnings were made in wartime in the attempt to reach the already huge populations of the Far East, the broadcasting effort to the Middle East and Latin-America, where it had all started, grew to an impressive scale. In the world-wide English Overseas Service, the heir to the pre-war Empire Service, the stimulus of war, by compelling a broadening of outlook and bringing about the injection of new blood, particularly from the Commonwealth, helped to sweep away the last remnants of that peculiar brand of comfortable English parochialism which had been such a feature of the old Empire Service, just as two decades later decolonisation and the growth of the Third World were in turn to prompt a further revolution in outlook. The Overseas Services, as they became known after the autumn of 1941 to distinguish them from the European Service, grew into just as vast and varied a grouping of broadcasting enterprises as the European operation, with their own News Service and programme departments and their own very distinctive feel, born of their wider and more diverse horizons.

As has been seen,[1] R.A. Rendall, the newly appointed Director of Empire Services, had moved rapidly in 1940 to redefine the objectives of the Empire Service, and by 1941 he was able to claim that it had become in effect a world service, split up into four daily segments, each under a separate director, with its own distinctive character and addressing itself primarily to listeners in a specific region of the globe, but mindful at the same time of the many listeners in other regions who would also be picking it up. News, under the skilled editorship of Bernard Moore, was a common ingredient, including 'Radio Newsreel', which offered 'a succession of vivid sound pictures of history in the making' and was originally designed by Peter Pooley in 1940 as a totally new concept of news broadcasting. The same was true of 'Listening Post', a daily programme presented by James Ferguson and Edgar Lustgarten in which they dealt with the inconsistencies of German propaganda to the English-speaking world. Talks by such distinguished regular contributors as Wickham Steed and J.B. Priestley were quite naturally given world-wide coverage since they were as valid for, say, an audience in Australia or New Zealand as for listeners in the United States.

In 1940, however, one of Rendall's most urgent tasks was to provide an antidote to the rampant anti-British and isolationist feelings prevalent at that time in America. As Maurice Gorham, who took charge of the North American Service in May 1941, put it: 'If isolationism and anti-British feelings triumphed in the United States, as well they might, not only would Britain probably be conquered and all Europe become a Nazi camp, but America herself would finally fall. Then, for the first time since the Pilgrim Fathers, there would be no resort of freedom, nowhere left for free men to go.'[2]

Until the summer of 1940 the Empire Service had contained no programmes aimed primarily at the American audience, even though it had long been established that it had a substantial following in the United States. Now, with Britain isolated and fighting for its life, there was an overriding need for 'calm reassurance' about British determination and capacity for survival and for a rapid extension of opportunities for Americans to hear the voice of Britain. Ernest Bushnell, the General Programme Organiser of the Canadian Broadcasting Corporation, was brought in on temporary secondment in the summer of 1940 to give the BBC the benefit of his close knowledge of American tastes. The CBC already had a substantially staffed office in London from which it was reporting the war. It was headed by H. Rooney Pelletier, a former Head of Programmes for the CBC Station at Quebec, and Canadians played a major role in setting up the new BBC service. Pelletier himself soon moved over to the BBC, with which he had spent six months on attachment before the war, to become North American Programme Organiser under Gorham. He was joined by Warren MacAlpine, who had been 'theologian, philosopher, politician and advertising man'[3] before becoming North American Talks Organiser.[4] Another Canadian, who was to become justly famous for his on-the-spot reports from the Arnhem battle in 1944, was Stanley Maxted, then working on 'Radio Newsreel' at Abbey Manor.

'Bush', as Bushnell was more generally known, was described by Gorham as 'tough, chunky and disrespectful', 'just the right man to put some new ideas into the BBC', and it was largely on his advice and through his influence that in the Overseas Services the BBC abandoned its somewhat casual pre-war attitudes towards timing and became professionally addicted to smooth presentation and rigorous, split-second precision. But it was more than a mere matter of cosmetic surgery. Although the first result of Bushnell's brief and hectic passage was a general tightening up of presentation, the elimination of gaps and silences, shorter and crisper news bulletins and the introduction of news commentaries on the American model, the substance of the service itself underwent a radical change. Whereas the pre-war Empire Service had tended to assume that it was in a seller's market and was, so to speak, doing the audience a favour, increased awareness of the need to attract the interest and attention of the American audience began to creep into the choice of pro-gramme ideas, there was a more purposive and competitive look about the whole output. The content was British, but the style, to some extent, was trans-atlantic. A new programme plan was introduced by Bushnell which included broadcasts by British stage and screen stars well known in the United States, record request programmes creating links between Britain and the United States, and plenty of Variety and light music, all designed to convince Americans that Britain wasn't going under but was cheerfully and valiantly carrying on.

American public reaction to the changes was immediately favourable. The New York Times commented: 'England's new short wave schedule indicates changed tactics in broadcasting. Most of the programmes are centred about Britain's preparations for invasion, and these are handed down the airlanes in such a variety of ways that something fresh is always coming to the ear. A review of the first new set of programmes showed that England isn't wasting time on fairy tales.'[5] The Princeton listening centre reported more tersely that it found the new programmes 'frank in tone, lively in pace and with no standoffishness'.[6] A Canadian announcer had been used in the early stages, but there was no mistaking the Britishness of the galaxy of distinguished speakers who contributed to the long-running series 'Britain speaks', intro-duced at that time. J.B. Priestley and other speakers such as Leslie Howard, Gerald Barry, Howard Marshall and Sir Philip Joubert put in regular appear-ances in this spot during 1940 and 1941, and perhaps the best known among the commentators, apart from Wickham Steed, whose talks on world affairs were transmitted each week throughout the war with only two interruptions, was Vernon Bartlett, Member of Parliament, writer and distinguished jour-nalist, who had been the first to give talks on international affairs for the BBC in the early twenties.

American listeners wrote in their hundreds to express their appreciation both to the BBC and to individual speakers like J.B. Priestley, whose 'unruffled calmness and courageous tone' were much admired, as were Vernon Bartlett's 'frank and informative' talks.[7] *Time* magazine commented at the end of July 1940: '"Britain speaks", now a fortnight old, is a vast improvement over the stodgy stuff that the BBC used to shortwave to North America. With swing bands and torch singers, brisk news and political comments, "Britain speaks" is at its best when novelist-playwright John Boynton Priestley holds forth.'[8]

American Radio commentators stationed in London, like Ed Murrow. of CBS and Fred Bate of NBC, who was injured by the Portland Place landmine in December 1940 just as he was about to go into Broadcasting House to transmit his daily despatch to America, did much to bring home to the American public the drama of life in the London blitz and made their own important contribution to the gradual shift of American sympathies in favour of Britain. Their graphic descriptions struck a responsive chord in American imaginations, gripped by the tense spectacle of the British with their backs to the wall. The North American Service supplemented their reports by documenting at first hand for American listeners what Londoners were going through by the simple device of taking microphones out into the streets and letting Londoners tell their own story of the blackout and the Blitz. 'London after Dark', designed for rebroadcasting by CBS, and 'London Carries on', designed for NBC, were remarkable for the fact that they were live and brought American listeners into immediate contact with the harsh realities of life at night in the London streets and shelters. BBC observers posted at various key points in the capital would take it in turns to provide descriptions, often at the height of air raids. An early edition of 'London after Dark' at the end of August 1940 started just as the air raid warning sirens were sounding. American listeners heard the sirens and the unhurried footsteps of the crowd at Trafalgar Square just by St Martin-in-the-Fields, making its orderly way to the shelters. 'That combination of sounds', Ed Murrow wrote afterwards, 'did more than pages of print or hours of radio news reporting to convince Americans that Londoners took their air raids without excitement or panic.'[9]

By the end of 1940 the BBC had achieved a major breakthrough in North America in securing substantial rebroadcasts by local stations. The Canadian Broadcasting Corporation was relaying two BBC news bulletins every day, as well as 'Radio Newsreel', 'Britain speaks', and a current affairs programme called 'Questions of the Hour'. All could be heard across the border in the United States. In addition to the CBS and NBC networks, the Mutual Broadcasting System was also relaying BBC news, and so were as many as eighty independent stations right across the United States.

Tony Rendall himself temporarily took personal charge of the North American Service after Bushnell had gone back to Canada and spent two months in Canada and the United States towards the end of 1940 to assess the impact of the new programmes. The proverbial 'old head on young shoulders', as Gorham described him,[10] he had a 'strong streak of the statesman in him' and the knack of attracting good people round him.[11] Gorham, who joined him as North American Service Director in May 1941, was certainly one of his most inspired if unorthodox choices. An Irish Catholic and a socialist with a bristling moustache, childlike charm and a healthy tendency to irreverence,[2] he had been Editor of the *Radio Times* for eight

years before moving over to programme direction. Lively, original, a great
beer drinker but suffering from a bad stammer, he was one of those who had
become impatient of the BBC's pre-war stuffiness and of the bureaucratic
stranglehold which he felt had increasingly gripped it after the move from
Savoy Hill. In his autobiography, *Sound and Fury,* he wrote characteristically:

> The war brought out the best in the BBC. During those years I think we saw how
> much good there was in the institution I had always criticised. But it did most good by
> making it break into new fields, do things in new ways and make use of a lot of people
> who would never have come to the BBC but for the war.[13]

That was certainly true of the North American Service, which under Gorham, Pelletier and MacAlpine, developed into one of the BBC's major and
most successful wartime enterprises. The service ran for seven and a half
hours each night, ending at 3 am. It involved an intricate network of relation-
ships with American radio stations and daily telephone conferences with the
BBC's increasingly busy New York office. By the autumn of 1942 the number
of American stations relaying BBC programmes had risen to 285, and a New
York survey showed that forty per cent of radio listeners heard one or more
BBC programmes each week on their own local stations. A whole array of
new programmes devised by Gorham and his staff had made their appearance
on the air, often the result of close consultations with the American networks
and tailored to their requirements. 'Britain to America', for instance, was
originally devised for NBC and was later also carried by ABC. Also heard on
the BBC Home Service, it brought to the microphone, with Leslie Howard as
compère, not only a whole array of stars of stage and screen and the works of
British composers played by the London Symphony Orchestra, but also
hundreds of ordinary British people, servicemen and civilians, to talk about
their wartime jobs and their experiences.

> They come to the microphone [wrote an American critic] and tell their own stories
> – dock workers, soldiers, housewives, girls who have replaced men in the war factories
> – and in their very understatement is an almost heart-breaking gallantry. The test of
> such programmes is, of course, whether or not they bring you closer, in understanding
> and emotion, to the people they describe. 'Britain to America' does precisely that.[14]

Some of the great names of what was to become the BBC Features Department under Laurence Gilliam lent a hand with 'Britain to America' in its
early days – writers and producers like Louis MacNeice, D.G. Bridson, Colin
Wills, Francis Dillon and Robert Barr. Great issues of war and peace were
discussed in 'Freedom Forum', an unscripted programme which was the first
of its kind to be broadcast by the BBC. Its regular team consisted of Ed
Murrow, G.M. Young and Harold Laski, who [Gorham noted] had a phenomenal knowledge of American affairs. Others like Sir William Beveridge
and Jan Masaryk would occasionally take part, and Ed Murrow himself took
the chair in the absence of the regular chairman, Sir Frederick Whyte. 'Trans-

atlantic Quiz', carried on both sides of the ocean, was also successfully launched at that time, while Hamish McGeachy, a Canadian journalist from Toronto, presented a regular Sunday news round-up in which he discussed world events with experts and war correspondents in Allied capitals. 'American Eagle Club' enabled Americans to hear the voices of their compatriots flying with the RAF in the Eagle Squadron, and in 'Children calling Home' British parents were able to talk to their children evacuated to the United States – an often moving experience for the American audience.

One of the North American Service's most successful and long-running ventures grew out of a conversation between Bushnell and Alan Melville over dinner at the Café Royal during the early stages of the Blitz in the autumn of 1940. This was 'Front Line Family'. The first of the British 'soap operas' and presenting the everyday life of an English middle-class family standing up to the strains of war, it ran continuously for six days a week throughout the war and in 1945 was taken by Gorham to the Light Programme, where as 'The Robinson Family' it ran until 1947. By May 1942 it seemed to have aroused more interest than any other overseas programme except the News, 'Radio Newsreel' and the talks by J.B. Priestley and Wickham Steed and was being broadcast all over the world. It was a firm favourite with the British troops, and gripped the imagination and affection of millions of listeners abroad. People would send cables when Mrs Robinson had a heart attack, 'threatening untold reprisals if she was allowed to die'. It was taken off after Gorham had moved from the Light Programme to take charge of television. 'The BBC killed it,' Gorham wrote. 'It had never been popular inside Broadcasting House.'[15]

Towards the end of the war a national survey conducted throughout the United States showed that in a sample week one-fifth of adult Americans with radio sets had heard at least one BBC broadcast. All four of the main radio networks, CBC, NBC, ABC and Mutual, were carrying at least one BBC broadcast regularly. On 'D' Day 725 out of a total of 914 American stations had rebroadcast BBC reports of the landings, and the numbers rebroadcasting King George VI's and Winston Churchill's addresses on VE Day was only slightly smaller. In the summer of 1945 the numbers of rebroadcasts was higher than ever before, and Verl Thomson, the Programme Director of stations KSOO and KELO in Sioux Falls, South Dakota, recalling that his two stations had carried more than 2,000 BBC relays since February 1944, summed up the feeling among American broadcasters:

In looking back now to the thousands of broadcasts carried and the hundreds of telegrams and letters from the New York Office of the BBC, we can see that international short wave broadcasting can be of tremendous service. People of this area have come to accept the English accent, that amused them at one time, as just a manner of speech. They feel a closer kinship and understanding of world problems better than ever before ...[16]

The same might have been said in any of the dominions. By the middle of the war, with the Overseas Services largely concentrated at 200 Oxford Street, a whole commonwealth broadcasting community had grown round Rendall and the revitalised world-wide English-language services. As in the case of Ernest Bushnell, Robert McCall, the Victoria Manager of the Australian Broadcasting Commission, had come over to start the first Pacific Service in 1940 and on his return to Australia was succeeded by George Ivan Smith, also an Australian, seconded from ABC, who subsequently became Head of the United Nations Information Services in New York. John Grenfell Williams, a bilingual South African trained as a medical missionary and with a deep commitment to the development of the black peoples of Africa, was African Service Director and later became Rendall's deputy. Z.A. Bokhari, later Director-General of All-India Radio, was in charge of Eastern Service programmes in English and Hindustani to India, where George Orwell worked as a producer. Regular commentators included Tahu Hole, a New Zealander who, at the outbreak of war, was the London correspondent of the *Melbourne Herald* and was soon contributing regular commentaries to the Pacific and Eastern Services,[17] the Canadian Hamish McGeachy, A.G. Mac-Donnell, the novelist, and Robert Fraser, later to become Director-General of ITA. Professor Denis Brogan was Gorham's intelligence adviser on American affairs – 'he could often tell you not only why something had happened but what was going to happen next'[18] – and wrote weekly reports on American opinion which were widely read throughout the BBC.

As with North America, broadcasting to Australia, New Zealand and South Africa was geared to the maximum amount of local rebroadcasting. A large number of programmes were 'made to measure' and shaped to fit agreed places in the schedules of the rebroadcasting country, and by 1943 Australia was relaying nearly two hours of BBC programmes daily, including 'Radio Newsreel' and three news bulletins, and New Zealand two and three-quarter hours including seven bulletins. Providing human links between Britain and the two Pacific Dominions was one of the main objectives. British cities were linked with Australian and New Zealand cities of the same name through the medium of broadcasting. Dominion troops in Britain had their own programmes in which they were able to speak to the folks back home. Radio was being used for bridge building and to enable people to speak to people at a time when so many had been scattered all over the world by the war and valued links with home. Something of wartime Britain, too, was being conveyed to the other end of the world through the voices of ordinary people speaking direct from farm and factory.

The African Service under Grenfell Williams, as well as providing a general service for the whole continent and in particular for what the Empire Service had regarded as its main audience, the white population of South Africa, was also now producing a large number of regular programmes specially designed for specific African colonies. The South African Broadcasting Corporation's rebroadcasts of BBC programmes were on a scale comparable with those of Australia and Canada – nearly two hours of programming each day – but there were also regular programmes for East and West Africa, Southern Rhodesia, and for the West Indies, Malta and Cyprus, and the Pacific islands, for whose broadcasting interests the African Service was also responsible. Grenfell Williams was probably the first to grasp the opportunities which radio offered of making a contribution to the solution of colonial problems. He could 'see Africa being born'[19] and a vast untapped audience coming up, and he sought to 'throw into the partnership between the United Kingdom and the colonies one valuable asset – the experience of the people of Britain in tackling some of their own problems, in the hope that this experience may be of some use to the people of the colonies in tackling similar problems.'[20] The title of one regular programme was 'Young Africa'. It was indicative of the new spirit at large in the BBC and a portent of the developments of a later decade.

Another sign of the times was that the term 'commonwealth' was being increasingly used as an alternative to 'empire', and there was much talk of commonwealth unity and solidarity. The Empire Service itself had been redesignated Overseas Service as early as November 1939 in recognition of its new wartime character, and by the middle of the war, with opportunites for development opened up by the introduction of new transmitters as well as the huge growth in the numbers of British and commonwealth troops serving overseas – particularly at first in the Middle East – the BBC began to explore the possibility of providing an alternative overseas service in English primarily for the forces. This began in a relatively small way in November 1942 with two hours of news and entertainment broadcast on short wave to the Middle East, and it was at this point that the title General Overseas Service was first used, to distinguish it from the specialised regional services which had grown out of the old Empire Service. Expansion was rapid. Two months after its inception the new service was transmitting six hours each day without interruption to the Middle East and the Mediterranean. By the end of 1943 it was on the air for twenty hours a day and could be heard practically all over the world, including the Western Hemisphere. Though when specifically providing a service for British troops it was referred to as the General Forces Programme its appeal was much wider. It was seen by the BBC as a Home Service for British listeners abroad, whether or not they were members of the forces, though, as had already begun to happen before the war with the old Empire Service, others for whom the programme was not intended could not be prevented from listening. One major consequence of its introduction was to enable the regional English services to concentrate more narrowly on their own intended audiences, leaving the General Overseas Service to cater for the needs of British expatriates. A further consequence was that the General

Overseas Service, unlike the regional services, was totally devoid of propaganda intentions, and this had its effect on its post-war character as it evolved into the World Service as we know it today.

This process of organic growth and transformation in response to external needs led to the decision, taken by the BBC's new Editor-in Chief, William Haley and approved by the Board of Governors on 13 January 1944, to make the General Overseas Service available to the home audience in Britain as its second domestic programme, replacing the Forces Programme which had been established in 1940. Haley had been on a visit to the forces in Italy late in 1943 and had returned convinced that what the troops wanted was to hear the same programme as the folks at home. But rather than transmit on short wave segments of the existing Home Forces Programme, as originally briefly envisaged, he went in the end for the bolder, reverse solution. Until the end of the war, therefore, when the Light Programme was created under Maurice Gorham, listeners in Britain had as an alternative to the Home Service, on medium wave, the same programme as was being broadcast to audiences all over the world. Many of its entertainment shows had of course previously been transmitted both at home and overseas, but many others had been specifically designed for overseas consumption and now found their way onto the domestic air, where they became firm favourites. Stemming from the endlessly fertile overseas entertainment unit run by Cecil Madden fom his base at the Criterion Theatre in Piccadilly Circus they included 'Variety Bandbox' and 'Merry-go-round' as well as the long-running 'Front Line Family'. All found their way onto the new Light Programme after the end of the war, as did also 'Radio Newsreel', brought there by Gorham and a major feature of domestic broadcasting until the end of the sixties. It survives intact to this day in the World Service, preceded by the same majestic signature tune – 'Imperial Echoes' – as in its early wartime days in the North American Service.

Though simultaneous rebroadcasting was the principal way in which BBC programmes achieved a deeper penetration in the United States and the commonwealth, transcriptions – that is to say programmes recorded in London and sent out on gramophone records to potential users – formed an increasingly important supplementary means of dissemination. Tentative beginnings had been made by the Empire Service in the mid-thirties,[21] when Malcolm Frost had successfully primed the pump in the course of a worldwide sales tour. But in the meantime complications had set in. A body called the Joint Broadcasting Committee had been set up early in 1939 under the auspices of the Foreign Office and quite separately from the BBC with, as its avowed purpose, 'to promote international understanding by means of broadcasting'. Its method was to 'place' British recorded programmes of a propaganda nature with foreign broadcasting organisations in Europe and elsewhere. The JBC's Director was Hilda Matheson, who had been BBC Director of Talks and a seminal figure in that field in the late twenties but had then fallen out with the BBC and resigned in 1931. The BBC saw the JBC's activities as a serious danger to its own position, not least because foreigners would not always be aware of the distinction to be made between BBC and JBC programmes. 'I am sorry to appear unduly persistent about the JBC problem', J.B. Clark wrote in January 1940, 'but there is increasing evidence to show that their growing activities are bound to trespass on what we regard as the BBC monopoly.'[22]

It took time for the problem to resolve itself, but after protracted discussions it was eventually agreed that the BBC would take responsibility for the activities of the JBC and final absorption took place on 1 October 1941.[23] The London Transcription Service – LTS – was born of the marriage. The natural successor to the old 'bottled programmes' scheme initiated by Frost, it grew to far larger proportions and encompassed a far wider range of programmes than it had ever done in the days of the JBC and assumed an increasingly important role as the war progressed, not only with commonwealth and American broadcasters but also in Latin-America. By the end of the war it was distributing programmes in nineteen languages, with those for Latin-America coming a close second to those intended for the English-speaking world. Entertainment and music had been added to the more serious cultural output. In the last year of the war over 500 stations all over the world were using LTS programmes, which accounted for a total of 48,000 hours of transmitted programme time in 1945 – or an average of 131 hours a day. It was a record unequalled by any organisation in the world and continued to be so until the financial cuts imposed by the Conservative Government in 1981 placed the whole operation in jeopardy.

The success of the Transcription Service in Latin America flowed naturally from that of the direct broadcasting operation in Spanish and Portuguese. It was a remarkable reversal of the unhappy situation which had been noted at the end of 1937 by Felix Greene, then BBC Representative in North America, in the course of an official visit to Latin America. 'We are facing damaging propaganda in all its forms,' he wrote on his return. 'Countless Brazilians, Argentinians and Chileans have told me how difficult it is to stand by and lift no finger to protect Britain's name and interests.' So far as information and therefore influence were concerned both Italy and Germany, as Greene had found, had established a dominant position in the South American continent, helped by the existence of large expatriate communities from both nations and by the apparent inertness of official British agencies.

The BBC Latin-American Service was to change all that in due course. Starting in March 1938 with a combined total of thirty minutes a day confined to news only, the service grew rapidly to nearly two hours a day in the first year. It then briefly reverted to news only at the outbreak of war on account of the acute pressure on available technical facilities created by the overriding need for a rapid expansion of foreign language services to Europe. Full transmissions were restored in July 1940, and by March 1943 had been doubled, from two and a half hours to five hours a day in both languages. At this point the introduction of the new transmitters at Skelton[24] made possible the long-desired splitting of the Portuguese and Spanish transmissions into two separate services operating simultaneously for part of the time, thus bringing to an end the uncomfortable arrangement which had made it necessary to switch from one language to the other as much as four times every night.

The change took place on 21 November 1943, when the combined output in both languages was doubled overnight. By the end of the war the BBC was transmitting in Spanish to Latin America for five and three-quarter hours each day, more than in any other foreign language in wartime except briefly in 1944, in French. This ensured that with the judicious use of repeats listeners in all four time zones covered by the service were able to receive all key programmes at a convenient time. The Brazilian Service rose at the same time to four hours a day, more even than the wartime Arabic Service and nearly as much as the Italian Service at the height of the war. Both services were to achieve further expansions immediately after the war before they were savagely cut by nearly half in the case of the Spanish Service and by nearly two-thirds in the case of the Brazilian Service as a result of reductions in the Government grant-in-aid in 1951.

In the earliest stages, when the service was confined to news, R.A. Calvert, who had been the *Christian Science Monitor*'s part-time correspondent in Madrid, was in charge of editing the bulletins under A.E. Barker, the Foreign Language Services News Editor. But as elsewhere, with the rapid expansion of the first year a separate programme unit was formed and J.A. Camacho, who had been in at the very start of the service as an announcer/translator, was made Programme Organiser, working to C.A.L. Cliffe, then Empire Programme Director. In the wider reorganisation of the Overseas Services which took place in the summer of 1940[25] Cliffe was appointed Director of the Latin American Service, a post he held until January 1942 when he left the BBC to join the RAF. His period of office is remembered as having been in many ways the happiest in the service's wartime history. Cliffe himself, a man of great intelligence (a former scholar and Captain of the School at Eton, a former ADC to the Governor of Nigeria, and later a classical scholar at Balliol), had learned Spanish in almost no time with Camacho's help. Gifted with an exceptionally comprehensive musical culture, he subsequently wrote the libretti of at least two of Arthur Benjamin's operas and used to solve *The Times* crossword puzzle in ten minutes. In later years he became a much loved performer on 'Round Britain Quiz'. He ran the service on a loose rein: 'He didn't interfere much and never gave orders', George Camacho remembers 'but he encouraged us, occasionally fought battles for us and sometimes expressed doubts.'[26] The service was expanding, the staff was enthusiastic and willing to work long hours, and there was the excitement of creating something new and the satisfaction derived from reports of growing audiences and increased numbers of rebroadcasts by local stations up and down the South American continent. There was also considerable talent at hand. Angel Ara, a young Spaniard, had been one of the earliest recruits. Strongly opposed to Franco and caught in England by the Spanish Civil War, he had been studying English at Nottingham University and was now beginning to reveal the skills which were to make him in due course one of the most outstanding producers of dramatised historical features of his day. The first of the service's dramatised offerings was not however, his work. Broadcast on 14 June 1940, the anniversary of Simon Bolivar's birth, it was an account, highly romanticised, of Bolivar's historic journey across the Andes from Venezuela into Colombia, written by Lionel Hale and produced by Archie Harding and Royston Morley. Camacho, who had played the part of Bolivar, was recruiting regular commentators for the service, like Geoffrey Crowther, H.V. Hodson and F.A. Voigt. Salvador de Mandriaga had already started his weekly broadcasts, which were to continue throughout the war. Wickham Steed's talks for the Empire Service were being regularly broadcast in translation, and Spanish-speaking commentators like Arturo Barca and Daniel Fernandez Shaw were also being drawn in.

Camacho's own weekly commentaries under the pseudonym of 'Atalya' – the watch tower – which were to become famous, started, as so often happened, out of accidental necessity rather than as a result of a positive editorial choice. The service was short of programme funds and Camacho, to make his limited resources go further, started building regular talks from material already broadcast on the Empire Service. This led to copyright difficulties and he began to write original commentaries of his own, first in English for translation and later, at Cliffe's urging, direct into Spanish. One of his colleagues suggested the pseudonym 'Atalya', which stuck. It was a whole year before the Overseas Service management discovered that he was contravening the rule which forbade staff from broadcasting commentaries in their own right, but by this time it was too late.[27]

A parallel development took place in the Brazilian Service, where a young Brazilian, Martin Pinheiro Neto, whom Cedric Cliffe had recruited in the course of a tour of Latin-America, started broadcasting regular commentaries under the pseudonym of 'P Xysto'. When he returned to Brazil his place was taken by one of the earliest members of the Brazilian Service, Manoel Antonio Braune, who broadcast under the pseudonym of 'Aimberé'.

The service had moved to Wood Norton at the end of September 1940 and the close proximity of the Monitoring Service produced its own benefits. In particular George Weidenfeld started contributing short talks on the internal

situation in Germany which were based on a careful analysis of the output of
the German Home Service and were intended in particular for the many
people of German origin who had settled in Latin-America. But apart from
the development of a rich and varied output, which also included music by
composers particularly favoured in Latin-America, there were more fundamental questions of style to resolve. Latin-Americans are brilliant, sponta-
neous broadcasters and favour an approach which reflects their predilection
for *personalismo*, and there were differences of opinion in the early stages
about whether the BBC should adopt a similar approach. Manoel Antonio
Braune persuaded Camacho that this would be mistaken and that a more
austere style would be more appropriate for the BBC and would win greater
respect.[28]

As the war progressed and the Latin-American Service moved on to its
more permanent base at Aldenham House in Hertfordshire, it was developing
its own distinctive character and appeal – 'quietly confident but frank about
failures; unbombastic, above all credible, accurate and reliable'.[29] An American survey conducted in 1941 had shown that two-thirds of short wave
listeners in the area gave the BBC the highest credibility rating.[30] By the
middle of 1943, with four BBC representatives at work in Latin-American
capitals, the amount of press and radio publicity for the BBC was on the
increase and one hundred local stations were relaying Latin-American Service
programmes on medium wave each day. A dramatic reconstruction of the
Battle of Britain was relayed by fifty-six stations, and seventy or eighty
stations were rebroadcasting BBC news. Norman Zimmern, who had succeeded Cedric Cliffe at the head of the service in 1942, wrote at the end of
1944 that the number of daily rebroadcasts had risen to three hundred and
that 'the majority of Latin-Americans automatically turn to the BBC for
accurate war news and for the confirmation or refutation of unofficial
rumours'.[31]

News, in fact, was, as always, what most attracted listeners, and next to it
were the widely rebroadcast weekly talks by Madariaga, Wickham Steed,
'Atalya' and 'Aimberé' – also reprinted in many newspapers. An attractive and
immediately successful addition to the Brazilian output after 1943 were the
war reports from the Italian front of Francis Hallawell – 'Chico Alabem' as
he was known to the Brazilian troops – the popular Latin-American Service
correspondent with the Brazilian forces in Italy.[32] 'Radio Newsreel', too, had
spawned Latin-American editions – 'Radio Panorama', in the Spanish Service
and 'Radio Gaceta' in the Brazilian Service. The programme was fed by line
every night in its original English version to Aldenham, recorded on wax
cylinders, transcribed, edited, translated and broadcast the same night in
Spanish and Portuguese. The climax, so far as news was concerned, came
with the Allied landings in Normandy on 'D' Day, when the BBC was the only
source available to Latin-American radio stations for rapid coverage and
interpretation of the dramatic events taking place in north-west Europe.

With the massive expansion of air time in November 1943 the service had become too large for one man to control the whole output directly. With intelligence, news and the overseas offices it now numbered close on 180 people. Separate organisers were then placed in charge of the two language services: W.A. Tate, who had been torpedoed twice on his way from Brazil to take over from Pinheiro Neto and as a result had taken five months to make the journey, took charge of the Brazilian Service, and Peter Wessel, of Anglo-Danish extraction but born in Chile, took over the Spanish output. Ara's dramatic output was going from strength to strength, partly adapted from Home Service programmes but mostly written by him, and he was now able to call on the services of a Spanish musician, Manuel Lazareno, for the incidental music for his features. Professional actors, too, were becoming available to reinforce the amateur cast of announcers, translators and secretaries. This led immediately after the war to Ara's most distinguished achievements, the 27-part 'Don Quixote', marking the 400th anniversary of the birth of Cervantes, and the 21-part 'Christopher Columbus', marking the 500th anniversary of Columbus's birth. Both series can still be found, forty years later, in the archives of radio stations up and down the South American continent and are occasionally brought out again as masterpieces in their own right.

There were some shadows in the picture. In particular there were disagreements at times between the news staff under W.J. Breething, the Latin-American News Editor (another *Daily Telegraph* man) and the programme staff under Camacho, who took the view that 'news must be straight and free from propaganda' and that humour, which sub-editors were seeking to inject in the bulletins, should be used only sparingly. An experiment with three-minute news talks written in the news room and inserted at the end of the shortened bulletins for a time in 1944 led to protests by the programme staff who had to translate them and read them at the microphone, on the grounds that they amounted to 'absurdly crude propaganda' and were 'wholly out of line with the principles that had guided the service and far worse than the Germans.'[33] J.B. Clark discreetly brought the experiment to an end when confronted with the facts.

On another front the story was a good deal happier. Philip Guedalla was one of those the BBC had to deal with on Latin-American matters at the Ministry of Information and proved a wise and friendly contact. The service was very largely left to its own devices, with Guedalla providing effective support when early in the war the BBC resisted Foreign Office pressure to broadcast a translation of Vansittart's *Black Book*. J.B. Clark was always there in the background, skilfully chairing the fortnightly meetings with ministry officials and deftly turning away their wilder suggestions.

At the same time friendly relations were being built up with the numerous Latin-American missions in London, not the least of the burdens borne by the service's senior staff, since the nineteen countries concerned each had two or three national feast days every year, invariably marked by special programmes and diplomatic receptions which had to be attended.

The reward came at the end of the war with Camacho's tour of Latin-American capitals in the autumn of 1945, which confirmed overwhelmingly the wide respect enjoyed by the service and revealed 'Atalya's' own huge personal popularity. He was 'dined, wined and fêted' everywhere 'like a victorious general' and received by ministers and presidents. His visit made front page news wherever he went. It was both a personal triumph and, at a deeper level, a welcome indication of the distance which had been travelled since Felix Greene's gloomy report of 1937. Zimmern might say, as he did, that the BBC's reputation in Latin-America was 'in a large measure due to the fact that London had been the centre of resistance to Germany and to a greater extent than ever before the real metropolis of the world.'[34] Indeed broadcasting, as elsewhere, can only have been one factor in the situation and the tide of history greatly assisted it, but its role in that distant continent had been crucial.

The Arabic Service, the first of the BBC's foreign language services to be launched, had started in inauspicious circumstances and inevitably came under closer official scrutiny than most in view of the immediate strategic importance of the Middle East to British interests. There had been the tough, protracted argument with Rex Leeper over editorial policy, and as has been seen difficulties had arisen over the divided loyalties of Calvert, the first Arabic Editor.[35] But though in its very early stages the service worked under a special regime which required its News Editor to attend daily meetings with the Foreign Office Middle East Department, this did not last and in any case Donald Stephenson, who succeeded Calvert as Editor, is clear that those meetings were of a purely informational character and that the pressures which might have been feared did not in fact materialise at that stage. 'J.B. Clark won his point', he said, and in his experience the policy of telling the unvarnished truth to the Arabs and to others in the region, in Iran and Turkey, was not questioned.[36]

However with the collapse of France, casting grave doubt, as it did, in the Arab world as elsewhere, on Britain's chances of eventual victory, the nervousness of British officials in Cairo and elsewhere in the region in the face of the flood of victorious broadcast propaganda from Bari and Zeesen led in the summer and autumn of 1940 to serious government misgivings about the effectiveness of Britain's response. There was a spate of criticisms from the Ministry of Information.[37] Complaints came pouring in from British representatives in the Middle East. BBC Arabic bulletins, it was claimed, lacked 'virility and incisiveness'.[38] They were, so it was alleged, repeating unconfirmed rumours from enemy sources. Anthony Eden, then Secretary of State for War, had been made aware of these views in the course of a Middle East tour and had cabled them back to London. Churchill himself became involved and asked for explanations. Later, again, there were complaints that Arabic Service bulletins were 'unimaginative and insufficiently dramatic'. Yet Stephenson, going through recent output, could find no trace of 'unconfirmed rumours', and the BBC was able to assert that there had been no deviation from official policy.[39] Frank Pick himself admitted that much of the criticism was 'unfair and prejudiced', and Duff Cooper, at that stage at any rate, was disposed to stand up for the BBC.[40]

The concern was largely misplaced, as Stephenson was able to demonstrate in a detailed paper in which he denounced the 'peevish and sketchily informed' criticisms of the Ministry of Information. It was the unfavourable course of the war, he wrote, which had led 'our harassed diplomats to look more and more to the BBC to turn "planned withdrawals" (i.e. "defeats") into victories'. 'Our propaganda is now as virile, and our style as powerful, though not as vulgar, as that of the enemy ... It would be a great mistake for the BBC to imitate the unrestrained abuse of Berlin.'[41] Later, after the North African victories of 1942–43, Sigmar Hillelson, the diminutive Director of the Near Eastern Service, who knew the Arab world better than most of his critics, was able to point out that the policy of restraint and dignity had been vindicated by events. By then Italian propaganda to the Middle East had ceased with the Italian surrender, and German propaganda had lost much of its punch and credit. To the criticism which had been made in 1940 that the BBC did not take sufficient account of the Arab 'mentality' and that, at that stage, Zeesen had greater appeal to 'the semi-educated and illiterate classes', he was now able to reply:

> We thought it more important to be accepted as sincere and truthful by the discerning few than to increase our audience at all costs. Compared with the fanfares and harangues of Berlin our truthful news bulletins were voted dull, and the story we had to tell in the early days brought little comfort to our friends. Victory has changed all that. We are no longer accused of dullness.[42]

By then the service was broadcasting for three hours a day, its wartime maximum. Though its mainstay was news and commentaries setting out the British interpretation of events, it had developed further its early policy[43] of giving ample space to Arab musicians and artists and to leaders of Arab thought, as well as to readings of the Koran. In doing so it was greatly assisted by the opening of a BBC office in Cairo in February 1943. There were fears on official quarters that it might become another Arabist organisation, but in fact its main function was to keep in touch with Arab opinion and to create increased opportunities for drawing on the literary and artistic talent of the Arab world. Poetry and later play competitions drew large numbers of entries from all over the Arab world. There were discussion programmes and a 'Listeners' Forum', which in one year quadrupled the number of letters received by the service. There were also English lessons, and an Arabic *Listener* was launched, edited by Nevill Barbour, who was in charge of intelligence and later became one of the most noted experts on Arab and North African affairs in Britain; and just as the service was providing Arab writers and musicians with a far wider audience in the Arab world than they could otherwise have hoped for, so it was also making its contribution to the growth of Arab consciousness through the dissemination of news of developments in the Arab world itself, which was not available from any other source. 'It was in the nature of things', Hillelson wrote at the end of the war, 'that an Arabic service from London should be metropolitan rather than regional and thus work in harmony with the Arab urge towards the strengthening of their common nationhood.'[44] He made sure, though that it never lost sight of its role as a British station speaking to the Arabs.

All the service's senior staff were fluent Arabic speakers. Stephenson, who became Hillelson's deputy, once worked out that he, Hillelson, Barbour and G.L.W. MacKenzie, the News Editor, had sixty years of practice of the Arabic language between them. Hillelson himself, who had spent twenty-two years as a colonial official in the Sudan and whose German-Jewish origins had caused some official hesitation over his appointment as Director in 1940, was a distinguished Arabic scholar and insisted on the highest linguistic standards, for which the sevice continues to be known to this day. Although a daily programme in Moroccan dialect was broadcast to French North Africa during the period of Vichy rule, it was the exception. Experiments with other Arab dialects in the early stages were not successful, and literary Arabic – the Latin of the Arab peoples, as Hillelson called it – was used exclusively.

The emphasis on Arab culture, Arab music and the Arabic language helped greatly in establishing the service's integrity. Axis broadcasts at the time were largely confined to political propaganda, whereas the BBC 'endeavoured to appeal to the intellect as well as to the emotions and cultivated the courtesies of life as well as the needs of day-to-day political warfare'.[45] Its success with the audience is perhaps best expressed in this extract from a letter from a listener in West Africa received in 1940:

Respectful greetings from one who admires and appreciates your humanitarian efforts on behalf of the Arabic-speaking people. Behold, your weekly programme guide reaches me regularly except when it is delayed in the post owing to the present war crisis brought about by that insubordinate house painter, that insatiable and low-born tyrant, that man-slayer, Hitler. May God destroy him and his adherents, and grant humanity rest from his evil craft – a task easy to God. Behold us here, constant auditors of your broadcasts, which are the greatest, best arranged, most richly expressed and most intelligible in language of all Arabic emissions.[46]

The Arabic Service loomed largest in the Near Eastern Service, and neither the Turkish Service, which had started in November 1939 with a single fifteen-minute bulletin each day, nor the Persian Service could compete with it in size and scope. Yet the Turkish Service, which in due course was transferred to the European Service, had grown by 1944 to four transmissions totalling an hour and a quarter each day. Like the Persian Service, as Hillelson observed, it was broadcasting to a country which was more remote from the war than the Arab states of the Middle East and with policies less close to those of Britain. There were few short wave sets – Turkey had only an estimated 46,000 receivers in 1938 – and the listening habit did not grow to quite the same level as it did in the Arab world. On the other hand the importance of broadcasting to Turkey lay not only in the amount of direct listening, which was inevitably small, but also in the use made of the BBC by the Turkish press as a source of news and in its readiness to publish the texts of talks broadcast in the Turkish Service. A frequent broadcaster was Brigadier Sir Wyndham Deedes, who was well known as a friend of Turkey and spoke fluent Turkish, even if not, as was alleged by the British Council representative in Ankara, of the right kind. He gave a weekly war commentary and talks on many aspects of British life. Like the more limited transmissions in Persian, the Turkish Service had its role to play in what was a sensitive area in strategic terms, particularly in 1941 and 1942 when the Germans were simultaneously threatening both the Caucasus and Egypt.

The Persian transmission, which started on a four-days-a-week basis in December 1940, did not become daily until February 1941 and then remained confined to a solitary fifteen-minute bulletin for another two years. This did not prevent it, evidently, from playing an important part, noted at the time by the BBC Overseas Control Board and in the press, in the toppling of Reza Shah from the Peacock Throne in September 1941.[47] It was the availability of news of what was taking place in the country as the Shah's military position crumbled which was responsible, rather than incitement, but the incident left a legacy of bitterness against the BBC in the mind of the new Shah, Mohammed Reza, who remained convinced throughout his life that the BBC was hostile to him and his dynasty. At the time the situation led to difficulties for the BBC as some members of the small Persian staff refused to appear at the microphone after British troops had marched into Persia at the end of August 1941, though they continued with their duties as translators. Their absence lasted only a few days and an explanation was broadcast when they returned. The incident appears to have been handled discreetly by the BBC, whose Overseas Control Board resolved a few weeks later to express its appreciation of the work of the Persian Service during the crisis and noted without comment that there was probably more listening in Persia than had been thought before the crisis developed.[48]

The case of India was altogether different. It was the finest gem in the imperial crown and Britain and India had been closely enmeshed for close on 200 years. The issue of India's future had played a central and divisive role in

British politics throughout the thirties and became increasingly critical during
the war. At the same time India's strategic importance in the British scheme
of things was second to none and for a time the country was under grave
threat from the Japanese. As has been seen Reith had been briefly tempted to
go out there himself in the thirties to develop Indian broadcasting.[49] Eventually Lionel Fielden had gone instead and in 1940 was more than ready to
come home. Having urged on the BBC and the Ministry of Information the
importance of broadcasting to India in Hindustani from as early as September
1939, he made a strong bid for the job of running it himself, warmly supported
by the Government of India. 'I regard him as one of the only two geniuses I
know,' P.J. Grigg wrote to Ogilvie from New Delhi: 'I do not find myself
unduly put off by the small tiresomenesses which are inseparable from gen-
ius.'[50] J.B. Clark, however, was less enthusiastic, and no amount of lobbying
was able to overcome his opposition. He had resolved that what was needed
was 'an ICS officer of long experience' who would have the necessary political
judgement which, in his view, Fielden lacked. Eventually the choice settled
on Sir Malcolm Darling. Fielden, reluctantly, came in as Indian sub-editor
and second-in-command to Darling, a position he found humiliating and
from which he resigned after only a few months. With him as Programme
Organiser came Zulfaqar Bokhari, one of the founding fathers of Indian
broadcasting, who had been Bombay Station Manager since 1935 and was
later to become Director-General of All-India Radio.

The case for a Hindustani programme had been strongly made not just by
Fielden – and Bokhari[51] – but also by the Government of India itself. A
memorandum from New Delhi pointed out that Indian opinion was largely
indifferent to the war. Indians might have little sympathy for Nazism but that
did not make them pro-British. They were ignorant, in any case, of the true
significance of Nazism. 'Indian opinion', the memorandum stated, 'is not
altogether sure of the grim necessity of the war, and a considerable section of
it has doubts about its justice.'[52] The broadcasts should not assume that they
were speaking to the converted. German propaganda to India was asking
why Indians should die for Britain and pointing out that while the British
talked of democracy India remained a subject nation. 'Obvious' propaganda
had to be avoided, and, as Sir Frederick Puckle, the head of the Government
of India's Information Board, strongly stressed, 'any suspicion that the Hindustani broadcast was being used as an instrument of propaganda in favour
of a particular policy in regard to the constitutional relations between Britain
and India would destroy its war value'.[53] Bokhari, for his part, felt that
propaganda to India needed to provide intellectual stimulus and to be 'leftist'
in character if it was to be convincing, bringing in as contributors such
personalities as H.N. Brailsford, Margaret Bondfield, Harold Laski and Ellen
Wilkinson.

The Hindustani transmission started at very short notice on 11 May 1940, the day after the start of the German offensive in the West. It was limited at first to a ten-minute daily news review but was soon increased to twenty minutes. By the end of the following year it had grown to an hour a day and by the end of the war had been expanded to two and a quarter hours. A weekly newsletter in Bengali was introduced in October 1941, and the following year similar transmissions were introduced in Marathi, Gujerati, Tamil and Sinhala.

The style and approach of the early Hindustani transmissions caused something of a furore in India. 'The present Hindustani broadcast does not conform to the high level of the Allied cause', an official report from New Delhi stated.[54] There were too many 'undignified quips and jibes' at the expense of the Nazi leaders. The bulletins were 'too light in tone and too flimsy in material' in comparison with German bulletins, which were felt to be giving more solid news and were attracting listeners because of their 'thrilling' accounts of German victories. Propaganda was no longer required. Instead the broadcasts should convey resolution and confidence and use reasoned arguments. The BBC, as well as being 'vulgar' and 'cheap', according to some, was felt by others to be 'too quiet and dignified'. Some also thought that the type of Hindustani used was too high flown and too close to Urdu. It should be colloquial Hindustani, in the view of those critics, and avoid difficult Persian or Arabic words. The official view clearly was that 'satire does not go down'.[55] The truth was, as Fielden wrote later, that 'when you are on the losing side your propaganda is always lame'.[56] Some of the criticism which was pouring in from India was almost certainly prejudiced and self-interested. Sir Malcolm Darling, for his part, had not yet arrived from India when the service was launched but made it clear when he did that British broadcasting should be 'courteous and non-committal'. Fielden disagreed but had to give way and left shortly after. The wave of criticism from India eventually subsided for a time, but there was never any likelihood that broadcasting to India would be able to operate free from the sharpest critical scrutiny from both sides of the divide. The BBC was not in a position to say what Indian nationalists wanted to hear, whereas Zeesen was, and in any case, from a military standpoint, the tide at the time was flowing in Germany's favour. It was easy, therefore, for the New Statesman, which gave support to Fielden's views, to claim that 'the Germans understand how to meet Indian tastes and susceptibilities' while suggesting that the British did not. In point of fact a good deal had been learnt about what Indians expected from London broadcasts. Laurence Brander, the service's Intelligence Officer, who knew India well, took the view that they did not want to hear Indians from London talking on intellectual subjects. Nor did they expect to hear Indian music, or, for that matter, British dance music. What was wanted, as Fielden himself had emphasised as far back as 1937,[57] was solid British cultural fare. It was the best antidote to the German tactics of broadcasting high-quality classical music with the aim of giving the lie to the claims that the Nazis were uncivilised barbarians. The Germans, it was said, had some success in this way; listeners had been switching over to Zeesen after the BBC news, and German propaganda to India had been making much of the low cultural level of broadcasting expected by the average British listener in India. The special English programme to India amounting to forty-five minutes a day and produced by Bokhari under the Eastern Service Director, Professor Rushbrook Williams, offered the obvious outlet for what Brander called 'the very best all-English product', 'sensible, cultivated, gracious and interesting'.[58] Once the General Overseas Service had been launched to cater for British troops and other expatriates it became possible to concentrate solely on the needs of educated Indians.

Brander had recommended that there should be more European classical music, more plays selected from among those which were used as set work by students in India, repeats of the best features from the Home programme, and more talks by English experts on Indian thought, art and music, which, it was felt, would have flattery value. As a result the English Service to India became in those years an early version of the Third Programme, designed for Indian ears. George Orwell produced a six-part series of talks on 'The world we hope for', with Vernon Bartlett, Julian Huxley, E.M. Forster, Osbert Sitwell, Harold Laski and C.E.M. Joad as his contributors. Stephen Spender, Herbert Read, T.S. Eliot and Edmund Blunden gave talks on English poets for Indian students, and E.M. Forster and Desmond MacCarthy regularly reviewed new books. Wickham Steed's weekly talks were included there as elsewhere, and so was a repeat of 'The Brains Trust'.

Early in 1943, with some degree of boldness, a major series of round-table discussions on India's future was planned and eventually broadcast towards the end of the year under the title 'India and the Four Freedoms'. With Wickham Steed in the chair it brought together speakers like Sir Ernest Barker, Professor Denis Brogan, Gilbert Murray, Lord Lytton, Sir Atul Chatterjee and a host of experts with special knowledge of India's problems. Bokhari in the meantime had started bringing British musicians to the studio to listen to Indian music and to comment on it from a European standpoint – one of the ways Bokhari was exploring of discovering a common basis of approach to the arts between East and West. The results were encouraging. One famous English novelist writing in one of the London weeklies commented that 'the best literary talks are not all on the Home Service. Many are on the Eastern Service, audible to Indians but not to us.'[59] Brander, for his part, felt able to say towards the end of 1943 that 'evidence accumulates that the policy of projecting Britain to India by talks and discussions of the highest quality procurable, carefully avoiding the second best, is correct'.[60]

As in the case of Cairo, the setting up of a Delhi office, to which Donald Stephenson was appointed on 1 February 1944, made closer contact with the

Indian audience possible at a time when Indian nationalism was becoming increasingly militant and broadcasting, to be effective, needed to be based on first-hand knowledge of the state of Indian opinion. The BBC had a difficult course to steer. To be credible it needed to be able to speak frankly about the situation as it was and to reflect the views and activities of Congress leaders, many of whom were strongly anti-British. On the other hand it had to take account of the views of the Government of India, which was maintaining ' a constant stream of suggestion, criticism and advice'.

It was as aware as were the propagandists of Zeesen and later of the Japanese-controlled stations in South-East Asia of the weaknesses of Britain's case in India. 'There is a great hatred of the British in this country,' wrote Ahmed Ali, a well-known writer of the Urdu Delhi school who was a lecturer in English at Lucknow. According to him they were regarded as 'just exploiters'.[61] It may have been an exaggeration, but Japanese and German Propaganda made the most of such feelings. Broadcasting from London could not provide an answer to the problems of India's future or to its immediate political difficulties. It could show, on the other hand, that there were people of distinction and influence in Britain who were prepared to discuss them positively and sympathetically. It could show, too, that beyond the immediate causes of conflict between Britain and India there was common ground of a more lasting kind between the English-speaking Indian intelligentsia and the world of culture and literature in Britain. This was a long term approach to the relationship between Britain and India through the medium of broadcasting, and the phenomenal growth of listening to the BBC in India and Pakistan in the sixties and seventies was to show that it had been soundly based.

According to estimates available at the time there were little more than 100,000 radio receivers in India in 1940 for a population which was already past the 400 million mark. In the Far East, including China and Japan, the potential audience was about 650 million – approximately one-third of the entire population of the globe at the time – but the total estimated number of radio sets was thought at the end of the war to be not more than half a million, half the number available in Scotland at the time for a population of only five million. By then the BBC was broadcasting bulletins daily in Standard Chinese, Cantonese, Japanese, Burmese and Thai, and there were less frequent broadcasts in Malay and Hokkien. The proportion of short wave receivers was probably lowest in Japan, where only a small number of privileged officials were allowed to own one and there were probably not more than one hundred listeners to the limited service of news in Japanese which was started in July 1943. The value of the broadcasts, in the view of the Ministry of Information, which had been pressing for their introduction since 1941, was that they would be monitored and summarised for senior govern-

ment officials and ministers and would therefore have some influence on
Japanese policy. John Morris, the newly appointed Head of the Far East
Service, who had lived in Japan and was working there as a Professor of
English Literature at the outbreak of war, attached more importance to
attracting listeners among the Japanese forces, where signals units would
have the necessary equipment and there would be a natural desire to know
what was happening on other fronts.

Broadcasting in Chinese had started with weekly news letters in May 1941
and did not rise to a daily pattern until September 1942. Output was at first
confined to news and commentaries, and it was only after March 1943, when
the daily programme in Standard Chinese was increased to thirty minutes,
that it became possible to include a wider range of material. This included
highly specialised scientific talks, mostly unintelligible to the general public,
which were intended to enable Chinese scientists cut off from the world
scientific community to keep up to date with the latest development in their
field. One such regular series took the form of a summary of the weekly paper
Nature, of which microfilm copies were also flown out and distributed to
Chinese universities. Of broader interest were the literary and cultural programmes arranged by William Empson, the poet and critic who had moved
from the Monitoring Service at Wood Norton to become a talks producer in
the Chinese Service. Even so the audience was limited by poor audibility –
broadcasts came direct from Britain and were not boosted on the way – and
by the very small number of short wave receivers available – only three
hundred in Chungking and not more than six thousand altogether in the part
of China controlled by the Nationalists.

With the important exception of India, therefore, the BBC, although it
made a start with vernacular broadcasting to Asia and established a presence
there, played only a limited part in the propaganda battle as compared with
the Japanese and the Germans. It was not until the mid-sixties, when output
in Standard Chinese, for instance, was doubled overnight to an hour and a
half a day, that it became a major factor. By then, of course, the transistor
revolution was well under way, bringing short wave broadcasting within
reach of millions in Asia, Africa and Latin-America who for the first time
would have access to information on a scale unimagined even as recently as
the Second World War.

Laying New Foundations

The story of the war had been one of constant if at times erratic expansion, and the results had amply vindicated both the policies and the scale of the effort. As the Report of the Drogheda Committee put it in 1954,

The British Broadcasting Corporation emerged after the war with a unique reputation for the quality and objectivity of its programmes and with all the immense prestige derived from having been during the darkest days the voice of freedom and the prophet of victory. It was also by far the greatest national broadcasting system in the world, the output of the Corporation's External Services in programme hours being more than that of any other two nations in the world added together.[1]

But in the next sentence Drogheda went on to say that 'this favourable situation could not last'. As will be seen, this marked the start of a period which has lasted to this day during which, down the years, the BBC has had to argue repeatedly the case for Britain to retain a major voice in international broadcasting and to resist time and again attempts to whittle down the scale of its effort. As Lord Strang, a former Head of the Foreign Office, put in a debate on external broadcasting in the House of Lords in February 1957, 'the art of hobbling an organisation without entirely crippling it is one which is well understood and practised in Whitehall'.[2]

Consideration of the possible scope of the BBC's Overseas Services in the post-war world started inside the BBC as early as 1943. There was no thought that the instrument which had been forged in wartime could be set aside once the war had been won. There was much emphasis on the role of broadcasting in helping to forge commonwealth unity, and even in Whitehall it was not envisaged that broadcasting in foreign languages to Europe would come to an end, though it was not envisaged that it would continue on the same scale.[3] W.J. Haley, who had succeeded R.W. Foot as Director-General in April 1944, was taking the view at that time that peacetime broadcasting to Europe would be confined to perhaps only four languages, which would include French, German and Spanish, and that so far as broadcasting in English to Europe was concerned relaying of the Home Service on short wave would probably be enough. Audiences in Europe would have their own sources of supply, he thought, and broadcasting from London would be likely to appeal to a much more restricted circle largely confined to what he called 'men of affairs'.[4] It was a far more limited view than was eventually to prevail. Haley foresaw that after the final defeat of Germany the Government would soon divest itself of its control over the European Service. The projection of Britain would become the main purpose of external broadcasting, with the provision of news as a central objective. Britain, he said, could give a powerful example, 'fortified by the great moral stature and prestige of wartime'. 'The British conception of news as something coldly impersonal and objective, having as its only touch-stone accuracy, impartiality and truth, is one of our great services to a civilisation in which speed of communications gives news an overwhelming importance it never had before.'

In the event, once the war was over, there were immediate reductions in the scale of broadcasting to Europe, though no single service was eliminated altogether. Almost no reductions took place elsewhere. PWE began to hand back its responsibilities for European broadcasting policy to the Ministry of Information even before the war was ended, and the ministry itself was wound up at the end of March 1946. By that time the Italian Service, to take an example, had been reduced from its wartime peak of nearly four hours a day to one and a half hours, the Austrian Service, which had been established as a separate service in March 1943 and was relayed after the war by Austrian Radio in Vienna, had its transmission time roughly halved, as had also the Belgian, Dutch, Portuguese, Spanish, Czech, Yugoslav, Swedish, Norwegian and Danish services. The Polish Service had also been substantially curtailed. Some of these reductions reflected the ending of broadcasts by Allied Governments in exile, but taken as a whole they represented a concerted scaling down of the BBC's European operations as a direct consequence of the ending of the emergency which had brought them into existence as well as for reasons of economy.

Even without the financial imperatives the return to peacetime conditions meant that the best of the long and medium wavelengths which had helped the BBC to make such an impact in Europe had had to be given up to enable the post-war reconstruction of BBC domestic broadcasting to take place. Moreover many of the best among the wartime broadcasters – the French team responsible for 'Les Français parlent aux Français' was perhaps the most notable single example – had returned home to their own countries. Henceforth, as Haley had indicated, the projection of Britain and its ways and achievements would become the principal task of the European Service, though impending political developments in Eastern Europe were shortly to create new demands and give new significance to external broadcasting in a way which at times came to be reminiscent of the war itself.

Not all services to Europe suffered. The French Service remained relatively unscathed until 1952, while the German Service was substantially expanded at the end of the war and again at the beginning of 1946 to provide, in effect, a domestic service for occupied Germany pending the full reconstruction of German broadcasting. In this latter process Hugh Carleton Greene, who was seconded to be Controller of 'Nordwest Deutscher Rundfunk' in August 1946, was to play a central role.

The reductions in broadcasting time to Europe which took place in June 1945 caused considerable public misgivings. These were widely echoed in the British press. *Tribune*, for instance, wrote that the war

made obvious the imperative for communication between peoples, and the BBC did much to supply that need. But what now? Is this link between ourselves and the peoples of Europe still needed? Certainly it is – more than ever. It is desperately necessary that Britain – Labour Britain – should retain or win their friendship and sympathy. The official language of diplomacy from government to government is not enough ... We cannot afford to throw away this vitally important weapon of democracy.[5]

It took time for the Attlee Government, beset as it was with far more momentous problems, to come to grips with the formulation of its post-war broadcasting policies. However it became clear from the discussions in which the BBC was involved with Whitehall departments in the winter of 1945-6 that the Government did not intend further reductions in broadcasting to Europe beyond those which were carried out immediately after VE Day. Indeed in a note to J.B. Clark in November 1945 Haley spoke of 'the Government's expressed intention to maintain European broadcasting indefinitely at its present level'.[6] The Colonial Office, for its part, was expressing a strong interest in maintaining the Overseas Services in English at their existing level and asking for special programmes for particular colonies or groups of colonies, while the Ministry of Information was particularly anxious that broadcasting to Latin-America should not be reduced. It saw the Latin-American Service as 'the most far-reaching means of presenting the British case, our ideals and our way of life and thought'.[7] The BBC, it said, was the best known, most liked and trusted external voice in Latin-America. This view was strongly supported by the Foreign Office, which, if anything, wanted more, not less broadcasting to Latin-America.[8] Under Treasury pressure that view was to be drastically reversed little more than five years later.[9]

The White Paper on Broadcasting which finally emerged on 2 July 1946 is a key document.[10] Not only did it set out in broad outline the Government's views on the scope of BBC broadcasting overseas in the post-war era, but it also sought to define in precise terms the nature of the peacetime relationship between the BBC External Services and the Government. That definition remains operative to this day. The White Paper laid stress on the importance attached by the Government to maintaining and developing what it called 'the Empire Services of the Corporation', 'in cooperation with the dominions,

India and the colonies'. It gave its blessing both to the BBC's efforts to achieve more rebroadcasting by commonwealth broadcasting stations and to the supply of transcriptions. So far as Europe was concerned, after paying tribute to the BBC's wartime role, the White Paper stated that the Government had concluded that 'in the national interest and in order to maintain British influence and prestige abroad, it is essential that many of the services should continue'. It recognised that the appeal of broadcasts from London could not remain what it has been during the war, but, it said,

The European Service retains a large audience and friends of this country on the continent are anxious that it shall continue. Moreover there are clear indications, at present, that other powers intend to continue to use the broadcasting medium to put their point of view before the European audience and we cannnot afford to let the British viewpoint go by default.

Although the Cold War had yet to break out, this was one indication that the Government was already concerned with the worsening international atmosphere.

On the question of the future relationship between the BBC External Services and the Government the White Paper was terse and to the point. The formula it adopted has been incorporated with minor modifications of wording in all subsequent versions of the BBC's Licence and Agreement.[11]

The Government [it said] intend that the corporation should remain independent in the preparation of programmes for overseas audiences, though it should obtain from the Government departments concerned such information about conditions in those countries, and the policies of His Majesty's Government towards them, as will permit it to plan its programmes in the national interest.

Herbert Morrison, then Lord President of the Council, went further into the Government's thinking on this point in the course of the parliamentary debate which followed the publication of the White Paper. He talked about 'the very British way in which we hope to reconcile the needs of foreign policy with the independence of the BBC'. 'Clearly', he said, 'it would be unthinkable for Broadcasting House to be broadcasting to Europe, at the taxpayer's expense, doctrines hopelessly at variance with the foreign policy of His Majesty's Government.' But, he went on, it would be 'equally undesirable that the Foreign Office should themselves become responsible for the foreign services'. Broadcasting, he said, required a different sort of experience and imagination from the conduct of diplomacy. 'We believe', he told the House, 'that the foreign services will better retain the respect of listeners abroad and of the public at home if, like the Home Services, they are removed as far as possible from the danger of being used to push the interests of political parties instead of the nation as a whole.'[12] The proposed compromise might result in occasional 'regrettable incidents', but, as Morrison put it, 'unless such incidents are to be much more numerous than we have reason to expect, they will, I think, be a small price to pay for letting the responsibility for broad-casting lie with those best qualified to exercise it'.

In the meantime the BBC itself was readjusting internally to the changed requirements arising from the transition to peacetime. Already, so far as Europe was concerned, the individual and highly autonomous foreign lan-guage services had been brigaded together under regional heads in April 1945. J.B. Clark, who had temporarily replaced Kirkpatrick as European Con-troller when the latter returned to the Foreign Office in 1944, now resumed his previous post as Controller, Overseas Services. Harman Grisewood, who had been Kirkpatrick's deputy during the war years, might have hoped to succeed to the European Controllership as of right, but was warned by Kirkpatrick, now in overall charge of Information at the Foreign Office, that his chances were slim. What was needed, Kirkpatrick told him, was someone from the outside world who had the confidence of Whitehall. He thought he had found the right man: it was Major General Sir Ian Jacob, who throughout the war had been Assistant Military Secretary to the Cabinet.[13] Grisewood returned to the very different world of Broadcasting House, which he had not liked when he had worked there before the war and found he liked even less after his wartime experience at Bush House. He resigned after a year but returned soon after to help found the Third Programme, of which he was the Controller during its seminal years. As Director of the Spoken Word in 1956 he was to be one of the key figures on the BBC side during the Suez row with the Eden Government.

This post, which had wide-ranging editorial policy functions at the very centre, had been created by Haley in 1947 as part of a major reorganisation of senior management. The structure which Haley had inherited from R.W. Foot in 1944 had been marked by a degree of decentralisation which was in stark contrast with the policy of tight control from the centre pursued by Reith from the earliest days. Haley was anxious to reduce the calls on the Director-General's time which arose from the large number of officials who reported direct to him, as well as to ensure that the organisational control and coordination of the BBC at the centre was both logical and efficient. This led him to propose to the board the creation of a senior executive body which, as Asa Briggs has put it, would 'keep under permanent review the whole of the corporation's activities'.[14] This new body, the Board of Management, met for the first time on 5 January 1948 under Haley's chairmanship. Its members were five newly-created Directors – Haley at this point reversed the previous BBC practice under which Controllers had ranked higher than Di-rectors and had been second only to the Director-General and his deputy. Each of the Directors was responsible for a broad grouping of activities – Administration, Technical Services, the Spoken Word, Home Output and Overseas Services, shortly to be modified to 'External Services'. In the latter case Haley had argued that all the BBC's broadcasting activities abroad, whether to Europe or to the world beyond, belonged together and should be brought under the control of an overall Director both on administrative and editorial grounds. He was also anxious that the organisational structure of the BBC should be such as to provide the Board of Governors with a sufficient choice of potential successors to himself, with adequate experience of the handling of BBC affairs at the most senior level. He saw the Director of External Broadcasting, as well as the Director of the Spoken Word and the Director of Administration, as three such potential successors. In the event it was Jacob, who had been appointed Director of External Broadcasting[15] in the autumn of 1947 after little more than a year as European Controller, who was to succeed him as Director-General when he departed to become Editor of *The Times* in 1952.

Both Haley and Jacob played a key role in setting the External Services on the course they were to follow in the post-war era. As has been seen, Haley, who, incidentally, was not greatly interested in external broadcasting and did not altogether approve of Bush House, saw the provision of 'an accurate, impartial and dispassionate flow of news' as the first aim of British overseas broadcasting. In a paper prepared for the Board of Governors in November 1946 he described the purpose of this news service as threefold:

It acts as a prime source of fact and information for any who care to take it, either professionally as journalists, publicists, politicians, or as private citizens. It makes the truth available in places where it might not otherwise be known. By its presence it forces newspapers and broadcasting in authoritarian countries themselves to approximate closer and closer to the truth. Within the commonwealth, where it is often rebroadcast, it provides a wider coverage of subject than local broadcasting services would otherwise enjoy and also a link between the parts of the commonwealth.[16]

Haley laid stress on comprehensiveness as well as accuracy, and while recognising that individual bulletins could be made up to take account of the interests of listeners in the particular countries or areas of the world for whom they were intended, he made it clear that 'it is not proper to "angle" the news to a particular country, either in the compilation of a whole bulletin or in the treatment of its parts'. Equally, he wrote, 'the treatment of an item in an overseas news bulletin must not differ in any material respect from its treatment in a current news bulletin for domestic listeners'.

As to talks, Haley laid down a number of guiding principles. 'It is not a function of the BBC's External Services', he wrote, 'to interfere in the domestic affairs of any other nation. The services do not exist to throw out governments or to change regimes.' More positively he saw the purpose of talks as providing a means of displaying the British way of life, projecting British enterprise and activity and demonstrating the British sense of values. In matters of international controversy, talks, he wrote, must ensure 'that the official British case is given due prominence, that opposing foreign views are also carefully explained and that conflicting opinions which have serious backing in this country are given weight as far as possible according to the strength of their backing'. This last directive, rigorously applied despite severe pressure from Whitehall and Downing Street, was to be the main source of conflict with the Eden Government during the Suez crisis in 1956.

Jacob, a brisk, businesslike, buoyant figure with an intimate knowledge of the workings of Whitehall, saw entirely eye-to-eye with Haley on the basic purposes of external broadcasting. He had stated in his earliest directive shortly after taking over the European controllership in 1946 that 'the spread of truth and the full ventilation of facts are highly desirable in themselves . . . Britain has to struggle against calumny and insidious propaganda poured out by upholders of a different way of thinking. Our part in counteracting this is not by refuting it but by seizing and retaining the initiative.'[17] He rejected the suppression of news merely on the grounds that it was 'inconvenient from a short-term political standpoint'. And he was equally firm on the subject of BBC independence. When heads of services visited the Foreign Office, he said, 'they should seek to learn all they can, they should listen to the views expressed, but they should not act on guidance received directly from Foreign Office departmental officials without testing it by our long-term standards, referring as may be necessary to me'. In a later directive, issued in October 1948 after he had taken over the overall direction of the External Services, he enlarged further on some of the points touched on earlier by both Haley and himself. In particular he stressed that 'the BBC has no views of its own on current affairs. It seeks to reflect British views.'[18] He posed the question whether the positive projection of British life and the exposition of British policies and British attitudes could be construed as meaning that the BBC was to conduct political warfare. 'The answer is that the BBC itself is not conducting anything. It is a mirror held to reflect the views and activities of the British people.'

Ernest Bevin, the Labour Foreign Secretary, for his part, gave full and robust support to the notion that the BBC, in its overseas broadcasts, must be left free to reflect conflicting views. Although there were then, as there were to be periodically down the years, charges of bias on one side or another on specific issues – Franco Spain was a case in point at the time – Bevin dismissed out of hand any idea that the Foreign Office should control or censor what was to be broadcast: 'I do expect the BBC', he told a questioner in the House of Commons, 'on matters of general policy for which His Majesty's Government are responsible and which we have issued, to have regard to that policy; but I am not going to interfere with anybody expressing his views one way or the other.'[19]

The underlying principles on which the BBC was to base its overseas operations down to the present day were thus clearly stated and widely accepted as the only possible choice for Britain from the outset, and whatever

public arguments might develop over their implementation in particular cases
it was only on the occasion of the Suez crisis in 1956 that they were seriously
challenged and placed at risk.[20] Even then the threat lasted no more than a
few weeks and the Suez dispute between the Eden Government and the BBC
led to no long-term changes in the ground rules which had been spelt out by
the Labour Government ten years earlier.

There were hints, however, in much that Haley and Jacob were writing in
1946 that the post-war climate in Europe was fast deteriorating. The Cold
War had not yet fully broken out, but already in February, only nine months
after the end of the war in Europe, Donald Hall, the Bush House Diplomatic
Correspondent, was noting in correspondence with Harman Grisewood, the
Acting Controller of the European Service, 'a rising flood of provocative
attacks on British policy in the Russian press and radio'.[21] At the urging of
the British Embassy in Moscow there had been discussion for some months
of the possibility of remedying the absence of any BBC Service in Russian,
which had stemmed from a desire not to upset the Soviet authorities in
wartime. Finally on 21 February 1946 Kirkpatrick wrote formally to Haley
to tell him that 'the Secretary of State has now instructed me to approach you
with a firm request for the initiation of Russian broadcasts'.[22] Haley told him
that the broadcasts could start in a month's time. In fact they began on
Sunday 24 March.
    Kirkpatrick's brief to Grisewood on the policy he hoped the BBC would
pursue is worth quoting extensively:

> We hope that the BBC's general aim will be to give an accurate impression of feeling
> in this country regardless of what we conceive to be the effect on the listener. We
> should give the impression of friendliness towards the Russian people and interest in
> things Russian ... but equally they [the broadcasts] should not give pro-Soviet press
> extracts more space than they earn on an objective review of the press. The aim of the
> BBC should be to get the proportions right, giving a dispassionate presentation of the
> facts, both of world events (which would include a great deal that is concealed from
> the Soviet public) and of British and world opinion about the Soviet Government and
> its policy, giving the true proportion both of favourable and unfavourable opinion.
> All this should be done against a background of friendly feeling for, and interest in the
> Soviet people, a great deal of weight being given to the intense desire of the Govern-
> ment and people of this country to achieve real cooperation on a frank and friendly
> basis with the Soviet Union if the Soviet Government's behaviour allows us to do
> so.[23]

The service started with three daily transmissions adding up to an hour and
a quarter. Early reactions to the first broadcasts were not altogether favourable and gave an indication of the numerous pitfalls awaiting broadcasters
from the outside attempting to come to terms with the Soviet audience. 'They
like the talking but not the music', reported the *Daily Telegraph* after the first

broadcast. 'The two marches played might have come from anywhere ...
They prefer English dance music.'[24] Other comments spoke critically of
'old-fashioned accents in rather old-fashioned Russian which gave a false
impression of hostility to the Soviet Union and of political nastiness'. One
report from the British Embassy in Moscow described the accents as the
Russian equivalent of 'exaggerated Oxford', which, it said, was very unpopular in Russia.[25] At that early stage the BBC's problem was its inability to
recruit speakers who had recently lived in the Soviet Union and had an up-
to-date knowledge of current spoken Russian. Only *émigrés* who had lived for
many years in the West were immediately available. However by August
matters appear to have improved considerably, and the British Embassy in
Moscow reported one Russian contact as saying that 'when you started off
you were full of political arguments and polemics, while now you have become
more objective'. The Embassy's view was that this comment did not arise
from any alteration in the substance of the broadcasts but from an improvement in the standards of translation and presentation. When the broadcasts
started, it said, Soviet listeners were *expecting* polemics. They heard speakers
who were clearly *émigrés*, judging by their style of speech, and automatically
took what they were saying to be polemical. Independent evidence became
available fairly rapidly and suggested that the broadcasts were attracting a
substantial following. David Tyrrell, the *Daily Express* correspondent in
Moscow, spoke of group listening and reported that there was no evidence
that people were seeking to conceal the fact that they were listening. 'Listeners
freely passed on to their neighbours what the London Radio had said,' he
wrote.

That situation was not to last. By 1949, following the Prague coup and the
Berlin blockade, the Cold War had reached its peak. Not only had Soviet
official attitudes to listening to foreign stations hardened but heavy jamming
of broadcasts from abroad had started in earnest. Systematic jamming of
'Voice of America' broadcasts in Russian to the Soviet Far East had begun as
early as April 1948. The jamming of the relays of 'Voice of America' broadcasts in Russian from the BBC transmitters at Woofferton followed in July,
and in April of the following year Soviet jammers were brought onto the
BBC's own Russian service. Jamming of 'Voice of America' and BBC services
to other countries behind the Iron Curtain, and even to some outside it like
Turkey, Israel and Finland, was introduced gradually over the following two
or three years.

Not surprisingly the worsening of the situation in Europe led to some
differences of opinion as to the best approach to adopt in addressing audiences
in the Soviet Union. For American broadcasters there could be no doubt that
what they were involved in was to them a 'crusade for freedom', and the style
of American broadcasting reflected that view. In Britain there was less enthusiasm for this new 'war of words' and the BBC remained wedded to the

view that a calm and rational exposition of the facts was likely to prove more effective in setting forth the British case than a more polemical approach. There was to be no incitement to subversion, no renewal of the 'V' campaign, only a forthright, 'incisive' statement of the democratic case. Where there was room for debate was over the question whether criticism of the Soviet Government and system was likely to be so unacceptable to the large majority of Russian listeners as to prove counterproductive. The British Embassy in Moscow tended to think it was. The attitude of Hugh Carleton Greene, who had returned from Germany in the late forties to become Head of the East European Service, was slightly different:

The Soviet audience [he wrote to Jacob in March 1949 in response to a letter from the Moscow Embassy] may be assumed to be at the very least tolerant of the regime and to be above all immensely patriotic. It seems however unnecessarily pessimistic to assume that our audience stands solidly behind the regime and resents any criticism of its present government. I am speaking of *our audience*, and not of the Russian people as a whole. There would also seem to be a fairly regular flow of political malcontents into the forced labour camps. Although listening is not forbidden in Russia we have evidence that members of the party have been expelled for listening to London, and it seems not unreasonable to suppose that most of our listeners feel that they are at least committing a misdemeanour by tuning in to the BBC. In such circumstances listening is by itself evidence of doubt and becomes more and more the first faint sign of opposition.[26]

Soviet analysts, for their part, were clear about the threat which this approach presented. Thus *Konsomolskaya Pravda*, in a 1957 article, wrote:

The foundation of BBC propaganda is the latest news, broadcast with emphatic objectivity. It should be noted that in selecting material for broadcasting to the USSR the BBC does not draw any conclusions of its own but leaves this to its listeners, who sometimes, through lack of experience or lack of knowledge, are hooked by those who for years have made it their practice to fish in troubled waters ... "White" propaganda is straightforward propaganda. It is waged by the enemies of communism quite openly, even though under the mantle of "impartiality" and "objectivity". But this does not lessen its hostile nature.[27]

However, even if there were no real doubts in Britain at that stage about the principles underlying the BBC's handling of its broadcasts to Eastern Europe, there were growing doubts about the scale of the British effort. Although the Russian Service itself was increased by an hour a day in 1949, shortly after the introduction of Soviet jamming, there were only minor corresponding increases in broadcasting in other East European languages, even though three new foreign language services, in Indonesian, Hebrew and Urdu, were introduced in 1949 at the Government's request. There had been moves in Parliament by a group of Conservative backbenchers led by Major Tufton Beamish calling for a strengthening of the European Service to enable it to 'hit back' more effectively against Communist propaganda. Yet precisely at that time Jacob and J.B. Clark, now his Deputy, were becoming alarmed at the financial constraints under which, increasingly, the External Services were being compelled to operate.

In its evidence to the Drogheda Committee at the end of 1952 the BBC set out with stark clarity what had happened to the financial position of the External Services since 1947. The Government Grant-in-Aid, which had covered both capital and running costs, had increased by only eighteen per cent in six years, whereas rising costs and developments precribed by the Government without additional funds being made available had accounted for an increase in overall expenditure of fifty per cent.[28] In the early years of the period Jacob had succeeded by dint of stringent economies in avoiding reductions in broadcasting services. There had been a cut of ten per cent in the cost of the External Services in December 1947, and for three years there had been no increase in the Grant-in-Aid despite rising costs.

Nonetheless in 1949 the External Services were still well ahead of their immediate competitors, with a total weekly output of 687 programme hours as compared with 434 hours for the Soviet Union and 214 for the United States. But the price paid for the maintenance of the service had been heavy. Many of the economies made had been undesirable, and taken cumulatively, as the BBC pointed out in its evidence to the Drogheda Committee, they had tended to weaken the fabric of existing operations. In particular there had had to be repeated deferments of capital expenditure. By 1956 the situation had still not been restored, so that the BBC was having to point out that with the exception of two transmitters at Tebrau, in Malaya, which had been brought into service in 1949, there had been no modernisation or addition to the BBC's transmitting facilities since 1942. 'The original transmitters and aerial installations are still in operation', it stated, 'and during a period when all other countries have been installing modern equipment of much greater efficiency the BBC has steadily gone downhill in the technical field for want of money.'[29] Moreover as part of the overall measures of economy prescribed by Jacob there had been a drastic reduction in the use of transmitters, so that there were now fewer transmitters in use for each hour of broadcasting, a measure which in the case of short wave transmissions was bound to produce a serious deterioration in the BBC's audibility. This was without taking into account the steps, known as 'the barrage', which had been devised to try to overcome Russian jamming: Western broadcasting organisations had agreed to concentrate the maximum possible number of transmitters, operating on different frequencies, to carry out simultaneous broadcasts in Russian, thus stretching to the limit the available Soviet jamming effort. This too had meant a considerable increase in expenditure.

But the difficulties which were confronting Jacob in the late forties were as nothing compared with what was awaiting him in 1950 and1951. He had had to make it clear in correspondence with the Foreign Office at the end of 1949 that he was now faced with having to cut services unless the Treasury agreed to meet the risen costs of the current year and to set the Grant-in-Aid for the following year at a level which took them into account. At the same time he pleaded for Treasury agreement to a three-year financial plan which would bring to an end the hand-to-mouth existence the External Services had had to endure over the preceding three years. In this he had the strong support of all three of the main sponsoring ministries, themselves concerned at the effect which wide cut-backs now proposed by the Treasury would have on Britain's ability to make her voice heard in the world. A report drafted by C.A.L. Cliffe, now working in the Cabinet Office, for a Ministerial Committee on which the Foreign, Commonwealth Relations and Colonial Offices were all represented, argued powerfully against any cuts at the present juncture: 'Politically', it said, 'in loss of prestige and influence upon overseas public opinion as well as in the Cold War, the harmful effects would in our view be great and increasing.'[30]

There was a partial reprieve when the matter came up before the full Cabinet, and throughout much of 1950 there were concerted efforts by the Foreign Office, the Commonwealth Relations Office and the Colonial Office to 'persuade senior ministers to adopt an entirely new attitude towards overseas information services and to agree that a considerable increase of effort was necessary'.[31] It had been pointed out repeatedly but in vain that it was 'illogical that the financial ceiling should be progressively lowered as our commitments are extended'. 'The struggle is world-wide', an official memorandum argued. 'It would be a mistake to concentrate only on the areas most immediately threatened.' There was an urgent need 'to keep the satellites in touch with the West, to combat defeatism in Western Europe, to check Communist infiltration in the Caribbean and in the colonial empire generally, and to forestall Communist efforts to drive wedges between ourselves, the Asiatic dominions and the United States'.[32] 'Special attention is being paid to the Armed Forces', the memorandum argued, 'and no doubt more money will be spent on them. It seems only logical to do the same with the overseas information services, on which we are spending at present little more than one-seventieth of what the fighting services cost us.' For Sir Robert Bruce Lockhart, writing in *Time and Tide* in October 1950, the External Services cost no more than a small cruiser, and for that price, he said, you could have the services of what amounted to a battle fleet.[33] It was not an argument to which the Treasury proved receptive.

In the event the top-level support of the Foreign Secretary, Ernest Bevin, and his colleagues in overseas ministries proved of no avail, and at a meeting at the House of Commons on 14 November the Chancellor of the Exchequer, Hugh Gaitskell, told relevant ministers that as a result of the heavy increase in defence spending occasioned by the Korean war and the worsening international situation he would have to make very substantial cuts elsewhere. The country could no longer afford what he called 'frills', and he felt that 'propaganda could be sacrificed without serious effect'. The Latin-American Service was an example of expenditure which, to his mind, was 'probably unjustified either by necessity or by result'. He envisaged a cut of roughly twenty per cent in the overseas information budget.[34] Translated into BBC terms, Jacob told the Foreign Office, this would mean making massive inroads into programme resources. The External Services would be brought 'to the brink of threadbareness'.[35] There was talk of cancelling all breakfast-time and lunch-time broadcasts to Europe except in Russian, of bringing to an end broacasting in Japanese, Afrikaans and subsidiary Indian languages, of reducing the Arabic, French and Brazilian Services to one and a half hours a day, the German Service to two hours (from five and a quarter), and the Spanish Service to Latin-America to three hours (from nearly six). The General Overseas Service in English would also be severely curtailed. To Sir Edward Bridges, the Permanent Secretary to the Treasury, Jacob described the proposed cuts as 'the height of folly in the present international situation', and to Sir John Slessor, the Chief of the Air Staff, whose support he was seeking, as 'an act of lunacy'.[36]

> It seems to me absolutely necessary for the future of this country [he wrote to Bridges] that its views should be in the vanguard of the struggle for men's minds in Europe. To my mind it is not a question of saving a few hundred thousand pounds; it is a choice between maintaining and expanding an asset of tremendous value to this country and to the free world, and throwing it down the drain. Either we mean business in the cold war or we don't.[37]

Rumours of the possible cuts reached the press early in 1951 and there was a flurry of critical editorials, as was to happen on many subsequent occasions of a similar kind down to the present day. Typical was the *Daily Mail*'s leader which observed: 'The "Voice of America" booms, the Voice of Stalin roars, the Voice of Britain must whisper.'[38] There were also protests on both sides in the House of Commons, with R.A. Butler, from the Opposition Front Bench, arguing that the arm of broadcasting was 'one of the most vital that we can use in our general defence arrangements'.[39]

It was all to no avail. The BBC's estimates for 1951/2 were duly cut from £5,330,000 to £4,750,000. To a special staff meeting which he called the following year to announce further cuts Jacob commented tartly that 'the level of Grant-in-Aid was fixed without any serious effort on the part of the Government to assess the value or otherwise of External broadcasting and to decide at what level it should be fixed and maintained. Each year the decision was on a purely financial basis.'[40]

The effects of the 1951 cuts – and of the further cuts made necessary the following year when the Conservative Government, now in office, refused to increase the level of the Grant-in-Aid to meet ordinary risen costs – were dramatic. The General Overseas Service was reduced to twenty-one hours a day and was not restored to a round-the-clock basis for another fifteen years. The Spanish Service to Latin-America was halved and the Brazilian Service reduced to little more than an hour a day. All transcriptions to Latin-America ceased, and all the BBC's offices in Latin-America were closed down, a grievous blow since it was thanks to this BBC presence on the ground that a high level of rebroadcasting by local stations had been achieved. The majority of breakfast and lunchtime broadcasts to Western Europe were eliminated, and the services to Belgium and Luxemburg discontinued. The Arabic *Listener*, a periodical with a wide readership in the Middle East, ceased publication, and nearly all capital expenditure, already reduced to the bare minimum, was deferred. Although there were limited increases in broadcasting in Arabic and Persian, and a bulletin in Vietnamese was introduced in January 1952, total weekly programme hours sank from 648 hours in 1950 to 540 hours at the end of March 1952. It was the most serious blood-letting the External Services were ever to know, and it took place at a time when in the space of three years the Soviet Union had nearly trebled its own external broadcasting output.

The Conservative Party, now in power, behaved no differently from its predecessor, notwithstanding the critical attitude it had adopted the previous year when in opposition. Its decision to freeze the budget of the External Services at its 1951 level, thus making further cuts inevitable, was as badly received in the House of Commons and in the press as had Gaitskell's announcement of swingeing cuts in 1951. Speaking in a House of Commons debate on 2 April 1952, Patrick Gordon Walker, who as Secretary of State for Commonwealth Relations, had fought hard behind the scenes against the Gaitskell cuts, asserted that the BBC was being drowned: 'In five years' time', he said, 'unless major projects in the form of relay stations, new technical developments, better signalling and the like are undertaken, its overseas service will be worthless.' The Opposition wanted an independent enquiry into 'this great national service' with a view to producing a long-term programme, and, in the meantime, a stay of execution.[41] Jacob, too, had been calling for a proper review, and the Government finally yielded and announced in July that it was setting up a small expert advisory committee under Lord Drogheda 'to furnish ministers as soon as possible with their considered views'.[42]

Even before Drogheda and his colleagues were appointed, Anthony Nutting, Parliamentary Under-Secretary at the Foreign Office, had announced the setting-up of a Cabinet Committee of officials under J. W. Nicholls, of the Foreign Office to look into the matter, In little more than two months it reported that the case for an intensification of overseas information work seemed proven, but that it was not qualified to decide 'whether, having regard to financial conditions, the 0.25 per cent of government expenditure now devoted to overseas information is excessive or inadequate'.[43]

Drogheda inclined to the latter view. His report, communicated to the Government in July 1953 but never published in full – only extracts were published, in April 1954 – covered the whole range of information work abroad. On broadcasting it placed the highest priority on the need for a large scale programme of capital investment – it recommended that £500,000 should be spent annually over five or ten years – mainly on the installation of overseas relays, made necessary by the increasing over-crowding of the short wave bands and the consequent difficulty of reaching distant audiences direct from the United Kingdom. This was more important, the report stated, than 'clinging on to wavelengths and keeping up services of doubtful peacetime value'.[44] The General Overseas Service in English, it urged, should be restored as a round-the-clock service. As to the drastic cuts in the Latin-American Service made over the preceding two years, these had been 'a grave mistake', it asserted. 'It is not too late to restore the position. We believe this should be done as soon as possible both as a matter of prestige and as a long term means of helping to build up our trade.'

For the BBC it was a welcome reversal of government policy, but it was a prime example of those switches of priorities which the BBC regarded as so detrimental to the long-term stability it required if its broadcasting operations were to be fully effective. The report also recommended an increase in Arabic broadcasting and an expansion of broadcasting to Asia, for which the linch-pin was to be the new relay station at Tebrau, in Malaya, where two additional transmitters were to be installed.

There was much in Drogheda for the BBC to be pleased with, but some of its underlying themes remained to haunt the debate on external broadcasting for many years to come. The price which Drogheda proposed for the increases in spending it was recommending was the total abolition of the French, Italian, Portuguese, Dutch and Scandinavian Services. The British Council, too, should be withdrawn from those countries. The money saved, Drogheda said, could be better spent on building up the Foreign Office Information Services in those countries and thus catering for the needs of the 'influential few' rather than for those of a mass audience.

If there was one concept in Drogheda to which the BBC took exception it was that of 'the influential few'. It accused Drogheda of mistakenly applying to broadcasting criteria which were irrelevent to it and contrary to its charac-ter. In particular, it said, the principle that 'information services should be directed at the influential few and through them at the many', while applicable to the work of the diplomatic service, was wholly alien to the nature of broadcasting. 'Wireless', the Board of Governors commented in a closely argued paper,[45] 'has given to governments direct means of access to audiences overseas which enables them to influence foreign governments by and through direct contact with the masses.' In any case, it said, audiences in Western Europe remained large: 'In France for instance, it is as if Britain possessed in its own right a daily newspaper with a circulation comparable to that of the *Daily Telegraph* in the United Kingdom.' To Drogheda's argument that those 'influential few' in Europe – provincial newspaper editors were specifically quoted as an example – who wanted to keep in touch with what London had to say could listen in English it replied that in France, for every one person listening to the BBC in English there were six listening to the French Service. In Italy the corresponding figure for the Italian Service was seven. But above all the BBC was anxious to safeguard the steady, long-term character of its operations, on which, it argued, its credibility was based. What Drogheda was proposing, it said, looked dangerously like 'following the tactical needs of the moment'. Was it not a fact that Drogheda had said that there were 'special reasons' why other language services should be retained, 'at any rate for the time being'? This applied, for instance, to Germany, Yugoslavia, Finland and Spain. To the BBC that smacked dangerously of short-term political opportunism and would do nothing for the BBC's reputation for stable responsibility which, the Board felt, 'precisely responds to the needs of Britain's international position'.

As it happened, however, the real danger lay elsewhere. It took nearly a year for extracts of the report to be published as a White Paper after it had reached ministers in its final form, and thereafter the months passed without any moves being made towards implementation. By the time the Suez crisis supervened a start had still not been made, and with Suez all bets were off and the BBC was going to have to ward off altogether more dangerous threats both to its independence and to its position as a world broadcaster.

12
Suez and its Aftermath

The nature of the problem which faced the External Services during the Suez crisis was well described by J.B. Clark, who succeeded Jacob as Director of External Broadcasting in 1952 when the latter became Director-General, and was therefore in charge throughout that period:

At no time since broadcasting began [he wrote shortly after] had there been such a lack of agreement in Parliament and in the country on a major matter of foreign policy. Never previously therefore had the BBC's tradition of objective reporting, in its external as in its home programmes, led it to show to the world a large part of the nation deeply critical of the government of the day on a matter of vital national concern.[1]

The post-war Labour Government had tolerated the reflection in the External Services of a largely critical press. But the points at issue had been domestic. They had never affected military action. The fact that the British nation had not been divided by any fundamental issue in foreign politics since before the war had made it possible for the BBC to reflect general support in Britain for any major step that was taken by the Government. This was not the case over Suez. Moreover there was an additional dimension in that the Anglo-French military action was massively condemned in most of the world. This made a convincing exposition of what lay behind the Government's actions doubly difficult for the BBC.

J.B. Clark was in no doubt about the policies which the External Services should pursue. He knew that there could be no difference between what the BBC was saying to its home and its overseas listeners. He was fully aware of the basic fact that sooner or later, from some source or other, the truth about the state of British opinion was bound to emerge, and that for the BBC to have been found for the first time suppressing important items of news – and it could not have done so unnoticed abroad – would have been to destroy its reputation without vindicating that of the Government. 'The harm done to the national interest in that event would have far outweighed any damage caused by displaying to the world the workings of a free democracy.'[2]

This was not the view from Downing Street and the Foreign Office. For Government ministers and officials the long term interest of the BBC in safeguarding its credibility could not possibly take precedence over what they asserted was the national interest. So throughout October there was mounting pressure on the External Services to play down the extent of opposition to the Government's handling of the crisis as well as expressions of increasing irritation from Downing Street with the fact that, as Eden saw it, the BBC was 'giving comfort to the enemy by reporting domestic divisions, thus weakening the credibility of our threats'.[3] As Asa Briggs has put it, 'Eden in 1956 expected the BBC to rally to a nation virtually at war, as it had rallied in 1939.'[4] Once British forces had been committed, Conservative MPs argued, it was wrong for the BBC to remain 'impartial', and Paul Grey, the Foreign Office Under-Secretary in charge of information policy, took the view that in such a situation it was not necessary to tell the whole truth and that certain news items should be suppressed in Arabic news bulletins. It was a distant echo of arguments which had been put forward by Rex Leeper nearly twenty years before when the start of Arabic broadcasting was being considered.[5]

Setting aside news policy, there were two specific aspects of the External Services coverage of the crisis which incensed the Government. The first was the daily press reviews which formed a routine part of the output of most services. These attempted to reflect in a fair and balanced manner the line taken by the editorials in the national and provincial dailies. The matter came to a head on 31 October, when following the Anglo-French ultimatum of the previous day and the start of the bombing of Egyptian airfields by the RAF the *Manchester Guardian* published a powerfully-worded editorial which described the course decided upon by the Government as 'an act of folly without justification in any terms but brief expediency'.[6] J.B. Clark, who had stood up on many past occasions for the most rigorous interpretation of the BBC's obligations, did so again on this occasion. He took the view that no honest press review of that day could ignore the *Manchester Guardian* leader and that the harsh judgement quoted above could not be omitted since it was the keynote of the editorial. That view was endorsed by the Chairman, Sir Alexander Cadogan, who was consulted and agreed that press reviews should continue normally.

The second issue which greatly exercised the Government concerned the Opposition's 'right of reply' following Eden's ministerial broadcast to the nation on Saturday 3 November, in which he explained why the Government had decided on its 'police action'. The BBC had made it clear to Downing Street that if Gaitskell, the Leader of the Opposition, asked for the right of reply, as he was entitled to do if in his view Eden's broadcast turned out to be of a controversial character, the Board of Governors, which was the final arbiter in the matter, would probably grant his request. Though it was argued in the event by Edward Heath, the Government Chief Whip, that Eden's broadcast had been 'the least controversial it could be in the circumstances',[7] he made it clear that no objection would be raised if the Governors decided to allow Gaitskell to reply. This they duly did. Like Eden's own broadcast, Gaitskell's, which went out the following night on all domestic channels, was simultaneously transmitted abroad by the General Overseas Service as well as being fully reported in translation in foreign language services, including Arabic. It was thus possible for British troops and air crews in Cyprus to hear it at the precise time when they were on their way for the assault on Suez.

Leaving aside the Government's increasing anger at the BBC's conduct in general, there was official concern on two specific counts. William Clark, Eden's public relations adviser, who resigned as soon as the crisis was over, had urged that the more 'inflammatory' passages in Gaitskell's broadcast should not be transmitted in the Arabic Service. More generally there was concern about the effect on the morale of the British troops involved of hearing not only Gaitskell's broadcast but accounts of the extent of opposition to the Government's action such as had been expressed in the *Manchester Guardian*. That danger was probably overestimated. An official of the External Services was in Cyprus at the time and in close touch with British commanders, but at no point did the latter raise the matter with him. Nor did the Ministry of Defence in London. Moreover one of the newspapers most widely available to the troops was the *Daily Mirror*, which itself was outspokenly critical of the Government's action. The troops, J.B. Clark felt, must have been well aware of the domestic political conflict, and in any case constituted only a tiny fraction of the General Overseas Service's total world audience.

Many bitter charges of bias and prejudiced reporting were levelled at the BBC by a group of Conservative MPs led by Peter Rawlinson in an angry debate in the House of Commons on 14 November, barely a week after a cease-fire had been declared. The Board of Governors called for detailed evidence of what had been said on the air in every instance and examined it exhaustively at its regular meeting on 22 November. The Governors concluded from their study that not one of the allegations made in the Commons could be made to stand up, though one or two Governors expressed some misgivings after the event about the possible effect on the troops of the press reviews carried in the General Overseas Service. Nonetheless the Board was unanimous in its conclusions, which Cadogan communicated to the Postmaster General, Dr Charles Hill, on 26 November. The BBC put out a public statement the next day, which was also posted up on all staff notice boards, saying that the Governors had found that the allegations against the staff were groundless and that the BBC had achieved 'a successful and creditable result during a period of great difficulty'.[8] On 6 December the Board went on to congratulate the External Services on their work during the Suez and Hungarian crises. There were indications even then that not all Conservative Ministers had taken the more extreme view of the inner Cabinet, as well as a growing recognition on the Government side that relations with the BBC had been badly handled.

In its Annual Report to Parliament the following year, the BBC, taking a retrospective look at what had taken place, made the point that evidence received since the crisis had shown not only that the BBC's continued adherence to honest reporting during the crucial period had won great praise abroad, but also that 'the vigorous presentation by BBC commentators of the reasons for Britain's actions in Egypt did much to promote a better understanding of it even among those who were bitterly opposed'.[9] The Foreign Office itself had acknowledged that the best justification of the Government's action seen until then had been a widely used central commentary written by Maurice Latey on 1 November. It had been described as 'a brilliant piece of work', and some of its arguments had later been used by the Government and by Eden himself in his broadcast to the nation on 3 November. 'Looking back in the long run', J.B. Clark wrote, 'it [the BBC] may be thought to have done well for the country.'[10]

It was not a thought which commended itself to the Government at the end of October. On 25 October Anthony Nutting, the Parliamentary Under-Secretary at the Foreign Office, had summoned Jacob and Tangye Lean, then J.B. Clark's deputy, to convey to them the Government's dissatisfaction with the External Services and to tell them of its decision to reduce the External Services Grant-in-Aid by £1,000,000. It was made clear that this was for punitive reasons, and given the timing of the move it is hard to resist the conclusion that it was a crude attempt to secure greater compliance with the Government's wishes at a point when the Suez assault was about to be launched. However by the next day the situation appeared to have changed. After the BBC's Chairman and the Director-General had been to see the Lord Privy Seal, R.A. Butler, the BBC heard that the proposed cut was to be reduced by half. The sequel was even more unexpected: the official Foreign Office letter confirming the cut which the BBC had been told to expect was never received, and with the appointment of Dr Charles Hill as Chancellor of the Duchy of Lancaster to conduct a wide-ranging review of overseas information services the matter was put in abeyance and was never heard of again. Nor indeed were the recommendations of the Drogheda Committee, which were quietly shelved.

There are two further aspects of the Suez crisis which are worthy of mention. The first concerns the use of the medium wave transmitter in Cyprus belonging to a British commercial company, the Near East Arab Broadcasting station, which broadcast in Arabic under the name of 'Sharq al Adna'. Its main programme output was straightforward news, commentaries – generally reflecting British views – and music interspersed with commercials. The BBC, for its part, had been vainly pressing the Government for sixteen years for medium wave relay facilities in Cyprus to enable it to extend the audience to its Arabic Service. It was, as Jacob put it, 'a classic example of false economy. Yet, when crises occur, there are complaints of failure of propaganda.'[11]

As the Suez crisis neared its climax towards the end of October steps were at last taken to fly a twenty-kilowatt medium wave transmitter to Cyprus – it was damaged in transit – and it was agreed that the Government would take over the 'Sharq al Adna' transmitter in the meantime to provide a relay for the BBC Arabic Service. However when the take-over was eventually announced on 30 October, the day after the Israelis had started their move into Sinai, it was officially stated that the transmitter would carry what was described as 'official announcements'. The BBC Arabic Service would be relayed 'as soon as circumstances permit'. The Station Director protested at the take-over and had to be removed at bayonet point, and virtually all the Arab staff refused to carry on under the new arrangements.[12] Nonetheless a Government propaganda operation of sorts was mounted, dubbed 'The Voice of Britain' and broadcasting entertainment records from Cyprus and news and talks originated by the Foreign Office. It was ingloriously wound up four months later, having achieved little, since its character was patently obvious and its output amounted to little more than crude propaganda.[13] At that point the transmitter was given over to the now expanded BBC Arabic Service, and the Foreign Office agreed to it being used to relay the General Overseas Service at other times.

The second matter concerned liaison between the Foreign Office and the External Services. At the meeting which Jacob and Lean had had with Anthony Nutting on 25 October, they had been told that the Foreign Office was proposing to appoint a special liaison officer with the External Services who would be stationed at the BBC Headquarters at Bush House. There was no intention, the Foreign Office said, to derogate from the BBC's authority under the Charter and Licence. The BBC would remain responsible for programme content as before. The purpose of the appointment would simply be to supplement the normal channels of communication between the Foreign Office, which would continue to operate as before. Under considerable pressure the BBC agreed to the arrangement, though only on an experimental basis. The Foreign Office official who was appointed to the job was J.L.B. Titchener – Bush House wags immediately dubbed him 'Titchener of Tartoum'. Pending his arrival from Tehran another official, Duncan Wilson,[14] took up the appointment on a temporary basis. He arrived on 2 November and his first assignment appeared to lie well outside the duties of the Liaison Officer as they had been defined by the Foreign Office: it was to examine the output of the Arabic Service to establish whether it was suitable for relaying by the 'Voice of Britain' transmitter in Cyprus. He concluded that it was not. It was clear to J.B. Clark that what the Foreign Office was after was what he himself had so decisively rejected in 1938 in the argument over Arabic news policy[15] – in other words distortion and suppression in a manner which had never been called for even during the war and would be quite contrary to the terms of the 1946 Government White Paper, frequently reaffirmed by Governments of both parties. For a change to be made, it was clear that there would have to be formal Government direction at the highest level.

The Liaison Officer survived at Bush House for a few months but in practice, as the BBC saw it, his presence tended to confuse the previously established channels of contact without yielding any compensating advantage. The arrangement was fiercely attacked in Parliament and in the press and there were vociferous public demands for Titchener's withdrawal. He was called back to the Foreign Office not long after, though an official working within the Information Policy Department continued for some time to be specially charged with day-to-day dealings with the External Services. 'It is well understood by all concerned', Jacob wrote in a note on the subject in 1958, 'that neither this official, who is sometimes termed a liaison officer, nor any other official of the Foreign Office, has any responsibility for the content of the programmes transmitted. This responsibility rests with the corporation itself and its staff.'[16]

It is clear in retrospect that the Government, having baulked at taking the final step of placing the External Services under its direct control, did what seemed at the time to be the next best thing. The arrangement, however, was bound to fail in its real purpose, since what was lacking on the BBC's part was not an awareness of the Government's policies but a readiness to fall in with its wishes. It was always a good deal less than likely that experienced BBC officials like J.B. Clark and his immediate subordinates could be persuaded to be more compliant by the mere presence of a middle-ranking Foreign Office official on the premises, even with threats of budgetary cuts in the background. Moreover a healthy spirit of independence and professional pride was too widespread among news editors and commentators for any departure from the basic editorial principles laid down by Haley and Jacob ten years before to have been possible without the most categorical instructions from the highest quarter. Even then it is unlikely that such instructions would have been observed without being seriously contested by the staff. It was, of course, always open to the Government to invoke the wide-ranging reserve powers written into the BBC's Licence and Agreement, but it did not do so. Harman Grisewood asserts that he was told by William Clark, Eden's adviser on public relations, that 'the Prime Minister had instructed the Lord Chancellor to prepare an instrument which would take over the BBC altogether and subject it wholly to the will of the Government',[17] and at least one other BBC official confirms quite independently that Clark did indeed say this, though it is conceivable that he may have given an exaggerated impression of what was afoot. Sir Ian Jacob, for his part, doubts whether matters could have gone so far, whatever might have been said in the heat of the moment:

They did, I'm sure, contemplate the idea of muzzling the dissent [Jacob said many years later], but it has to be recalled that all the decisions in relation to the Suez adventure were taken by a small group of inner ministers, not by the Cabinet as a whole. I think it would have been very difficult to have proceeded to extremes, if those few ministers had wanted to do so, against the BBC's independence. This would have meant yet more trouble from all the other ministers, let alone the public and the Opposition, and the whole proceeding was so unlike the normal methods of government in this country that one tends, as I do, to regard it as an aberration and something that one forgets about.[18]

Several important points emerge from the Suez crisis. The first is that the long-term consequences of the BBC's stand can now be seen to have been wholly advantageous not just for the BBC's own reputation and credibility in the world at large but in terms of the national interest in the broadest sense. Except in France, the military assault on Egypt aroused almost universal hostility, and it was largely through the BBC that the world – and more particularly the newly emerging non-white Commonwealth – became aware of the extent to which British public opinion had been opposed to the Government's actions. The lucid and detached analysis by BBC commentators of the reasons why the Government had acted as it did also helped to mitigate the damage and, as J.B. Clark put it, to 'lighten the atmosphere in which the British Government has had to move'.[19] Something of Britain's blighted reputation was salvaged as a result.

A second point concerns the long-term effect of the Suez episode on the relationship between the External Services and the British Government. Suez is sometimes regarded as having marked a turning point in that relationship, after which things were never the same again. Sir Ian Jacob himself does not believe this to be true. For him Suez had no particular effect on the future of the BBC. What it did, however, was to provide an opportunity for the BBC to reaffirm in a particularly vivid way that the principles governing its broadcasts overseas could not be sidestepped or modified for the sake of momentary political convenience. It also provided important evidence of the very real obstacles which lie in the way of a government wishing to bend the BBC to its will in a situation which falls short of war and in which national consensus does not exist. Future generations of BBC officials would henceforth have before them a precedent which illuminated with stark clarity the precise nature of the BBC's constitutional obligations and of its relationship with the Government. There could have been no more effective demonstration that the External Services were truly as independent as they claimed to be. If anything, therefore, the BBC came out of the ordeal immensely strengthened. However it was some time before the sense of bitterness against the BBC among some Conservatives vanished altogether.

As has been seen, within a few weeks of the end of the crisis it emerged that Dr Charles Hill, the Postmaster General, was to become Chancellor of the Duchy of Lancaster and minister in charge of the coordination of government information services. In that capacity he was to conduct a wide-ranging review of all overseas information services, including the BBC External Services. Already it had become clear that not all ministers had shared the animus of the Prime Minister against the BBC. There was anxiety in the Commonwealth Relations Office, for instance, about the possible loss of the Indian vernacular services, and at least one senior British Ambassador in the Middle East has staunchly supported the BBC's line. The Conservative Central Office, for its part, had carefully steered clear of giving its support to the hue and cry in the House of Commons in November, aware as it was that many of the allegations being made against the BBC were based on hearsay and were without real substance. As the dust settled wiser counsels were beginning to prevail. When the House of Lords debated the issue of the External Services on a motion by Lord Strang early in February 1957, Lord Gosford, speaking for the Government, confirmed that there would be no change in the Government's policy on objectivity in the External Services. By that time it had also become clear that the threat of a punitive cut in the Grant-in-Aid had been lifted: 'In deference to representations made by Parliament and by the BBC', Lord Gosford said in the same debate, 'no decision has been taken up to now to terminate these seven West European languages.'[20] The matter would be examined urgently by Dr Hill. The languages under threat since late in October were Danish, Norwegian, Swedish, French, Italian, Portuguese and Dutch. At least twelve other language services had then also been listed as expendable, including the Latin American Service and all vernacular services to India.

It was clear from the start of Dr Hill's enquiry that the Suez fiasco had caused a major turnabout in the Government's view of the importance of overseas information. Britain's image had been badly dented, and a major effort was needed to restore it. In the BBC it was hoped that the steady whittling away would now stop and that an attempt would be made to arrive at a settled policy so as to bring to an end the annual financial wrangles which had so bedevilled the previous decade.

It had been obvious since Drogheda, however, that the Government was thinking of a major redeployment of effort in the direction of Eastern Europe, the Middle East and the Far East, and Jacob remained apprehensive, despite the general reassurances he was receiving, that broadcasting to the rest of Europe remained vulnerable. He was only too well aware from his own experience at Bush House that even if some minor adjustments might be necessary the wholesale elimination of services to Western Europe would have a disastrous effect and would finally destroy the confidence of the staff. Moreover he believed passionately, as he had made clear in many conversations with ministers and officials, in the importance of the External Services as a national asset and was deeply disturbed by what he saw as the failure of post-war governments to give them proper support: 'We had no idea', he once said bitterly, 'whether anyone believed in our work.' He was strengthened in his resolve by the critical reaction in the European press to the published recommendations of the Drogheda Report two years earlier. One Dutch newspaper, the *Harlems Dagblad*, was typical of the response the other side of the Channel: 'Surely it is a mistake', it wrote, 'for Britain to fail in her task of keeping Western Europe informed of her point of view at the very moment when one would like to see the ties between the continent and the British Isles become closer.'[21] Another, the *Algemeen Handelsblad*, wrote that Drogheda 'has tried to gain support for an expansion of propaganda to countries behind the Iron Curtain and in areas where the British feel less certain of themselves at the expense of good will in other countries, which may be less automatic than the Committee imagines'.[22] *Le Monde*, in Paris, spoke of 'the illusion, very prevalent in Great Britain, that European countries are "necessarily" friends and that it would be superfluous to give these countries a clearer idea of the attitude of the British Government'.[23]

That the External Services had sunk to a parlous condition by the mid-fifties emerged clearly from a paper which Jacob prepared for the BBC's General Advisory Council in January 1957. The cumulative cuts which had been made in the Grant-in-Aid since 1949 had caused the loss of services equivalent in value to £1,000,000 a year – or over twenty per cent of the annual budget.[24] Overall costs in the previous ten years had risen by fifty per cent whereas the funds made available had increased by only twenty per cent. The staff had been reduced by 400. For reasons of economy transmitters were heavily underused and no funds were available for their modernisation. The original pre-war and wartime transmitters and aerials were still in operation, and at a time when other countries were installing modern equipment of much greater efficiency the BBC had gone steadily downhill in the technical field for want of money. None of the increases in expenditure recommended by Drogheda, themselves amounting to nearly £1,000,000 annually, had been implemented. On the contrary the External Services had been 'eaten away year by year'.[25] In the past the BBC's policy had been to maintain at least the skeleton of the machine so that growth could start again immediately if the cuts were restored. From now on, Jacob made clear, any failure to reverse the trend would mean abandoning that policy:

External Broadcasting [the paper for the General Advisory Council said] is a long term operation. It should be founded on principles that will stand the test of all situations ... To seek to save the cost of a particular language on the grounds that problems are unlikely to arise in that particular area is like an attempt to pick out the notes of a piano keyboard which will not be wanted ... [It was tempting to] do away with services for friendly nations where no trouble is seen to be brewing, and start new services for countries where trouble is visibly afoot. But trouble can arise for Britain, as for hardly any other country, in almost any part of the world. And broadcasting cannot contribute usefully to a solution of such troubles magically after they have developed. What is needed is time and stability of service to promote friendship on the one hand and to eat into totalitarian situations by the steady action of truth on the other.

It was the classic statement of the BBC's approach to external broadcasting, which was to guide all Jacob's successors both in the Director-General's chair and at Bush House down to the present day.

The Government White Paper embodying Dr Hill's proposals was published on 15 July 1957,[26] too near the start of Parliament's summer recess to enable a proper debate to take place. In any case, as was made clear to the BBC, it was intended that it should be implemented immediately. Some of its recommendations had already been carried out. The doubling of the daily output of the Arabic Service to nine and a half hours – closing the stable door after the horse had bolted, as some Bush House wits put it – had taken place at the end of March with the handing over to the BBC of the 'Voice of Britain' transmitter in Cyprus. There had been talk with the Colonial Office during the summer and autumn of the previous year of introducing broadcasts to Africa in three of the principal vernaculars, Hausa, Somali and Swahili, in response to the growing radio propaganda effort from Cairo. Treasury support was secured in February. Local British colonial stations in East and West Africa would relay the twice-weekly fifteen-minute programmes with which it was proposed to make a start and thus ensure a wider audience. The Hausa broadcasts started in March, Swahili in June and Somali in July. The White Paper was recommending that these services should become daily as soon as possible, and this duly took place the following year. Hill also recommended that the General Overseas Service should revert to being a round-the-clock service, though in the event this was not achieved until ten years later. Finally there were to be minor increases in broadcasting in Russian and Polish – an additional fifteen minutes a day in Russian had already been introduced in November 1956, and there was a similar increase in Polish in September 1957, bringing both up to two hours and fifteen minutes per day.

Seen in the perspective of time and against the background of the world-wide developments then taking place, particularly in the activities of the BBC's rivals, the proposed redeployment of resources seems remarkably modest. Overall it produced a reduction of the BBC's total hours of broadcasting, and it is the doubling of the Arabic Service's time on the air, prompted by the immediate need to restore Britain's influence in the Middle East, which stands out as its most significant feature, though the introduction of African vernaculars at the behest of the Colonial Office, followed as it was to be at the start of the sixties by a rapid expansion of specialised English-language broadcasting to Africa, can now be seen as having been both significant and timely. All three services rapidly gathered a large following which they retained after the independence of the countries concerned eventually brought an end to re-broadcasting. But the Drogheda Report's urgent recommendation for an increased effort in South East Asia and for the restoration of the swingeing cuts in the Latin-American Service made in 1951 and 1952 was not taken up.

Nor was the BBC's own recommendation that there should be a substantial increase in broadcasting to China and to the Indian sub-continent. Whatever importance the Government might have attached to the Cold War at the time, and notwithstanding the appearance of the first cracks in the façade of East European Communism in 1956, the BBC's broadcasting effort to Eastern Europe was clearly regarded in Whitehall as broadly adequate, subject to the minor increases recommended in Polish and Russian.

The price the External Services had to pay for the change of emphasis which the Government had decided upon was a heavy one and the BBC lost no time in making it clear that it deplored it. Indeed J.B. Clark thought it right to say that in his view there had not been the degree of consultation called for in the spirit of the relevant clause in the BBC Licence.[27] Seven services altogether were to be abolished. These were the Swedish, Norwegian, Danish, Dutch, Austrian, Portuguese and Afrikaans Services. The French and Italian Services were reprieved, but the French Service was reduced by half, to less than two hours a day, and the Italian Service to one and a half hours a day. As the White Paper put it, 'Western Europe is an area with which we possess many other effective means of communication.' But there were also to be substantial reductions in the North American Service. Moreover the Hill Committee declined to endorse the BBC's bid for funds to develop television transcriptions, with which the External Services had made a modest start in 1952 on a self-financing basis. For the time being the Central Office of Information would be charged with negotiating rights for particular pro-grammes with the BBC and the commercial television companies where a showing was not commercially profitable. In other words, so far as television was concerned, there was to be no equivalent of the BBC's Transcription Service in radio, making the best of BBC Radio available the world over in recorded form. The total savings to be achieved by the curtailment of services proposed amounted to £200,000. The cost of the increases in Arabic and elsewhere came to £258,000. The net increase in recurrent expenditure on broadcasting was therefore to be £58,000. It was a far cry from the £500,000 the BBC had said it needed to restore the cuts made in the early fifties, and it contrasted starkly with the increase of £900,000 proposed by the White Paper for the British Council.

In its comments on the White Paper the BBC pointed to the large audiences which the services to be abolished continued to enjoy – the total audience to the Norwegian Service, for instance, was still equivalent to twenty per cent of the population in 1955, even after the service had been reduced to less than forty minutes a day. Poland alone, the BBC said, was now broadcasting more to Western Europe than the BBC. Moscow had increased its broadcasting effort in Norwegian precisely at the time when the BBC was reducing its own, and more generally the Soviet Union and its satellites were involved in a massive programme of expansion.

Almost immediately there was a strong public reaction in the countries to which the BBC was now to cease broadcasting. The Copenhagen newspaper *Dagens Nyheder* wrote: 'With some regret and a touch of dismay it must be affirmed that it is the voices of the West which are disappearing and becoming muted. And it is the propaganda blast of the East – where no dictator needs to request Congress or Parliament for grants – which is increasing in stridency.'[28] In Portugal the barrage of press criticism continued for nearly a month. 'Every night', the *Diario de Lisboa* wrote on 1 August, 'the BBC came into our homes without needing to ask permission. It was a member of the family.'[29] The *Diario de Noticias*, recalling that in the course of the royal visit to Portugal in February the Queen had said that 'Portuguese friendship is a source of strength to Britain,' wondered whether 'perhaps the British Government does not agree with Her Majesty'.[30] Reuters reported 'considerable indignation and disappointment' from Lisbon and quoted one newspaper as saying that 'friends need at least to be treated as friends. Otherwise one had the right to suppose that their friendship is insufficiently appreciated.'[31] In Britain too the response was critical. A leader in *The Times* under the title 'Lost Voices' commented: 'The protests against the decision – notably in the case of the Portuguese Service – have been weighty and reasoned';[32] while in a long article in the *Manchester Guardian* entitled 'Silence from London', Cecil Sprigge spoke of 'the mournful ceremony enacted on 9 August' (the date when the condemned services were closed down).[33] James Cameron, writing in the *News Chronicle*, itself so soon to disappear, was characteristically outspoken: 'Who else but this Government', he wrote, 'would argue that your friends are the one group you snub . . . By economising on one seventieth part we amputate the best limb our information has got.'[34] There were moves in Parliament in an attempt to cause the Government to have second thoughts. John Harvey, Labour MP for Walthamstow, took up the matter on the Consolidated Fund Bill on 31 July and drew the Government's attention to 'the considerable adverse reaction in so many influential organs of the press in almost every country concerned'. 'There was,' he told Ian Harvey, the Joint Parliamentary Under-Secretary at the Foreign Office, 'such a fund of good will towards the BBC among so many of our friends in Western Europe that we should not lightly take the risk of throwing this away.'[35]

The protests were of no avail, though there were signs that privately the Government was particularly shaken by the strength of the reaction from Portugal. The service was to be reinstated six years later, a prime example of the kind of switching on-and-off against which the BBC had always warned.

There are two ways of looking at the outcome of the 1957 review. In one sense the BBC could consider itself fortunate that the drastic and punitive surgery with which it had been threatened at the height of the Suez crisis had not taken place. Even if at a grievous cost there had been some valuable additions to its broadcasting effort which were to stand the test of time. The

French and Italian services had survived. A major plan for the replacement of outdated transmitters and the building of new relay stations, particularly in the South Atlantic, had been agreed in principle. More money had been put into programmes, into the Transcription Service, and into the teaching of 'English by Radio', and, most important of all, perhaps, the Government had unequivocally reaffirmed its commitment to the editorial independence of the External Services: 'In the Government's view', the White Paper stated, 'the impartiality and objectivity of the BBC is a national asset of great value and the independence which the corporation now enjoys should be maintained.' There was also a welcome modification of the stand taken by Drogheda on the issue of the 'influential few': 'While the sympathy of the influential few must always be sought', the White Paper stated, 'it is no less important, in many areas, to seek to enlist the good will of the general population.'

But to the BBC the gains were bound to seem insufficient to outweigh the heavy losses it had suffered. There was less broadcasting in 1958 than in 1957, and a start was not made with reversing the trend – and then only very slowly – until the early sixties. Yet in the field of international broadcasting the fifties were precisely the period during which, all over the world, rapid growth began to take place and the BBC's lead, substantial until 1950, had been wiped out by the end of the decade. During that period the Soviet Union's output abroad doubled and had overtaken the BBC's by 1955. So had the combined output of the countries of the Warsaw Pact, which increased by one hundred per cent between 1950 and 1955. China had overtaken the BBC by 1960, and both the United States and, more surprisingly, Egypt, trebled their output between 1950 and 1955.

Equally significant was the fact that it was in the 1950s that there began what can only be described as the Transistor Revolution, which rapidly brought cheaper and more efficient receivers within reach of even the poorest in what was beginning to be known as the Third World. Radio set ownership trebled in Communist Eastern Europe in the ten years between 1955 and 1965. In the Middle East it grew five times in the same period, in China six times, in black Africa and in India twelve times. Tangye Lean, Assistant Director of External Broadcasting under J. B. Clark, noting the decline in the BBC's own broadcast output since 1950, commented that it had been dictated 'not by policy considerations but by a series of accidents in connection with the immediately varying financial situation from year to year. And it is not, of course, the financial situation of the country as a whole but simply twists and eddies within the information vote and our own budget.'[36] Jacob himself, replying to a letter from Woodrow Wyatt, who had just returned from Liberia where he had been impressed by the BBC's following, observed wearily:

It is a curious thing that practically every foreigner and practically every Englishman who travels abroad with his eyes and ears open says the same thing on this subject. The only people who seem to be incapable of grasping the true facts of the situation are ministers and officials in this country, and this seems to go for all governments here.[37]

The 1950s, as Tangye Lean noted at the end of the decade, marked the change-over, in the field of international broadcasting, from the dominance of the West to the dominance of the East. Even though it averted the worst, the 1957 review did little to arrest the decline in Britain's relative position, a sign that Treasury expenditure priorities had not changed in spite of the growing evidence of international competition. The question whether Britain seriously intended to remain in the field, so often posed by Jacob in his conversations with ministers, was not answered. There were to be further cuts, in particular the abolition of the Thai Service, in 1960, before a wider vision began to prevail and limited expansion was resumed after the decline of the postwar years. Perhaps it would have been too much to expect that such a reversal of policy could have taken place in the immediate aftermath of Suez, even with such a man as Dr Hill, who is known to have stood up in defence of the rights of the BBC during the Suez crisis, in charge of the post-Suez review.

13
The Sixties and After

If, from the point of view of the External Services, the fifties can be regarded as a period of decline and lost opportunities, the sixties were marked by a distinct reversal of the trend. Whereas in the first fifteen years after the war the BBC barely succeeded in keeping its head above water and suffered heavily, in terms of its effectiveness, from the failure of successive governments to heed its advice that capital investment had fallen dangerously low, something about the climate of the next decade brought about a radical change in official policies which became perceptible right from the start of the period. It stemmed in part from an appreciation of the political significance of developments in Africa and Asia, where decolonisation was proceeding apace and the Third World was gaining in consciousness and discovering its voice, at the same time becoming an object of competition for influence by the great powers. Britain, for its part, was adjusting to the loss of imperial power, so vividly driven home by the Suez fiasco. Influence, in the future, given the reduced means available and the changed international circumstances, would have to be wielded by other means than through military presence on the ground and political control. From then on Britain's capacity to make an impact on the world scene would have to depend, in the first place, on her general standing, closely linked to the strength of her position as an industrial and trading nation. But it was also realised that in the new age which was beginning no country which wished to play a significant role on the international stage could afford to neglect the projection of its image beyond its frontiers. Public opinion overseas, as well as governments and top people, needed to be addressed direct. Britain, in many respects, was uniquely well placed. She had a wide network of connections and friendships the world over which had survived the passing of empire. She had a culture, institutions and political ways which evoked respect and set standards, in terms of the freedom of the individual and the rule of law, which were widely aspired to by others less privileged. In the continuing ideological conflict she had a strong hand to play, in which broadcasting was one of her most effective cards. At the same time increased domestic prosperity contributed to a greater feeling of optimism. Harold Macmillan's 'Wind of Change' speech in Cape Town in 1960 set the tone for the decade in one respect, but so also did his famous remark that 'You've never had it so good.'

The wind of change was also felt in Bush House, where the whole of the External Services broadcasting operation was finally brought together under one roof in November 1957, and in the BBC at large, where the appointment of Hugh Greene, one of the first of the Bushmen, to be Director-General in 1960 spelt the start of renewal and of a freer, more adventurous outlook which filtered through to the External Services when they themselves were not taking the lead.

The first tangible consequence of the new climate, so far as the External Services were concerned, was a readiness on the part of the Government to consider a considerably increased level of capital expenditure, as had been recommended by both Drogheda and Hill. The modernisation of domestic transmitters had started on a limited scale as an immediate sequel to the 1957 White Paper, but by the early sixties the Government was showing signs of wanting, as a matter of the highest priority, to make a concerted effort to improve audibility, more particularly in Africa and Asia. Successive official reviews, in 1961, 1965 and 1967, reiterated the need for the comprehensive replacement of obsolete transmitters by more high-powered equipment and for the setting-up of new relay stations overseas. These were seen as essential if the new transistor audiences in the Third World were to be in a position to listen to London now that decolonisation was likely to lead to a gradual decline in local rebroadcasting of the BBC. Though Treasury constraints due to economic difficulties, particularly in the second half of the sixties, reduced the level of investment to well below what was desirable and caused the deferment of many projects, major steps were taken then which transformed the technical position of the External Services. They made possible the BBC's greatly increased impact in the seventies, as measured by all the available yardsticks.

By the early seventies four out of the five short wave transmitting stations in the United Kingdom had been re-equipped. Nearly half the senders in those stations now had an output power of 250 kilowatts. Twenty-six of the UK transmitters were of modern design, though the twelve remaining war-time transmitters at Skelton, in Cumbria, had still not been replaced at the beginning of 1982, forty years after they were originally installed. The Government's first priority of the early sixties, Africa, and particularly its West Coast, led to the building of a high-power short wave relay station on Ascension Island, in the South Atlantic. Equipped with four 250-kilowatt transmitters, the station was in full service by May 1967 and provided improved coverage both of Africa and, when not in use for that purpose, Latin-America. In the Middle East, following earlier spells of operation on medium wave from Berbera in the Somali Republic and later from Perim

Island in the Aden straits, a powerful new medium wave relay operated by the Diplomatic Wireless Service on behalf of the BBC was built in 1969 on the island of Masirah in the Indian Ocean. It provided coverage of Pakistan, North West India, Iran, Afghanistan and the Persian Gulf and was responsible for a steep rise in listening in the area, making the BBC in Arabic, Farsi, Urdu and Hindi as well as English as easily accessible in many areas as the local domestic service. In the Middle East, too, the Cyprus transmitter taken over in 1957 from 'Sharq al Adna' and the small transmitter which had been hastily installed during the Suez crisis were supplemented by a new fifty-kilowatt medium wave transmitter in 1969. Increased short wave capacity was added in the mid-sixties in the shape of four 100-kilowatt transmitters. They were to be supplemented in the seventies by two 500-kilowatt medium wave transmitters of the latest model, which placed the BBC in a commanding technical position over a wide area of the Middle East. At the start of the eighties a further four 250-kilowatt short wave transmitters were being added to the Cyprus complex, thus turning it into the largest of the overseas installations relaying BBC programmes. It too was operated by the Diplomatic Wireless Service. In the Far East the modernisation of the relay station at Tebrau, in Malaysia, was completed in 1972 with the installation of four 250-kilowatt and four 100-kilowatt transmitters, while in 1976 a project which had first been considered thirty years before and had repeatedly been shelved for want of funds came to fruition in the Caribbean. The site which had first been considered for a Caribbean relay was at Georgetown, in Guiana, and its purpose in the years that immediately followed the war would have been to improve the BBC's signal in North America and Australasia as well as in the Caribbean. However, the final choice fell on Antigua, where in the early seventies the BBC went into partnership with Deutsche Welle to put up four 250-kilowatt transmitters, which are jointly operated and provide a boost for signals to Central America, the Caribbean and the northern tier of South America.

These were crucial developments, producing, as they did, much evidence of increased listening, and providing the journalists and programme makers at Bush House with the spur that comes from the knowledge that the technical means more nearly match the quality of the broadcast output. However the slowing down of investment in the late sixties, and the further reductions in capital spending imposed by the Chancellor of the Exchequer at the end of 1973 following the dramatic rise in the price of oil, led in the late seventies to a situation which bore a marked similarity to the predicament in which the BBC had found itself twenty years before. Too many projects had been deferred, and the funds available were now insufficient to maintain the BBC's technical competitiveness in the face of massive investment by its rivals. It was hard to persuade governments of whatever party, in the midst of the economic crisis of those years, that external broadcasting is, in part at least, a capital-intensive activity and requires a minimum of regular investment if it is to remain technically effective. In the case of short wave broadcasting, matters have been complicated by the increasing overcrowding of the broadcasting bands which can only be overcome by stepping up the power of the transmitters. The first Empire Service transmitters at Daventry had a power output of ten to fifteen kilowatts and were described then as 'high-power'. By the sixties many of the transmitters being installed were 250-kilowatt models, and by the mid-seventies the Soviet Union, the Federal German Republic and France, amongst others, were all re-equipping with 500-kilowatt senders. Complaints about the worsening audibility of the BBC – attributable as often as not, it has to be said, to natural phenomena rather than to any inadequacies in the output of the transmitters themselves – inevitably led to pressures for a crash programme of modernisation such as the one which was eventually agreed by James Callaghan when Prime Minister in 1977 following the report of the Central Policy Review Staff. However, by the time such programmes received serious government consideration the need to catch up on the neglect of past years made the sums involved seem so large, relatively speaking, as to cause the Treasury to call for compensating economies in broadcasting activities. Leaving aside the Thatcher Government's major cuts in public expenditure announced in the summer of 1979, the rows between the BBC and the Government over cuts in broadcast services in the late seventies and early eighties were all caused by this problem. The BBC – supported by many members of both Houses of Parliament and leader writers in the national and provincial press – would argue tenaciously that it should not have to pay through cuts in foreign language services, with the disproportionate damage that this involved, for the failure of successive governments to make adequate continuing provision for the minimum essential level of capital investment. The Government would respond by saying that whatever the rights or wrongs of what had or had not been done in the past the amount of money available at a particular time was finite and broadcasting overseas had to be seen in the overall context of the Government's expenditure priorities, in which it clearly figured fairly low down the list.

At the end of the fifties all this was yet to come. Already inside the External Services there were the stirrings of change and renewal as the implications of the transition from empire to commonwealth and the growth of non-alignment were being assessed. The role of broadcasting was changing, new audiences in Africa and Asia were emerging which had no first-hand knowledge of Britain and would not necessarily take its values for granted. As far back as 1957, Donald Stephenson, Controller, Overseas Services, who had represented the BBC in New Delhi during the war and knew India well, was making the case to J.B. Clark for an increase in broadcasting in the Indian vernaculars, under threat at the time of the Suez crisis. At the same time he was arguing that the regionalised English services, which had dominated pre-war and war-time broadcasting, were becoming increasingly irrelevant: 'The more the BBC's short wave broadcasts in English can be consolidated into a single service', he wrote, 'the more authentic and emphatic is likely to be their impact.'[1] He saw the new General Overseas Service as a 'round-the-clock and round-the-world information service of the liveliest and most authoritative kind'. Time might not yet be ripe for what he called the 'assimilation' of the services to Africa, North America and the Pacific into what was generally referred to in everyday conversation as 'the GOS', but their days, he thought, were numbered. The GOS should in any case be renamed the World Service, a change which did not finally take place until 1965. He argued strongly with J. B. Clark for a change in the GOS's conception of its audience, which would in turn mean a radical shift in programme policy and in the editorial attitudes of producers and broadcasters: 'I do not think we give best value to the UK taxpayer', he wrote, 'by a disproportionate concentration on preserving the bonds of sentiment with the Englishman abroad today ... We do better by encouraging the Englishman to realise that he is part of a new kind of commonwealth.' He proposed that the new brief of the GOS should be 'to take full cognisance of English-speaking but foreign native audiences' at all times when it was not broadcasting primarily to Australasia and North America.

The main architect of the new GOS – and the creator of the World Service as it is today – was R. E. Gregson, who headed the network for thirteen years from 1958. A Lancastrian who had been a classical scholar at Liverpool University, he had first joined the BBC in Manchester in the late forties and had been the founder of the long-running Home Service programme 'Gardeners Question Time' before joining the Overseas Services in the early fifties. A man of sharp and complex intelligence, he had the uncommon ability needed to master the intricate technicalities involved in planning a network which throughout the twenty-four hours of the day was serving constantly shifting combinations of audiences in different parts of the world as local peak listening times came up. He could hold his own, as few people could, in discussions with the Bush House engineers, themselves expertly involved in the optimum use of transmitters and frequencies. Under his direction there was a radical shift of emphasis to news, comment and the background discussion of world affairs. With the recruitment of a new generation of highly-professional young producers in the Overseas Talks and Features Department, of which this writer was then the Head, a fresh tradition of current affairs broadcasting was forged which has continued to this day. The accent shifted from the longer, more leisurely talks to a livelier journalistic presentation in which impromptu everyday speech took over from the polished, scripted microphone performances of the past. A new spirit of intellectual enquiry was at large, a sense of breaking new ground and creating a new role for the BBC, as well as a fascination with the developments which were transforming the world and an urge to explore their significance for the benefit of the predominantly non-British audiences which the network was now seeking to attract.

At the same time the interests of listeners in the developing world were increasingly catered for in regular programmes on agriculture, science, technology, medicine and public health designed to provide information of practical use to specialists working in these fields. A truly international flavour was creeping in, and Britain, as reflected in the programme output, was losing its imperial image and acquiring a new one, more in tune with the spirit of the times – the image of a country rich in skills and experience, the home of a culture and a language that held universal appeal, whose voice, now that it was no longer a world power of the first rank, could be regarded as disinterested – a purveyor of the truth and a source of practical wisdom in world affairs.

These developments coincided with a substantial redeployment of resources in the direction of Asia and Africa which reflected increased government concern with those areas as decolonisation gained momentum. As Donald Stephenson had foreseen, all but one of the regionalised English services which had played such an important role in wartime were phased out to make possible increases in broadcasting towards the Third World both in English and in foreign languages. 'London Calling Asia', a daily transmission specially tailored for listeners in the Indian sub-continent and South East Asia, was integrated into the General Overseas Service largely, as Stephenson had argued, because the diversion of frequencies necessary to carry it diminished the BBC's overall signal strength in the area and there was no evidence that it attracted a wider and more significant audience than the main network. A single voice from London would be more effective, though with the proviso that there would be what Stephenson had called 'a consciousness of Asia' in the GOS at certain peak Asian listening times. The North American Service was brought to an end in 1962, though for the BBC this meant a sad loss of rebroadcasting by American stations, which had remained at a remarkably high level throughout the fifties, and was not retrieved, at least in part, until the mid-seventies.

As against these losses the Thai Service, taken off the air in 1960, was reinstated in 1962 in one of those about-turns of official policy which left the BBC with the onerous task of reconstituting a programme team and regaining an audience which by then had been lost. The following year the same happened with the Portuguese Service, one of the casualties of the 1957 review, which now returned after a silence of six years. At the same time there were increases in broadcasting in Russian and in Burmese – the Burmese Service being doubled overnight in 1960.

It was in broadcasting to Africa, however, that the most important developments of those years took place. The 1960s, in a sense, were the decade of Africa. They saw the creation of a large and separate BBC African Service and a steep increase in the interest taken by the External Services in African affairs, itself a reflection of the march of events and of the Government's own priorities. Close and friendly relations had been built up in the post-war years between the BBC and the nascent broadcasting organisations of anglophone Africa under the sympathetic influence of John Grenfell Williams. Many of these organisations had been set up, and were now run, by BBC men on secondment. Among the first was Tom Chalmers, who had given up the Controllership of the Light Programme to go and lay the foundations of broadcasting in Nigeria and had then gone on to do the same in what was then Tanganyika. Many members of the staff of African radio stations – and this was also true in other parts of the new commonwealth – had been trained by the BBC. Hundreds, in fact, had been through the overseas courses run by the BBC at its staff training school, and much good will and a feeling of belonging to the solidarity of commonwealth broadcasters had thus been fostered, as well as an understanding of BBC traditions and values. It had been one of Britain's relatively unnoticed invisible exports. At the same time rebroadcasting of BBC programmes by stations in African colonies had been at a high level, and within the External Services there was a fund of experience of African affairs and of good will towards the new nations which was reinforced by the recruitment at that time into the ranks of the External Services of former members of the colonial service whose careers had been cut short by decolonisation but whose expertise and dedication the BBC was now able to exploit.

As has been seen, it was expected that with the advent of independence the level of rebroadcasting would be bound to decline. Direct listening to London would assume greater importance. The decision to build a relay station on Ascension Island, taken in the early sixties, came as a direct consequence. With it there came a steep increase in broadcasting to Africa, both in English and in the vernaculars. Broadcasting, it was felt, could do much to assist in maintaining links of friendship with the new black nations. There was a need, too, to break down the artificial barriers between African states left behind by the colonial era and to inform African audiences about developments elsewhere on the continent. Broadcasting was thus going to become one of the agents working towards the creation of an African consciousness. The title 'Focus on Africa' given to a daily current affairs programme started by the African Service in those early years was symptomatic of this continental approach, and the programme itself did much, through interviews with African personalities and reports from its many correspondents throughout Africa, to give its listeners an awareness of the wider continental context.

By 1963 all three of the African vernacular services, Hausa, Swahili and Somali, had been increased to an hour a day. A daily bulletin in French for Africa was introduced in June 1960, and it was not long before the French Language Service (as it was renamed at that time) was once again being expanded after being halved in size as a consequence of the 1957 White Paper. By 1961 it had been restored to its 1951 level of four hours a day, of which the bulk could be heard in Africa as well as in Europe and nearly half was specially geared to the interests of listeners in francophone Africa – a development which would have been impossible to achieve quickly and effectively had the Drogheda recommendations – let alone the closure threatened during the Suez crisis – been immediately implemented.

There was a parallel development in English. The grounds for offering African listeners a substantial alternative to the General Overseas Service gave rise to much debate in Bush House in view of the limited transmission facilities available at the time. For Donald Hodson, who had succeeded Stephenson as Controller, Overseas Services in 1958, the case was strong. The GOS, by its very character as a worldwide service, was 'not accessible to any but the best educated Africans, linguistically and educationally'.[2] A greater degree of regionalisation for those for whom English was, so to speak, one of the local vernaculars would be bound to increase the BBC's overall effectiveness. The GOS, the British High Commissioner in Accra argued, was 'not close to and in harmony with the environment of the audience'. Special daily programmes for West Africa had long been a feature of the BBC's output, but there had been no comparable effort in the direction of East Africa. As the former East African colonies and protectorates gained their independence after 1961, therefore, a new pattern of special programmes for the region was introduced on a daily basis. But it took time before resources became available to do much else than transmit to East Africa material originally intended for West Africa. As Hodson put it to the Colonial Office in making the case for additional funds, this tended to be 'too sophisticated. Linguistic levels are not always suitable and the content is conceived, of course, in terms of the original audience.'[3]

Other problems, stemming fundamentally from the shortage of transmitting facilities, proved hard to resolve until more transmitters and frequencies became available with the coming into service of the Ascension Island Relay early in 1967. Elliot Watrous, the energetic Head of the African Service, supported by the Commonwealth Relations Office, felt strongly, as he told Hodson, that programmes for West Africa needed to be broadcast at the peak evening hours if they were to reach the maximum intended audience. He took the view that much of the GOS's programming between 5 and 9 pm, the peak listening period in West Africa, was of limited appeal to West African listeners. Why not insert programmes specially built for Africa by the African Service into the GOS for an hour every night, he suggested. 'Would this not lead to the greater popularity of the GOS in a part of the commonwealth where English is the first language of many millions of people?'[4] The debate on this point ran on fiercely for some time, pitting the advocates of regionalism against those who felt, as Stephenson had argued in 1957, that London could speak more effectively with a single voice and that the dispersal of scarce technical resources was not the way to build an audience. In any case, as Gregson, the Head of the General Overseas Service argued, it was not true to say the programmes broadcast in his network were not relevant to the interests of African audiences. Audience research data showed that on the contrary they were widely followed. The GOS record request programme 'Listeners' Choice' received more letters from West Africa than from any other part of the world. Moreover at peak West African listening times there was a good deal of listening in other parts of the world, where the proposed concentration on African interests would be unacceptable and would affect the GOS's following. On the technical side, it was argued that 'a suitable evening time' for African programmes 'could not avoid being most damaging to existing services', and the Audience Research Department, in a thoughtful paper, took the view that to try and fit in a full regional service in the evening would involve weakening the GOS's strong position in the area. Moreover, it warned, 'efforts to create a distinctive identity for the regional service need to be carefully handled for fear of arousing suspicions of propaganda or ulterior motives – suspicions which the General Overseas Service, as a world-wide service, is free from'.[5]

In the event the problem was resolved when the Ascension Island relay came into service and it became possible to inject a special and expanded stream of programmes for Africa into the World Service as relayed on Ascension Island transmitters. The building of the Ascension Island relay station revolutionised the BBC's position in west Africa as well as bringing about substantial improvements in audibility in Latin America. In Nigeria, Ghana and Sierra Leone it was now possible to reach a mass audience on a scale with few parallels anywhere in the world except the Middle East and the Indian sub-continent and rivalling the following of the local domestic services.

In the arguments about the limits of regionalisation, which were always in the end arguments about the extent to which the BBC could afford to be suspected of ulterior motives and of speaking with more than one voice, a fine line had to be drawn between two quite different conceptions of the role of broadcasting. On the one hand there could be no objection to addressing audiences in particular areas in terms which they would immediately understand and on subjects of obvious relevance where a more general English service might not be in a position to provide the sharpness of focus of which a foreign language service, with its precisely delineated audience, was capable. On the other hand, there was always the danger, as Cecil Graves and J.B. Clark had feared when the introduction of foreign language broadcasting was being considered in the late thirties, that the singling out of a particular audience for special attention could become suspect in the minds of the intended listeners, particularly in circumstances in which political motives were more likely than not to be present.

Issues of this kind were much to the fore in 1965 when after the Rhodesian unilateral declaration of independence the Wilson Government asked the BBC to undertake a special broadcasting operation directed at White Rhodesians. This was intended to stress their isolation and vulnerability and the likely consequences of the Smith regime's illegal action. The relays of the BBC's programmes by the Rhodesian Broadcasting Corporation had been brought to an end a week before UDI, and except through the World Service's transmissions on short wave the Rhodesian audience was therefore largely cut off from any awareness of how the world was reacting to UDI save for the highly tendentious version put out by the Rhodesian media. To achieve better penetration of the white Rhodesian community the British Government set up a fifty-kilowatt medium wave transmitter just south of the Rhodesian border at Francistown in Botswana, together with a low-power short wave transmitter. There was talk in government circles of 'an aggressive exercise in psychological warfare' and 'calling in the propaganda experts', perhaps intended to make up for any really effective government action against the rebel regime. Tangye Lean, now the BBC's Director of External Broadcasting, secured an assurance from the Government that the BBC would be the sole user of the Francistown transmitter. There would be no question of another 'Voice of Britain' exercise such as had taken place during the Suez crisis, and it is clear that the Government itself took the view that the BBC was the best instrument available for the operation because of its reputation for objectivity and impartiality. Psychological warfare experience, it was said, had shown the importance of those qualities. There was to be no vilification or personal abuse, which were regarded as having little value as a propaganda weapon, and no incitement to violence or subversive material was to be broadcast.

Early reports from Rhodesia suggested that the Francistown signal, while audible at night throughout most of the country, could not be heard by day much beyond Bulawayo. In January the *Guardian* reported that Francistown was inaudible and that the BBC admitted it, and it is true that at that stage there were some sharp differences of opinion on technical issues between the BBC's own engineers and the Diplomatic Wireless Service, who were operating the transmitter. On the other hand the broadcasts were audible enough to have caused the Rhodesian authorities to ban listening in public places as well as frequently to take the trouble to refute what had been said on the air. By the end of March 1966 the frequencies used at Francistown were being heavily though selectively jammed, the main target of the jammers being 'The World and Rhodesia', a special programme transmitted five times a day which carried the main burden of the effort to persuade white Rhodesians of the error of their ways. The programme was transmitted as part of the World Service on frequencies beamed to Central Africa, a fact that helped to give it a more balanced image in the minds of those Rhodesians who managed to hear it, but the evidence available suggests that even this did not succeed in disposing of the widespread conviction in Rhodesia that it was no more than a government-inspired propaganda operation. The BBC was accused in Salisbury of being 'a political arm of the Socialist Government'. W.P. Kirkman, a journalist with extensive knowledge of Africa reported on returning from Salisbury that 'even among sympathisers with what the BBC are doing there is a fairly general feeling that the programmes are propaganda'. 'Nothing the Rhodesian Broadcasting Corporation puts out is half as objective as "The World and Rhodesia" ', he said, 'but the average Rhodesian doesn't think it is objective.' There were risks, too, in talking about the internal situation in Rhodesia itself, since anything that was even slightly wrong was immediately spotted and used to discredit the programme. Much comment on Rhodesian topics, he felt, was not in tune with local conditions. Ian Smith himself made violent attacks against the BBC, but a *Financial Times* report in March took the view that there was not much in Smith's charges: 'It takes more than a little local difficulty to swerve the BBC from its belief in balance. It is hard to see Bush House, that bastion of Reithian ethics, as a sinister mind bender.' Other British journalists took a more critical view. Jim Biddulph, who had been a correspondent in Salisbury over a number of years, felt that 'some of the views reported in "The World and Rhodesia" were too extreme and might cast doubt on the credibility of BBC news programmes'.

By 1967 it was clear that the medium wave signal from Francistown had been rendered practically inaudible and that the audience to it was probably very small. Most Rhodesians who listened to the BBC did so direct from London on short wave. The transmitter was eventually closed down on 31 March 1968 after having operated for nearly two and a half years. Charles Curran, who had succeeded Tangye Lean as Director of External Broadcasting at the beginning of 1967, wrote to the *Scotsman* in reply to a report from a correspondent from Botswana who had claimed that the BBC's reputation had been tarnished. He asserted that 'while there is no doubt that the regime found BBC broadcasts objectionable – not surprisingly since these broadcasts were directed against the censorship which was denying the facts to Rhodesians – there was never any question of the BBC applying different editorial standards in these broadcasts'. There were people in Bush House at the time who did not share that view. At all events the operation did not succeed in its object, as was perhaps inevitable, and the BBC had come close – some felt too close – to allowing itself to be used for a purpose which some regarded as lying well outside its proper function. The Francistown episode was in every respect an isolated incident. If anything it demonstrated once again that radio propaganda cannot be a substitute for policy, as Jacob never tired of pointing out in his day, and by itself can seldom bring about political change where other, more potent forces are not already at work.

In the wider context, whatever judgement may be cast on the negligence and lost opportunities of the first fifteen years after the war, by the early

seventies the BBC's position in international broadcasting was well on the way
to being restored, even if there could be no question of emulating the Soviet
Union, the United States and China in terms of sheer volume. Although the
BBC had fallen well behind its major rivals, who were continuing to grow and
had known none of the setbacks which it had experienced, it had at least held
its own and remained the dominant force in international broadcasting.
Though there might be parts of the world where others had more listeners
and could be better heard, it was the most widely listened to, and the most
trusted. The policy of building new overseas relay stations, wisely accepted as
right by one official review body after another, led to vastly increased audiences, particularly in Africa, Asia and the Middle East. It also made possible,
in most though not in all cases, substantial increases in foreign language
broadcasting to the areas served by the new stations. Thus the coming into
service of the Ascension Island relay led not only to the increased broadcasting effort in the direction of Africa, but also, in 1967, to the partial restoration
of the cuts in the Latin-American Service which had been imposed in 1951
and 1952, just as the building of the medium wave relay station at Masirah,
in the Indian Ocean, led to substantial increases in broadcasting in Hindi,
Urdu, and Farsi to Iran and Afghanistan. There were further increases in
broadcasting in most Asian languages when the modernisation of the Far
East Relay in Malaysia was completed in 1972. At the end of their fortieth
year the External Services, with nearly 750 hours of weekly output in forty
languages including English, were broadcasting more than at any time since
the war and nearly 200 hours a week more than at their nadir in the mid-
fifties. There were some losses along the way, however, in particular the
Albanian and Hebrew Services, which had been under threat for some years
and were eventually abolished in 1967 and 1968 respectively, though it is hard
to believe that the minimal economies thus achieved can have made a worth-
while contribution to solving the economic difficulties which the Government
was experiencing at the time.

Nonetheless, as the External Services looked back on their first forty years,
they could feel that they were better equipped to face whatever challenge the
future held in store than at any time since the war. Moreover the potential
audience for international broadcasts had vastly increased since the war and
was continuing to do so. The total number of radio sets in the world at large
had risen more than five fold in that period, and whereas the vast majority of
the 150,000,000 sets available in 1945 had been concentrated in western
Europe and North America, the proportion to be found in Eastern Europe,
China and the developing world had grown by leaps and bounds in the
following twenty-five years. At the start of the eighties the world figure was
approaching 1,500 million, ten times what it was at the end of the war and
well over fifty per cent more than in 1972.

There was growing evidence, too, that as one international conflict followed another and the world became an ever more dangerous and unstable place, accurate and dependable information was increasingly at a premium. The BBC's calm, dispassionate and professional presentation and careful back-grounding of developments was attracting an expanding following, not only among those with a professional interest and involvement in events but among ordinary people the world over who sought an understanding of what was taking place. During the Second World War it had been a case, in the most dramatic of circumstances, of maintaining morale in the occupied countries and slowly sapping the enemy's will to continue the fight. Now the BBC's role was more diffuse but no less important, and the decisive policy direction given by Haley and Jacob in the first years after the war, with its firm emphasis on news, was being vindicated. Even if in a wider sense Britain, to quote Dean Acheson, remained a country which had lost an empire but had failed to discover a role, the field of external broadcasting, at any rate, was one in which, thanks to the prescience of such as Haley and Jacob, Britain could continue to make an important contribution to a sane and rational approach to the affairs of the world.

Yet it is precisely at that juncture that the External Services entered what was to prove to be the most precarious period in their existence since the fifties. The immediate and fortuitous trigger was the economic crisis caused by the rise in oil prices at the end of 1973. This led to a succession of almost yearly demands for budgetary cuts as part of the Treasury's policy of reducing government expenditure, with consequent squeezes on already slender pro-gramme resources, the slowing down of capital investment and reductions in hours of broadcasting, which by 1980 has declined to just over 700 per week. The BBC could never claim that it was entitled as of right to remain immune from the pressures resulting from the country's economic predicament, but it could and did attempt to persuade successive governments, as it had done on many previous occasions, that the value of its activities had to be seen in a long-term perspective and that stability of output was necessary if it was to fulfil the role expected of it. The scale of the economies demanded, small if not minimal in the context of total government expenditure, was often such, when seen as a proportion of the External Services' own budget, as to threaten disproportionate damage to an operation which had long ago shed all its fat. The problem was compounded by the fact that because of the high level of permanent overheads involved in the broadcasting operation, very heavy cuts in broadcast services have to be made before the cost of overheads begins to fall. This meant that reductions in broadcasting activities were inevitably out of all proportion to the savings achieved.

So the BBC found itself repeatedly confronted from the mid-seventies onwards with attempts by the Government to identify services deemed to be 'marginal' in terms of what was considered at the time to be the national interest, and therefore expendable. Fearful that once a number of so-called marginal services had been eliminated a further group of services would become the expendable marginal services of tomorrow, it felt bound to point to the occasions when services which had been judged expendable at one stage were later reinstated, presumably for good reasons of overall strategy, and to stress that stop-go policies in broadcasting carried heavy penalties. The closing down of services was resented in the countries concerned, as had been made clear in the case of the Portuguese Service; trained staff were dispersed and audiences lost. More important, a means of British influence had been abandoned. Yet it remained true, as Jacob had argued twenty years before and as had been argued many times since, that it was impossible to predict when the ability to broadcast to an already existing audience in a particular country might not become of crucial importance. As the BBC's Annual Report to Parliament for 1955-56 had put it, referring to individual foreign language services, 'it is regrettable that too often their importance is recognised only when conditions of crisis and tension developing in different parts of the world throw into relief the urgency of presenting the British point of view'.

The BBC could also argue that had it quietly accepted, as some felt it should have done, the demise of particular services and not fought hard and successfully for their retention, those services would not have been available at a subsequent time of crisis, when their role was recognised as important. Thus the Turkish Service, reprieved *in extremis* in 1979, found itself being expanded in 1981 following the Turkish military take-over. Thus also the Persian Service, heavily attacked from Tehran in 1976 and 1978 and a source of recurrent difficulties in official Anglo-Iranian relations, was expanded in 1980 following the Soviet invasion of Afghanistan. The Indian vernacular services, regarded as expendable on more than one occasion going as far back as the Suez Crisis, gained such plaudits for their role during the period of emergency rule imposed by Mrs Gandhi in 1976 that a special reference was made to them in Mr Callaghan's speech to the Indian Parliament when he visited India as Prime Minister in 1977 after the end of the emergency.

For many years standard procedure adopted by Whitehall when faced with a complex situation requiring difficult choices, has been to set up a committee of enquiry or official review body. There had been two such enquiries in the fifties, Drogheda and Hill, and a further three internal Governmental reviews in the 1960s, whose reports were never published. Towards the end of the decade, as the pound was being devalued and the Wilson Government found itself in increasing economic difficulties, it decided to resort to yet another independent enquiry into the overseas information services, this time to be conducted by a small committee of three under Sir Val Duncan, a leading figure in the City. He was assisted by Sir Frank Roberts, a senior retired ambassador, and Andrew Shonfield, a distinguished journalist and academic and an able broadcaster who was later to become Director of the Royal Institute of International Affairs.

Already in 1964 the Plowden Report on Representational Services Overseas had begun to cast doubt on the continued capacity of a declining Britain to play a world role now that she was withdrawing from her overseas commitments: 'There must not be an incongruity', Plowden wrote, 'between Britain's powers of influence in the politico-military and economic fields and the size of her propaganda effort. Political propaganda cannot in our view be effective if conducted from an inadequate power base.'[6] There was abundant evidence in the short wave bands that this view was not shared in the rest of the world. Nor was it corroborated by the BBC's own experience in the field.

The Duncan Report[7], published in July 1969, followed a similar line. It recommended that there should now be a major switch of emphasis in Britain's information effort abroad from attempts to explain Britain's political policies to commercial and cultural promotion. 'There can be no hope', it said, 'of reaching mass audiences effectively from within the resources available.' Once again the Drogheda view was resurrected: 'Our efforts', Duncan said, 'should be directed towards the influential few.' Like Plowden, Duncan – wrongly as the BBC saw it – linked influence with political power: 'Political motives for a direct interest in Britain on the part of mass audiences [in the Third World] will diminish as Britain's political influence in these areas is reduced and her military forces are withdrawn.' It then went on to its most controversial conclusion and one which, like the concept of 'the influential few', had periodically come up whenever there was talk of economies:

It seems fair to predict [it said] that in many countries the BBC's External Services will have the greatest effect upon the educated and professional classes, for whom English will often be the main lingua franca. These classes will have a broad interest in the whole range of subjects affecting their countries and will therefore take an interest in their countries' relations with Britain.

It was essentially an élitist view, in which public opinion in the broad sense played no part. It was also in direct conflict both with the Haley view of the importance of accurate news *per se* as a force for good in the world at large and with the realities of broadcasting as they were known to the BBC. But it led to Duncan's principal recommendations on external broadcasting: there should now be a concentration of effort on broadcasting in English. Foreign language broadcasting should be given a lower priority except in Eastern Europe and the Middle East. All foreign language services to the rest of Europe should be abolished, and there should be swingeing cuts in overseas foreign languages, from which the Latin-American Service, for example, was not to be exempt, the Committee having taken the highly debatable view that 'an increasing proportion of the educated classes understand English', and that Latin-America was 'not an area in which British interests were involved to such a major degree'. Like its predecessors, the Duncan Report placed great stress on the need for an increase in capital investment, overlooking the fact that its technical recommendations, which included the strengthening and modernisation of relay stations overseas, and an improvement in reception in Western Europe on medium wave were in conflict with its policy recommendations.

There was wide agreement between the BBC and the Foreign Office that the logic of Duncan's thinking was shaky and many of its conclusions questionable, and there was no dispute at the time about the fact that, real though the spread of English undoubtedly was, there were many parts of the world where influential people either did not understand English at all or had an insufficient command of it to be able to listen profitably. Moreover the capital programme proposed by Duncan, with its rapid stepping up of investment, particularly on medium wave transmitters, was not a practical proposition at the time. There was no urgent need, therefore, so the Foreign Office argument went, for cuts in foreign language services to pay for an immediate increase in capital expenditure. There might be a further review of foreign language services in due course, but the Foreign Office firmly took the view, which was accepted, that further studies with a view to economies were inappropriate, that the end of the line had been reached as far as savings in the overseas information services were concerned, and that the BBC and others should now be left to get on with the job. The outcome, in the end, was a minor, largely cosmetic redeployment of resources from foreign language broadcasting to English which left few traces. Two years later increases in broadcasting in Asian languages planned to exploit more fully the potential offered by the new high-power transmitters just installed at the Far East Relay were duly implemented.

The final verdict on the Duncan Report was delivered by Oliver Whitley, the son of J.H. Whitley, Chairman of the BBC Governors at the time of the start of the Empire Service. Writing to the Foreign Office as Managing Director of the External Services in April 1970, he brought the debate back to more fundamental issues:

The main value of the External Services is not that they may help to sell tractors or nuclear reactors, nor even that they so influence people in other countries, nobs or mobs, as to be more amenable to British diplomacy or foreign policy. Their main value is that because they effectively represent and communicate this British propensity for truthfulness or the adherence to the individual right to the perception of reality, they help to increase the instability of political systems based on the total inversion of morality and reality for ideological purposes. Countries which have such political systems are for that reason less amenable to British diplomacy, more difficult to trade with, and particularly if powerful or proliferating, liable to be a military threat to Britain, whose contrasted liberties constantly give the lie to their fictitious universe.[8]

Seen in retrospect, the Duncan Report turned out to have been of doubtful value, largely because the conclusions it drew from its interpretation of the realities of the world in which Britain had to exist were highly debatable. Like Drogheda it left few traces as far as the BBC was concerned.

Much the same was to happen seven years later, though the circumstances were to be a great deal more dramatic. Once again the country's worsening economic situation led the Government to call for a fundamental and critical review of the assumptions on which Britain's representation overseas was based and for recommendations for change. But this time the job was given not to an independent committee of wise men but to Downing Street's own Central Policy Review Staff – 'the Think Tank' – a body which had been created by Edward Heath when Prime Minister in the early seventies and was now headed by Sir Kenneth Berrill, a senior Whitehall official with a Treasury background. The BBC saw little of those of its members who were assigned to look into its activities, though it produced much written material for their benefit, and, as the BBC's Annual Report for 1977/8 put it, 'it is probably true to say that at no time in the history of the External Services has such a comprehensive body of detailed evidence been brought together and made available ... The CPRS was almost certainly better and more thoroughly informed than any of its predecessors.'[9] What part the study of this evidence played in assisting the CPRS in formulating its conclusions is impossible to say at this stage, though there was a distinct impression inside the BBC that these conclusions had been reached in broad outline weeks before the detailed evidence became available. Thereafter the CPRS struggled in an attempt to make the realities of short wave broadcasting fit in with its pre-conceptions. The BBC, for its part, thought it right, when informed in advance of the review's likely conclusions, to seek a meeting in order to emphasise not only that they were deeply flawed on the technical side but that the major damage they would undoubtedly cause to the BBC's continuing effectiveness would be bound to cause a public outcry. The warning was brushed aside.

The CPRS Report, when it emerged at the beginning of August 1977, received an even more hostile reception than had been predicted. Put succinctly it recommended that the External Services should cease to broadcast each day between 8 pm and 4 am and that they should no longer seek to be heard in North America and Australasia. All broadcasting in European languages should cease except to communist Eastern Europe. Outside Europe broadcasting in Japanese, Burmese and Somali would be abolished, and the amount of broadcasting in Arabic and in Spanish to Latin-America would be halved. The BBC should in general concentrate its efforts on those parts of the world where freedom of information was restricted. Even accepting this judgement, however questionable, the proposal to close down transmissions between 8 pm and 4 am would have gravely affected the BBC's ability to act accordingly: had it been implemented it would have meant losing the large breakfast-time audiences for the BBC's English and vernacular broadcasts to the whole of Asia from Baghdad to Tokyo, including parts of the Soviet Union, as well as in East and Central Africa and in Central and Southern Europe. Expensive transmitters would lie unused during large parts of the

day and frequencies would be placed at risk. Altogether, a reduction of forty
per cent in the total output of the External Services would result, yielding
savings of no more than ten per cent of operational costs. In return there was
to be a much needed speeding-up of capital expenditure on new transmitters
and on the technical infrastructure needed to feed the BBC's programmes to
its overseas relay stations by satellite, with a consequent improvement in
audibility.

As seen by the BBC, implementation of the CPRS recommendations would
have spelt disaster for the External Services. The BBC's Chairman, Sir Michael
Swann, lost no time in making this clear at a packed press conference at
Broadcasting House attended, amongst others, by over one hundred foreign
journalists. The vast majority of British newspapers saw it the same way. So
did many editorials published in newspapers all over the world. Indeed there
can have been few issues in recent times which caused such a unanimous
reaction. The *Economist*, at the end of a leader entitled 'Think Small', expressed the general view when it tersely asked for 'more think, less tank,
please'.[10] The *Daily Mail* headlined an article by Peter Walker, a past and
future Conservative minister, with the words 'Too wet, too shallow *and* out
of their depth',[11] and The *Guardian's* leader was headlined 'So far away, so
sadly out of tune.'[12] The *Birmingham Evening Mail* wrote:

> The point that worries us most is the suggestion that the BBC's External Services
> should be cut to sixteen hours a day and concentrated on certain defined areas. The
> World Service broadcasts and their vernacular companions in thirty-nine other lan-
> guages are a model to the world – 'free' or otherwise – and should if anything be
> stepped up. They are probably the best ambassadors Britain has.[13]

Anthony Howard, writing in the *New Statesman*, commented that 'the net
result of any such cut-back would be to relegate the BBC to the same status as
'Radio Liberty' and 'Radio Free Europe', in other words to make it an overt,
anti-communist propaganda agency'. 'Nothing', he wrote, 'could be better
calculated to destroy "at a stroke" the reputation for editorial integrity and
political independence that the BBC has patiently (and sometimes, as at the
time of Suez in 1956, painfully) managed to build up over the years.'[14] *The
Times*, for its part, reported on 13 August: 'Even allowing for the grinding of
personal axes, the number of letters to this newspaper has been remarkable.'[15]
For three weeks hardly a day passed without some of these letters – a small
proportion of the total, *The Times* stated – appearing in its correspondence
columns. 'Even more remarkable', *The Times* added, 'is that such a large
correspondence has been almost unanimous. Scarcely a single letter has come
to the defence of the Think Tank's report.' The BBC itself received 2,500
letters from listeners, 1,700 of them relating to vernacular services. As the
BBC's Annual Report to Parliament for 1977/8 commented,

> It is ironic that a report whose purpose was to reduce Britain's external broadcasting

effort to a level appropriate, in the view of its authors, to the country's reduced
circumstances should have produced as one of its principal results such a striking
reaffirmation by those for whom our broadcasts are intended of the importance they
continue to attach to them.[16]

The eventual outcome was, in effect, a rejection by the Government of the
CPRS's recommendations on external broadcasting save for the proposed
programme of increased capital investment, which was based on the BBC's
own recommendations and was in due course given the go-ahead by the
Callaghan Government.

That the BBC was not out of its troubles is recent history. There was equally
vocal opposition in the summer and autumn of 1979, both at home and
abroad, when the new Conservative Government announced that it required
a cut of £4,000,000 – or about ten per cent of operating costs – to be made in
the budget of the External Services for the following year. Vociferous parliamentary and public pressure compelled it first to reduce the cut to £2,700,000
and later, under threat of defeat in the House of Commons caused by a
large-scale revolt of Conservative backbenchers, to reprieve – at least for the
moment – the seven services which had received their sentence at the beginning
of November. They were the French, Italian, Greek, Turkish, Spanish,
Maltese and Burmese Services. The savings would be found, for the immediate
future at any rate, from the proposed capital programme. Parliamentary
defeat was averted.

It is perhaps not to be wondered at that subsequently the Government,
baulked for a time in its determination to get its way but resolved to assert its
right under the Licence and Agreement to be the final judge of which languages the BBC should broadcast in and for how long, should in the end have
decided to impose its will. Early in 1981 it announced that it would now
require the continuing year-by-year saving which it had imposed in 1979 to
be achieved not by further deferments in capital expenditure but by cuts in
broadcasting services. The French Service to Europe, it said, would have to
go. So would the Spanish, Italian, Maltese, Somali, Burmese and Brazilian
Services. The funding of the Transcription Service would be withdrawn and
it would have to pay its way on a commercial basis, a proposition which was
clearly unrealistic in a world market in which most other countries were
offering their recorded material for use without payment.

Equally, it came as no surprise that notwithstanding the Government's
efforts to persuade peers and MPs as well as the press that it was in fact
increasing overall expenditure on external broadcasting to make possible a
long-term improvement in audibility, it still had to face a major row in
Parliament and threats of rebellion by Conservative backbenchers. Once
again the press, both at home and abroad, was filled with critical articles. At
the end of a debate in the House of Lords on 30 July the Government was
roundly defeated by a majority of thirty-seven. Nonetheless there was no sign

at the start of the summer Parliamentary recess of any readiness on its part to give way. It was only in the autumn, with the sudden and unexpected imminence of a debate in the Commons in Opposition time, that a compromise which proved acceptable to the majority of Conservative backbenchers was hastily put together, thus saving the Government from further Parliamentary difficulties. The French Service for Europe and the Brazilian Service were reprieved, though much reduced, the Somali and Burmese Services, both unique in their impact on communities for whom the BBC is the only voice which reaches them from the West, survived intact, and only the Spanish, Italian and Maltese Services were finally condemned.

Less than a year later the Falklands crisis, with its sharply divisive effect, was calling into question the wisdom of having abolished the Italian and Spanish Services and reduced the Brazilian Service. In all three countries both governments and public opinion were sharply critical of British policies and rallied to Argentina's side in the name of Latin solidarity. The need for the British version of events to be made available and for British policies to be explained can seldom have been plainer. It was a time to remember what Sir Ian Jacob had written to Sir Edward Bridges thirty years before at a similar time of crisis: 'to my mind it is not a question of saving a few hundred thousand pounds. It is a choice between maintaining and expanding an asset of tremendous value to this country and throwing it down the drain.'[17]

Although, over the years, questions of survival loomed large, at intervals, in the collective mind of the External Services and took up more of the time of senior executives than most others, they were not the only concern, nor indeed, the main ones. Day-to-day decisions of editorial policy were inevitably the one continuing preoccupation of senior news and programme staff, and potentially this was the area where the gravest conflicts could arise, particularly when the interests of diplomacy and journalism seemed opposed. Suez was the only instance of a major row on editorial policy between any British post-war government and the External Services, but there were many other occasions when Bush House found itself under attack by interested parties, whether at home or abroad, for what it was alleged, often wrongly, to be saying, or for what it was accused of failing to say. Accusations of bias, misrepresentation or inaccuracy are, of course, expected by broadcasters as a normal feature of daily life, but just occasionally there are more fundamental criticisms which call into question the very assumptions on which the broadcasters have been basing their work.

There were two cases of this kind in the late fifties, when the *Spectator* conducted a virulent campaign against the policies of the Russian Service and later those of the Yugoslav Service. Essentially the charge against the Russian Service was that it was trimming its sails in order not to displease 'even the touchiest of its listeners'[18] and, so it was claimed, to secure the lifting of jamming. British sovietologists who joined in the attack felt the service was 'more concerned with the Soviet establishment than with the growing number of Russians who are aware that there is much wrong with communist rule'.[19] It was, they said, using the language of diplomacy and appearing to be taking the diplomatic professions of the Soviet state seriously. Peter Wiles, a Fellow of Nuffield College, Oxford and the leading and most bitter critic, went further. He accused the service of 'moral compromise and appeasement' and its Programme Organiser, Anatol Goldberg, of 'esoteric right-wing Marxism'. These were serious charges, and the BBC took them seriously. It opened its files of scripts to Wiles to enable him to study at first hand what had been broadcast and replied to the charges point-by-point in the columns of the *Spectator*, though its rejoinders were never allowed to stand on their own without further editorial comment by the *Spectator*. It was essentially a clash of attitudes and of interpretation of recent events in the Soviet Union, and there was about it something of the acrimony of major religious or philosophical disputes. For Wiles, nothing had really changed since the death of Stalin and the rise of Khruschev, nor did the real nature of Marxist-Leninism make any change possible. It was a fundamentalist and dogmatic view which suffered no contradiction. Goldberg, who was deeply critical of Wiles's view of history and was faced with the task of speaking convincingly to a Soviet audience whose national pride was intense, took a different line: 'The line we have adopted since Stalin's death', he wrote, 'has been to welcome any change for the better and to suggest openly or by implication that the politically minded Soviet citizen should ask for more.' There had been no failure, the BBC said, to condemn Stalin's atrocities, as was alleged by Wiles, and it produced abundant evidence to prove it. Neither the *Spectator* nor Wiles, however, seemed disposed to soften their stance. Indeed the *Spectator* failed, for reasons which were never cleared up, to publish a letter from a distinguished sovietologist, Thomas Preston, who defended the BBC's policies, though it had earlier given him an assurance that it would be published. The campaign became so persistent and its tone so extreme as to suggest a personal vendetta. It finally died out in January 1958. Goldberg went on to become the BBC's most effective and respected voice in the Soviet Union until his death in 1982, though dissidents like Solzhenitsyn and Bukovski continued to feel that his tone was not sufficiently polemical. Other Soviet listeners did not: two Leningrad ladies wrote to the BBC some years ago to say that they frequently amused themselves by creating imaginary world governments; Goldberg invariably figured on the list of ministers.

Thomas Preston had argued in his unpublished letter to the *Spectator* that 'the subtlety, restraint and authoritative voice of the BBC would eventually pay big dividends'.[20] There can be little doubt that his judgement was correct and that a more polemical approach would have defeated its own object. The audience studies conducted by the Munich-based American Station 'Radio

Liberty' suggest that it has been successful in reaching a much wider audience
than could be found among the small dissident groups and that among its
estimated regular audience of some fifteen million there are many members
of the Soviet intelligentsia and of the managerial classes. Its regular following
is, indeed, the largest after that of the 'Voice of America', whose transmission
time is three times as long.

The charges against the Yugoslav Service, which followed in the columns
of the *Spectator* in 1959 and were couched in equally vehement terms, were of
a broadly similar nature. Maurice Latey, who was Head of the East European
Service at the time as well as a noted commentator, dismissed the campaign
as 'organised and partly written by a known Yugoslav *émigré* group which has
in the past sought to bring pressure to bear to change the policy of the
Yugoslav Service'.[21] Hugh Greene, by now Director-General of the BBC,
writing to the *Spectator* on 18 March 1960, attributed it to '*émigré* resentments
and faction squabbles' and described it as 'an extraordinary mixture of
untruths, half-truths, trivialities, and a few, a very few valid points on which
it would be possible to argue that the BBC had made an error of judgement.'[22]
Desmond Clark, who had been a respected commentator in the Yugoslav
Service over many years, argued that since it was the policy of the Western
powers to uphold and assist the Tito regime the BBC was bound to reflect this
and should seek to 'foster liberalisation tendencies in Yugoslavia with tact
and intelligence', 'It is easy enough', he wrote, 'to churn out elementary
anti-communist propaganda which will satisfy the pressure groups with interests in Bush House and serve to keep the inquisitors at bay. But it will
cause the people we want to reach to turn off their sets, not in indignation but
from sheer boredom.'[23]

Debates of this kind went right to the heart of the BBC's conception of its
role in broadcasting to the Communist societies of Eastern Europe, which
has remained unvaried in its essentials to this day, and needs to be in keeping
with the BBC's wider editorial stance. The frequent attacks against the BBC in
the Russian media have been one proof that *Komsomolskaya Pravda*'s assessment of 1957[24] continued to hold good in the Soviet official mind. So was the
laborious and painstaking interest which Soviet academics took in analysing
the propaganda methods which, according to them, the BBC employed to
mislead its listeners.[25] Jamming, resumed at the time of the Hungarian rising
in 1956 after a brief interruption but gradually relaxed in the sixties, was
resumed again after the Soviet intervention in Czechoslovakia in 1968. It too
was proof of the danger which the Soviet leadership saw in the access to
Western ideas and information which the BBC's broadcasts, together with
others, offered to Soviet listeners. Jamming was lifted in September 1973 at
the start of the process which led to the Helsinki Final Act, but it was resumed
again even more vigorously at the end of August 1980 during the strikes in
Gdansk which led to the creation of the Polish Solidarity movement, a sign

that those events were causing profound apprehension within the Soviet Union and that contagion was genuinely feared.

There was at least one occasion when BBC broadcasting to the Soviet Union threatened to cause difficulties in the official relations between the Soviet and British Governments. This took place in 1967, on the eve of the Six Day War in the Middle East, when the impending transmission of a reading from Stalin's daughter, Svetlana Alliluyeva's *Letter to a Friend* caused the Soviet Government to threaten to break off talks in Moscow with George Brown, Foreign Secretary at the time, which had been arranged in an attempt to find ways of averting the war. The BBC, under pressure from No. 10 Downing Street, agreed to defer the transmission so as not to jeopardise the efforts for peace but restored it forty-eight hours later when, the talks having ended unsuccessfully, the Foreign Secretary returned to London.

It was one of the two occasions in the last fifteen years when serious pressure was brought to bear by the Foreign Office on the BBC to abandon a programme for the sake of the national interest. The other took place in 1975, when it was represented to the BBC that an interview on the subject of Uganda which it was proposing to broadcast in its African Service might place British lives at risk. The incident related to a book on President Idi Amin by David Martin, a journalist from the *Observer* who had been the BBC's stringer in East Africa. It was held that the interview, in which David Martin talked about his book, would so incense Amin that he might well seek revenge on British nationals in Uganda. The BBC agreed on this occasion to defer the broadcast, but its own subsequent review of the situation led it to feel satisfied three weeks later that whatever risk there might have been had now passed, and the interview was duly broadcast. It provoked no reaction.

The infrequency of such incidents was an indication that the characteristically British convention that the External Services must be left free of government interference in the editorial field was, generally speaking, scrupulously observed. Individual Foreign Office officials might occasionally allow themselves to suggest informally, for instance, that it would be unfortunate if this or that foreign government were to be irritated, on the eve of a British ministerial visit, by the reflection in BBC press reviews of critical Fleet Street editorials. But such suggestions were usually made with no great hope that they would cause the BBC to modify its normal practice. Individual ambassadors, exposed to the angry representations of the Government to which they were accredited about a BBC broadcast which had caused displeasure, sometimes found it difficult to persuade their foreign counterparts that they were not answerable for the BBC. Some occasionally felt that the relevant BBC vernacular service was not serving the British national interest as they saw it. But such reactions seldom led to anything more than the BBC being informed of them without comment.

Even at the height of the Iranian crisis in the last few months of 1978, when

a concerted campaign was mounted from Tehran against the BBC Persian
Service for allegedly subverting the Shah's regime and aiding its enemies, the
Foreign Office, whose policy was one of support for the Shah, scrupulously
refrained from intervening. The campaign reached a degree of intensity seldom experienced by the BBC and was taken up in London by senior executives
of British firms with contracts in Iran, as well as by some politicians with
Iranian connections. However the scrutiny of scripts of programme items
which had been incriminated convinced two Conservative MPs with a personal
knowledge of Iran, Eldon Griffiths and Peter Temple-Morris, at the time
respectively Chairman and Secretary of the Anglo-Iranian Parliamentary
Group, that the charges were unfounded and that the Persian Service had
scrupulously abided by the BBC's obligation to remain impartial and had
applied the most rigorous journalistic standards in reporting the crisis. In fact
much of the material which came under fire, and of which corrupt transcripts
emanating from Tehran were circulating in London, consisted of news stories
and correspondents' despatches which had also been transmitted in English
in the World Service, where they had failed to arouse the same reaction. It
was one indication out of many of the impact of vernacular broadcasting,
particularly at times of crisis, when listeners tend to turn to the BBC to find
out what is going on in their own country because their own media cannot be
depended on. It was also an indication of the effect which the mere accurate
reporting of events is sometimes held to have on the way a crisis situation
develops. This placed a heavy burden of responsibility on news and programme staff, who were well aware of the possible worldwide repercussions
of their handling of news and comments but knew that accuracy, as Reith
and later Haley and Jacob had stressed all those years ago, was the only
criterion by which their work should be judged.

Examples abound in the history of the last thirty-five years of the reliance
placed by listeners on BBC news. One instance will suffice as an illustration. In
March 1975 a *Guardian* correspondent in Vietnam reported on what he called
'the God-like authority of the BBC' with both sides in the conflict and described how the great flight of the South Vietnamese, civilians and military
alike, from the Central Highlands started when rumours that the Saigon
Government was planning to abandon the area to the Vietcong were confirmed by the BBC Vietnamese Service. 'The authority of the BBC Vietnamese
language service', he wrote, 'is difficult to comprehend for those who have
never visited Vietnam, but for a variety of reasons it is trusted by the Vietnamese, who are not a trustful people, like no other news source.'[26]

At the start of the eighties that hard-won reputation remained untarnished,
and Reith himself, were he alive today, would almost certainly see it, despite
the vast changes of the last fifty years, as the vindication of his own vision
and of the tradition of which he was the begetter. Success, as measured not
just by reputation but by the size of the BBC's world-wide following was

indisputable. By the most conservative and scrupulous estimates one hundred million people the world over were regular listeners, more than two-thirds of them in foreign languages, and this was without counting listeners in China. This was more than at any time in the BBC's fifty years of external broadcasting, more, much more than during the BBC's finest hour in the Second World War, and more than the following of any other external broadcasting organisation, even the largest. Indeed in many parts of the world there was more listening to the BBC than to all other external broadcasters added together. This was a subject for quiet pride at Bush House, where the spirit of sturdy independence, whose birth in the Second World War was so well described by Harman Grisewood, was still at large, as vigorous as ever. The conclusion, that there has somehow to be an end to the repeated questioning and uncertainty and the start of a new and more secure era, is inescapable. This is a matter for government. A few years ago a distinguished American foreign correspondent[27] coined a phrase to describe the role which the External Services have come to play. They are to the free mind, he said, what Oxfam is to the hungry. It was a description which was liked in Bush House. It seemed to say it all.

Bibliography

In researching for this book I have turned in the first place to the BBC's Written Archives, whose files, going back to the earliest days, contain a wealth of internal memoranda, reports, minutes of meetings and conversations, correspondence with Government Departments and private individuals and Government White Papers on broadcasting matters, as well as scripts, details of programmes as broadcast, and wartime intelligence reports and directives. BBC Yearbooks, Handbooks and Annual Reports to Parliament have also been an important source, both for factual information and for indications of the BBC's public attitudes on matters of current concern. I have supplemented these primary sources with extensive conversations with many retired BBC officials, among them some of the earliest members of the first foreign language services and many who worked in the European and Overseas Services in wartime.

In addition I have consulted the following books and have quoted extracts from some of them:

Amouroux, H., *La Vie des Français sous l'Occupation* (two vols) (Paris: Arthème Fayard, 1961).

Aron, R., *Histoire de Vichy 1940-1944* (Paris, Arthème Fayard, 1954).

Aron, R., *Histoire de la Libération de la France, Juin 1944-Mai 1945* (Paris: Arthème Fayard, 1959).

Beachcroft, T.O., *British Broadcasting* (London: Longman, Green and Co., 1946).

Beachcroft, T.O., *Calling all Nations* (London: British Broadcasting Corporation).

Boyle, A., *Only the Wind will Listen* (London: Hutchinson, 1972).

Boyle, A., *'Poor, dear Brendan' - The Quest for Brendan Bracken* (London: Hutchinson, 1974).

Bramsted, E.K., *Goebbels and National Socialist Propaganda 1925-1945* (London: The Cresset Press, 1965).

Briggs, A., *Governing the BBC* (London: British Broadcasting Corporation, 1979).

Briggs, A., *The History of Broadcasting in the United Kingdom*: Volume I: *The Birth of Broadcasting, 1961*; Volume II: *The Golden Age of Wireless*, 1965; Volume III: *The War of Words*, 1970; Volume IV: *Sound and Vision*, 1979; (London: Oxford University Press).

Browne, Donald, R., *International Radio Broadcasting* (New York: Praeger, 1982).

Bruce Lockhart, Sir Robert, *Comes the Reckoning* (London: Putnam 1947).

Bruce Lockhart, Sir Robert, *The Diaries of Sir Robert Bruce Lockhart, Volume 2, 1939–1965* Ed. Kenneth Young (London: Macmillan, 1980).

Crémieux-Brilhac, J-L. (Ed.), *Les Voix de la Liberté – Ici Londres 1940–1944* (five vols) (Paris: La Documentation Française, 1975).

Cruickshank, C., *The Fourth Arm. Psychological Warfare 1938–1945* (London: Oxford University Press, 1981).

Dalton, H., *The Fateful Years: Memoirs 1931–1945* (London: Muller, 1957).

De Gaulle, C., *Mémoires de Guerre* (three vols) (Paris: Plon, 1954, 1956 and 1959).

Delmer, S., *Black Boomerang* (London: Secker and Warburg, 1962).

Dougall, R., *In and Out of the Box* (London: Collins and Harvill Press, 1973).

Duff Cooper, A., *Old Men Forget* (London: Rupert Hart-Davis, 1954).

Fielden, L., *The Natural Bent* (London: André Deutsch, 1960).

Fraser, L., *Propaganda* (London: Oxford University Press, 1957).

Gordon Walker, P., *The Lid Lifts* (London: Victor Gollancz, 1945).

Gorham, M., *Sound and Fury* (London: Percival Marshall, 1948).

Greene, Sir Hugh, *The Third Floor Front* (London: The Bodley Head, 1969).

Grisewood, H., *One Thing at a Time* (London: Hutchinson, 1968).

Katz, E. and Wedell, G., *Broadcasting in the Third World* (London: Macmillan, 1978).

Kirkpatrick, I., *The Inner Circle* (London: Macmillan, 1959).

Laqueur, W., *Europe since Hitler* (London: Weidenfeld and Nicolson, 1970).

Lean, E.T., *Voices in the Darkness* (London: Secker and Warburg, 1943).

Lichtheim, G., *Europe in the Twentieth Century* (London: Weidenfeld and Nicolson, 1972).

Lochner, Louis P., (Ed.) *The Goebbels Diaries* (London: Hamish Hamilton, 1948).

Newsome, N., *The 'Man in the Street' (of the BBC) Talks to Europe* (London: P.S. King and Staples, Ltd, 1945).

Nicolson, H., *Diaries and Letters* (London: Collins, 1967).

Oberlé, J., *Jean Oberlé Vous Parle* (Paris: La Jeune Pargue, 1945).

Pawley, E., *BBC Engineering 1922–1972* (London: BBC Publications, 1972).

Reith, J.C.W., *Broadcast over Britain* (London: Hodder and Stoughton, 1924).

Reith, J.C.W., *Into the Wind* (London: Hodder and Stoughton, 1949).

Rolo, C.J., *Radio goes to War* (London: Faber and Faber, 1953).

Taylor A.J.P., *English History 1914-1945* (London: Oxford University Press, 1965).

Taylor, P.M., *The Projection of Britain: British Overseas Publicity and Propaganda 1919-1939* (Cambridge: Cambridge University Press, 1981).

Zeman, Z.A.B., *Nazi Propaganda* (London: Oxford University Press, 1964).

Notes

Chapter 1

1 BBC Archives.
2 J.C.W. Reith, 'Diaries', 19 December 1932, BBC Archives.
3 Edward Pawley, *BBC Engineering 1922–72*, p. 179.
4 BBC Archives.
5 BBC Archives.
6 Minutes of the Colonial Conference, 15th Meeting, BBC Archives.
7 Ibid.
8 Ibid.
9 Eckersley to Captain Ian Fraser, MP, 28 June 1927, BBC Archives.
10 BBC Archives.
11 Ibid.
12 *The Times*, 11 August 1927.
13 Minutes of the Colonial Conference 15th Meeting, 20 May 1927, BBC Archives.
14 Sir Edward Appleton quoted in T.O. Beachcroft, *Calling All Nations*, p. 58.
15 I am indebted for much of the information on which this paragraph is based to the chapter on short wave broadcasting in Edward Pawley, op. cit., p. 126 ff.
16 Donald R. Browne, *The Voice of America: policies and problems*, Journalism Monographs No 43, (Lexington, Kentucky, Association for Education in Journalism).
17 Information from Radio Nederland.
18 J.C.W. Reith, *Into the Wind*, p. 207.
19 J.C.W. Reith, 'Diaries', 10 April 1925, BBC Archives.
20 J.C.W. Reith, *Into the Wind*, p. 113.
21 Murray to Reith, 21 June 1927, BBC Archives.
22 Reith to Murray, 11 July 1927, BBC Archives.
23 *Hansard*, Vol. 208, No 97, 11 July 1927.
24 Reith to Murray, 28 July 1927, BBC Archives.
25 Murray to Reith, 22 July 1927, BBC Archives.
26 Gerald Beadle, Notes on Empire Broadcasting, 12 May 1927, BBC Archives.
27 *The Times*, Letters, 11 August 1927.
28 C.F. Atkinson, Memorandum on Empire Broadcasting, May 1927, BBC Archives.
29 Minutes of the Colonial Conference, op. cit.
30 Edward Pawley, op. cit., p. 179.
31 C.F. Atkinson, op. cit.
32 R.H. Eckersley, *The Times*, Letters, 11 August 1927.
33 BBC Memorandum on Empire and World Broadcasting, June 1929, BBC Archives.
34 Leech (GPO) to Reith, 24 September 1929, BBC Archives.
35 Undated manuscript memorandum by Admiral Carpendale, BBC Archives.

36 Ibid.
37 Chief Accountant to Carpendale, 22 August 1929, BBC Archives.
38 Eckersley to Reith, 7 August 1929. BBC Archives.
39 BBC Memorandum on Empire Broadcasting, November 1928, BBC Archives.
40 Colonial Office to BBC, 7 February 1930, BBC Archives.
41 Minutes of Meeting at the Colonial Office, 11 March 1930, BBC Archives.
42 Reith to Atkinson, 21 March 1930, BBC Archives.
43 Minutes of Colonial Conference, 30 June 1930, BBC Archives.
44 Internal Memorandum, 16 October 1930, BBC Archives.
45 Report of the Proceedings of the Imperial Conference, 1930, BBC Archives.
46 Australian Broadcasting Co Ltd to BBC, 23 April 1931, BBC Archives.
47 Reith to Colonial Office and Reith to GPO, 16 February 1931 BBC Archives.
48 Note of a meeting with Sir Samuel Wilson, 1 May 1931, BBC Archives.
49 Wilson to Reith, 2 May 1931, BBC Archives.
50 Wilson to Reith, 20 July 1931, BBC Archives.
51 Reith to Wilson, 21 July 1931, BBC Archives.
52 J.C.W. Reith, 'Diaries', May 1931, BBC Archives.
53 Board of Governors Meeting Minutes, 16 September 1931, BBC Archives.
54 Wilson to Reith, 31 October 1931, BBC Archives.
55 Minutes of the Board of Governors Meeting, 28 October 1931, BBC Archives.

Chapter 2

1 C.G. Graves, 'Looking Backwards', BBC Empire Broadcasting, Coronation number,
    7 April 1937.
2 J.C.W. Reith, *Into the Wind*, p. 131.
3 J.C.W. Reith, 'Diaries', 10 October 1932, BBC Archives.
4 J.C.W. Reith, *Into the Wind*, p. 168.
5 J.C.W. Reith, 'Diaries', 29 December 1932, BBC Archives.
6 J.C.W. Reith, *Into the Wind*, p. 169.
7 Graves to Ashbridge, 3 March 1933, BBC Archives.
8 Ashbridge to Graves, 13 March 1933, BBC Archives.
9 Ashbridge to Reith, 2 May 1934, BBC Archives.
10 Ibid.
11 Edward Pawley, op. cit., p. 133.
12 *BBC Year-Book 1934.*
13 C.G. Graves, 'Review of the Empire Service', April 1934, BBC Archives.
14 *BBC Annual 1935.*
15 J.B. Clark, 'Draft for Parliamentary Report for 1934, BBC Archives.
16 Graves to Reith, 11 December 1934, BBC Archives.
17 In December 1931 Reith had finally obtained the withdrawal of the opposition of the News
    Agencies, the Newspaper Proprietors Association and the Empire Press Union to the
    broadcasting of news in the Empire Service. For much of the duration of the Chelmsford
    experiment no news had been included because of that opposition, until Sir Roderick Jones
    of Reuters agreed to a one-month free experiment from 22 April 1930. Regular news
    broadcasts were able to start from Chelmsford on 4 January 1932. However the relaying of
    BBC Empire news bulletins continued to be banned because of fears that the relaying of BBC
    news would constitute a threat to the existence of newspapers in the Commonwealth. The
    ban was temporarily lifted during the Munich crisis in 1938 but was not abolished
    altogether until the start of the Second World War.
18 *BBC Year-Book 1934.*
19 *BBC Annual 1936.*

20 BBC *Annual 1936*.
21 Sir Noel Ashbridge, Private and Confidential Report on the Empire Service, 1 October 1937, BBC Archives.
22 Ashbridge to Reith, 2 May 1934, BBC Archives.
23 Ashbridge to Reith, 23 August 1934, BBC Archives.
24 J.C.W. Reith, 'Diaries', 28 August 1934, BBC Archives.
25 Reith to Cunliffe-Lister, 5 July 1934, BBC Archives.
26 Graves to Reith, 12 July 1934, BBC Archives.
27 Reith to Cunliffe-Lister, 12 January 1935, BBC Archives.
28 Sir Cecil Graves, Internal Memorandum on the Empire Service, April 1934, BBC Archives.
29 Post Office Minute of 25 February 1935.
30 Note by Graves for Reith's lunch with Malcolm MacDonald, 19 September 1935.
31 BBC Introductory Memorandum on Broadcasting and the Colonial Empire, October 1935, BBC Archives.
32 Memorandum on the Empire Service by Lionel Fielden, 15 July 1937, BBC Archives.
33 Memorandum on the Empire Service by Felix Greene, 15 July 1937, BBC Archives.
34 Graves to Reith, 20 August 1937, BBC Archives.
35 J.B. Clark became Director of External Broadcasting in 1952 and held that position until his retirement in 1964. He was knighted in 1958.
36 Report by Malcolm Frost, 21 October 1937. Frost had been in at the very start of the Empire Service in a junior capacity under Graves and Clark. He was now Head of the Empire Press Section and eventually rose to become, first, Head of the Monitoring Service and finally General Manager of the Transcription Service.
37 Sir Noel Ashbridge, Private and Confidential Report on the present position of the Empire Service, 1 October 1937, BBC Archives.
38 Felix Greene, Internal Memorandum of 8 June 1938, BBC Archives.
39 Ullswater Committee, Minutes of verbal evidence, BBC Archives.
40 Vernon Bartlett received a very large mailbag following this talk. The vast majority of letters were favourable.

Chapter 3
1 Its President over many years was also a BBC man, Admiral Carpendale, Reith's deputy.
2 League of Nations Assembly Council, Circular Letters and Documents 1936-9, Category XIIA, 1936, C37 (1936), quoted in Philip M. Taylor, *The Projection of Britain*, p. 190.
3 League Convention concerning the use of broadcasting in the cause of peace, 23 September 1936, in ibid. C399, M252 (1936) XII C Article 1, quoted in Philip M. Taylor, op. cit., p. 190.
4 Lord Avon, *Memoirs: Facing the Dictator*, p. 182.
5 Ullswater Committee, Minutes of verbal evidence, BBC Archives.
6 J.C.W. Reith, *Into the Wind*, p. 290.
7 J.C.W. Reith, 'Diaries', March 1935, BBC Archives.
8 Ullswater Committee, Minutes of verbal evidence, BBC Archives.
9 Ibid.
10 Introductory Memorandum on Broadcasting and the Colonial Empire, October 1935, BBC Archives.
11 Cmd 5091 (1936), 'Report of the Broadcasting Committee', §121 and 122.
12 Draft BBC Memorandum on Foreign Language Broadcasting, 18 May 1936, BBC Archives.
13 Greene to Clark, 19 April 1936, BBC Archives.
14 *Indianapolis Star*, 5 June 1936.
15 Dudley to Greene, 11 June 1936; Greene to Clark, 23 June 1936, BBC Archives.
16 Private and Confidential Paper on Foreign Languages and the Empire Service, June 1936, BBC Archives.

17 Morrison to Reith, 17 June 1936, BBC Archives.
18 Reith to Morrison, 19 June 1936, BBC Archives.
19 Morrison to Reith, 24 June 1936, BBC Archives.
20 These official reports are all in the BBC Archives.
21 'The Press, the Public and Broadcasting – Sir John Reith on their relationship and future', *Yorkshire Post*, 26 May 1937.
22 J.C.W. Reith, *Into the Wind*, p. 278.
23 Foreign Office Memorandum, 'Proposed Broadcasting Station in Cyprus', 29 July 1937, CAB 27/641, ABC (37)4, quoted in Philip M. Taylor, op. cit., p. 196.
24 Minutes of Cabinet Sub-Committee on Arabic broadcasting, 4 October 1937, BBC Archives.
25 Minute by Leeper, 14 June 1937, FO 395/547, P2682/10/150, quoted in Philip M. Taylor, op. cit., p. 194.
26 Record of conversation between Graves and Leeper, 7 July 1937, BBC Archives.
27 Minutes of Cabinet Sub-Committee on Arabic broadcasting, 15 September 1937, CAB 27/641, ABC (37), quoted in Philip M. Taylor, op. cit., p. 198.
28 BBC Paper on Foreign Language Broadcasting, March 1937, BBC Archives.
29 Record of conversation between Graves and Leeper, 7 July 1937, BBC Archives.
30 Paper prepared for BBC Control Board, September 1937, BBC Archives.
31 Phillips, Director of Telecommunications, GPO to Reith, 20 September 1937, BBC Archives.
32 Reith to Admiral Carpendale and others, 1 October 1937, BBC Archives.
33 Carpendale strongly urged Reith to include Graves in the BBC party, even though he was hostile to BBC involvement. It is clear that, initially at any rate, Reith was disinclined to attend in person. Cf. 'Diaries', 30 September 1937, BBC Archives.
34 J.C.W. Reith, *Into the Wind*, p. 291.
35 J.C.W. Reith, 'Diaries', 4 October 1937, BBC Archives.
36 Official Report of Cabinet Sub-Committee on Arabic Broadcasting, 4 October 1937, BBC Archives. See also J.C.W. Reith, *Into the Wind*, pp 291–2.
37 Ibid.
38 Internal note by Graves, 11 November 1937, BBC Archives.
39 Clark to Graves, 31 December 1937, BBC Archives.
40 Note by Reith of interview with Calvert, 7 January 1938, BBC Archives.
41 Leeper to Graves, 5 January and 18 January 1938, BBC Archives.
42 Clark to Calvert, January 1938, BBC Archives.
43 *Hansard*, Vol. 328 (1937), Col. 501.
44 J.C.W. Reith, *Into the Wind*, p. 292.
45 BBC Archives.
46 J.C.W. Reith, 'Diaries', 5 November 1937, BBC Archives.
47 J.C.W. Reith, 'Diaries', 1 November 1937, BBC Archives.
48 Minute by Leeper, 8 January 1938, FO 395/557, P. 292/2/150, quoted in Philip M. Taylor, op. cit., p. 206.
49 Clark to Calvert, January 1938, BBC Archives.

Chapter 4

1 Hermann Rauschning, *Germany's Revolution of Destruction*, quoted in C.J. Rolo, *Radio Goes to War*, p. 18.
2 Ewald Banse, *Germany, prepare for war!*, quoted in C.J. Rolo, op. cit., p. 21.
3 'Black' radio stations purported to be operating on enemy soil but in fact broadcast from transmitters in England, chiefly 'Aspidistra', the big medium wave transmitter at Crowborough. 'Black' operations were controlled by SOI, based at Woburn, under the overall control of Rex Leeper.
4 Sir Hugh Greene in BBC Television programme 'Battles of Broadcasting', 1980. As Hugh

Carleton Greene he became German Editor in October 1940 and was in charge of the German Service as a whole from 1941 on. He rose to become Director-General of the BBC in 1960.

5 Cf. pp. 118 and 177.

6 This was the broadcast in which Chamberlain referred to Czechoslovakia as 'a far-away country of which we know little'.

7 Internal Report by J.B. Clark, 24 October 1938, BBC Archives.

8 Philip M. Taylor, op. cit., p. 211.

9 Internal Report by J.B. Clark, op. cit.

10 Internal Report by J.B. Clark, op. cit.

11 *The Listener*, 6 October 1938.

12 Notes on coverage of the Czech crisis, 1938, BBC Archives.

13 *The Listener*, 6 October 1938.

14 J.C.W. Reith, *Into the Wind*, p. 192.

15 Ibid.

16 Letter by E.J. Hodsoll, 29 October 1934, quoted in Asa Briggs, *The Golden Age of Wireless*, p. 626.

17 J.C.W. Reith, 'Diaries', 25 October 1935, BBC Archives.

18 Draft paper on 'The position of the BBC in War', July 1935, BBC Archives.

19 Lindsay Wellington became Director of Broadcasting Relations at the Ministry of Information in 1940. A.P. Ryan became Liaison Officer with the Department of Enemy Propaganda ('Electra House') at the outbreak of war. He became Controller (Home), BBC, in April 1940, moved across to the Ministry of Information to become Home Adviser to the BBC in March 1941, but returned to the BBC in October of the same year as Controller, News Coordination, later to become Controller, News. 'Throughout the whole of this period', according to Asa Briggs, 'he had been the leading figure in most of the BBC's dealings with the ministry and with the armed forces.'

20 Minute of the 322nd Meeting of the Committee of Imperial Defence, 12 May 1938, BBC Archives.

21 Official Paper by Sir Stephen Tallents, October 1938, BBC Archives.

22 J.C.W. Reith, *Into the Wind*, pp. 304-5.

23 Asa Briggs, *The War of Words*, p. 91.

24 Memorandum on an interview with Sir Horace Wilson, 21 July 1939, BBC Archives.

25 *Hansard*, Vol. 351, Col. 1491.

26 *The Times*, 23 October 1939.

27 Asa Briggs, *The War of Words*, p. 337.

28 He was thought to have made too many enemies among rival Whitehall Departments. Cf. Philip M. Taylor, op. cit., p. 281.

29 Lionel Fielden, *The Natural Bent*, p. 208.

30 Ibid.

31 Sir Robert Bruce Lockhart, *Diaries 1939-65*, p. 41. There was a strong feeling in the Foreign Office that the job of Director-General of the Ministry of Information should have gone to Rex Leeper, who had done most of the pre-war preparatory spade work on British overseas propaganda. Instead Leeper, from being Head of the Political Intelligence Department at the Foreign Office, was put in charge of the secret propaganda set-up at Woburn.

32 Quoted in Andrew Boyle, *Poor dear Brendan*, p. 266.

33 Monckton and Radcliffe to Duff Cooper, Memorandum on Propaganda Policy, June 1941, BBC Archives.

34 Ryan to Monckton, 4 June 1941, BBC Archives.

35 Listener's letter to Sir Stephen Tallents, 29 December 1940, BBC Archives.

36 Ogilvie to Sir Samuel Hoare, Sir Edward Bridges, Sir Kenneth Lee and Col Aylmer Vallance, 26 December 1939, BBC Archives.

37 Ogilvie to Sir Kenneth Lee, 25 March 1940, BBC Archives.
38 *New York Times*, 19 March 1940.
39 *Evening Standard*, 20 March 1940.
40 Ogilvie to Sir Kenneth Lee, 25 March 1940, BBC Archives.
41 A.P. Ryan, Note on the release of news, 6 April 1941, BBC Archives.
42 Information to the author from Leonard Miall.
43 Ibid.
44 J.C.W. Reith, *Into the Wind*, p. 367.
45 Hugh Dalton, *The Fateful Years, 1931-1945*, p. 378.
46 Sir Robert Bruce Lockhart, *Comes the Reckoning*, p. 96.
47 Ibid, p. 117.
48 Ibid, p. 118.
49 Andrew Boyle, op. cit., p. 265.
50 Information to the author from Harman Grisewood.
51 Andrew Boyle, op. cit., p. 266.
52 Ibid. p. 300.
53 Hugh Dalton, op. cit., p. 378.
54 Even Reith, then Minister of Information, seems to have heard about it at second hand from a Press Lord, who had had it some hours earlier from the First Lord of the Admiralty. Cf. *Into the Wind*, p. 379.
55 Newsome to A.E. Barker, 5 May 1940, BBC Archives.
56 J.C.W. Reith, *Into the Wind*, p. 438.
57 Ivone Kirkpatrick, *The Inner Circle*, pp. 149-50.
58 Wellington to Ogilvie, 28 September 1940, BBC Archives.
59 Note by Ogilvie, 22 November 1940, BBC Archives.
60 Note by Sir Stephen Tallents of a meeting at the Ministry of Information, 21 January 1941, BBC Archives.
61 Powell to Duff Cooper, 6 May 1941, BBC Archives.
62 Record of a conversation between Monckton and Ogilvie, 1 January 1941, BBC Archives.
63 Duff Cooper to Powell, 17 June 1941, BBC Archives.
64 Minutes of the Board of Governors meeting, 10 July 1941, BBC Archives.
65 Minutes of the Board of Governors meeting, 17 July 1941, BBC Archives.
66 Ibid.
67 Ibid. 24 August 1941.
68 *Hansard*, Vols. for 1941.

Chapter 5

1 Information to the author from Harman Grisewood.
2 Harold Nicolson, *Diaries and Letters*, p. 207
3 Asa Briggs, *The War of Words*, p. 34.
4 Information to the author from A.E. Barker.
5 Note by Kirkpatrick, 21 October 1941, BBC Archives.
6 Information to the author from Martin Esslin.
7 Reminiscences by Jean Oberlé, from BBC programme marking the twenty-first anniversary of the French Service, 27 September 1959, BBC Archives.
8 Salt to Tallents, 16 December 1940, BBC Archives.
9 Clark to Tallents, 14 May 1941, BBC Archives.
10 Information to the author from A.E. Barker.
11 Harman Grisewood, op. cit., p. 142.
12 Ivone Kirkpatrick, op. cit., p. 156.
13 Salt subsequently returned to his pre-war job as Programme Director in Manchester, but died soon after.

14 Information to the author from Clare Lawson Dick.
15 Bracken to Powell, 2 October 1941, BBC Archives.
16 Sir Robert Bruce Lockhart, *Diaries 1939-65*, 11 September 1941, p. 118.
17 Note on the organisation of the European Division, 21 October 1941, BBC Archives. Newsome in fact was made Director of European Broadcasts.
18 Kirkpatrick to Bruce Lockhart, 22 November 1941, BBC Archives.
19 Sir Robert Bruce Lockhart, *Diaries 1939-65*, 24 July 1941, p. 111.
20 Information to the author from Harman Grisewood.
21 Harman Grisewood, op, cit., p. 134.
22 Ibid., p. 140.
23 Kirkpatrick left the BBC in 1944 to become Deputy Commissioner (Civil), Control Commission for Germany. He returned to the Foreign Office in 1945. He became United Kingdom High Commissioner for Germany in 1950 and Permanent Head of the Foreign Office in 1953. On retirement in 1957 he was made Chairman of the Independent Television Authority.
24 Harman Grisewood, op. cit., p. 134.
25 Robert Bruce Lockhart, *Comes the Reckoning*, pp. 205 and 290. (By permission of Robin Bruce Lockhart.)
26 Information to the author from Elizabeth Barker.
27 Harman Grisewood, op. cit., p. 145.
28 Quoted in Asa Briggs, *The War of Words*, p. 34.
29 *BBC Year Book 1941*.
30 Hillelson to Clark, 6 December 1941, BBC Archives.
31 Ibid.
32 Internal Memorandum by J.B. Clark, 21 July 1942, BBC Archives.
33 Information from Sir Hugh Greene.
34 Leonard Miall, who was also present on that occasion and to whom I am indebted for his story, told the Queen that he was engaged in the 'dirty' side of the work. 'The rest of the BBC is concerned with raising the morale of its listeners. Here we're trying to lower the morale of ours.' Much anxiety was caused to the senior BBC officials present. They saw the King laughing uproariously with Lindley Fraser and overheard the word 'dirty' used in conversation with the Queen without knowing the cause of the one or the context of the other.
35 'The Bushmen', a Bush House-based cricket and dining club with a wide membership throughout the BBC, still flourishes.
36 Information from Sir Hugh Greene.
37 Robert Bruce Lockhart, *Comes the Reckoning*, p. 226.
38 Note by F.W. Ogilvie of a speech by Lord MacMillan at the first meeting of the Ministry of Information's Advisory Council, 7 September 1939, BBC Archives.
39 Lindley Fraser, *Propaganda*, p. 89.
40 Information to the author from Donald Edwards.
41 T.O. Beachcroft, *British Broadcasting*, p. 20.
42 Information to the author from F.L.M. Shepley.
43 Information from Sir Hugh Greene.
44 Information to the author from Donald Edwards.
45 Ibid.
46 T.O. Beachcroft, *British Broadcasting*, p. 21.
47 Harman Grisewood, op. cit., pp. 143-4.
48 Information to the author from Donald Edwards.
49 Information to the author from F.L.M. Shepley.
50 Harman Grisewood, op. cit., p. 141.
51 Ibid. p. 148.

52 Information to the author from F.L.M. Shepley.
53 Alan Bullock, 'The Time of my Life', BBC Radio Four, 28 January 1966.

Chapter 6

1 Information to the author from A.E. Barker.
2 Ibid.
3 Darsie Gillie returned to journalism after the war and became the *Manchester Guardian*'s Correspondent in France. Donald Edwards stayed on with the BBC and became Editor News and Current Affairs in the sixties. After retiring from the BBC, he became Managing Editor Independent Television News. Hugh Carleton Greene was Director-General of the BBC in the sixties.
4 Information to the author from Maurice Latey.
5 Undated note by J.B. Clark, BBC Archives.
6 From the start it was accepted by the BBC and by the Foreign Office that the same broadcasts could not serve audiences both in the Iberian Peninsula and in Latin-America.
7 Record of conversation between Graves and Perth dated 10 July 1939, BBC Archives.
8 Information to the author from Maurice Latey.
9 Harman Grisewood, op. cit., p. 130.
10 Felix Greene, Internal Memorandum on the Empire Service, 15 July 1937, BBC Archives.
11 Asa Briggs, *The War of Words*, p. 15.
12 Information to the author from Konrad Syrop.
13 See p. 38.
14 *BBC Year Book 1940*.
15 Much of this information is derived from Edward Pawley's admirably exhaustive *BBC Engineering – 1922-1972*.
16 The possibility of introducing a Russian language bulletin was considered early in 1940 but the matter was shelved for the time being because it was felt that the number of short wave receivers in the Soviet Union was too small and there was tight control of listening in apartment blocks. Cf. Overseas Board Minutes, 1 February 1940, BBC Archives. Churchill's broadcast of 22 June 1941 was broadcast by the BBC in a Russian translation, in circumstances not unlike Chamberlain's Munich broadcast of 27 September 1938, i.e. at very short notice. The possibility of regular Russian broadcasts was again discussed in 1941 but again set aside on account of likely Russian hostility and of the evidence that radio sets were being confiscated. Cf. Overseas Board Minutes, 3 July 1941, BBC Archives.
17 *BBC Year Book 1941*.
18 Halifax to Duff Cooper, 3 October 1940, BBC Archives.
19 Cf. p. 60.
20 Note by Ogilvie, 3 October 1940, BBC Archives.
21 Clark to Salt, 2 October 1940, BBC Archives.
22 Note of a Meeting at the Ministry of Information, 15 October 1940. BBC Archives.
23 These included Lindley Fraser, R.H.S. Crossman, F.A. Voigt, Sefton Delmer and Hugh Carleton Greene himself.
24 Information to the author from F.L.M. Shepley.
25 Charles de Gaulle, *Mémoires de Guerre: L'Appel*, p. 131.
26 Ibid.
27 Information to the author from Robin Scott.
28 See a note by Kirkpatrick of 31 December 1941 setting out some of the controversial issues.
29 European Divisional Meeting Minutes, 30 December 1941, BBC Archives.
30 Michael Winch was transferred to the Portuguese Service.
31 Asa Briggs, *The War of Words*, p. 466.
32 Information to the author from Gregory Macdonald.
33 Ibid. Gregory Macdonald took over as Polish Editor in February 1942.

34 Information to the author from Konrad Syrop, Clare Lawson Dick, Halvor Olsson and F.L.M. Shepley. The Council Chamber on the second floor of Broadcasting House is a large, semi-circular room where the meetings of the BBC's central advisory bodies normally take place.
35 Overseas Board Minutes, 24 October 1940, BBC Archives.
36 Maurice Gorham, *Sound and Fury*, p. 95.
37 Information to the author from W. Galbraith, F.L.M. Shepley and Cecilia Gillie.
38 The decision to prepare Maida Vale for use in emergency by Overseas staff had been taken in June. (Overseas Board Minutes, 20 June 1940, BBC Archives).
39 Overseas Board Minutes, 12 December 1940, BBC Archives.
40 Information to the author from Josephine Gaman.
41 Information to the author from F.L.M. Shepley.
42 Overseas Board Minutes, 5 December 1940, BBC Archives.
43 Overseas Board Minutes, 30 January 1941, BBC Archives.
44 The BBC first became interested in Bush House in September 1940, when it took over a studio belonging to the J. Walter Thompson Company. The decision to move the European Service there was taken in January 1941.
45 Overseas Board Minutes, 30 January 1941, BBC Archives.
46 Sir Robert Bruce Lockhart, *Diaries 1939-1965*, 24 July 1941, p. 111.
47 Information to the author from W. Galbraith.
48 Edward Pawley, op. cit., p. 249.
49 Information to the author from T.R.P. Hole.
50 The 'Y' Unit of the Monitoring Service was charged with keeping a continuous watch on broadcasts in English from Germany to check rumours of threats. Additionally it monitored the BBC's own domestic wavelengths for signs of attempts by the Germans to use those wavelengths to communicate with the British listening public. The 'Y' unit was merged with the reception unit of the Monitoring Service in 1943.
51 Interview with Oliver Whitley. Whitley returned to the BBC after the war and served in a number of senior capacities in the Overseas Services. He eventually became Chief Assistant to the Director-General, Managing-Director, External Broadcasting and Deputy Director-General. Marriott also returned to the BBC and became Controller, Northern Ireland, and, eventually, Assistant Director, Radio.
52 Cf. p. 104.
53 *BBC Year Book 1942*.
54 Overseas Board Minutes, 14 November 1940, BBC Archives.
55 Ibid.
56 Cf. p. 149.
57 Sir Alan Barlow to Monckton, 9 May 1941; Monckton to Ogilvie, 13 May 1941, BBC Archives.
58 Monckton to Ogilvie, 18 June 1941, BBC Archives.
59 J.B. Clark to Overseas Services Directors, 1 September 1941, BBC Archives.
60 Monckton to Ogilvie, 11 September 1941, BBC Archives.
61 Ogilvie to Monckton, 19 September 1941, BBC Archives.
62 Board of Governors paper G12/41 dated 7 April 1941, BBC Archives.
63 Powell to Duff Cooper, 9 July 1941, BBC Archives.
64 Board of Governors Paper G12/41 dated 7 April 1941, BBC Archives.
65 Ashbridge to Fraser, 12 June 1941, BBC Archives.
66 Minutes of Meeting of the Board of Governors, 17 July 1941, BBC Archives.

Chapter 7

1 Asa Briggs, *The War of Words*, p. 441.

2 Jean Marin left the BBC French Service in 1943 to join the Fighting French Navy, but later returned to broadcasting as the first director of the newly liberated radio station at Rennes in August 1944. He subsequently became director of *Agence France Presse*.

3 Michel Saint-Denis, unpublished papers, quoted in Cecilia Gillie, unpublished M/S History of the BBC Wartime French Service, BBC Archives.

4 Cecilia Gillie, op. cit.

5 Information to the author from Robin Scott.

6 Tangye Lean, *Voices in the Darkness*, p. 157.

7 Michel Saint-Denis, unpublished papers, quoted in Cecilia Gillie, op. cit.

8 Information to the author from Robin Scott, and Cecilia Gillie, op. cit.

9 Cecilia Gillie, op. cit.

10 Michel Saint-Denis, unpublished papers, quoted in Cecilia Gillie, op. cit.

11 Jean Oberlé, *Jean Oberlé Vous Parle*, Paris.

12 Jacques Brunius, unpublished film scenario, BBC Archives.

13 Tangye Lean, op. cit., p. 157.

14 Information to the author from Robin Scott.

15 Quoted in BBC European Intelligence Report, 12 December 1940, BBC Archives.

16 BBC European Intelligence Report, 10 February 1941, BBC Archives.

17 Quoted in Asa Briggs, *The War of Words*, p. 255.

18 Ibid., p. 256n.

19 Quoted in Tangye Lean, op. cit., p. 149.

20 BBC Monthly Intelligence Report, Europe, November 1940, BBC Archives.

21 Maurice Schumann's first broadcast was read at the microphone for him by Jacques Duchesne because his voice was thought at the time to be too high pitched for broadcasting. He was later persuaded to pitch his voice deeper because, he was told, it would then cut through the jamming more effectively.

22 *Neue Züricher Zeitung*, 26 November 1940.

23 BBC European Intelligence Report, 23 April 1941, BBC Archives.

24 Ibid., 18 June 1942, BBC Archives.

25 Ibid., 16 September 1941.

26 Ibid., 17 October 1942.

27 Information to the author from Robin Scott.

28 Based on accounts by Jacques Duchesne and Cecilia Gillie, quoted in Cecilia Gillie, op. cit.

29 Quoted in Henri Amouroux, *La Vie des Français sous l'Occupation*, Vol. II, p. 325.

30 'Broadcasting as a new weapon of war', a BBC paper by Douglas Ritchie, BBC Archives.

31 Quoted in Charles Cruickshank, *The Fourth Arm*, p. 124.

32 Ritchie had also overlooked the fact that for the Flemish population of Belgium 14 July was not a day for celebrations. It symbolised the dominance of the French-speaking element in Belgium.

33 Charles Cruickshank. op. cit., pp. 52 and 128; Sir Robert Bruce Lockhart, *Diaries 1939-65*, p. 163.

34 One of the ditties invented by van Moppès ran: '*Un amiral nommé Darlan est garanti pro-Allemand*', after the popular advertising slogan for Levitan furniture: '*Un meuble signé Levitan est garanti pour longtemps*'.

35 It is interesting to note that the interruption of 'Honneur et Patrie' appears to have passed almost unnoticed in France. According to one listener described by the European Intelligence Department as 'exceptionally reliable', 'for almost everyone in France the English radio and the de Gaulle radio are one and the same thing'. He maintained that 'the BBC continues to be listened to everywhere and is universally trusted. The Darlan episode has not undermined our reputation or the confidence in our broadcasts.'

36 Quoted in Cecilia Gillie, op. cit.

37 BBC European Intelligence Report, 25 February 1943, BBC Archives.

38 Sample of actual *messages personnels* from a list in the BBC Archives.

39 Letter from Darsie Gillie to Emmanuel d'Astier, quoted in Cecilia Gillie, op. cit.

40 For a full account see Robert Aron, *Histoire de la Libération de la France*, Deuxième Partie, Chapitre II, p. 140 ff. De Gaulle himself claims in his memoirs that 'the Allied High Command viewed with some misgivings the general spread of guerilla fighting. Moreover it assumed that battle would be prolonged and would have preferred the resistance to hold its hand except in the immediate vicinity of the bridgehead'. See Charles de Gaulle, *Mémoires de Guerre*, Vol. II, *L'Unité*, p. 280.

41 Cecilia Gillie, op. cit.

42 Charles de Gaulle, op. cit., p. 225.

43 De Gaulle's broadcast had been due to be transmitted at 2.30 pm. but because of delays in obtaining policy clearance it did not go out until 5.30. It was repeated five times during the following few hours. For a full first-hand account of the day's events in connection with de Gaulle's broadcast see Sir Robert Bruce Lockhart, *Diaries 1939–65*, 6 June 1944, p. 319.

44 Charles de Gaulle, op. cit., p. 227.

45 Cecilia Gillie, op. cit.

46 BBC *Year Book 1945*, p. 14.

Chapter 8

1 E.K. Bramsted, *National Socialist Propaganda 1925–45*, p. 309.

2 A P. Ryan, '*Principles of Propaganda as followed in Broadcasts to Germany*', March 1940, BBC Archives.

3 Nicolls to Wellington, 9 April 1940, BBC Archives.

4 Wellington to Nicolls, 17 April 1940, BBC Archives.

5 Lindley Fraser, op. cit., p. 95.

6 *Die 30 Kriegsartikel für das Deutsche Volk, Das Reich*, 26 September 1943, quoted in E.K. Bramsted, op. cit., p. 287.

7 Lindley Fraser, 'BBC Sonderbericht, Germany after the war', 28 June 1943.

8 Ibid.

9 Lindley Fraser, 'BBC Sonderbericht', Tehran Talk, 6 December 1943.

10 E.K. Bramsted, op. cit., p. 314. See also for the same point Hugh Greene, 'Psychological Warfare', Lecture at NATO Staff College, Paris, 9 September 1959.

11 A.P. Ryan, loc. cit.

12 Ibid.

13 Department EH, Memorandum to the BBC on Broadcasts in German, 25 February 1940, BBC Archives.

14 BBC Overseas Board Minutes, 9 May 1940, BBC Archives.

15 Ibid., 23 May 1940.

16 See pp. 88–9, 91.

17 BBC Overseas Board Minutes, 8 February 1940, BBC Archives.

18 Ibid., 31 October and 14 November 1940, BBC Archives.

19 Information to the author from Martin Esslin.

20 Sefton Delmer, *Black Boomerang*, p. 16f.

21 Duckworth Barker to A.E. Barker, 20 September 1939, BBC Archives.

22 German Section to Duckworth Barker and A.E. Barker, 21 February 1940, BBC Archives.

23 Notes of meetings with a deputation of German translators, 17 May and 24 May 1940, BBC Archives.

24 Duckworth Barker to A.E. Barker, 31 May 1940, BBC Archives.

25 Handwritten comments on the above.

26 A.P. Ryan, loc. cit.

27 Information to the author from Martin Esslin.
28 Ibid.
29 See p. 83ff.
30 Information to the author from Martin Esslin.
31 Anonymous Electra House Memorandum, 6 June 1941, BBC Archives.
32 Ibid. See also Memoranda by Hugh Carleton Greene, 17 July, 24 September and 16 October 1941, BBC Archives.
33 Undated Memorandum by Hugh Carleton Greene and Basil Thornton, probably late 1941, BBC Archives.
34 E.K. Bramsted, op. cit., p. 246.
35 Quoted in C.J. Rolo, op. cit., p. 213.
36 Information to the author from Martin Esslin.
37 Quoted in E.K. Bramsted, op. cit., p. 297.
38 E.K. Bramsted, op. cit., p. 307.
39 Information to the author from Martin Esslin.
40 BBC Monthly European Intelligence Reports, 1943.
41 Information to the author from Martin Esslin.
42 Ibid.
43 Quoted in Tangye Lean, op. cit., p. 71.
44 Tangye Lean, op. cit., p. 71.
45 Ibid.
46 Ibid, p. 58.
47 Quoted in Ibid, p. 52.
48 Lindley Fraser, 'The BBC versus Goebbels', Address to the Royal Empire Society, 18 April 1945.
49 Tangye Lean, op. cit., p. 59.
50 Quoted in C.J. Rolo, op. cit., p. 121.
51 Ibid.
52 Ibid.
53 H. Wiedermann, Contribution to BBC Programme marking the 21st Anniversary of the German Service, October 1959.
54 E.K. Bramsted, op. cit., p. 291.
55 Quoted in Asa Briggs, *The War of Words*, p. 10.

Chapter 9

1 Memorandum by Count Balinsky-Jundzill tabled at a BBC liaison meeting, 22 November 1940, BBC Archives.
2 Kisielewski to Kirkpatrick, 2 December 1941, BBC Archives.
3 Clark to Haley, 19 January 1945, BBC Archives.
4 Roberts to Clark, 14 December 1944, BBC Archives.
5 Guyatt to Clark, 1 January 1945, BBC Archives.
6 Kirkpatrick to Makins, 24 December 1941, BBC Archives.
7 Marks to Clark, 29 July 1941, BBC Archives.
8 *Daily Herald*, 3 June 1941. See also Labour Discussion Notes produced by the Socialist Clarity Group, June 1941.
9 BBC Output Report, 15–21 March 1942, BBC Archives.
10 Grisewood to Kirkpatrick, 15 October 1943, BBC Archives.
11 Kirkpatrick to McCann, 19 October 1943, BBC Archives.
12 BBC Output Report, 15–21 March 1942, BBC Archives.
13 Duckworth Barker to Kirkpatrick, April 1942, BBC Archives.
14 Asa Briggs, *The War of Words*, p. 479.

15 Soteriades to Newsome, 22 November 1941, BBC Archives.
16 Note by Richard Law, Parliamentary Under-Secretary at the Foreign Office, of a conversation with Michalopoulos, 29 April 1942, BBC Archives.
17 Ibid.
18 Kirkpatrick to Bruce Lockhart, 16 April 1942; Pierson Dixon to Kirkpatrick, 1 May 1942; and Kirkpatrick's reply to Dixon, BBC Archives.
19 BBC Survey of Greek output, 26 May 1942, BBC Archives.
20 Noel Paton to Kirkpatrick, 12 January 1944, BBC Archives. D.E. Noel Paton succeeded George Angeloglou as Greek Editor in March 1942. He had been Director of the British Institute in Athens.
21 Kirkpatrick to Bruce Lockhart, 16 April 1942, BBC Archives.
22 Soteriades to Newsome, 22 November 1941, BBC Archives.
23 Kirkpatrick to Murray, 15 December 1941, BBC Archives.
24 Kirkpatrick to Bruce Lockhart, 16 April 1942. BBC Archives.
25 Noel Paton to Kirkpatrick, 12 January 1944, BBC Archives.
26 Noel Paton to Grisewood, 5 May 1943, BBC Archives.
27 Robert Bruce Lockhart, *Comes the Reckoning*, p. 333.
28 *The Diaries of Sir Robert Bruce Lockhart, 1939–65*, 23 December 1944, p. 380.
29 Ibid., 14 December 1944, p. 378.
30 Kirkpatrick to Greenway, 7 August 1942, BBC Archives.
31 Murray to Greenway, 9 August 1942, BBC Archives.
32 Ibid.
33 Ibid.
34 Kirkpatrick to Newsome and others, 23 June 1942, BBC Archives.
35 Quoted in Rendell to Pierson Dixon, 20 October 1942, BBC Archives.
36 Ibid.
37 Ibid.
38 Ibid.
39 Sargent to Rendell, 31 October 1942, BBC Archives.
40 Pierson Dixon to Murray, 31 October 1942, BBC Archives.
41 Howard to Rendell, 17 February 1943, BBC Archives.
42 Harrison to Brown, 23 January 1943, BBC Archives.
43 Howard to Kirkpatrick, 17 February 1943, BBC Archives.
44 Kirkpatrick to Howard, 18 February 1943, BBC Archives.
45 Kirkpatrick to Sendall, 26 May 1943, BBC Archives.
46 Memorandum by Gordon Fraser.
47 Ibid.
48 Ivone Kirkpatrick, *Mussolini, Study of a Demagogue* (1964), p. 508, quoted in Asa Briggs, *The War of Words*, p. 437.
49 Information to the author from F.L.M. Shepley.
50 Newsome to Harrison, 7 February 1943, BBC Archives.
51 Information to the author from F.L.M. Shepley.
52 Ibid.
53 Note by A.P. Ryan, 16 July 1940, BBC Archives.
54 N.F. Newsome, General Directive, 31 March 1943, BBC Archives.
55 Information to the author from F.L.M. Shepley.
56 Ibid.
57 Shepley, Report of an interview with Sir Noel Charles, 13 October 1944, BBC Archives.
58 Ibid.
59 Kisielewski to Kirkpatrick, 2 December 1941, BBC Archives.
60 Roberts to Belinsky-Jundzill, 22 July 1941, BBC Archives.
61 Grant Purves, European Intelligence, 22 May 1941, BBC Archives.

62 Kirkpatrick to Bowes Lyons, 22 January 1941, BBC Archives.
63 Macdonald to Clark, 2 November 1944, BBC Archives.
64 Quoted in BBC Output Report, 19–24 February 1943, BBC Archives.
65 Note by Moray Maclaren, 9 June 1944, BBC Archives.
66 BBC Output Report, 19–25 February 1943, BBC Archives.
67 Draft Secret BBC Report on Broadcasting by Foreign Governments, undated, probably mid-1943, BBC Archives.
68 Unpublished article on BBC Polish Broadcasts during the war, 2 November 1946, BBC Archives.
69 Quoted in unpublished letter from Gregory Macdonald to Martin Esslin, 13 January 1979.
70 *Hostages of Colditz*, by Giles Romilly and Michael Alexander (London: Sphere, 1977); originally published under the title of *Privileged Nightmare* by Weidenfeld & Nicolson, 1954.
71 Macdonald, loc. cit.
72 Ibid.
73 Tangye Lean, op. cit., p. 207.
74 Ibid. p. 206.
75 Masaryk to Ogilvie, 20 January 1941, BBC Archives.
76 Draft Secret BBC Report on Broadcasting by Foreign Governments, BBC Archives.
77 Robert Bruce Lockhart, *Comes the Reckoning*, p. 112.
78 BBC Output Review, Bulgaria, 26 April–2 May 1942, BBC Archives.
79 BBC Output Review, Hungary, 19–25 April 1942, BBC Archives.
80 Ibid.
81 Kirkpatrick to Graves, 9 January 1943, BBC Archives.
82 Report by Duckworth Barker, 20 March 1940, BBC Archives.
83 Young to Kirkpatrick, 7 July 1941, BBC Archives.
84 Report by Duckworth Barker, 28 December 1939, BBC Archives.
85 Clark to Macgregor, 29 December 1939, BBC Archives.
86 Asa Briggs, *The War of Words*, p. 684.
87 Hillar Kallas, Paper on Finnish Service policy, 12 November 1943, BBC Archives.
88 Clark to Warner, 27 November 1944, BBC Archives.
89 Memorandum by Dr Raestad and Dr Sommerfelt, 3 July 1940; Report of a meeting between Ogilvie, Tallents, Raestad and Sommerfelt, 21 June 1940, BBC Archives.
90 Ibid.
91 Report of a meeting between Clark, Barker, Salt, Sommerfelt, Øksnevad, Miss Benzie and Kenny, 28 August 1940, BBC Archives.
92 Winther to Grisewood, 7 May, 1943, BBC Archives.
93 Ibid.
94 Quoted in Tangye Lean, op. cit., p. 203.
95 Reactions to BBC broadcasts to Denmark, 1 April to 30 June 1940, BBC Archives.
96 BBC Output Report, Denmark, 17–23 May 1942, BBC Archives.
97 Quoted in Asa Briggs, *The War of Words*, p. 476.
98 Information to the author from Halvor William-Olsson.

Chapter 10

1 See p. 105.
2 Maurice Gorham, op. cit., p. 99.
3 Ibid., p. 105.
4 Both Pelletier and MacAlpine stayed on with the BBC after the war. Pelletier became Controller of Programme Planning, in overall charge of both the Home Service and the Light Programme. MacAlpine was Controller, Overseas Services, in the early fifties.

5 *New York Times*, 14 July 1940.
6 Quoted in BBC *Year Book 1941*.
7 Ibid.
8 *Time*, 29 July 1940.
9 Quoted in BBC *Year Book 1943*.
10 Maurice Gorham, op. cit., p. 97.
11 Information to the author from Tom Chalmers.
12 Ibid.
13 Maurice Gorham, op. cit., p. 101.
14 Quoted in BBC *Year Book 1943*.
15 Maurice Gorham, op. cit., p. 107.
16 Quoted in BBC *Year Book 1946*.
17 Tahu Hole joined the staff of the Overseas Services shortly after and later became Editor, News and Director of Administration.
18 Maurice Gorham, op. cit., p. 111.
19 Information to the author from Tom Chalmers.
20 J. Grenfell Williams, 'Broadcasting to the Colonies', in BBC *Year Book 1945*.
21 See p. 28.
22 Clark to Nicolls and Graves, 30 January 1940, BBC Archives.
23 Overseas Board Minutes, 25 September 1941, BBC Archives.
24 See p. 102.
25 See p. 81.
26 Information from J.A. Camacho, to whom I am indebted for much of the first-hand information on the Latin American Service in wartime on which this account is based. Camacho rose to be Head of Talks and Current Affairs Group, Radio, in the sixties.
27 Ibid.
28 Ibid.
29 Asa Briggs, *The War of Words*, p. 518.
30 BBC *Year Book 1942*.
31 BBC *Year Book 1945*.
32 Hallawell was later fêted and decorated in Brazil, became a pillar of the British community in Rio, and was made an OBE.
33 Information to the author from J.A. Camacho.
34 Zimmern to Clark, 20 September 1944, BBC Archives.
35 See p. 51.
36 Information to the author from Donald Stephenson.
37 See pp. 74-5.
38 Duff Cooper to Ogilvie, 7 November 1940, BBC Archives.
39 Ogilvie to Duff Cooper, 16 November 1940, BBC Archives.
40 Pick to Tallents, 18 November 1940, BBC Archives.
41 Memorandum on the Arabic Service by Donald Stephenson, 12 July 1940, BBC Archives.
42 'Allies and friends throughout the Middle East', by S. Hillelson, BBC *Year Book 1945*.
43 See p. 101.
44 S. Hillelson, op. cit.
45 BBC *Year Book 1946*.
46 Quoted in BBC *Year Book 1941*.
47 Overseas Board Minutes, 18 September 1941, BBC Archives.
48 Ibid., 25 September 1941.
49 See p. 7.
50 P.J. Grigg to Ogilvie, 25 January 1940, BBC Archives.
51 Note by Z.A. Bokhari, 8 September 1940, BBC Archives.
52 Government of India Memorandum on the proposed Hindustani Service by the BBC, 4 April 1940, BBC Archives.

53 Puckle to Findlater Stewart, 16 February 1940, BBC Archives.
54 Telegram from Government of India Home Department to Secretary of State for India, 24 May 1940; Official weekly report by the Government of India, 25 May 1940, BBC Archives.
55 Ibid., 31 May and 7 June 1940, BBC Archives.
56 Lionel Fielden, op. cit., p. 218.
57 See p. 36.
58 Report on Indian programmes by Laurence Brander, 11 January 1943, BBC Archives.
59 Quoted in BBC Year Book 1946.
60 Overseas Quarterly Reports, Empire Services and USA, 10 September 1943, BBC Archives.
61 Note by Ahmed Ali, 17 February 1943, BBC Archives.

Chapter 11

1 Summary of the Report of the Independent Committee of Enquiry into the Overseas Information Services, Cmd 9138 (1954).
2 House of Lords Debate, 6 February 1957.
3 Asa Briggs, Sound and Vision, p. 144.
4 W.J. Haley, Broadcasting to Europe, 9 October 1944, BBC Archives.
5 Tribune, 31 August 1945.
6 Haley to J.B. Clark, 9 November 1945, BBC Archives.
7 Ministry of Information, Latin American Division, Paper on the BBC Latin American Service, 13 November 1945, BBC Archives.
8 Meeting at the Ministry of Information, 11 December 1945, BBC Archives.
9 Cf. p. 223.
10 White Paper on Broadcasting, Cmd 6852 (1946).
11 Ibid.
12 Quoted in Board of Governors Paper G68/46, 14 November 1946: The Principles and Purposes of the BBC's External Services, Note by W.H. Haley, BBC Archives.
13 Harman Grisewood, op. cit., p. 157.
14 Asa Briggs, op. cit., p. 122.
15 Sir Ian Jacob's original designation was 'Director of Overseas Services'. This was changed soon after to avoid confusion.
16 Board of Governors Paper G68/46.
17 Statement of Policy for the European Service, 29 July 1946, BBC Archives.
18 'The Task of the Overseas Services of the BBC', Paper OS 48/2 by Director of Overseas Services, 4 October 1948, BBC Archives.
19 Hansard, Vol. 423, Cols 312-13, 22 May 1946.
20 Cf. Chapter 12.
21 Hall to Grisewood, 28 February 1946, BBC Archives.
22 Kirkpatrick to Haley, 21 February 1946, BBC Archives.
23 Kirkpatrick to Grisewood, 23 March 1946, BBC Archives.
24 Daily Telegraph, 25 March 1946.
25 Report from British Embassy, Moscow, 29 March 1946, BBC Archives.
26 Greene to Jacob, 22 March 1949, BBC Archives.
27 Komsomolskaya Pravda, 3 January 1957.
28 Drogheda Committee, BBC Paper No. 1: 'The Financial Policy of the last five years and its results', 7 November 1952, BBC Archives.
29 BBC Memorandum, 31 May 1956, BBC Archives.
30 'Revised Three-Year Plan for the Overseas Information Services', Cabinet Committee on Colonial Information Policy, 2 December 1949, BBC Archives.
31 Minutes of meeting chaired by E.A.J. Davies, Parliamentary Under-Secretary for Foreign Affairs, 26 July 1950, BBC Archives.

32 Memorandum on the case for an increase in Overseas Information expenditure, 21 July 1950, prepared for the above meeting, BBC Archives.
33 *Time and Tide*, 28 October 1950.
34 Note of Meeting, 14 November 1950, BBC Archives.
35 Jacob to A.E.C. Malcolm, Foreign Office, 18 January 1951, BBC Archives.
36 Jacob to Air Chief Marshal Sir John Slessor, 29 November 1950, BBC Archives.
37 Jacob to Sir Edward Bridges, 3 January 1951, BBC Archives.
38 *Daily Mail*, 31 March 1951.
39 *Hansard*, Vol. 484, Cols. 1268-72, 21 February 1951.
40 Minutes of special External Services meeting, 6 February 1952, BBC Archives.
41 *Hansard*, Vol. 498, Cols. 1685-1806, 2 April 1952.
42 *Hansard*, Vol. 504, Cols. 1486-8, 30 July 1952.
43 Cabinet Committee Paper, 14 July 1952, BBC Archives.
44 Cmd 9138 (1954).
45 Comments on the Report of the Drogheda Committee, Board of Governors Paper G94/53, 25 September 1953, BBC Archives.

Chapter 12

1 BBC Annual Report to Parliament, 1956-7, p. 15.
2 Ibid., p. 16.
3 William Clark, 'Suez, an inside story, *Observer*, 3 October 1976.
4 Asa Briggs, *Governing the BBC*, p. 214.
5 Cf. p. 50.
6 *Manchester Guardian*, 31 October 1956.
7 Asa Briggs, op. cit., p. 212; Harman Grisewood, op. cit., p. 203.
8 Board of Governors, Minutes, 22 November 1956; BBC Statement, 27 November 1956.
9 BBC Annual Report to Parliament, 1956-7, p. 16.
10 Quarterly Report to the Board of Governors by Director of External Broadcasting for period 1 September to 30 November 1956, 27 November 1956.
11 Minutes of Director-General's Liaison Meeting, 16 October 1956.
12 Information to the author from Michael Sumner, who was News Editor of 'Sharq al Adna' at the operative time.
13 Ibid. See also House of Lords debate on a motion by Lord Strang, 6 February 1957, in which Lord Glyn described the station's output as 'amateur attempts at propaganda which were absolutely laughable and brought this country into contempt'. *Hansard* HL 10 C5, Cols. 537 ff.
14 Duncan Wilson was well known to the BBC, where he had many friends. He later became HM Ambassador at Belgrade and Moscow and, after his retirement, Master of Corpus Christi College, Cambridge.
15 Cf. pp. 51-2.
16 Internal note by Director-General on the relationship between the BBC and the Government, 28 July 1958.
17 Harman Grisewood, op. cit., p. 199.
18 Information from Sir Ian Jacob to Andrew Walker, March 1980.
19 Quarterly Report by Director of External Broadcasting, loc. cit.
20 House of Lords Debate, 6 February 1957, loc. cit.
21 Quoted by John Harvey MP in House of Commons Debate, 31 July 1957, *Hansard* 32 Q 27, Cols. 1456 ff.
22 Ibid.
23 Ibid.
24 GAC Paper 214, 4 January 1957.

25 BBC Memorandum, 31 May 1956.
26 White Paper on Overseas Information Services, Cmd 225 (1957).
27 Note by J.B. Clark of a telephone conversation with Ralph Murray, 24 July 1957.
28 Quoted in House of Commons Debate, 31 July 1957, loc. cit.
29 *Diario de Lisboa*, 1 August 1957.
30 *Diario de Noticias*, 29 July 1957.
31 Reuters dispatch from Lisbon, 9 August 1957.
32 *The Times*, 8 August 1957.
33 *Manchester Guardian*, 10 August 1957.
34 *News Chronicle*, 19 July 1957.
35 John Harvey MP to Ian Harvey, Parliamentary Under-Secretary of State for Foreign Affairs, 1 August 1957.
36 Tangye Lean to J.B. Clark, 28 July 1960.
37 Jacob to Woodrow Wyatt, 29 January 1957.

Chapter 13

1 Undated draft notes from Donald Stephenson to J.B. Clark.
2 Hodson to J.B. Clark, 4 November 1959.
3 Hodson to Owen Morris, 14 August 1961.
4 Watrous to Hodson, 29 October 1963.
5 Overseas Audience Research Department, 'African Service in English: the question of an evening placing', 27 November 1963.
6 Plowden Report on Representational Services Overseas, Cmd 2276 (1964).
7 Cmd 4107 (1969).
8 Whitley to Cape, 6 April 1970.
9 BBC Annual Report to Parliament 1977-8 (incorporated in *BBC Handbook 1979*), p. 44.
10 *Economist*, 6 August 1977.
11 *Daily Mail*, 5 August 1977.
12 *Guardian*, 3 August 1977.
13 *Birmingham Evening Mail*, 3 August 1977.
14 *New Statesman*, 5 August 1977.
15 *The Times*, 13 August 1977.
16 BBC Annual Report to Parliament 1977-8, loc. cit.
17 Jacob to Bridges, 3 January 1951.
18 *Spectator*, 21 June 1957.
19 Leonard Shapiro, in the *Spectator*, 16 August 1957.
20 Thomas Preston, unpublished letter to the *Spectator*, 30 August 1957.
21 'Z. Marn' in the *Spectator*, 30 October 1959; Memorandum by Maurice Latey, 5 January 1960.
22 Hugh Greene in the *Spectator*, 18 March 1960.
23 Desmond Clark in the *Spectator*, 6 November 1959.
24. Cf. p. 220.
25 *The BBC – History, Apparatus and Radio Propaganda Methods*, by Vladimir Artemov and Vladimir Semenov (Moscow: Iskusstvo, 1978).
26 BBC Annual Report to Parliament 1974-5 (incorporated in *BBC Handbook 1976*), p. 53.
27 Malcolm Browne, of the *New York Times*.

Index